Marketing
Investment
Real Estate

Director of Publishing—Llani O'Connor
Book Editor—Peg Keilholz
Production—Meg Givhan

Marketing
Investment
Real Estate

Finance
Taxation
Techniques

Stephen D. Messner
Irving Schreiber
Victor L. Lyon

NATIONAL ASSOCIATION OF REALTORS®
developed in cooperation with its affiliate, the
REALTORS NATIONAL MARKETING INSTITUTE®
of the NATIONAL ASSOCIATION OF REALTORS®
Chicago, Illinois

International Standard Book Number: 0-913652-07-5
Library of Congress Catalog Card Number: 75-25213
REALTORS NATIONAL MARKETING INSTITUTE® Catalog Number BK 116

Printed in the United States of America
First printing, 1975, 10,392
Second printing, 1976, 10,400
Third printing, 1977, 9,957
Fourth printing, 1978, 10,438
Fifth printing, 1979, 10,610
Sixth printing, 1980, 10,154
Seventh printing, 1980, 10,000

Foreword

This book concerns itself with how to effectively fit real estate into a total investment program to achieve the investor's goals. While primarily addressed to the
commercial-investment real estate broker to provide information to use in marketing real estate to clients, it will also have appeal to the investor and the members of
his team. Accountants and attorneys will also find this book a reference of great
value in their work for real estate investment clients.

Income-producing and/or speculative real estate have long been recognized as
having a useful investment potential for a broad range of investors with different
needs and investment objectives. Of the many forms of direct and indirect investment media, few offer both the flexibility and return potential of real estate when it
is properly structured.

Real estate is widely used as a hedge against inflation. In addition, real estate is
often purchased because of the various tax advantages it holds for certain categories of investors. Finally, real estate has long been linked with high leverage
financing.

Revolutionary change has characterized the real estate market over the past
several years. Financial institutions now have more flexibility in making real estate
loans with the result that more complex and varied packages are being put together
and more financing vehicles such as sale-leaseback or participation financing are
available today. New and more complex tax legislation has been enacted. New
forms of real estate ownership, with syndication in the forefront, have made it
possible for investors to limit the total amount of their investment as well as their
personal liability and thus to move into types of real estate investment until then
unavailable to most investors.

Investors are more sophisticated, have more discretionary funds and there is an
increase in the number of investors interested in real estate.

All these developments create new opportunities for well-qualified investment real
estate brokers to provide counsel to a growing number of clients to meet their
investment objectives. It is clear that the broker must be aware of market developments and be equipped with the specialized tools of analysis necessary to cope with
the ever-changing market conditions.

Understanding and knowledge of the new techniques and tools presented here will
assure the broker a viable role in the client team—attorney, accountant and
REALTOR® (as depicted in the cover logo). The broker's role is multifaceted: it
could be the traditional representation as the seller's agent or representation as the
buyer's agent or one of providing counselling services for which a fee rather than
a commission is paid.

Thorough mastery of investment principles and techniques and their applications
can best be achieved through the educational courses which lead to the professional
designation CCIM (Certified Commercial Investment Member) of the REAL-
TORS® National Marketing Institute. These courses constitute the best in professional education and training and produce some of the most competent real
estate investment brokers in the country. This book is the primary textbook for
these courses.

However, *Marketing Investment Real Estate* is also intended to be an independent
entity. It can be used before, during and after the courses or can stand on its own.
In any case, it is intended to be read from cover to cover so that the comprehen-

siveness of a thorough, uniform analytical approach is understood. Only then should it be used as a reference in checking a particular tax treatment or a specific financing technique to be applied to a particular property.

It is the authors' hope that this book will make it easier for real estate professionals who understood and practiced the old cash flow and equity build-up analysis techniques to make a smooth transition to the new techniques of discounting cash flows to calculate Internal Rates of Return.

By using the methods described in this book knowledgeable brokers will be able to extend their skills to serve many more clients than in the past and serve all their clients in a more professional manner than has ever before been possible.

About the authors

The writing of such a comprehensive book requires a wide variety of expertise and knowledge. Each of the three major sections in *Marketing Investment Real Estate* was primarily written by an authority in that area. The total planning, review and coordination of material was worked on by the three as a team, with consultation by two investment brokers.

Stephen D. Messner, D.B.A., is head of the Finance Department, Professor of Finance and Real Estate and Director of the Center for Real Estate and Urban Economic Studies at the University of Connecticut. He has authored several books, articles and monographs and has written for RNMI's magazine, *real estate today®* as well as consulted on RNMI's Commercial-Investment Council courses.

Irving Schreiber, B.B.A. and J.D., is a certified public accountant and a member of the New York bar. Currently he is President of Panel Publishers and Professor of Accountancy and Taxation at The School of Professional Accountancy, C. W. Post Center, Long Island University. He has served as author and editor for numerous publications in the tax planning field.

REALTOR® Victor L. Lyon holds the following RNMI designations: Certified Commercial-Investment Member and Certified Residential Broker as well as the Member Appraisal Institute from the American Institute of Real Estate Appraisers and the Counselor in Real Estate from the American Society of Real Estate Counselors. He is President of Tacoma Realty, Inc., Tacoma, Washington and is currently Chairman of RNMI's Editorial Committee, a Senior Instructor for the Commercial-Investment Council courses and serves both on RNMI's and the National Association's Board of Governors. He has also served as Chairman of RNMI's Commercial-Investment Council.

REALTORS® Howard M. Benedict, Certified Commercial-Investment Member and Certified Residential Broker of New Haven, Connecticut and Jay Levine, Certified Commercial-Investment Member of San Francisco, served on the planning committee for the book. Both are members of RNMI's Commercial-Investment Council and Board of Governors.

Llani O'Connor, RNMI's Director of Publishing, and Peg Keilholz, Book Editor, were responsible for publishing and editing the book.

Contents

Section I

Real Estate Investment and Finance

Chapter 1

Nature and Scope of Investments

1

This is a text about real estate investments, the impact of the Federal Income Tax on such investments and a rational approach to analyzing and comparing the relative benefits of real estate investment opportunities. It is appropriate at the outset, however, to consider the broader spectrum of investment, including how and why investing is undertaken, the problems of investment risks, basic investment characteristics or attributes and investment alternatives.

Doing this will enable the real estate broker or investor to compare different types of investments available and the expected results of each. The real estate broker must be familiar with the entire spectrum of investments to make a meaningful analysis of the present or potential position of a client or prospect.

Nature of investing

What is an investment?

The answer to this question is probably understood by most people in only a very general way. The dictionary, for example, defines an investment as an "expenditure of money for income or profit; capital outlay." Most people understand that investment involves the commitment of money or other property (the capital outlay) in the hope of earning future income or profit on that outlay. However, specific investments and the elements affecting them raise more complex questions for which answers may not be as readily available.

The range of possible investments is, of course, very broad. Placing money into a savings account is an investment, as is the purchase of corporate or government bonds. The purchase of life insurance is considered an investment insofar as there is a build-up in cash surrender value. Similarly, the purchase of an annuity is a form of investment. If an individual buys stock in a corporation or a mutual fund he considers that he has made an investment. He might equally consider the contribution of capital to his sole proprietorship or partnership as an investment. Last, but not least, are the many forms of investments in real estate.

The profit or income an investor expects from his investment can take two basic forms: (1) income earned in the form of interest, dividends or rents; (2) profit realized from the appreciation in value (when the investment property is sold for more than it cost).

Who invests?

One quite remarkable thing about the economic system of the United States with its vast ability to produce an enormous and varied quantity of goods and services is the fact that a major portion of this capacity is made possible by private investments. In a private enterprise economy such as ours, the buildings and machines necessary for production are purchased by sacrifices in present consumption, by the desire and ability of some to save and to invest these savings for the future.

The overwhelming majority of our population are engaged in some form of investing. As disposable personal income in the United States has risen, so has the number and proportion of people who have funds in excess of their current consumption requirements. Indeed, the number of savers and investors has grown at a rate much higher than our rate of population growth during the past several decades. Today in our economy, savings and investment capital emanate not from a select few but from the large and growing middle-income individuals and families. Concomitant with this growth in the number of investors has been the growth in our financial intermediaries: the banks, life insurance companies, savings and loan associations, pension funds, etc. Even here recent changes have been seen whereby increasing numbers of investors are channeling their funds directly into investments such as real estate and open-market securities (U.S. Treasury Bills). The forecast for the future seems clear enough: there will be even greater numbers of investors; investors will be more sophisticated and will have increasing amounts of information and media to aid them in their investment pursuits; finally, there will be an ever-increasing number of investors who will seek to invest their funds directly rather than utilize a financial intermediary.

Why do people invest?

While the answer to this question seems all too obvious, the point should be emphasized that "making a profit" is neither definitive enough nor comprehensive enough as a goal to be helpful in assessing the rationale for investing. In our free enterprise economy, individuals interact with business firms by supplying both labor and capital in exchange for wages, salaries, interest and dividends. The cash receipts from business are then used by individuals to meet and satisfy basic consumption needs and desires. Consumption, however, has a variety of prices and while food and clothing can typically be purchased from current earnings, other items such as housing, automobiles, education, etc. can only be purchased through borrowing and/or saving. Most individuals save a portion of current income so that they might provide for future consumption and as a result face investment decisions regularly. *Thus it is to make possible future consumption that people save and invest in the present.*

Investment alternatives

There are a large number of investment alternatives available to the typical investor and these can be categorized in a number of ways. Smith and Eiteman[1] offer one scheme that is most helpful.

I. Direct Investment Alternatives
   A. Fixed—principal investments
      1. Cash
      2. Savings accounts
      3. Marketable savings certificates
      4. Corporate bonds
      5. Government bonds
   B. Variable—principal securities
      1. Preferred stocks
      2. Common stocks
      3. Convertible securities
      4. Warrants

[1] Smith and Eiteman, *Essentials of Investing*, pp. 4–7.

13

     5. Options
   C. Nonsecurity investments
     1. Real estate
     2. Mortgages
     3. Commodities
     4. Business ventures
     5. Art, antiques and other valuables
II. Indirect Investment Alternatives
   A. Pension funds
   B. Insurance company portfolios
   C. Investment companies
   D. Trust funds

The primary division between types of investments, direct and indirect, differentiates between those investment alternatives in which the individual makes the actual investment decisions for himself. Of the former type investments, the fixed-principal investments refer to those in which the principal amount or terminal value is known (fixed) with complete certainty. Perhaps the best example of this class is the bond which has a set value at maturity.

Variable-principal securities have no fixed or certain terminal value and the laws of supply and demand produce periodic changes in principal value (price). Common stock, for example, has neither a fixed income nor a fixed market price.

Nonsecurity investments include a broad range of investment types but their common characteristic is that while they are direct investments under the definition used by Smith and Eiteman, they are not classified as securities. One might argue that the mortgage instrument is a near security in that it is traded in secondary markets but there are many types of mortgage loans and many different ways to invest directly in mortgages. The other nonsecurities are more clearly of the tax-sheltered variety in which certain of the income tax provisions can offer significant tax advantages to classes of investors.

Finally there is the classification of indirect investment alternatives in which individuals have virtually no (or at least very little) influence or control over the actual selection of investments. Some have called this the "money management industry" which is growing very rapidly in our economy.[2]

Investment attributes or characteristics

There are a variety of reasons why individuals and institutions invest even though in general it is accurate to observe that the primary reason is to provide for future consumption. Because particular investors have different needs and desires concerning the investments they undertake, it follows that there are basic factors or attributes of investments that somehow relate to the ability of the investment to meet the objectives of investors. Also, as a practical matter, many institutional investors are restricted to some extent in the types of investments they may make. In some cases they are legally restricted but equally important to individuals as well as institutional investors are such factors as habits, historical precedent, tradition and simply sound judgment which prompts investors to limit their selection to certain types of investments.

Investment attributes are directly related to investment objectives. Rational financial planning requires that each investor carefully consider and specifically

[2] *Ibid.*, p. 7.

identify his investment objectives within the context of his personal needs and/or any legal restrictions he might face when he invests for others. Thus, we might think of attributes in terms of the ability of an investment to provide investment benefits.

The five most important investment attributes to the typical investor are the following.

Degree of safety; degree of risk
Liquidity
Return: dollar and rate
Manageability
Taxability

Degree of safety and risk

Safety is defined in terms of degree of certainty with which the return from the investment is expected. An extreme example would be cash which remains uninvested; the return is absolutely certain to be zero and therefore there is complete safety. In terms of relative importance, this may be the most important attribute of an investment to most classes of investors. It should also be noted that by "safety" most investors think of certainty of receiving principal invested back as their highest priority and are concerned secondarily with receipt of income.

Risk is in essence the exact opposite of safety for it measures the uncertainty of return from an investment; both principal and income. Risk may be further defined in terms of types of risk, which are generally divided into four distinct categories.

Purchasing power (price-level) risk   This form of risk relates to the extent to which an investment is subject to losses (or gain) in the purchasing power of dollar amounts received as income or as return of principal. Experience shows that price levels have tended to move upward steadily and thus most investors have come to think of this form of risk as almost entirely uncertainty as to *loss* of purchasing power, referring to this as "inflation risk." It should be remembered, however, that there have been periods of downward price movement (during the Great Depression of the 1930s and even some isolated instances in the mid-1970s) and during these periods purchasing power actually increased.

Most commonly, high purchasing power risk is associated with those types of investments that have a fixed income even though this risk affects both income and principal in the same way. The most frequently cited examples of specific investments which are subject to a high degree of purchasing power risk are bonds, mortgages, savings accounts and other fixed (or limited) income investments. Common stock and real estate are generally considered the most practical and effective protection against this form of risk.

Financial risk   This form of risk is measured in terms of the uncertainty concerning the financial ability of the investment to return principal and income in the future. The popular rating systems such as Moody's and Standard and Poor's base their grading system of securities in terms of the relationship between the amount of funds an issuer has to satisfy security holders and the amount of funds required to meet these demands.

Business risk   This form of risk is often confused with "financial risk" because they are so closely interrelated. Business risk, however, refers to the uncertainty

15

associated with the profit potential of the property or business, while financial risk relates to the capital structure that is used to finance the assets of the firm.

Interest rate (money rate) risk   This relates to the impact of changes in future interest rates on investment value. When interest rates fall, the market price of existing mortgages increases; conversely, when interest rates rise, the value of existing mortgages falls. Even the most secure investments from the standpoint of financial risk. U.S. Government Bonds, are highly subject to changes in interest rates as evidenced by the significant drop in long-term government bond prices during 1968–69 and 1973–74 when interest rates hit new highs. In general, the greater the financial safety of the investment, the greater the interest rate risk. For example, high grade bonds suffer most from changes in interest rates.

Liquidity

Another attribute important to many investors is the ability to liquidate an investment rapidly but with a minimum loss of principal. An example of a highly liquid investment would be a savings account. Liquidity is important to both individuals and institutional investors since liquid assets may be needed to meet unexpected expenses or take advantage of unpredictable opportunities that are particularly favorable.

Return: dollar and rate

Not surprisingly, the *periodic income* from and the *appreciation* of the investment is one of the most important attributes of an investment. Generally speaking, both income and appreciation are combined into a measure of return that can be expressed as a periodic dollar amount or as a periodic rate measured as a percentage of amount invested.

All investors are pressured to seek the highest return on their investment possible commensurate with the risk they are willing to assume and other important attributes they desire.

Manageability

The manageability of an investment is the extent to which it requires "care and feeding" over time. As a rule, real estate investments require much more management than the investment alternative of a savings account or even the purchase of common stocks. It is possible, however, to acquire the services of professional management and thereby reduce the burdens and risk of management.

Taxability

The effect of the income tax is well known for it is only the after-tax dollar that is spendable by the investor. The Federal Government (and many states) takes its share of income via the income tax and the investor gets what remains. Not all types of income are taxed alike however. The tax on some types of profit may even be deferred as in the case of exchanges. Also, some investments have certain built-in tax advantages (such as depreciation) which reduce the tax impact on the income produced by those investments.

Impact of investment attributes
Risk

It is generally accepted that risk and return on the investment have a direct relationship to each other. That is, the higher the expected return, the greater the risk. In contrast, risk is low when guaranteed (or practically guaranteed) returns are involved. Thus the risk factor is low for savings accounts, life insurance and annuities. The risk is also relatively low for corporate and municipal bonds. The effective interest rate (not necessarily the rate called for by the bond but the effective rate determined by the combination of the interest rate called for by the bond, the price at which the bond is selling and the time left to maturity of the bond) will reflect the relative risk that is attributed to the bond.

Corporate stock is more difficult to classify with respect to risk since it may have widely varying degrees of risk. Stock of a regulated public utility is generally considered less risky than the stock of a new, unproven company that is entering the field. The latter may have more "action" among stockholders looking for dramatic increases but the risk is also more substantial.

Partnerships, syndicates and other forms of ownership in business ventures also have varying degrees of risk. Again the risk and rate of return are directly related. Investments in speculative oil drilling, for example, may be very risky (in terms of the percentage of wells that do strike oil) but the return may be substantial. The cost of an investment in a proven well will be much higher than in a wildcat venture because the risk is much less.

Real estate investments also run the gamut of degrees of risk. A property with a long-term lease from a national tenant is considered far less risky than one with a lease that has three years to go. Some other factors that affect the degree of risk in a real estate investment may be unknown at the time the investment is undertaken. Changes in the economic viability of the neighborhood, changes in zoning, increases in real estate taxes, possible condemnation of the property by public authorities and increases in interest rates are all examples of factors that affect risk.

Liquidity and marketability

Money in a savings bank, investment bonds, life insurance and annuities are all considered to be relatively liquid. They are already in the form of cash or may be be converted into cash very quickly and generally with little or no loss of principal. This is in contrast to the characteristic of "marketability" where there is a ready and active market for the investment and therefore may be sold quickly, even though the sales price may be well below the original amount invested. Investments in common stocks listed on the New York Stock Exchange may be highly marketable but the price at which they are traded may fluctuate widely from week to week; thus it would be considered marketable but not liquid.

Investments in oil, cattle and any other business ventures may not be liquid nor marketable. An interest in a closely-held business (especially a minority interest) may be difficult to sell at any price.

Real estate is generally not considered to be very liquid and is often not marketable as compared with other investment alternatives. Certaintly it is not as readily salable as stock trading on the New York Stock Exchange. However, cash is often available from a real estate interest without sale. Real estate, traditionally, is among the best type of security for a loan; mortgages on real estate are generally readily available. If property has increased in value, the immediate availability on this increase to the owner may be realized without actually selling the property; he can generally borrow against by refinancing the property.

Management

Probably every investment has a charge for management built into it when it does not require direct management by the investor. An investment in a savings bank does not seem to require management by the investor at all. However, the bank has to select the properties on which it will grant mortgage loans and determine what other investments and loans it may make. The cost of this management reduces the net return to the bank and, therefore, to the investor. Admittedly, this management cost is almost negligible as far as each individual depositor in the bank is concerned.

Stocks and bonds require careful and constant management regarding both the selection of individual stocks or securities and the timing of purchase and sale. The management may be supplied by the investor himself or by professional management available from brokers or from professional managers hired for a fee. An investor may try to avoid the management problem and, in effect, hire professional management by investing in mutual funds. But here too professional management must be paid since each mutual fund has a professional management advisor who is paid a fee based upon the size of the fund's portfolio.

Other types of investments (oil, gas, cattle, etc.) require management and the investor is often not experienced in this role. Hence, built into the fee he pays for his investment and the arrangements thereafter is a charge for management.

In the case of real estate, management is again generally required. In small properties the investor may be his own manager. In larger properties he will generally need professional management help and should take this fact into consideration when analyzing the return he can expect from his investment.

Capital appreciation

Fixed income investments, while relatively free of risk, generally have no appreciation factor. The return on the investment is there (in the form of interest or dividends) but the dollar value of the capital investment remains unchanged. If you deposit $10,000 in a savings bank and receive 5% interest per year, the original $10,000 investment grows only by the amount of interest earned. If you buy an annuity which pays $100 a month for the rest of your life, that is what you will receive for the rest of your life (except in the case of variable annuities whose periodic payouts are geared to the value of the equity securities in which the annuity company invests).

The amount payable at the maturity of a bond is generally its face amount. So unless the bonds were purchased at a discount there is no capital appreciation. During the life of the bond it pays interest but when it matures you get back what was originally paid for the bond.

Stocks may have a substantial appreciation factor. This will vary according to the nature of the stock, the industry involved, the expectations of investors for that type industry, the position of the company in that industry, the inflation factor in the economy and many other intangibles that continue to baffle students of the stock market. Many stocks have been known to double, triple and quadruple in value in comparatively short periods of time; others have nosedived in similarly short periods.

Investments in oil, gas, cattle, etc. (or in other forms of businesses) may have some appreciation, especially if the price of the end products is influenced by inflation and other market conditions.

Real estate, especially over the past 25 years, has shown remarkable increases in value due to a variety of factors such as increasing population and wealth, limitations on the quantity of land available, the availability of mortgage money, inflation and the special tax advantages available to real estate investors.

Income tax

In general, dividends, rents and interest are taxable as ordinary income, with the exception of the interest on municipal bonds. However, the accounting measure of taxable rental income is reduced by depreciation deductions (which require no cash outlay) which, in turn, can boost after-tax cash flows to the investor.

Annuity income is partially taxed (since part of the annuity is merely a return of the capital investment). However, the taxable portion is taxable as ordinary income.

Income from the participation in a business venture as a sole proprietor or partner is taxable as ordinary income. Income from the sale of oil or gas (or other minerals) is subject to ordinary income but a depletion allowance (22% of the income from the sale of oil, for example) reduces the income subject to tax.

Gain from the sale (or exchange when applicable) of investment property is generally taxable as capital gains. That means that these gains are taxable at about half the rate that applies to ordinary income and in no event at a rate exceeding 25% for gains of up to $50,000 and at a rate not exceeding 35% thereafter for gains in excess of $50,000.

In addition to the special tax advantages enjoyed by real estate through the use of the depreciation deduction and the availability of capital gains treatment on the sale or exchange of real estate at a profit, another tax advantage lies in the availability of the tax-deferred exchange. Real estate that has appreciated in value may be exchanged for other real estate with the tax on the appreciation deferred to a later time. (The income tax on the appreciation may be avoided altogether if the property acquired in the exchange or some other property acquired in still another exchange for this acquired property is held until death.)

Inflation

Fixed income investments are not protected against inflation or loss of purchasing power. Once an annuity with a fixed dollar amount is purchased, that is the dollar amount that will be received regardless of changes in the purchasing power of dollars received. This also holds true for the interest rate called for in bonds; only the amount specified by the bond will be paid at each interest period. Furthermore, the amount received at maturity will be the amount paid for the bond except when purchased at a discount. Preferred stock falls into the same category as bonds since the dividends called for are generally fixed as a percentage of the par value of the stock.

Common stock, on the other hand, is deemed to be a hedge against inflation on the theory that the market value of the stock will reflect any inflationary factors in the economy. This may hold true for the entire spectrum of common stocks but may not apply to any one particular stock. Furthermore, when interest rates increase, common stock prices may decline in an inflationary period, as was dramatically demonstrated in 1974.

Various types of business investments may reflect the pressures of inflation since the price at which the products or services are sold by the business will be subject to the same inflationary pressures.

Real estate prices generally have reflected the inflationary spiral in recent years. It has also become quite common for real estate leases to have escalation clauses calling for increased rents to offset increases in the cost of living.

Chapter 2

Real Estate Investments

2

The previous chapter dealt with the various characteristics found in all forms of investments. This chapter will focus specifically on the nature and scope of real estate investments. The real estate broker must deal with and therefore be aware of a number of investor and user needs and desires. These "needs and desires" may be satisfied by acquiring interests in a wide variety of investment properties, ranging in type from raw land to small duplex multi-family units to massive shopping center developments. The interests that may be acquired in this large array of alternative properties may also take many forms such as lessee, sub-lessor, equity owner, mortgagee, etc. The overwhelmingly large number of combinations open to the broker in meeting the objectives of his client or prospect makes his task both complex and challenging.

Spectrum of income-producing property

The spectrum of real estate investments is quite broad, ranging from residential income property to commercial and industrial properties and to farms and land. The following list is illustrative of the real estate investment spectrum. It should be recognized that these properties could be owned by users or held by investors for rental income.

Residential income
    Apartment houses
        Garden
        High-rise
    Hotels
    Motels
    Rest homes
Commercial
    Professional buildings (doctors, lawyers and other professions)
    Office buildings
    Shopping centers
        Regional
        Community
        Local
    Single purpose buildings
        Theatres
        Bowling alleys
        Free-standing retail stores
        Service stations
Industrial
    Warehouses
    Industrial parks

Manufacturing facilities

Utility company buildings—power plants, steam generating plants

Farms and land

Recreation land—residential lots for single family

Subdivision land

Residential lots zoned for multiple dwellings

Commercially zoned land

Industrially zoned land

Raw acreage

Farms

Ranches

Types of clients

Being knowledgeable about the types of properties in the market is only a portion of the real estate investment broker's responsibility. He must also be aware of the people in the market and what motivates them.

On one hand are the sellers of property or even more broadly conceived are the disposers of property. These people provide the basic inventory for the broker.

In many cases the disposition of the property is by sale or exchange and usually the principal motivation is that the property no longer meets the investment goals of the owner. In other cases, the disposition is accomplished by leasing the property to others to create an income stream for the owner.

Purpose of acquisition

The other portion of the real estate market is that which includes the acquisition of real estate. Real estate can be acquired as inventory for resale. This is what a dealer in real estate does. His profit on the resale is treated as ordinary income. Typical dealers in real estate are developers who buy to improve and resell the property. Speculators bring liquidity to the marketplace in exchange for a potential profit.

On the other hand, real estate may be acquired for investment. Here, investments are divided into two categories. Property used in the investor's trade or business is one form of real estate investment. In this category, for example, would be the factory building acquired by a manufacturer for his own use in producing manufactured goods.

Another category is property held for the production of income. Income may be further divided into two categories.

Ordinary income which, in the case of real estate, is rental income.

Capital gain, the income realized from the disposition of real estate at a price higher than the seller's adjusted basis.

The latter case of capital gain is the realization of the appreciation in value of the real estate while it was held by the investor.

It might be noted that the tax law has a somewhat different distinction between trade-or-business property and production-of-income property because it treats the ownership of an apartment house, for example, as a trade or business. That leaves production-of-income property almost exclusively to vacant land held for appreciation insofar as real estate is concerned. It should be noted, however, that

21

this tax distinction creates no practical differences in figuring the tax consequences of an investment since depreciation deductions and capital gain treatment are available whether the property is held for production of income or in a trade or business.

Types of interest in real estate

In addition to the types of property involved in the real estate investment spectrum, it should be noted that real estate interests can be divided in a number of ways. One form is a fee ownership interest which is the outright ownership of the property (subject, in many instances, to encumbrances due to loans for which the property is security).

Parts or all of the fee, however, may be leased to lessees who, in turn, may sublease part or all of their leasehold interests. A lessee may also construct improvements on the leased property (for which he may be entitled to deduct depreciation or amortization expenses). However, at the termination of the lease, the improvement reverts to the lessor unless otherwise provided for in the lease contract.

There is also the interest of the lender, the mortgagee. He may be entitled to foreclose on the mortgage loan, acquire the property and sell it, should there be a default on the loans on that property. In the case of mortgagees, there may be several mortgagee positions, each with a different interest. The first loan on the property has the first lien. If a second lender has also made a loan, he stands in line behind the first mortgagee and has no claim against the property until the first mortgagee's loans have been satisfied.

In addition, there may be other liens against a property. For example, should the owner have a judgment against him, the judgment holder may have a lien against the property, which means he has a claim against the proceeds of sale for the amount of his lien. There may also be a mechanic's lien against the property for unpaid amounts to those who have made repairs or have done other work on the property.

Finally, the property may be subject to easements, the right of others to make certain use of the property. An example would be the right of a telephone company to string telephone lines across part of the land.

Forms of ownership

The ownership of a fee or other interests may be by a single individual or by several persons in the form of joint ownership, a partnership, trust or by a corporation. The manner in which real estate, or an interest in real estate, is owned often has great tax significance, as illustrated in Chapter 8.

An individual investor generally seeks to have tax losses generated by the real estate investment available to offset his other taxable income. An individual or partnership form of ownership accomplishes this purpose best. On the other hand, if real estate is producing ordinary income and the investor already has considerable taxable income, it may be preferable to have the income taxable to a corporation.

Corporate ownership presents other problems. The corporation is a separate entity and pays its own tax on any income it earns. However, the income remaining after tax, if paid to the stockholders by way of dividends, is taxable to the stockholders so that income may be taxed twice.

Accumulating after-tax income in the corporation may not be the long-term solution either. The corporation may become subject to a penalty tax for unreasonably accumulating earnings and profits. There are also problems of disposing of corporate-owned property or getting that property back into the hands of the stockholders. Many of these problems can be solved but advance, astute planning is required prior to acquisition.

The tax problems and tax-saving opportunities that evolve from the proper form of ownership are mentioned here to alert the reader to the importance of the ownership form. Too often, not enough attention is paid to this aspect of real estate investment; too often it is done automatically, without regard to all of the consequences, only to discover at some later date that the investor is faced with possible tax liabilities that could have otherwise been avoided.

Factors affecting real estate investments

In the previous chapter, the investment factors of risk, appreciation, marketability and liquidity and management were discussed. These factors will be discussed in more detail here with respect to how they affect real estate investments.

Risk

Risk is one of the most vital factors to consider in any investment. As previously indicated, in virtually all cases the greater the risk element the greater the expected return must be in order to attract investors. This element of risk is itself composed of component parts; namely the quantity, the quality and the durability of the future income stream produced by the property.

Quantity If all other factors are equal, a property which is estimated to produce $6,000 of income will be less valuable than a similar property which is estimated to produce $10,000 of income over the same period of time with equal probability of attainment.

Quality A rooming house for transients and a small industrial warehouse both producing the same amount of net income are not necessarily worth the same amount. The warehouse will normally be deemed more valuable because the quality of its income stream is more reliable than that of the rooming house.

Durability A parcel of property having two years remaining on its lease may not be as valuable as one with fifteen years still to run on its lease. The concept of "durability" may also be related to the economic life of the property.

In essence, then, risk is the chance an investor takes that he will not earn as much as he anticipates. His return from his investment will vary directly with the degree of risk. High risk will tend to yield high income and low risk will tend to produce low income.

Appreciation

Another characteristic inherent in real estate investments is that of increment or appreciation. Part of the reason for this is due to inflation, the decrease in the value of money. In the case of land, much of this appreciation is caused by the law of supply and demand. For the most part, there is only a fixed supply of land. Except for certain limited instances where man has been able to reclaim land from the sea and lakes, there is only a certain amount of land on earth; this cannot be increased. At the same time, the population of the earth is increasingly steadily. There is, therefore, an increased need or demand for whatever land is available. As the ratio of supply and demand changes so does the value of the commodity, in this case land. Because of these factors, it is often true that the value of land and buildings can increase, appreciate, even though there is physical deterioration to the improvement occurring at the same time.

Liquidity and marketability

Liquidity is another basic characteristic of real estate investment property which is important to bear in mind. This includes two elements: the loan potential and the sale potential. Real estate is particularly well-suited to financing. The property is virtually immovable in the case of buildings and virtually indestructible in the case of land. Traditionally, lending sources have been willing to make loans secured by real estate. After the income from a parcel has enabled its owner to pay off his mortgage loans, it is possible for him to place a new mortgage on the property. Proceeds of this new loan will be tax-free to him at that time.

Often, with respect to real estate, there is the lack of an instant market. An owner desiring to sell his real estate must often wait for a considerable period of time before he gets his desired price. This differs markedly from the case of an owner of a listed security who can merely telephone his broker and have the sale of his stock completed within minutes of his instructions to sell. By the same token, perhaps because of the slowness of the real estate market, real estate is not usually subject to short cycles, upward and downward trends in prices, as is the securities market.

Sources of financing are as varied as man's imagination. Conventional sources are the commercial banks, savings and loan associations and insurance companies. In addition, there are union welfare funds, pension, profit-sharing and other kinds of employee-benefit and retirement funds (both public and private) and some charitable and educational institutions which may be interested in placing such loans for their investment portfolios. Not to be overlooked is the seller of the property. He may be willing to take a purchase money mortgage which will provide sufficient financing to complete a transaction. In some cases, the necessary financing can come from the brokers handling the transaction.

Management

A sometimes neglected characteristic of a real estate investment is the requirement of management. This is necessary in varying degrees, from the mere receipting of one check a month to the full-time occupation of caring for a large building. In some cases, the investor may be buying himself a full-time job.

In computing return on investment, it is important for the investor to remember to charge a cost for management, even if he does it himself and has no cash outlay, in order to determine true return on the capital invested. Often professional management is worth the out-of-pocket cash outlay. Professional management usually knows when to increase or decrease rents and provides protection for the lessor that he would not ordinarily think of such as tax escalator and cost-of-living index clauses. Professionals have the ability to guide and counsel the investor on proper timing for selling or exchanging. On the other hand, sometimes the personal attention of owner-management can counteract the forces of a depressed market. It depends on the management skills of the professional or the owner.

Special factors affecting real estate

Three special factors particularly applicable to real estate investments should be noted. They are depreciation, leverage and exchanging potential.

Depreciation This is the depreciation deduction allowed for tax purposes. The depreciation deduction is based on the entire adjusted basis of the improvement on the property which includes the amount of any loans on the property. Thus, if a property were purchased and the improvement was worth $100,000, $10,000 cash and $90,000 mortgage, the depreciation is computed on the $100,000 and not the $10,000. Furthermore, depreciation may often be computed by accelerated methods which permit the recovery of basis for tax purposes in a relatively short time since, under accelerated depreciation, deductions in the early years are large and diminish as the property gets older.

The importance of the depreciation deduction is that it requires no cash outlay yet it reduces the income from the property subject to tax. Further, depreciation taken can exceed real depreciation in the property thereby creating tax-free dollars because of income tax savings. (If the deduction exceeds the income from the property, the excess deduction may be applied to reduce the other taxable income the property owner may have). Since a dollar of tax that does not have to be paid is, in essence, a form of income, the depreciation deduction helps produce more after-tax dollars from a real estate investment than would be available were the same amount of income earned from another form of investment that does not allow for depreciation deductions.

Leverage It has already been pointed out that real estate is well-suited to financing; it has traditionally been very good security for loans. This means that real estate can be acquired or carried with a smaller percentage of cash outlay by the owner than most other investments. The ability to finance the purchase or carrying of real estate gives rise to leverage. Leverage arises because all of the appreciation of the property belongs to the property holder even though there may be substantial loans against the property. Similarly, all of the income belongs to him regardless of the amounts of the loan.

To illustrate leverage, assume a property is available for $100,000. Five years later the same property can be sold for $150,000. If the property were bought in the first instance for $100,000 cash, the buyer would subsequently realize a $50,000 profit or a 50 percent increase of his investment. Suppose, however, the buyer were able to obtain a $90,000 mortgage. He would then be required to use only $10,000 of his own money. Subsequently, when he sold the property for $150,000 and paid off the $90,000 mortgage he would be left with $60,000 or a 500 percent increase of his investment. (The cost of the transaction and the loan for the five-year period has been ignored for the purposes of keeping the example simple.)

Leverage has its negative side, too. If the investor put up $10,000 of his own money and borrowed $90,000 and then the value of the property went down to $90,000, his entire $10,000 investment would be wiped out.

Leverage is also present in terms of the current income from the property. Suppose, for example, the net operating income from the property in the previous example amounts to $5,000. If the investor had put up $100,000 in cash, that would be a 5 percent return on his investment. Had he only put up $10,000 in cash, that would be a 50 percent return on his investment. (Again, the cost of the loan and the effect of income taxes have been ignored in order to illustrate the principle of leverage.)

Exchange of Property Investment real estate can be exchanged on a tax-deferred basis, a possibility not available in many other popular investment alternatives. This gives owners an additional factor to consider prior to disposition.

25

Chapter 3

Discounted Cash Flow Analysis

3

Valuation of income-producing properties

Meaning of value

Of central importance in the analysis of investments is the determination of "value." Likewise, in the field of real estate, brokers, appraisers, investors and users are concerned with estimates of value for existing or proposed property developments. A variety of purposes is represented by those desiring an estimate of value and thus there is also a variety of definitions for value. In essence, the definition of value is a function of the purpose for which an estimate of value is sought.

For example, the well-known real estate appraiser, Alfred Ring, lists the following as representing only *a few* of the many types of "value" in common use today.[1]

Economic value	Sale value
Stable value	Salvage value
Appraised value	Intrinsic value
Potential value	Extrinsic value
Book value	Tax value
Sound value	Use value
Fair value	Rental value
Real value	Speculative value
True value	Reproduction value
Depreciated value	Nuisance value
Warranted value	Liquidation value
Face value	Mortgage value
Cash value	Improved value
Capital value	Insurance value
Exchange value	Leasehold value

The economist typically views "value" as the point of intersection between a supply and demand curve. The residential broker may consider the value of a property he represents as being the price the property will bring after reasonable exposure in an active and competitive market. The appraiser may view the value of a property in a variety of ways: (1) as having the same value as a comparable property already in existence and sold in the marketplace; (2) as having a value equal to the cost of reproducing a given property with equivalent utility; and (3) as having the same value as an investment with a similar income stream. These are all related concepts of "market value." To the typical investor, however, "value" is the present worth *he* places on the anticipated future income stream or benefits that would accrue to him if he were to acquire the investment. To the user of the property, "value" is related to the specific purpose to which he has put a property and the productivity that he has achieved in this use. In this book the primary focus is on

[1] Ring, *The Valuation of Real Estate*, p. 6.

"investment value." To the extent that the investor is "typical" of investors in the market who are most likely to purchase the subject property, investment may be the same dollar amount as market value.

Amenity versus income-producing properties

For amenity properties, such as owner-occupied homes, the value of the property is most often derived from the right to use the realty and payment for the property is typically from income and/or wealth totally unrelated to the property itself. Even the approval of a mortgage loan on such a property is generally based on the owner's ability to meet mortgage payments.

In contrast, income-producing properties provide a stream of payments from the rental of the property that may be used as the basis of its purchase price and as the security for mortgage financing. Typically, the investor collects rents from which he pays the necessary expenses of operation such as property taxes and maintenance. The remainder is available to pay financing charges and a return to the investor for assuming the risk of ownership. Even if the investor himself chooses to use the property rather than rent it, the rental payments that he would have to pay to obtain a comparable property represent a savings to the investor-owner. These savings in turn may be used to support the purchase and financing of the property. In either case, the investor who rents the income property to another or the investor who uses the property himself, the value of the property may be derived as the present worth of the estimated income from rents to be received by the investor, whether it is actual or imputed rent, plus the present worth of the estimated proceeds from the sale of the property.

In the case of real estate investments, like all other forms of investments, the investor is concerned with *cash* received in the future in return for cash or its equivalent invested in the present. Tax benefits from the ownership of real estate, the impact of financing and financial leverage, depreciation, etc. are all factors which influence the after-tax cash flows that accrue from a property. Once the after-tax cash flows are determined or estimated, it is still necessary to determine which alternative stream of future income is most valuable to a specific investor.

Capitalization of income

The basis for the value of income-producing real estate is the potential income it can produce in the future. The process of converting future income into a single present value is called "capitalization." In this sense, value is directly a function of income and as anticipated future income changes, so does the capitalized value (present value) of the income.

Future income streams are "capitalized" into single values so that investors may have a consistent basis to compare investment alternatives. The primary selection criterion of the investor should be based upon some measure of comparison of the stream of income from rental payments and from the eventual sale of the property to the initial cash (down payment) he must invest in order to receive this future income. Reduced to its simplest terms, the cash that a buyer is willing to invest for an income-producing property is directly related to the income that is estimated to be received and the rate of return that is desired. For example, an income of $10,000 per year "capitalized" at 10 percent return suggests that the *investment value* of such a future stream of income is $100,000. Alternatively viewed, if $100,000 were invested today at an annual rate of interest of 10 percent, the investment would accrue to a value of $110,000 by the end of the first year. If this total amount is considered to represent both returns *of* the original investment ($100,000) and return *on* the investment ($10,000), the "return on" portion is indeed 10 percent and the earnings may be withdrawn and enjoyed with no effect on the original investment. This process of earning and withdrawal can take place endlessly as long as (1) only the "return on" portion is withdrawn and (2) the original investment amount ($100,000) can be reinvested each and every year at 10 percent.

This example represents the most simplistic form of income capitalization, perpetuity capitalization. That is, the income stream is treated as beginning at the end of one period (usually one year but not necessarily so) from the time of the initial investment and lasting each year thereafter for infinity. Symbolically this may be stated as follows.

$$V = \frac{I}{R}$$

V = value or present worth of the future rights to periodic income
I = periodic net income
R = rate of capitalization

This formula represents the most basic building block to an understanding of the investment process. However, the preceding illustration deals with the very simple case of capitalization in perpetuity where the principal is assumed to remain unchanged over an indefinite period. Although raw land may provide an excellent example of a form of realty that could possess this characteristic, the more common investment situation involves capitalization over a finite period of time. In order to better understand this process whereby income received for a finite period of time is capitalized into a single present value, it is necessary to introduce the concept and techniques of compound interest and discounting.

Compound interest and discounting

For many years the fields of mortgage lending, banking, corporate finance, securities investment, etc. have used compound interest and discount techniques to analyze their loans and/or investments. Nearly all investments are (or can be) evaluated in terms of their annual return on invested capital, with compounding when invested capital is not returned within one year but left to reinvest per period. From the standpoint of the investor these techniques are critically important because they provide a means of: (1) measuring the return from a particular investment; (2) comparing alternative investments, both real estate and other forms; and (3) reflecting the investor's "time value" of invested capital.

Time value (or cost) of money

The fact that interest or borrowing charges are paid for the use of money points up the fundamental principle of the "time preference" for money. It is widely observed that a rational person always prefers a sum of money in the present rather than the same sum at some time in the future, even if the future money is virtually certain to be received. This behavior among investors simply represents the inherent "opportunity cost" of waiting to receive money and the related opportunities that must be foregone while waiting. A more specific example would be the widely observed practice whereby an investor places a lower *present value* on $1,000 guaranteed to be received one year from today as compared with receiving $1,000 today. This is because, among other things, if he had $1,000 today he could invest it at some earnings rate, say 6%, and thus would have $1,060 one year from today. In this case, then, the true equality is $1,000 today with $1,060 one year from today. In more general terms, this case with the specified opportunity cost of 6% illustrates a situation whereby *any* amount to be received one year from today would be *discounted* by the same proportion.

$$\frac{\$1,000}{\$1,060} = .943396 \text{ or } 94.34\%$$

Thus, the present value of $10,000 to be received one year from today is as follows.

$ 10,000.00 (to be received one year from today)
x.943396   (discount factor, 6%, one year)
$ 9,433.96 (present value—value today of $10,000 to be received one year from today when the opportunity cost of waiting is 6%)

Viewed from the standpoint of the investor, he would be willing to pay no more for a future amount to be received than that present amount that could be invested so as to grow to an amount equal to the future amount to be received.

$9,433.96 (amount invested today)
     .06 (annual interest earned)
$ 566.04 (amount earned during the year)

Clearly, $9,433.96 invested today at 6% annual interest will grow to $10,000 ($9,433.96 plus $556.04) by the end of one year. Thus, $9,433.96 today equals $10,000 one year from today if the opportunity cost of invested capital is 6 percent.

Compound interest

In the example, the time period used to illustrate the time value of money was one year, with interest paid only once during the one-year investment period. This is generally referred to as "simple interest" since interest was earned only on the original investment. However, investment opportunities are generally available where periodic earnings may be reinvested along with the original investment. Under these circumstances it is difficult to compare alternative investments with differing investment periods.

Suppose, for example, that two investment alternatives were presented as follows: (1) an investment of $100 that returns $140 at the end of five years; or (2) an investment of $100 that returns $108 at the end of one year. One simple means of comparing these two investment alternatives is to convert the five-year investment to an annual simple rate. Since the investment returns 40% per five-year period, the average annual rate is 40% divided by 5 or 8% per annum. Since the one-year investment likewise returns 8% per annum, it would appear that the two investments have the same return.

What is not taken into account in this comparison is the possibility of reinvesting both principal and interest at the end of each year for five years when selecting the one-year investment. This is exactly the same investment amount and duration as the five-year investment case since annual interest earned is not withdrawn but reinvested. Both investments would then involve the commitment of $100 for a duration of five years with no returns to the investor until the end of the fifth year. In the case of reinvestment each year, the following would occur.

Year	Investment Beginning of Year	Interest Rate	Interest Earned During Year	Investment Amount Plus Interest Earned
1	$100.00	.08	$ 8.00	$108.00
2	108.00	.08	8.64	116.64
3	116.64	.08	9.33	125.97
4	125.97	.08	10.08	136.05
5	136.05	.08	10.88	146.93

Thus, if the one-year investment is selected *and* the investor is able to reinvest the annual proceeds at the 8% rate over the five-year term, his $100 investment would grow to an amount of $146.93 or $6.93 more than the simple five-year investment which returns only $140.

The rate of return for nearly all types of investments may be measured in terms of *annual return* on invested capital, with compounding assumed when the capital invested is not returned within one year. Thus the concept of compound interest and discount is fundamental to evaluating investments in general and real estate investments in specific. Compound discounting not only reflects the investor's preference for returns sooner rather than later but also includes in the cost of waiting the assumption that the investor has the opportunity to reinvest both principal and earnings.

If the investment choice is simple, such as the choice of investing $1,000 today and receiving either $1,100 one year from today or $1,100 two years from today, no measurement is actually needed. Investment alternatives are seldom that simple. For example, consider the problem of measuring the annual rate of return for the following investment alternatives, each of which costs exactly $10,000 each.

Cash Receipts from Alternative Investments

End of Year	Discounted Mortgage	Five-Year Note	Stock	Insurance Annuity	Land
1	$ 1,627.45	–0–	$ 1,000	$1,000	–0–
2	1,627.45	–0–	1,000	each	–0–
3	1,627.45	–0–	1,000	year	–0–
4	1,627.45	–0–	1,000	to	–0–
5	1,627.45	$16,105.10	1,000	perpetuity	–0–
6	1,637.45	–0–	1,000		–0–
7	1,627.45	–0–	1,000		–0–
8	1,627.45	–0–	1,000		–0–
9	1,627.45	–0–	1,000		–0–
10	1,627.45	–0–	11,000		$25,937.42
Total Receipts	$16,274.50	$16,105.10	$20,000	∞	$25,937.42

The problem here is converting each of these cash flows to a common base so that they may be compared. In order to deal with this type of measurement problem, compound interest and discount tables must be used.

Use of the compound interest and discount tables

Proper use and understanding of compound interest and discount tables is pre-requisite to the measurement of investment rates of return, present value and a number of other calculations commonly used in the field of real estate. For this reason a rather detailed presentation will be made of such tables, their construc-tion, useful modifications and real estate applications. In addition, Appendix A contains selected compound interest tables from Part II of the third edition of Ellwood's *Tables for Real Estate Appraising and Financing*. The sample pages shown are 5% and 10% (monthly, quarterly, semi-annual and annual factors) and 15%, 20% and 25% (annual factors) and are used for purposes of illustration. The reader may also use them to follow the examples in this chapter. The full set of tables contained on pages 1–166 of Ellwood has monthly, quarterly, semi-annual and annual factors for rates of interest in .25% increments from 3% to 12%. In addition, factor tables in 1% increments are available from 13% through 30%. Each table contains six columns as follows.

Column	Factor
1	Amount of one at compound interest
2	Accumulation of one per period
3	Sinking fund factor
4	Present value, reversion of one
5	Present value, ordinary annuity of one per period
6	Installment to amortize one

1. Amount of one at compound interest   The fundamental building block of all compound interest and discount factors is the simple example of a time deposit or savings account. Suppose that $10,000 were invested today at a savings institution that promised to pay 5% interest each year. This means that the institution would deposit 5% of $10,000 (or $500) in the account containing the original deposit at the end of one year. The balance in the account at End of Year (EOY) 1 could be calculated as follows.

$$\$10,000 + (\$10,000 \cdot .05) = \$10,500$$

$$\$10,000\,(1 + .05) \qquad\ = \$10,500$$

$$P\,(1 + i) \qquad\qquad\ = S$$

P = amount invested at the present
i = interest rate paid per period (effective rate)
S = amount to which P will grow by the end of one period

If the entire balance of the account were allowed to remain in the account (that is, reinvest the entire balance of the account) for a second year, the balance at EOY 2 might be calculated as follows

$$[\$10,000\,(1 + .05)] + [\$10,000\,(1 + .05) \cdot .05] = \$11,025$$

$$\uparrow \qquad\qquad\qquad \uparrow \qquad\qquad\qquad \uparrow$$

EOY 1 Balance   5% of EOY 1 Balance   EOY 2 Balance

$$\$10,000\,(1 + .05)\,(1 + .05)$$

$$\$10,000\,(1 + .05)^2$$

$$P\,(1 + i)^n = S^n$$

n = number of periods "i" is earned (compound periods)
S^n = amount to which P will grow in "n" periods

The funtion $(1+i)^n$ is the most important and the most basic expression in the study of the compound interest tables. Note that this expression is found in the calculation of all six column factors. In the context of investment analysis, it incorporates both *return on* and *return of* the investment.

$$S^n = P(1 + i)^n$$

return
of "P"

return
on "P"

Assume $10,000 were invested for two years at 5% per annum.

$$S^n = \$10,000 (1 + .05)^2$$
$$S^n = \$10,000 (1.1025)$$
$$S^n = \$11,025$$

Turn to the annual compound interest table for 5% (page 280) and note that in Column 1, across from the second year, the factor is 1.102500. Obviously this represents the factor $(1+i)^n$ where $(1+.05)^2$. Note also that the "effective rate" is 5%. This means that the rate applied at each compounding period is 5%. Finally, note that the "Base" is equal to $(1+i)$; thus, in this case it is $(1+.05)$ or the value 1.05.

When compounding occurs more frequently than once per year, both the "i" and the "n" are modified to reflect this fact. Assume semi-annual compounding of the same two-year investment.

$$S^n = \$10,000 (1 + .05/2)^4 = \$11,038.13$$

Here, "i" becomes the annual rate (5%) divided by the number of times compounding takes place each year. The "effective rate" is so named because it is the rate actually applied to the outstanding balance *each* compounding period. Also, "n" becomes 4 rather than 2 in this case because it represents the actual number of times that interest will be paid over the two-year investment period.

This same approach applies to quarterly and monthly compounding. The following exhibit summarizes the two-year investment of $10,000 at a 5% annual rate with the various forms of compounding.

5% Annual Rate—Two Years

Form of Compounding	Effective Rate (%)	"n"	Table Factor	S^n
Annual	5.0	1	1.102500	$11,025.00
Semi-Annual	2.5	2	1.103813	$11,038.13
Quarterly	1.25	4	1.104486	$11,044.86
Monthly	0.4166	12	1.104941	$11,049.41

To again illustrate the use of Column 1 factors, suppose that $325.43 were invested for 25 years at a 5% rate compounded monthly. The problem of determining the amount to which this investment grows is solved as follows.

$$S^n = P(1 + i)^n$$

$$P = \$325.43$$
$$i = 5\% \div 12 \text{ or } .0041666$$
$$n = 25 \text{ years} \cdot 12 \text{ or } 300 \text{ months}$$

$$\$325.43 (1 + .0041666)^{300} = \$1,132.92$$

or use the Column 1 Factor, 5%, Monthly Compounding for 25 years which is 3.481290.

$$S^n = \$325.43 \cdot 3.481290 = \$1,132.92$$

(Note that for compounding periods less than annual, "Years" appears on the left side of the table and the appropriate compounding period on the right side of the table.)

2. Accumulation of one per period Column 2 provides factors for use in determining the future amount to which a series of equal periodic investments will grow. More specifically, this involves the assumption of investing an amount *at the end of one period* and that same amount each period thereafter for a total of "n" periods at "i" interest rate. This factor is solved by the following.

$$S_n = p\left[\frac{(1 + i)^n - 1}{i}\right]$$

S_n = the future balance of a series of "n" equal investments earning "i" interest rate.
p = the amount of the equal periodic investments.

Suppose that $1,000 were invested at 10% per annum *one year from today* and each year thereafter for a total of 8 years. The amount accumulated by EOY 8 is

$$S_n = \$1,000\left[\frac{(1 + .1)^8 - 1}{.10}\right] = \$11,435.89$$

or use the Column 2 Factor, 10%, Annual Compounding for 8 years which is 11.435888.

$$S_n = \$1,000 \cdot 11.435888 = \$11,435.89$$

Certain characteristics of this factor are worth special attention. First, the investment stream begins *not* at the present but at the end of the first compounding period. This may be seen by the fact that the value of the factor found at the first period (at EOY 1 for annual compounding, at the end of the first month for monthly compounding, etc.) is always 1.000000. This is because the first investment is made at the end of the first period and thus the value accumulated at that point is exactly the amount just invested since no interest has been yet earned. This characteristic is always present in the Column 2 Factor in that the accumulated value will always contain an investment amount that has not yet earned any interest.

The second point is that the number of investments is always equal to the number of compounding periods. Thus, in the preceding example eight years of annual compounding means that eight investments of $1,000 each were made over the eight-year investment period. A total of $8,000 was invested and the last $1,000 invested has not yet earned any interest.

To again illustrate the use of Column 2 Factors, suppose that $25 per quarter were invested for twelve years at a 5% rate compounded quarterly. If the first $25 amount were invested at the end of one quarter, how much would be accumulated by the end of twelve years? This may be solved as follows.

33

$$S_n = p\left[\frac{(1 + i)^n - 1}{i}\right]$$

p = \$25
i = 5\% ÷ 4 or .0125 →→→→→→↓

n = 12 years·4 or 48 quarters
thus, ↙←←←←←←←←←←↙

$$\$25\left[\frac{(1 + .0125)^{48} - 1}{.0125}\right] = \$1,630.71$$

or use the Column 2 Factor, 5%, Quarterly Compounding for 12 years which is 65.228388.

$$S_n = \$25 \cdot 65.228388 = \$1,630.71$$

3. Sinking fund factor Column 3 provides Factors for use in determining the amount of equal periodic investments that would be necessary to grow to an amount "S_n" by "n" periods when the money invested earns "i" interest rate per period. Note that this is the same general type of problem that was outlined for Column 2 Factors except that the periodic investment amount is sought here rather than the future amount accumulated. Thus, Columns 2 and 3 are reciprocals.[2] This factor is solved by the following.

$$p = S_n\left[\frac{i}{(1 + i)^n - 1}\right]$$

In order to relate this to the previous problem, suppose that the investment goal is to accumulate the exact amount of \$11,435.89 by the end of 8 years. How much must be invested each year, beginning one year from today, if the funds invested earned 10% per annum?

$$p = \$11,435.89\left[\frac{.1}{(1 + .1)^8 - 1}\right] = \$1,000.00$$

or use the Column 3 Factor, 10%, Annual Compounding for 8 years which is .087444.

$$p = \$11,435.89 \cdot .087444 = \$1,000.00$$

4. Present value—reversion of one Column 4 provides Factors that are the reciprocal of Column 1 Factors; thus, rather than solve for the future value of an investment when "P" is invested for "n" periods at "i" interest rate, the future value (S^n) is known and the present value (P) is calculated. The Column 4 Factor is solved.

$$P = S^n\left[\frac{1}{(1 + i)^n}\right]$$

[2] The reciprocal of any number "N" is 1 ÷ N.

Relating this to the earlier problem involving Column 1 Factors where $10,000 was invested at 5% compounded annually for two years, the future amount (S^n) was $11,025. Suppose instead that an investor was offered an opportunity to purchase an investment which promised $11,025 two years from today. If the investor could typically invest his capital at an interest rate of 5% compounded annually, the present value (P) of the investment is

$$P = \$11,025\left[\frac{1}{(1 + .05)^2}\right] = \$10,000$$

or use the Column 4 Factor, 5%, Annual Compounding for 2 years which is .907029.

$$P = \$11,025 \cdot .907029 = \$10,000$$

The logic employed here is that if the investor had $10,000 today and could invest it at 5% per annum, it would grow to the sum of $11,025 by the end of two years. Thus, at a 5% discount rate (the compound interest rate at which future sums to be received are "discounted" to the present) the investor should be indifferent between $10,000 today and $11,025 two years from today.

5. *Present value of an ordinary annuity of one per period*   Column 5 Factors are simply the summation or cumulative value of the Column 4 Factors and represent the present value of a series of uniform payments received each period for "n" periods when discounted at "i" interest rate. The Column 5 Factor is solved by the following.

$$a = p_n\left[\frac{1 - \dfrac{1}{(1 + i)^n}}{i}\right]$$

a = present value of a level annuity
p_n = uniform payments to be received per period

Suppose that $100 were to be received at the end of one year and each year thereafter for a total of 10 years. The present value of this level or ordinary annuity when discounted at 15% is

$$a = \$100\left[\frac{1 - \dfrac{1}{(1 + .15)^{10}}}{.15}\right] = \$501.88$$

or use the Column 5 Factor, 15%, Annual Compounding for 10 years which is 5.018769.

$$a = \$100 \cdot 5.018769 = \$501.88$$

6. *Installment to amortize one*   Column 6 Factors are the reciprocal of Column 5 Factors; thus, these factors are used to solve for the periodic equal payments necessary to amortize a given present value. The Column 6 Factor is solved by the following.

$$p_n = a\left[\frac{i}{1 - \dfrac{1}{(1 + i)^n}}\right]$$

35

In order to relate this to the previous problem suppose that someone wishes to borrow exactly $501.88. A lender is willing to lend this amount for a period of ten years at 15% interest per year but requires that the loan be completely repaid (amortized) with equal annual payments.

$$p_n = \$501.88 \left[\frac{.15}{1 - \dfrac{1}{(1 + .15)^{10}}} \right] = \$100.00$$

or use the Column 6 Factor, 15%, Annual Compounding for 10 years which is .19252.

$$p_n = \$501.88 \cdot .199252 = \$100.00$$

Summary of compound interest and discount factors

COLUMN 1—Amount of One at Compound Interest

$S^n = P \cdot F_i$
S^n = Future sum to which P will grow
P = Amount invested at the present
F_1 = Column 1 Factor for "n" periods at "i" interest rate

COLUMN 2—Accumulation of One per Period

$S_n = p \cdot F_2$
S_n = Future sum to which a series of equal investments will grow
p = Amount invested *per period*, beginning at the end of the first period
F_2 = Column 2 Factor

COLUMN 3—Sinking Fund Factor

$p = S_n \cdot F_3$
p = Amount that must be invested per period, with the first investment at the end of one period
S_n = Future sum to which a series of equal investments will grow
F_3 = Column 3 Factor

COLUMN 4—Present Value, Reversion of One

$P = S^n \cdot F_4$
P = Present value of a single future sum to be received
S^n = Future sum to be received
F_4 = Column 4 Factor

COLUMN 5—Present Value, Ordinary Annuity of One per Period

$a = p_n \cdot F_5$
a = Present value of a series of future sums to be received
p_n = Future amount to be received per period
F_5 = Column 5 Factor

COLUMN 6—Installment to Amortize One

$p_n = a \cdot F_6$
p_n = Amount of equal periodic payments required to amortize a present amount
a = Present amount to be amortized
F_6 = Column 6 Factor

Real estate applications of the compound interest tables

There is a wide variety of applications for the compound interest tables that was demonstrated in the preceding. Nearly every financial investment employs such applications since investment analysis involves the comparison of cash flows that occur at different times. This portion of the chapter will illustrate some specific types of applications to the field of real estate in order to provide reinforcement in training in the use of the tables. In addition, it will concentrate on types of calculations useful in the analysis of real estate investments.

Future Values

Column 1 problem   A survey of land sales over the past fifteen years indicates that comparable land to a subject site has increased at a rate of 5% annually. If this trend continues, what would the estimated sales price be in five years for a property worth $15,000 today?

Column 1, 5% Annual Compound Interest Table, $n = 5$
Factor $1.276282 \cdot \$15,000 = \$19,144.23$

Another form of Column 1 type problems is illustrated in a situation in which an investor pays $5,500 for a building lot in January 1967. In January 1975, he sells the lot for the amount of $11,789.74. At what annual compound rate of interest did the value of the land increase?

$$S^n = P \cdot F_1^8$$

$$\$11,789.74 = \$ \ 5,500 \cdot F_1^8$$

$$F_1^8 = \frac{\$11,789.74}{\$5,500} = 2.143589$$

Then the question becomes at what annual compound interest rate does an 8 year, Column 1 Factor equal 2.143589. Inspection of the tables shows that this occurs at exactly 10%.[3] This procedure is the equivalant of calculating

$$i = \left[\sqrt[n]{\frac{S^n}{P}} - 1 \right]$$

or

$$i = \left[\sqrt[8]{\frac{\$11,789.74}{\$5,500}} - 1 \right] = 10\%$$

Column 2 problem   Suppose that a land owner just leased his land for use as a parking lot. The lessee agreed to pay all expenses including property tax in his net lease contract. The lessor is to receive a ground rental of $180.00 per month for 9 years with the first payment to begin one month after signing the lease. If the lessor were to invest his monthly rental proceeds at an annual rate of 5%, compounded monthly, how much would he have in his investment account by the end of the term of the lease?

Column 2, 5% Monthly Compound Interest Table, $n = 108$
Factor $136.043196 \cdot \$180.00 = \$24,487.78$

Column 3 problem   An investor purchases an apartment property that is projected to require a new roof costing $10,000 five years from the date of purchase. How much must be set aside from monthly rental income at 5%, compounded monthly, to be assured of having the necessary capital for the roof?

Column 3, 5% Monthly Compound Interest Table, $n = 60$
Factor $.014705 \cdot \$10,000 = \$147.05$ per month

---

[3] Calculation when the "rate" does not fall exactly on rates provided by the Ellwood Tables is discussed in Appendix B under the portion entitled "Interpolation."

Note that 60 investments of $147.05 would be made for a total investment of $8,823.00; thus, $10,000 less $8,823 or $1,177 is the amount of interest earned over the five-year period.

Present values

Column 4 problem   An investor is considering the purchase of a "remainder" (the interest in a property which matures after the end of another estate). The property is under leases for seven years and the investor estimates that the value of the fee interest at the end of the lease will be $50,000. What should the investor be willing to pay for the remainder interest today if he requires a rate of return on his invested capital of at least 15% per annum?

Column 4, 15% Annual Compound Interest Table, n = 7
Factor .375937·$50,000 = $18,796.85

Alternatively viewed, if the investor were to invest $18,796.85 today at 15% compounded annually, it would grow to the amount of $50,000 by the end of seven years.

Column 1, 15% Annual Compound Interest Table, n = 7
Factor 2.660020·$18,796.85 = $50,000.00

Column 5 problem   What is the present value of a leasehold interest of $2,650 per year for four years when discounted at 10%?

Column 5, 10% Annual Compound Interest Table, n = 4
Factor 3.169865·$2,650 = $8,400.14

Now, suppose that the same stream of income were available in an investment (that is, $2,650 per year for 4 years) but that the first payment would begin three years from today rather than one year from today. In essence, this problem could be solved in three different ways, as follows.

Method 1
(Addition of Reversion Factors)

EOY	Column Factor (10%)	Cash Flows	Present Value
1	—	–0–	–0–
2	—	–0–	–0–
3	.751315	2,650	$1,990.98
4	.683013	2,650	$1,809.98
5	.620921	2,650	$1,645.44
6	.564474	2,650	$1,495.86
Total	2.619723	—	$6,942.26

2.619723 · $2,650 = $6,942.27

Method 2
(Subtraction of Annuity Factors)

This approach may be viewed as removing or subtracting out those periods for which no cash flows are received.

Column 5 Factor 10%, n=6	4.355261
Column 5 Factor 10% n=2	−1.735537
	2.619724
	×$ 2,650
	$6,942.27

Note that the factor çalculated by subtracting annuity factors is the same as that arrived at in "Method 1" by adding reversion factors.

Method 3
(Calculating Deferred Annuity)

The logic employed in this method is that at a 10% discount rate

n	$		n	$
1	–0–		1	–0–
2	–0–		2	$8,400.14
3	2,650	equals		
4	2,650			
5	2,650			
6	2,650			

Column 5 Factor 10%, n=4	3.169865
Column 4 Factor 10%, n=2	×.826446
	2.619722
	×$ 2,650
	$6,942.26

Column 6 problem   What is the monthly payment for a $25,000 mortgage loan at 5% for a term of 30 years?

Column 6, 5% Monthly Compound Interest Table, n=360
Factor .005369 · $25,000 = $134.23

Another example of the use of Column 6 factors would be a situation where a portion of a real estate investment must be recovered over a finite time period. Assume a situation where an investor pays $10,000 for a site and builds a $90,000 warehouse on it. Assume that the land value remains stable to perpetuity and that the warehouse has an economic life of 25 years. What would be the proper *annual net rental* on a twenty-five year contract if the investor requires a 10% return before taxes.

This may *seem* much more complex than the previous problem but in reality it is not. The $90,000 structure in this problem is treated as though it were a loan to be repaid with interest over its economic life. Thus the annual rent must include the following.

Rental—(10% of $10,000)		$1,000.00
Rental on Structure	$90,000	
(Col. 6 Factor, 10%, n=25)	×.110168	+9,915.12
Required Annual Net Rental		$10,915.12

Perpetuity problem   In the previous problem it was presumed that the site would produce $1,000 net rental to the site each year to perpetuity. Thus, at a 10% discount rate, the present value of the site is $10,000 ($1,000 ÷ .10). But what of a case where the stream of income to perpetuity is deferred? For example, what is the present value of a perpetual income stream of $1,000 which begins at EOY 5 instead of EOY 1 when discounted at 10%?

Method 1
(Subtraction of an Annuity)

n	$		n	$
1	1,000 received *each year* to perpetuity	minus	1	1,000
			2	1,000
			3	1,000
			4	1,000

or

3.169865   (Col. 5, 10%, n = 4)
× $1,000
$10,000 minus $3,169.87   = $6,830.13

The logic employed is that the present value of an ordinary perpetuity assumes that the income stream begins at EOY 1. If it begins at a later time, the present value of the amounts not received must be subtracted from the present value of an ordinary perpetuity.

Method 2
(Calculating Deferred Perpetuity)

The logic employed in this method is that at a 10% discount rate

n	$		n	$
1	–0–		1	–0–
2	–0–		2	–0–
3	–0–	equals	3	–0–
4	–0–		4	10,000
5	1,000	received *each year* to perpetuity		

Thus, the calculation becomes that of a simple single sum reversion of $10,000 to be received at EOY 4.

Present Value of Ordinary Perpetuity	$10,000
Column 4 Factor, 10%, n = 4	× .683013
Present Value of Deferred Perpetuity	$6,830.13

Mortgage calculations

Calculation of the size of periodic (generally monthly) payments over a given term necessary to fully amortize a mortgage loan has already been illustrated. Another very useful application of the compound interest tables is the calculation of mortgage balances over the term of the loan.

The typical mortgage loan contract can be considered from the standpoint of both the lender and the borrower. To the borrower, the mortgage loan represents a loan amount received in the present in return for level payments in the future over a specified period. In contrast, the lender views the loan as an investment outlay in the present which promises to return a series of equal cash flows over a specific term in the future.

In the previous section the example was used of a mortgage loan of $25,000 at 5% with monthly payments for a term of 30 years. Here it was found that the monthly payment necessary to amortize this loan is $134.23. From the standpoint of the investor (lender) in this example, the initial mortgage loan amount represents the *present value* of the thirty-year stream of monthly payments of $134.23.

Column 5 Factor		186.281617	
(5%, Monthly Compounding, n = 360)			
Monthly Payments		$134.23	
		$25,000.00	

(Actual calculation is $25,004.58 because of rounding cents in the payment)

Since the periodic payments on a mortgage loan can be viewed as an ordinary annuity, it is very simple to calculate the balance of the mortgage loan to any point in time over the life of the mortgage. It is the present value of the remaining stream of payments when discounted at the mortgage lending rate. For example, after 10 years of payments (120 payments of $134.23) have been made, 20 years (240 payments) remain. Therefore, the balance of the mortgage loan at EOY 10 is as follows.

Column 5 Factor	151.525313
(5%, Monthly Compounding, n = 240)	
Monthly Payment	× $134.23
Mortgage Balance, EOY 10	$20,339.24

In the analysis of real estate investments, it is often necessary to calculate both future mortgage balances and annual interest. This may be done as follows.

Year	EOY Mortgage Balance	Principal Reduction	Annual Payments	Interest Expense
0	$25,000.00	–0–	0	
1	24,635.67	$364.33	$1,610.76	$1,246.43
2	24,247.89	387.78	1,610.76	1,222.98
3	23,840.27	407.62	1,610.76	1,203.14
4	23,411.79	428.48	1,610.76	1,182.28
5	22,961.39	450.40	1,610.76	1,160.36
6	22,487.95	473.44	1,610.76	1,137.32
7	21,990.28	497.67	1,610.76	1,113.09
8	21,467.16	523.12	1,610.76	1,087.64
9	20,917.27	549.89	1,610.76	1,060.87
10	20,339.24	578.03	1,610.76	1,032.73

The procedure used to construct the preceding table was (1) calculate the mortgage balances for each of the ten subsequent periods using the remaining terms of 29 years through 20 years respectively; (2) subtract each year and balance from the previous year-end balance to obtain the second column, "Principal Reduction"; (3) calculate amount of annual payment by multiplying 12 times the monthly payment; and (4) find "Interest Expense" by subtracting the principal reduction from the "Annual Payment."

Conclusion

This chapter has been devoted to a systematic presentation of the concepts and techniques of compound interest and discounting. The tools and applications presented here can serve as a regular reference and guide to the real estate investment broker.

It simply is not possible to understand the ever-changing world of real estate finance and investment without a thorough working knowledge of the compound interest and discount tables and their many applications. There is no doubt that the investment problems and instruments of tomorrow will be different than those of today; however, the tools discussed in this chapter will be used to create the many innovations of the future. The time spent now in mastering these tools should be considered a sound *investment* which will pay great dividends in the future.

Chapter 4

Measuring Investment Returns

4

One of the most critical considerations in the analysis of real estate investments is the measure of investment desirability. Over the years, many measures have been used to indicate the relative profitability of alternative real estate investments with the interesting dilemma that different approaches or methods of measuring investment returns (relative investment desirability) produced both different relative rankings and different indicators of investment returns. It is not the purpose of this chapter to critique all past practices and techniques of analysis since this topic has already been discussed in various publications.[1] It is worthwhile noting, however, some of the principal weaknesses of traditional techniques.[2]

Investment in real estate involves making choices among investment alternatives. These choices must be made within the context of investment objectives. Real estate investors, like other investors, are concerned with providing for future consumption for themselves and/or others by limiting present consumption. Their selection of a particular investment to meet this end of future consumption takes into account several investment characteristics such as risk, return on investment, timing and duration of cash flows and other attributes. Most traditional measures of return are ill equipped to provide a clear and unequivocal indication of investment desirability in view of the variety of investment characteristics that may be important to a single investor.

A general shortcoming of traditional methods of measuring investment returns from real estate is the failure to account for the realities of the market place. There are several instances of this weakness in evidence. For example, it is common to measure the return on a real estate investment on a before-tax basis. This may be extremely misleading since each real estate transaction offers unique income tax effects. Although most investors are aware that the Federal income tax is a significant expense item of most investments, it is often ignored in selecting an investment. This may be because small, middle-income investors assume that they are not really tax sensitive or believe that all investments are affected proportionally by the income tax. Also, the returns of the most common investment alternatives to real estate are stated in before-tax terms. Many investors considering savings accounts or Certificates of Deposit as investment alternatives tend to forget that the annual interest will be treated as ordinary income for tax purposes. Even common stocks and corporate bonds are evaluated by many investors on the basis of before-tax yields.

---

[1] For an exposition of some of the traditional and conventional methods of measuring the return on real estate investments and their shortcomings, see Cooper, *Real Estate Investment Analysis*, Chapter 1 and Roulac, "Truth in Real Estate Reporting," *Real Estate Review*, pp. 90–95.

[2] Much of the following discussion is taken from Messner and Findlay, "Real Estate Investment Analysis: IRR Versus FMRR," *The Real Estate Appraiser*, pp. 5–20.

In addition, some techniques ignore the timing of cash flows from the investment while others "stabilize" a single-year income and thus distort the importance of timing. Still other techniques utilize non-market rates as "opportunity costs" in a practical world where markets exist. Finally, other approaches omit consideration of the impact of financing when measuring returns to the equity investor.

Present value and internal rate of return

Because of the many shortcomings related to those techniques which distort or disregard the timing of cash flows, there has been a significant move toward the use of the Internal Rate of Return (IRR) as the standard measure of return on equity investments in real estate. This widespread acceptance can be explained by the seeming advantages offered by this measure of return.

1. It is simple to understand and compute.

2. The measure is the "standard" among most financial institutions and has been widely used for mortgage loan rates, bond rates, etc.

3. The measure is provided in a convenient form, a rate, which can be readily used as the criterion of comparison for alternative investments.

In Chapter 3, the following investment alternatives were presented.

Cash Receipts from Alternative Investments

End of Year	Discounted Mortgage	Five-Year Note	Stock	Insurance Annuity	Land
1	$1,627.45	–0–	$ 1,000	$1,000	–0–
2	1,627.45	–0–	1,000	each	–0–
3	1,627.45	–0–	1,000	year	–0–
4	1,627.45	–0–	1,000	to	–0–
5	1,627.45	$16,105.10	1,000	perpetuity	–0–
6	1,627.45	–0–	1,000		–0–
7	1,627.45	–0–	1,000		–0–
8	1,627.45	–0–	1,000		–0–
9	1,627.45	–0–	1,000		–0–
10	1,627.45	–0–	11,000		$25,937.42
Total Receipts	$16,274.50	$16,105.10	$20,000	∞	$25,937.42

By now, with the illustration of the use of the compound interest and discount tables, it should be clear that each of the alternative investments has a present value of $10,000 when discounted at an annual rate of 10%. Since the cost of purchasing each alternative is exactly $10,000, the rate of return to the investor is 10%; that discount rate which reduces the sum of all future amounts to be received to exactly the amount of the initial investment.

Cash flows as the focus of analysis

All real estate investments may be viewed as cash flows. Subsequent chapters of this text are devoted to methods of determining or estimating the cash flows from real properties with particular emphasis on the effect of method of depreciation, form of ownership, age and type of property and various other factors that influence the after-tax cash flows. It is then the function of the compound interest and discount factors to determine both investment value and/or rate of return on the various investment alternatives available to the investor.

Within the context of the present value tables, estimated cash flows from real estate investments are treated as though they are *sums certain to be received*. That is, when future cash flows are discounted to the present, the discounting process makes no specific allowance for risk. Even the use of relatively higher discount rates, while having the effect of producing relatively lower present values, does not actually take into account the element of risk associated with the specific property. When comparisons are made among the present values and/or rates of return among investment alternatives, the alternatives should represent cash flows of similar risk and duration.

Future cash flows are also treated as though they represent dollars with the same purchasing power as those of the present. Since future cash flows are discounted to the present and compared with present dollar outlays, such comparisons are valid only when constant dollars are assumed.

Present value

The present value or present worth of an interest in a real property investment may be defined as the sum of all future benefits accruing to the owner of the interest when such benefits are discounted to the present by an appropriate discount rate. In the case of investment real estate, "future benefits" are expressed as *cash flows* which may be both receipts and outlays. As a general proposition, the present value of any interest in real estate may be estimated if the *amount* and *timing* of cash flows and the appropriate *discount rate* are known.

Any form of cash flow, level, decreasing, increasing and variable, may be converted to a simple present value figure. Negative cash flows are discounted in the same manner as positive cash flows and the sum of such flows are subtracted from the sum of positive flows. For example, compare the following present value calculations of different cash flows discounted at 15%, all of which total $100,000 to be received over a 6-year period.

Present Value of Cash Flows

EOY	A		B		C	
	CF	PV	CF	PV	CF	PV
1	$ 85,000	$73,913	$ 1,000	$ 870	$ 25,000	$21,739
2	5,000	3,781	2,000	1,512	25,000	18,904
3	4,000	2,630	3,000	1,973	25,000	16,438
4	3,000	1,715	4,000	2,287	(25,000)	(14,294)
5	2,000	994	5,000	2,486	25,000	12,429
6	1,000	432	85,000	36,748	25,000	10,808
	$100,000	$83,465	$100,000	$45,876	$100,000	$66,024

Internal rate of return

The typical investor is concerned with, in addition to the complete return *of* his invested capital, an adequate return *on* his investment. In general, this return on invested capital is expressed as an annual rate. The calculation of "rate of return" or "yield" of a real estate investment is an important measure of investment worth because it provides one basis for selecting among alternative investments. Since it is calculated from cash flows relating only to a specific investment (the initial investment outlay and the future cash flows) it is frequently called the Internal Rate of Return.

The IRR of an investment may be defined as *that rate of discount at which the present worth of future cash flows is exactly equal to the initial capital investment*. Three forms of IRR calculations are common in the analysis of real estate investments. The first represents the most simple form of investment return: a single sum returned for an initial investment.

For example, find the IRR of an investment of $15,000 that returns $39,900 in 7 years.

$$S^n = P \cdot F_1^7 \qquad \text{or} \qquad P = S^n \cdot F_4^7$$
$$\$39,900 = \$15,000 \cdot F_1^7 \qquad \$15,000 = \$39,900 \cdot F_4^7$$
$$F_1^7 = 2.660000 \qquad F_4^7 = .375940$$

Thus, the solution will be found by looking for a Column 1 Factor for 7 years that equals 2.660000 or a Column 4 Factor for 7 years that equals .375940. These are found at an annual rate of approximately 15%. Thus, the IRR of this investment is 15% because at this discount rate the present worth of the future amount to be received is equal to the initial investment.

Another common form of investment return is a level stream of income (ordinary annuity) in return for an initial investment. For example, find the IRR of an investment of $15,000 that returns $3,600 each year for 7 years.

$$a = p_n \cdot F_5^7 \qquad \text{or} \qquad p_n = a \cdot F_6^7$$
$$\$15,000 = \$3,600 \cdot F_5^7 \qquad \$3,600 = \$15,000 \cdot F_6^7$$
$$F_5^7 = 4.166667 \qquad F_6^7 = .240000$$

As in the previous problem, the solution is found by looking for a Column 5 Factor for 7 years that equals 4.166667 or a Column 6 factor for 7 years that equals .240000. These are found at an annual rate of approximately 15%.

Calculation of the IRR of the investment forms illustrated may be accomplished directly because the basic solution equation involves only one unknown. Variable cash flows, however, cannot be solved quite as readily and a "trial-and-error" process must be used to find that rate which discounts the future cash flows such that their sum equals the initial investment. Most conventional income properties produce variable after-tax cash flows. For example, find the IRR of an investment of $15,000 that produces the following cash flows.

n	$
1	3,000
2	3,000
3	3,000
4	2,000
5	2,000
6	2,000
7	13,700

This case is similar to many real estate investments in which variable cash flows are received for a period after which the property is sold, creating a single sum reversion. The method of finding the IRR is to systematically calculate the present values of the future income stream at successively higher rates, searching for that rate which will equate the present value of the cash flows with the initial investment. The following indicates the present value of these variable cash flows at different discount rates.

Present Values of Cash Flows

	Alternative Discount Rates			
	5%	10%	15%	20%
Present Value of Cash Flows	$22,611	$18,228	$15,003	$12,581

Clearly, the 15% discount rate reduces the future cash flows quite closely to the initial investment of $15,000. Thus, the IRR of this investment is approximately 15%. See appendix B under "Interpolation" for treatment of problems where the IRR falls at rates other than those for which factors are provided in the available compound interest and discount tables.

Problems with the use of IRR

Although IRR is widely used as a measure of investment return, there are a variety of problems connected with the reliance on IRR as the exclusive criterion of investment desirability. Before moving to a summary critique of some of the procedural problems inherent in quantifying the relative yield advantage of one real estate investment alternative over another, the reader is reminded again of at least two other considerations that should be taken into account when selecting (or guiding the selection of) investments: risk and non-financial elements. In the case of the former, risk, it should be noted that the following discussion is based upon the assumption that investments being compared are of *similar risk* so that an explicit measure of risk is not necessary. As indicated earlier in this text, present-value discount factors are not an acceptable means of adjusting for the risk inherent in an investment.

Turning to the particular weaknesses of the IRR as a measure of investment desirability, five problems are apparent.

Lack of unique yield

Conventional investments involve an initial outlay of capital with future receipts. For such investments, there can be one and only one IRR. For non-conventional investments, where the future net cash flow stream contains both receipts and outlays, the calculation may become more complex. Under certain circumstances, a given investment may have multiple IRR's or no IRR within the realm of real numbers.[3] Whenever this occurs, it is clear that the use of the IRR as the criterion of investment selection can be misleading.

Discounting negative cash flows

In the standard approach to the calculation of IRR, negative cash flows are discounted at the same internal rate as positive cash flows. However sound this approach may be from a mathematical standpoint, it generally makes little financial sense. The discount rate for negative cash flows should be that rate at which funds could be invested at the present period so as to be available to meet future outlay requirements. It would seem most reasonable to discount future negative cash flows by that rate which represents the best estimate of the investor's after-tax yield on relatively safe investments so that the amount set aside in the present would have a reasonable guarantee of increasing in value to the amount needed as an outlay in the future.[4]

---

[3] *Ibid.*, p. 9. See pages 8 and 9 in Messner and Findlay for numerical examples of non-conventional investments and the phenomenon of multiple yields.

[4] *Ibid.*, pp. 9–11.

Initial investment

Directly related to the procedure of discounting future outlays is the problem with the IRR of improperly identifying the true initial investment. In the typical IRR approach, the outlay in the present is the measure of the investor's initial investment. However, this does not take into account outlays (investments) in the future that may be necessary to continue the investment. The typical real estate investor is concerned not only with the initial capital investment needed to acquire an interest in the real estate but he is also most interested in future capital requirements that may not be met by either borrowing and/or by positive cash flows that occur prior to the future obligations.

For example, suppose that a developer is considering a project that offers the following cash flows after taxes and after borrowing.[5]

n	$	
0	($230,000)	Initial Investment
1	($500,000)	Future Outlays
2	($500,000)	
3	$2,000,000	Future Receipt

The IRR on this investment is approximately 30%. However, note that the investor is, in effect, discounting one million dollars of future outlays at 30% so that they represent a present "cost" of only $680,000. The key question here is: Could the developer reasonably expect to invest $680,000 in the present so as to meet solid obligations of $500,000 in one year and $500,000 at the end of the second year? The answer is, of course, only if he could invest the $680,000 in some form of investment that is relatively liquid and has an after-tax yield of 30%. Without belaboring the argument, it would seem clear that an *after-tax* rate of between 5% and 7% would be more realistic. If 5% were used, the "adjusted" rate could be calculated as follows.

n	$
0	($230,000) + ($929,705) = ($1,159,705) Adjusted Initial Investment
1	–0–
2	–0–
3	$2,000,000

Adjusted IRR = 20%

The substantial drop in IRR took place because of the different manner in which negative cash flows in the future were discounted. In addition, the initial investment is increased by $929,705. It is the contention here that these adjustments represent a significant improvement over the simple IRR procedure.

Reinvestment of cash proceeds

When the IRR is used to choose between mutually exclusive investment alternatives, there is the implicit assumption that the cash proceeds from the investments can be reinvested at the calculated IRR. If the timing of the cash flows differs among the investments being compared, the IRR may provide an invalid indicator of investment desirability. For example, consider the following choice problem between two investments.

---

[5] *Ibid.*, pp. 10–11.

Investments

n	A	B
0	($10,000)	($10,000)
1	–0–	$11,000
2	–0–	–0–
3	–0–	–0–
4	–0–	–0–
5	$20,114	$2,074

If the IRR is calculated for each of the alternative investments, the yield of "A" is 15% while the yield of "B" is 20%. The investments look quite similar; they both require the same initial investment and they are both for a duration of five years. Using IRR as the basis for investment selection, "B" is preferable to "A". However, this presumes that the investor's goal is to maximize rate of return or at least choose that investment alternative among several which has the highest IRR. What this neglects to consider are the reinvestment opportunities that should be taken into account in most investment decisions. In the previous example, Investment A involves only one cash flow received in the future while Investment B involves two. The question that should be asked when making investment comparisons of this type is: At what rate can the investor invest his intermediate cash flows? Suppose that the investor could hope to achieve a yield of only 10% on the EOY 1 cash flow from Investment B. A direct comparison of the result would be as follows.

Investments

n	A	B	
0	($10,000)	($10,000)	
1	–0–	$11,000	
2	–0–	–0–	Reinvested
3	–0–	–0–	at 10%
4	–0–	–0–	
5	$20,114	$ 2,074 + $16,105 = $18,179	

Clearly, the investor would have increased his future wealth position by a substantially greater amount by selecting Investment A rather than Investment B *if* he could reinvest his intermediate cash flows at a rate of only 10%. In order to make investment choices that reflect true market conditions, the reinvestment rate should be explicitly considered in the analysis of alternatives and it should not be assumed that the rate to be earned on reinvested funds is exactly equal to the IRR.

Size differences in investments

The size of an investment can influence the return in a number of ways. Implicit in the use of IRR is that investments being compared are both *divisible* and *replicable*. That is, the use of IRR implicitly assumes that any size cash flow can be reinvested at the constant IRR and that a given investment may be undertaken or replicated at any time and on any size scale. Obviously, this is seldom possible in the real world.

For example, assume the following mutually exclusive investment alternatives.

Investments

n	A	B
0	($10,000)	($15,000)
1	–0–	–0–
2	–0–	–0–
3	–0–	–0–
4	–0–	–0–
5	$30,518	$40,541

If the IRR is calculated for each of the alternative investments, the yield of "A" is 25% and the yield of "B" is 22%. If we rely exclusively upon IRR in the selection of one of these investments, "A" would be selected because it has the higher IRR. However, the real issue here is what would the investor do with the incremental investment (the $5,000 difference between the two initial investments) if he were to select Investment A? If we assume that the investor could select either "A" or "B", we must likewise assume that he has the larger of the two investment amounts available to invest. Under these circumstances, it is critical to the investment decision to make an explicit estimate of the rate of return that the differential investment might earn and incorporate that rate in the decision. For example, if the investor could earn only 10% on the differential $5,000 initial investment, the following case would result.

Investments

n	A Original (25%)	+ Differential (10%)	= Total	B
0	($10,000) +	($5,000) =	($15,000)	($15,000)
1	–0–	–0–	–0–	–0–
2	–0–	–0–	–0–	–0–
3	–0–	–0–	–0–	–0–
4	–0–	–0–	–0–	–0–
5	$30,518 +	$8,053 =	$38,571	$40,541

Thus, the investor would have been better off selecting Investment B with the lower IRR than selecting Investment A and investing the remaining $5,000 at 10%. The key question again is: What is the actual market rate that the investor can expect to invest his differential cash flows?

Another size-related issue is the implicit assumption made using the IRR as an investment criterion for mutually exclusive investment alternatives that any future cash flow, (negative or positive) *regardless of size*, can be reinvested at the IRR. Within the realm of real world investment opportunities it is clear that the dollar size (as well as the duration) of an investment is related to the yield. This market phenomenon is well known and widely observed, yet is ignored by the IRR measure.

Calculation and use of financial management rate of return

In view of the various shortcomings and deficiencies of the use of IRR with many forms of investment decisions, an alternative model called the Financial Management Rate of Return (FMRR) was developed.[6] This model was specifically developed around the assumption that the primary goal of the investor is to maximize his long-run wealth position. Although this may not be his only goal, it is generally consistent with other goals he may have. This model is based upon the terminal value rate of return concept which has existed in the economics and finance literature for some time and has recently been suggested for use in analyzing real estate investments.[7]

In particular, the FMRR is a specialized version of the geometric mean rate of return and is thus directly consistent with the goal of long-run wealth maximization.[8] It is described as "specialized" because the structure of the model has been modified to include as many of the unique characteristics of the real estate market as possible. FMRR makes the following assumptions.

1. *Only cash flows after financing and taxes from the property under evaluation are considered.* The fact that other sources of cash (such as other properties owned by the investor) may be available in future years to meet cash outflow requirements on the given property is ignored, as is the possibility of the investor meeting such payments through the use of unsecured credit.

2. *It is assumed that funds can be invested at any time in any amount at a safe after-tax rate (i_L) and withdrawn when needed.* This would represent highly liquid holdings at modest after-tax yields comparable to a savings account. The key points here are safety to principal and stability of interest with the ability to make any size investment, however small.

3. *It is assumed that funds can also be invested in "run of the mill" real estate projects of comparable risk at after-tax rates (i_R) above the safe rate.* The stipulation here is that such investments must be in minimum quantities of "R" dollars and such investments may not be liquidated to meet other cash requirements during the period under analysis.

These assumptions were included in the model to give recognition to the reality of the market and to stimulate the actions of a rational financial manager. Real investments are *not* completely divisible; they require a certain minimum level of investment and typically cannot be liquidated without suffering significant loss. At the same time, these returns are higher than those of the safe rate. The variables are defined in terms of "run of the mill" projects so that i_R will represent the minimum acceptable return at the given level of risk for an investment of R. Defined in this manner, i_R also represents the minimum return which could be earned by reinvesting cash thrown off early in a project's life. Hence, the main test of whether the i_R used in a given application of the model is appropriate is whether the analyst is confident that numerous projects would be available yielding at least that rate; if not, i_R should be lowered until such confidence is achieved.

---

[6] The FMRR was developed by M. Chapman Findlay and Stephen D. Messner of the School of Business Administration, the University of Connecticut, Storrs, Connecticut, in 1973. Jay W. Levine, working with Realtron Corporation, assisted the originators to relate and adapt their model to problems found in the real estate investment market. An explanation of this model was first published as *Determination and Usage of FM Rate of Return*, 1973, by Realtron Corporation, Detroit. An expanded version was presented by Findlay and Messner at the Eastern Finance Association meetings in April 1975, at the University of South Carolina.

[7] Dilmore, *The New Approach to Real Estate Appraising*, pp. 122–23.

[8] Latane, "Criteria for Choice among Risky Ventures," *Journal of Political Economy*, pp. 144–55.

Derivation of the basic FMRR model

A simple example can be used to demonstrate the calculation and use of the FMRR model, using only after-financing and after-tax cash flows to show how they are treated within this model. The FMRR was designed to overcome all of the deficiencies outlined previously. More specifically, it is designed to do the following.

1. Avoid the possibility of a non-unique solution by converting the cash flows into a conventional investment format.

2. Make explicit those assumptions implicit in the use of IRR regarding the discounting of outflows and the reinvestment of inflows. In essence, this eliminates the problems associated with cash flow reinvestment assumptions, variations of rate with size of investment and reinvestment and recognition of true initial investment.

To illustrate the FMRR model, the following example is provided.

n	$	
0	($10,000)	
1	($50,000)	
2	($50,000)	
3	$30,000	IRR = 25.2%
4	($20,000)	
5	$30,000	
6	$250,000	

Step 1. *Remove all future outflows by utilizing prior inflows where possible.* In this example, if $19,048 of the $30,000 received at EOY 3 were invested at a safe rate (i_L) of 5%, it would grow to $20,000 by EOY 4 and be available to meet the $20,000 outflow requirement at that point in time.

The cash flows are changed as follows.

n	$
0	($10,000)
1	($50,000)
2	($50,000)
3	10.952
4	–0–
5	$30,000
6	$250,000

Step 2. *Discount all remaining outflows to the present at the safe rate.* In this example, the $50,000 payments at EOY's 1 and 2 are discounted to the present at a rate of 5%. The cash flows are changed as follows.

n	$
0	($10,000) + ($92,971) = ($102,971)
1	–0–
2	–0–
3	$10,952
4	–0–
5	$30,000
6	$250,000

Note that this reflects the fact that the actual investment amount to be made or assumed by the investor is $102,971, not $10,000.

Step 3. *Compound forward those positive cash flows remaining at the appropriate rate.* In this example, assume R is equal to $10,000. Thus, cash flows received at EOY's 3 and 5 will be compounded forward at $i_R = 10\%$. The cash flows are changed as follows.

n	$
0	($102,971)
1	–0–
2	–0–
3	–0–
4	–0–
5	–0–
6	$250,000 + $14,577 + $33,000 = $297,577

FMRR = 19.4% (the rate at which $102,971 grows to $297,577 in 6 years)
IRR   = 25.2% (the rate which discounts all future cash flows such that the sum of the present values is equal to $10,000.)

The difference between the two measures of yield is entirely explained by the explicit estimates made for the various rates utilized within the FMRR calculation as compared with the assumption of the IRR approach in which all relevant rates are exactly equal to the calculated IRR.

Other applications of the FMRR

There are several other applications of the FMRR that can be most helpful in real estate investment decision-making. It is not within the scope of this chapter to detail such applications but the concerned reader is referred to the Messner-Findlay article for such extensions or modifications of the basic FMRR model.[9]

One of the more interesting and useful applications of the FMRR is in determining the "optimal holding period" of the investment. This is particularly true in view of the fact that the holding period of a real estate investment has generally been determined by the IRR, which is especially ill-suited to the task. In addition, the FMRR can be used in selecting among mutually exclusive alternative investments and in selecting from a mix of alternatives when investment funds are rationed.

   [9] *Ibid.*, pp. 18–20.

Chapter 5

Estimation of Real Estate Cash Flows

5

Thus far the major emphasis of this text has been on the process of converting forecast future cash flows (income receipts) into present value estimates by means of the mathematical process of compound discounting. The mathematical logic employed in discounting future cash flows is fundamentally essential in analyzing real estate investments. Of equal importance, however, is the process by which the future cash flows of a specific property (or group of properties) is estimated. Generally speaking, this process stands in marked contrast to the inexorable precision of the discounting process. Since estimates of cash flows generated by real estate necessarily involve estimates of the future, they are more often than not significantly less precise than the mathematical technique used to discount them to the present.

The estimation of future cash flows for income-producing real estate requires a variety of judgments and assumptions concerning the future. Among these are judgments concerning the property itself, the future of the neighborhood in which it is located, the general market conditions that will prevail in the future and their impact on the specific property, future developments in the federal income tax laws that may influence the after-tax cash flows of the property and myriad other factors which may affect the cash flows of the specific property over time. The point is that the task of income estimation typically requires both experience in and knowledge of the operation of the real estate market. It is not simply an extrapolation of the known market behavior of preceding years nor can the estimation problem be refined completely to objective statistical probabilities. In its final form, the estimate of future benefits from an investment in real estate must relate to the *amount*, *timing*, *duration* (or term) and the *stability* of after-tax cash flows to be received by the investor.

This process may be viewed as more an art than a science because of the variety of types of real estate income. The income from a long-term net lease is simplest to define because the lease itself usually states the rental stream. This estimation could become more complicated if a percentage rent is also required. At the other extreme, the income from a vacant portion of land, encumbered with debt, can account for a negative income stream created by the real estate taxes and the loan payments until sold.

Between these extremes is the apartment, the store building or other improved real estate with short-term leases where the owner pays all or most of the expenses. Other examples include vacant buildings as well as properties to be developed where all income and expense items must be estimated and projected.

Income estimation as a brokerage tool

Distinction between residential and investment property

At the outset, it is important to recognize the differences between marketing investment property and residential property. By understanding the differences, the broker presenting an investment property can readily see the most effective means of presenting a potential investment.

Residential properties are paid for from income unrelated to the property and are purchased to satisfy the functional and structural arrangement needed by the purchaser. These properties must have the floor plan and amenities that are of personal importance to the buyer. He is interested in the size of the home, the number of bedrooms and the room arrangement. Neighborhoods, the local school system, available transportation, churches, shopping, social and recreational facilities and, perhaps, the view from his living room window are important considerations. Real estate brokers stress these items in showing residential property.

In selling residential properties, a market data approach is typically used in determining market value and/or price. In other words, market value is determined by the sales price of similar properties. In some cases, replacement costs and the amount of actual depreciation that the property has already undergone might be considerations that influence residential property buyers.

When income-producing property is involved, the amenities, churches, neighborhood and view, are all secondary considerations. Income-producing properties are purchased for their ability to produce an income stream, whether that income is operating income or potential capital gain on resale or both and are paid for with the income generated by the property. The amenities and other factors that are so important in connection with residential properties have importance, insofar as income-producing property is concerned, only if they influence the stream of cash flows. Do they add to the quantity of that income; do they make the quality or the durability of that income any better?

Many brokers make the mistake of stressing only the physical characteristics of an investment property and/or its replacement cost when the purchaser is really interested in the future income benefits of property. The fact that the present owner has invested considerable sums in the property does not necessarily influence the potential buyer of investment property. If the income produced by the property will only justify a sale price of $175,000, the buyer does not care that the owner has actually invested $300,000 in the property and is "willing to let it go" for $250,000.

If, then, buyers purchase investment property for future income, it is absolutely imperative that the broker have all of the financial information about a property prior to marketing it. Just as a stock broker cannot market his stock without a prospectus (operating history), a real estate broker cannot intelligently present a property if the owner will not produce an operating statement until a qualified buyer is found.

Appraiser versus investment broker

The task of the real estate appraiser is most often that of estimating the *market value* of a property; that is, the most probable selling price of the property under "normal" exposure to the market and under financing terms generally available for properties of the type being appraised. Under the somewhat rigid definition utilized for market value, particularly in the legal context imposed by institutional mortgage lenders, property tax authorities and others, there is a single value at any point in time. Obviously, different opinions of market value among appraisers may prevail but in concept there is only one correct market value for a given property at a specific point in time.

In contrast, the investment broker is generally concerned with the value of a property to a specific potential investor. Under these conditions, the analysis of value takes into account the estimated after-tax cash flows, the desired or required rate of return on the equity investment and the financing terms available on the property to the specific investor. This value estimate is *investment value*: it may be less than, equal to or greater than market value. For example, *if* the potential investor is also "typical" in terms of the group of investors most likely to purchase the property under the competitive market conditions required under the definition of market value, investment value will be exactly equal to market value.

Collection of property data

The first step in estimating the future cash flows that will be generated by a specific property is to collect the most recent operating data from the present owner. Obtaining the financial information about previous years' operations, however, is not the broker's only responsibility. He must also be able to analyze and evaluate the information, process the information in an operating statement, convert the income stream to an estimate of value and, finally, be able to interpret to the owner or client what the consequences of ownership of the property under present and alternate financing arrangements mean.

Gathering operating data

Interview with owner   The broker, in his interview with the owner, must be firm and adamant in his quest for information. Many owners are reluctant to divulge financial information about their property. Most agree to supply the information "when a qualified buyer is found."

It is only when the broker truly understands that buyers are buying the future income rather than the structure that he can insist on obtaining proper information from the owner before any potential purchaser is contracted. It certainly follows that when owners also understand what truly motivates a buyer that they will usually supply the necessary information. No one buys securities without a prospectus. Thus, the public cannot be expected to purchase income property without a past history of its operations.

The broker cannot always depend on the owner's memory and should therefore insist on previous years' statements. The best information is usually obtained when the broker gets written authority from the owner's accountant for all the information needed. The owner's records will have validity but income tax statements will provide the best information. It is rare for income tax records to overstate income or understate expenses.

Property inspection   Although the property will be sold mainly on the basis of the financial data, it is necessary that the broker obtain physical data on the property. This will include type of construction, condition of the property, the size and area of the land and improvements. This information will be used as an aid in verifying incomes and expenses and for estimating value.

It is also important that the broker inspect the neighborhood and observe if it is economically stable, dying or growing.

If it is important, depending on the type of property, the broker will also investigate the following facilities.

Public transportation
Highways
Freeways
Interchanges
Power
Utilities
Rail transportation
Schools
Taxation procedures
Any other necessary data

Revision of property data   The information that the broker has obtained from the owner may or may not be valid. It may be 100% truthful and still not be valid. The owner, even if he is truthful, can only report what the property took in for the previous year or years and what expenses were incurred during the same years. The owner is not in a position to evaluate the data. This is the broker's task since he is interested in developing an operating statement that will more closely reflect what the property might be expected to do under average management conditions during future years. Buyers are paying for the future potential, not for past income.

It is possible that during the previous year rents could have been unusually low or high. It is the broker's job to find out what rents should be for this type of property. It is possible that last year's maintenance costs or taxes or any particular expense might have been ususually high or low and the broker must determine typical costs. It is possible that when all adjustments and revisions have been completed, not a single item of expense or income will be the same as indicated for previous years. However, the statement will more closely reflect what the building can be expected to do in the future.

The first step is to analyze the information obtained from the owner and make some of the following obvious adjustments.

If the owner is occupying the building, it is necessary to determine what rent he should be paying. Even if at this time the broker is unable to evaluate what the rent should be, a notation should at least be made that the owner is not paying rent.

The expenses should be evaluated to determine if they include any of the owner's personal expenses. It is possible that they could be legitimate tax deductions for the present owner but still not be expenses involved in obtaining the rent for the building under study.

Obtaining market data   In order to make the necessary adjustments to the historic operating data the broker must investigate and/or be familiar with the following market data.

Rental information must be obtained. What do similar properties rent per square foot per month or per year? Is a percentage rent applicable and, if so, how much? What are typical rent terms and provisions? How valid are the owner's stated rents as to quantity, quality and durability? What vacancy and credit loss factor should be applied? Are utilities included in the rent or are they paid for by the tenant? Do the comparable rent schedules have comparable services or furnishings?

Expenses must be analyzed individually and totally. Are the expenses indicated by the owner valid or should they be adjusted upward or downward? Are sufficient amounts allowed for taxes in districts that need new schools and other facilities? Are there proper amounts allowed as maintenance and repair expenses? Is the total expense ratio to income adequate?

The broker should also obtain from his own files, contractors or other sources reconstruction costs for the type of building under study. The broker must search the market for recent sales of similar properties and similar land. They will be needed for estimating market value.

Financial data indicated or omitted from the Owner's Statement must be verified. The broker will determine exact encumbrances, payments, interest rates and due dates. He will find out whether existing financial arrangements are by mortgage, trust deed or contract and determine the order of the liens. He must also determine if the existing loans may be assumed by a prospective purchaser and on what terms.

He will try to determine if there is any refinancing available and in what amounts, terms and rates. He will discover whether the seller will carry back any financing on a resale and at what terms.

Other important items of information the broker should include on the statement are assessed values of land, improvements and personal property as well as the present owner's basis and depreciation schedule.

Organization of property data

For purposes of investment analysis, *cash flows* are used rather than accrual accounting concepts to measure benefits. Thus, noncash flow "expenses" such as depreciation are *not* included in the measure of cash flows (although the impact of depreciation may be reflected through reduced tax outlays) while the cash outflow of debt repayment through mortgage amortization is not recorded as an accounting expense.

The typical cash flow statement for real estate is divided into the major categories of Gross Income (or Scheduled Gross Income), Gross Operating Income (Effective Gross Income), Operating Expenses, Net Operating Income, Before-Tax Cash Flows and After-Tax Cash Flows. Each of these major categories will be discussed in some detail.

Gross income (gross scheduled income)

This is generally defined as the "rent roll" or annual market rental for the entire capacity of rentable space in the property. If the property is owner-occupied, a market rental would be imputed; if the property is under long-term lease, the contract rent would be the most appropriate measure of the rent receipts. The main point here is that present rents for the property may be higher, lower or approximately equal to market rentals. It is important to determine (estimate) the most probable rent levels in the future because this is a critical first step in determining the future cash flows that the potential investor might expect to receive.

Gross operating income (effective gross income)

As indicated, Gross Income is the annual amount that the property would produce *if* all rentable space were rented. In most cases, it is not reasonable to assume 100% occupancy of the property. In any case, the "vacancy and credit losses" of similar and competitive properties must be compared with the subject property so that reasonable expectations of the future rate can be made. In general, the rate is measured as the annual percentage of total rentable space that is vacant. This rate is then converted into an annual dollar amount and subtracted from Gross Income.

Another factor that may influence Gross Operating Income is "Other Income." This is income related to the property but not derived directly from the rental of space. Examples would be income from the rent of parking space or income from concessions. Such income is added to Gross Income to obtain Gross Operating Income.

Operating expenses

As Gross Operating Income was defined, it represents the total cash inflows to the property that are available to pay operating expenses including income taxes, cover annual debt service and provide for a return on investment as well as a complete return of the investment over time. Operating Expenses typically include the following.

Taxes   The major tax paid on real estate is the property tax. This is a "fixed" expense in that it does not vary with occupancy but does (or can) change over time. Factors such as trends in the local or state property tax and the frequency of re-assessment can help in estimating likely future tax payments.

Insurance   Current quotations or estimates are needed in the case of multi-peril insurance for the property. The "prudent man" test should be applied to determine the extent of coverage.

Utilities   Utility costs may be increasing so that actual costs for the past year may understate significantly probable future costs. Utility companies may be able to provide some estimates for the future based upon past levels of consumption.

Licenses, permits and advertising   A check should be made to determine what licenses and/or permits are needed, if any, to operate the property and their annual cost. Local property management companies and other owners can provide some comparable information on the annual cost of advertising with signs, newspapers and other publications.

Management   There are two kinds of property management: professional and resident. Professional management is generally available and charges a percentage of Gross Operating Income. The resident manager is required in many areas and is generally used when a large number of units is involved and/or when day-to-day requirements call for constant supervision. Market data is usually available on the cost of such management.

The real problem in this category of operating expense is the tendency to omit this expense when the present owner and/or prospective buyer serves as the manager.

Payroll and payroll taxes   Regular employees used in operating the property must be paid and, in addition to the payroll expense, there is also the cost of payroll taxes, such as social security tax and workmens compensation insurance.

Supplies   This category of expense will vary significantly from one type of property to another but similar properties should have similar relative supply expenses.

Services   Special services required by the property such as rubbish collection and pool service must be included as an operating expense. Typically this category of expense is relatively small but as in the case of "supplies" can vary greatly from one type of property to another.

Maintenance Actual maintenance and repair expenses for the subject property for the past few years can be used as a starting point for estimating future expenses in this category. However, market experience should be compared with recent past history. Market data can generally be obtained from local management firms; in addition, there are published data on several types of income-producing properties providing average annual maintenance costs per unit of space.

Replacements Equipment and building parts with relatively short lives must be replaced periodically over the term of investment. Typical appraisal practice calls for prorating or "stabilizing" such outlays on an annual basis. This is accomplished by dividing the replacement cost by the forecast economic life to obtain the annual amount needed to cover replacement.

This appraisal treatment is technically incorrect for two reasons. From the standpoint of income tax calculations, the cost of replacements is a capital expenditure, *not* an expense, and must be depreciated over the economic life of the asset. Also, the practice of prorating the cash outlay over several annual periods distorts the actual cash flows used to measure investment value and return. Thus, proper practice for investment analysis is to forecast actual cash flows.

Net operating income

Net Operating Income is obtained by subtracting Operating Expenses from Gross Operating Income. This is *the* key measure of income used by appraisers, mortgage lenders, etc. when market value is sought. This is because it is the measure of return *before* financing, taxes and capital recovery.

Before-tax cash flow

As indicated, Net Operating Income (NOI) represents an estimate of the typical year's income return to the *entire* property. When the property is financed with a mortgage loan, the NOI must provide for the Annual Debt Service associated with the loan. Thus, Before-Tax Cash Flow is obtained by subtracting the Annual Debt Service from the NOI.

After-tax cash flow

This is the true "bottom line" of the annual returns of the investment. Each year's income tax liability is subtracted from Before-Tax Cash Flows to obtain After-Tax Cash Flow. The calculation of income tax liability will be considered in subsequent chapters but it is important to note that this may be (in fact, typically is) a negative figure. That is, accounting losses (because of the noncash depreciation expense) may be used to reduce taxes that would be paid on other income.

Illustration of cash flow statements

The following illustration is intended to show how data collected from both the present owner of an apartment property and from the market place may be used to develop cash flow estimates.

Owner's property data

The accounting records of a 28-unit apartment building for the past year reflected the following.

Rental Receipts		$51,000
Expenses		
Property taxes	$7,956	
Insurance	4,203	
Utilities	2,669	
Supplies	1,173	
Services	1,511	
Depreciation	5,000	
Interest	9,076	
		−31,588
Taxable income (accounting income)		$19,412

A physical inspection of the property indicated the following information.

The apartment buildings contained	26,500 sq. feet
garages	6,900 sq. feet
land 270 × 200	54,000 sq. feet
apartment rooms	100

All this information is listed on the Owner's Statement.

The owner's mortgage loan record indicates that the original mortgage loan of $200,000 is now eight years old. The interest rate of loan is 6%, payable monthly and the term of the loan is twenty years. Monthly payments on the loan are $1,432.80 and the present balance of the loan is $146,825.81.

Based upon this accounting record of the past year's income, NOI for the past year for the owner would be as follows.

Taxable Income		$19,412
Plus:		
Depreciation	$5,000	
Interest	9,076	
		+14,076
Owner's NOI		$33,488

Broker's cash flow estimate

Up to this point the only thing that has been accomplished is the organization of the owner's accounting data relating to the apartment in a form that will allow comparison with market data. The next step is to compare the past year's performance with the performance of other similar apartment properties in the same market area.

The information that was submitted by the owner reflects the results of last year's operations. Last year's results might or might not be an indication of results in the future. Consequently an analysis must be made of what the potential income of the property is, in terms of quantity, quality and durability, because the purchaser is buying the future potential benefits of the property.

To test the validity of the income information submitted by the owner, the broker reconstructs a new operating statement based upon the Owner's Statement and market area.

The first item calls for Gross Scheduled Income. This is the income that the property would produce if rented at market or economic rents 100% of the time. To estimate Gross Scheduled Income it is necessary to know what the typical rentals in the area are for this type of apartment. Studies may have to be made to determine unit rents on a square or cubic foot basis or per-room or per-apartment basis. In this case the broker's study indicates rents at $2.40 per square foot annually.

In addition, the study indicates that garage space rents at $96 per year. Thus, an estimate of Gross Scheduled Income would be as follows.

(26,500 sq. ft.) ($2.40)	$63,600
14 garages @ $96 per year	1,344
Gross scheduled income	$64,944
	or
	$64,950

The broker's studies also indicated that vacancies and credit losses are to be estimated at 6% or $3,897 (or $3,900). This is subtracted from Gross Scheduled Income resulting in Gross Operating Income.

Next, an analysis of the expenses is in order. The taxes submitted on the Owner's Statement were $8,000. An analysis of the tax situation must be made to determine whether that figure will hold for the next several years. (For example, are all the schools in the neighborhood adequate? Are there other improvements in the offering?) In this case the broker estimates an annual tax cost of $8,400.

The broker asks his insurance agent to check the owner's reported premium of $4,200. It was determined that this amount was for a three-year policy, the average annual cost being $1,500.

A check with the utilities companies for the last several years indicated an increase in utilities costs over those submitted by the owner. Therefore, the broker increased the utility costs to $2,700.

The broker determined that the present owner managed the property, collected the rents, did minor repairs and kept the lawn and gardens. Investigation indicated that typical management costs were a 5% management fee plus an onsite manager rental allowance of $50 per month, say approximately $3,700 per year.

Supplies were estimated at $120 per month or $1,400 per year. Services were estimated to be $175 per month or $2,100 per year. Maintenance costs are estimated at $140 per year per unit and miscellaneous costs at $50 per month.

It is now possible to calculate Net Operating Income for this property for a typical investor.

Gross Scheduled Income		$64,950
Less: Vacancy and credit losses		−3,900
Gross Operating Income		$61,050
Less: Operating expenses		
Taxes	$8,400	
Insurance	1,500	
Utilities	2,700	
Management	3,700	
Services	2,100	
Supplies	1,400	
Maintenance	3,920	
Other	600	
		−24,320
Net Operating Income		$36,730
	or	$36,700

Obviously, the broker's cash flow estimate for the property is significantly different from the owner's accounting of the past year's income for the property. The reasons are numerous and affect both rent receipts and operating expenses. It must be noted that the broker's estimate is based primarily on current market conditions. Thus, the estimate of cash flow is essentially a "one-year" estimate for the property. Whether or not this may be safely extrapolated into the future beyond the first year depends upon the specific circumstances. In later chapters of this text further examples will be provided of the process whereby the future income stream of a property is estimated.

Chapter 6

Real Estate Financing

6

General characteristics

Real estate, like most other forms of economic goods, may serve as collateral for loans. A key difference, however, is that real estate provides unique advantages to both lender and borrower that tend to make borrowing the rule of the real estate investment market rather than the exception. Of key importance to the lender is the fact that as security for a loan, most real estate has a long life (both physical and economic) and a fixed location. The borrower is concerned with financial leverage and, at times, simply supplementing his equity investment in order to meet the sizable purchase price of the property.

Certain outstanding characteristics are obvious as one views the financing of real estate that tend to set it apart from other types of financing. The relatively *long-term* nature of loans on real estate is unique. Of course short-term construction loans are typical for development projects but this is only a form of interim financing until the permanent loan is made. The durability of the property and its fixed location have made such long-terms a standard of the industry. Long terms mean relatively small principal returned per annum and increased cash flows for the investor in real estate.

Related to the long-term nature of real estate loans are the special risks associated with such long-term commitments. A wide variety of factors in the neighborhood where the property is located, the urban area that provides the demand for the property services and the national economy which is responsible for changes in purchasing power, federal government spending and monetary policy all affect the income-producing potential of a specific property. These must be taken into account by both the lender and the borrower-investor in making real estate finance decisions.

Also important to an understanding of real estate financing is the predominant instrument used in the market: the mortgage. The legal complexities surrounding the mortgage contract have tended to make real estate transactions relatively cumbersome and costly. In addition, terms, rates and conditions may vary significantly from location to location.

Finally, real estate may be financed in a variety of ways other than simply through mortgage loans. Partnerships, syndicates and trusts may be created to accumulate the necessary equity funds. In addition, leasing is a popular alternative means of financing real estate.

Sources of real estate funds

The major sources of mortgage loans for real estate investments are life insurance companies, commercial banks, mutual savings banks and savings and loan associations. Other important financial operatives in the market are mortgage brokers and companies, real estate investment trusts and individual lenders.

Life insurance companies

Life insurance companies specialize in large long-term loans on major real estate development projects. They represent the most important source of debt financing for major shopping center developments, office buildings and large multi-family projects. They have been the leaders in innovative financing techniques in this country and have in recent years used lender participations with a high degree of sources.

Commercial banks

Commercial banks also play a highly specialized role in real estate financing and have extended the scope of their activities in recent years. Although commercial banks do make mortgage loans, this has not been the area where they have had the greatest impact on the market. They are closely regulated with respect to their mortgage lending practices and by policy have not been as aggressive in mortgage lending as some other financial institutions even though their mortgage portfolios have increased in recent years. Their primary significance in the real estate market is in the area of short-term lending where they supply the vast majority of interim financing for real estate. They lend not only to developers during the construction phase of the project but they also finance other real estate lenders and investors such as mortgage brokers and companies.

Mutual savings banks

Most mutual savings banks are found on the East coast where they invest a major portion of their total portfolio in real estate. They are quite active in home mortgages and are also important area lenders for commercial and investment real estate. Like the insurance companies, they have been somewhat innovative and creative in their lending procedures and are helped by somewhat less regulation than other mortgage lenders.

Savings and loan associations

Savings and loan associations are "home loan" specialists who originate most of their mortgage portfolios locally. They are by far the most important sources of single-family mortgage loans in this country and have historically restricted the majority of their loan portfolios to this type of loan. In recent years, however, they have moved to diversify into other types of real estate investments including an emphasis on financing multi-family housing projects.

Mortgage banking

The primary function of mortgage brokers and companies is to channel mortgage funds from large institutional investors to developers and other real estate owners and users. The "broker" serves as an intermediary between borrower and lender and receives a fee for his services. Mortgage bankers on the other hand use their own funds (or warehoused funds borrowed from commercial banks) to make mortgage loans.

Real estate investment trusts

REITs have grown in number dramatically in the past few years and now represent a substantial source of funds for real estate investment. They operate and are governed much like closed-end mutual funds. Their performance throughout the early 1970s has been less than encouraging, however, and their future importance in the field of real estate financing is not clear.

Analyzing the impact of financing

In the case of real estate, particularly income-producing property, the typical informed purchaser (user and/or investor) uses mortgage financing. He does this for a number of reasons but the principal one is to take advantage of leverage. In addition, the purchaser also borrows because he may need to supplement his equity capital to meet the relatively large investment amount usually required in the real estate market. However, even if the knowledgeable investor had the necessary funds to buy a real estate investment on a "free and clear" basis, he generally would *not* do so.

Small investors, both individuals and syndicated groups formed to buy real estate investments, may absolutely require mortgage financing because they lack the necessary cash to buy on a completely equity basis. Business firms, however, that acquire income-type properties for their own use can frequently pay for the property from cash available within the firm. They usually elect not to do so because of their need for working capital for the business and because of their belief that their funds are more profitable when used in the business. Investors, whether users of the property or not, recognize that the *interest rates* on mortgages are usually lower than the overall rate of return on the property (NOI divided by selling price). When they borrow as much as they can, they accomplish the two-fold objectives of (1) enhancing their equity yield (the rate of return per annum on each dollar of equity funds invested) over what it would be without the use of borrowed funds and (2) extending their available funds into more leveraged investments, producing higher yields on those funds.

Leverage

Definition The term "leverage" refers to the use of borrowed funds that have a fixed cost to the borrower (or at least that have a portion of the borrowing cost fixed as in the case of equity participations) to complete the purchase of an investment type property. As a general proposition, the larger the percentage or ratio of borrowed funds to total value (or purchase price), the greater is the amount of leverage.

Financing Structure When borrowing is undertaken to finance the purchase of a real estate investment, several variable items are crucial.

Rate of interest

Ratio of loan to value

Term of the loan (period over which the loan is made) and method of amortization

Ratio of annual debt service to net operating income

Amount of loan in dollars

Impact of financing structure on equity yield

Rate of interest The interest rate paid for the use of money is one of the key variables in analyzing loan packages. The idea of increasing equity yield through borrowing is based upon expectation that money can be borrowed at a rate of interest that is lower than the overall rate of return produced by the property. If this expectation is realized, that proportion of the total investment financed by the mortgage produces an additional amount that is available to the equity investor.

If a $100,000 property produces $10,000 income per year and remains stable in value over the foreseeable future (that is, no allowance for capital recapture of principal is necessary), an equity investor will earn 10% per annum per dollar invested if he invests the entire $100,000 to buy the property.

    Total Investment: $100\% \times .10 = 10\%$ Overall Yield

If, however, the investor can borrow $60,000 at 8% interest (assume an interest-only loan with a 100% balloon payment at the time of maturity), his return each year during the period that the loan is outstanding is $5,200 on his $40,000 equity investment.

Total investment   100% × .10 = 10.00%
Mortgage interest   60% × .08 =   4.80
                                 5.20

Return on equity $= \dfrac{5.2\%}{40\%} = 13\%$

In this case, borrowing at a mortgage interest rate *below* the overall rate resulted in an increase in the equity yield from 10% to 13% per dollar of equity capital invested. This is because, in addition to earning $4,000 on the $40,000 of equity capital invested, the equity investor also received the *excess* of earnings over cost from the borrowed funds. This amounted to $1,200 since the $60,000 borrowed earned $6,000 and only cost the equity investor $4,800. This is an example of *positive leverage*.

Alternatively, if the equity investor could borrow at an interest cost of 10%, borrowing would have no effect on the equity *rate of return* but would reduce the amount of equity investment.

Total investment   100% × .10 = 10.00%
Mortgage interest   60% × .10 =   6.00
                                  4.00

Return on equity $= \dfrac{4.00}{40.00} = 10\%$

This is an example of *neutral leverage*.

Finally, the use of borrowed funds may actually reduce the return on equity if the *interest rate* exceeds the overall rate of return. For example, if the interest rate on borrowed funds were 11%, the equity investor would receive only $3,400 per year on his $40,000 investment, a rate of return of 8.5%.

Total investment   100% × .10 = 10.00%
Mortgage interest   60% × .11 =   6.60
                                  3.40

Return on equity $= \dfrac{3.40}{40.00} = 8.5\%$

This is an example of *negative leverage*.

Loan to value percentage   The percentage that the loan represents of the property value or purchase price can also influence equity yield. The higher the proportion of total investment represented by borrowed funds, the *greater* the leverage. The *leverage factor* is another means of expressing this and is simply the reciprocal of one minus the loan-to-value percentage. In the preceding examples, all loans were 60% of value; therefore, they each have the following leverage factor.

$$\frac{1}{1 - .6} = 2.5$$

In other words, the equity investment goes into the total investment 2.5 times. If an equity investor had $10,000 to invest and he found that he could borrow 60% of value, his leverage factor times his equity position determines the size of total investments.

$$2.5 \times \$10,000 = \$25,000$$

Under conditions of *positive leverage* (i.e. when the mortgage interest rate is less than the overall rate), the larger the leverage factor the higher the return on equity.

Total investment $100\% \times .10 = 10.00\%$
Mortgage interest $\underline{70\% \times .08 = 5.60}$
4.40

Return on equity $= \dfrac{4.40}{30.00} = 14.67\%$

or

Total investment $100\% \times .10 = 10.00\%$
Mortgage interest $\underline{80\% \times .08 = 6.40}$
3.60

Return on equity $= \dfrac{3.60}{20.00} = 18.00\%$

or

Total investment $100\% \times .10 = 10.00\%$
Mortgage interest $\underline{90\% \times .08 = 7.20}$
2.80

Return on equity $= \dfrac{2.80}{10.00} = 28.00\%$

It should be obvious at this point that there is an infinite variety of interest rate/ loan to value combinations that could be produced at any given equity yield. For example, as in the earlier case of an 8% interest and 18% equity yield, there are *many* other combinations that can produce the same equity yield.

$.85 \times .0859 = .0730$ $.90 \times .0911 = .0820$
$\underline{.15 \times (.18) = .0270}$ $\underline{.10 \times (.18) = .0180}$
$.1000$ $.1000$

$.80 \times .08 = .0640$
$\underline{.20 \times (.18) = .0360}$
$.1000$

$.75 \times .0733 = .0550$ $.70 \times .0567 = .0460$
$\underline{.25 \times (.18) = .0450}$ $\underline{.30 \times (.18) = .0540}$
$.1000$ $.1000$

Amortization method and term   The "term" of the loan is the length of time over which there will remain some outstanding balance on the loan. The amortization of the loan is the periodic repayment of the principal balance in addition to payment of interest for funds loaned. Three general types of amortization are present in the market.

1. Straight mortgage loan—Only interest is paid over the term and the entire amount of the original mortgage amount is paid at maturity.

2. Fully amortized mortgage loan—This is the typical loan payment method whereby periodic (most often monthly) equal payments are made such that the loan is completely paid back at maturity.

3. Partially amortized mortgage loan—This is a case in which the periodic payments of debt service are not sufficient to completely amortize the loan by its maturity, such that a lump sum payment, generally called a balloon payment, must be made to complete the return of all principal. This is often done by establishing the maturity of the loan for one period and setting the debt service payments for a longer period.

The examples of financing on equity yield thus far have considered only a "straight mortgage" where there was no amortization over the term. The typical long-term mortgage loan involves full amortization, however. The same $100,000 property produces an NOI of $10,000 and assumes that there is an $80,000 mortgage loan with an 11% mortgage constant.

Given: $100,000 Property which retains a constant value over time for 10 years
$80,000 Loan
$10,000 NOI
$8,800 Annual debt service (annual payments)

4. Examination of mortgage constant—

A Band of Investment Analysis

$$.80 \times .11 = .088$$
$$.20 \times .06 = .012$$
$$\overline{\hspace{1.5cm}.100}$$

Indicated Equity Yield = 6% *only* if the loan is 11%, interest only: if the loan has an annual constant of 11%, it may have an infinite variety of interest rate-term combinations. Some of these are as follows.

Percentage Interest	Term in Years	Mortgage Balance EOY 10
5	12.4	$19,626
6	13.5	$27,277
7	14.9	$35,787
8	16.9	$45,232
9	19.8	$55,691
10	25.2	$67,250
11	0	$80,000

B Equity Yields
The related equity yields of the lending terms presented above are calculated as follows.

5%

Invest $20,000 initially for a return of $1,200 per year for ten years plus an equity reversion of $80,374 ($100,000 less mortgage balance) at the end of ten years. IRR = 18%

6%

$1,200 per year for 10 years plus $72,723 at EOY 10. IRR = 17%

7%

$1,200 per year for 10 years plus $64,213 at EOY 10. IRR = 16%

8%

$1,200 per year for 10 years plus $54,768 at EOY 10. IRR = 14%

9%

$1,200 per year for 10 years plus $44,309 at EOY 10. IRR = 13%

10%

$1,200 per year for 10 years plus $32,750 at EOY 10. IRR = 10%

11%

$1,200 per year for 10 years plus $20,000 at EOY 10. IRR = 6%

C Generalizations

Certain observations and generalizations can be made from the preceding example.

a The "simple" band-of-investment example which indicated an equity yield of 6% is only valid for an interest-only loan that has an interest rate that is *equal* to the annual mortgage constant.

b The equity yield of the investment is greater than the overall rate of the investment if the interest rate on the loan is less than the overall rate.

c As the interest rate on the loan goes down relative to the overall rate, the equity rate rises.

d Even though the mortgage constant is greater than the overall rate, there are still loan terms that can result in equity yields that exceed the overall rate of returns on the property.

e Even lower debt service (mortgage constant) may not result in higher equity yields.

$$
\begin{array}{r}
.80 \times .10 = .08 \\
.20 \times .10 = .02 \\
\hline
.10
\end{array}
$$

Hence, the mortgage constant has been reduced to 10% from 11%, thereby increasing cash flow from $1,200 to $2,000. If the terms of the loan were 9.5%, 33 years, the balance of the loan at EOY 10 would be $73,776. The IRR to equity for this loan is calculated as follows:

$2,000 per year for 10 years and $26,224 to be received at EOY 10. IRR = 11%

Obviously, this return to equity is less than most of the equity returns shown in the preceding material *in spite of the fact that this loan has a lower constant.*

Even a 9% interest rate loan with a 10% constant has only a *13% equity rate of return*, still well below rates shown with an 11% constant.

Alternative Equity Yields with the Same Annual Debt Service and Loan Amount

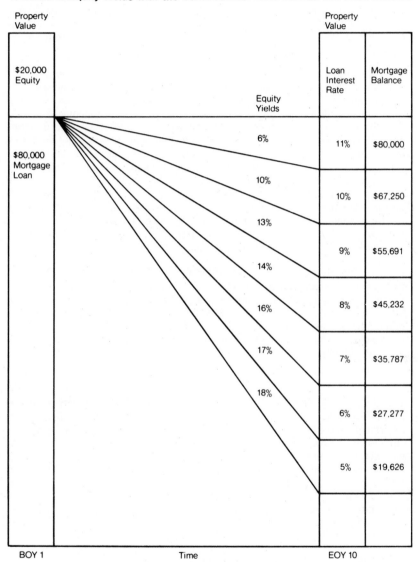

Thus, while some generalization can be made, the specific alternative terms and conditions of the mortgage contract should be compared in order to test for relative yield.

Ratio of annual debt service to net operating income   Most lenders who finance investment real estate projects are concerned more with the relationship between Net Operating Income and Annual Debt Service than they are with the loan to value percentage. The reason for this is the general lack of agreement concerning the value of the property and/or the overall rate that is used to capitalize Net Operating Income.

The foundation of the Market Value or Investment Value of income-producing real estate is the future stream of income. The key to estimating the present value of this future income rests in estimates of the *size, timing, duration* and *stability* of future income flows. The process of converting these future income flows to a present value is a simple matter of capitalization at the appropriate rate. In the area of mortgage lending, the *appropriate* rate can sometimes present quite a problem, particularly when the overall rate on the property combines such factors as the marginal tax rate of the typical investor, typical financing terms, recapture, etc. In any case, the lender is not really interested in acquiring the property. That, in essence, is his *final* step in protecting his loan capital. The first line of protection for the loan is the *income stream*, for it is from the income stream that the lender will receive both interest on the loan and periodic principal payments. Thus, the lender is much more concerned with a careful examination and analysis of the validity of estimates of NOI than his estimates of the present market value of the property.

Lenders typically specify "coverage ratios" for Annual Debt Service (ADS). Thus, the lender may require that NOI be 1.25 times ADS. Alternatively stated, the lender is requiring a 20% margin between NOI and ADS. For example, with the $100,000 property used previously, the NOI was forecast as $10,000. If the lender's requirements (based upon his experience in lending on properties of a similar type) were that there must be a 12% margin (ADS must be 88% of NOI) his coverage ratio would be as follows.

$$\frac{\text{ADS}}{\text{NOI}} = 88\% \text{ or } \frac{1}{.88} = 1.14 \text{ coverage}$$

In either case, the margin of safety is found by the extent to which NOI could drop (in this example, by 12%) and still have adequate coverage to meet the ADS requirements. If the NOI is highly stable and can be forecast with a high degree of accuracy with respect to size, timing and duration (as in the case of a long-term, complete net lease with an AAA tenant) the lender should require relatively less margin between NOI and ADS.

Amount of loan   The amount of the loan can be determined by either the loan-to-value ratio once value is established from NOI using an overall ratio or by capitalizing ADS with an appropriate mortgage constant. In general, the latter method has greater validity and accuracy than the former.

A typical mortgage loan analysis might proceed in the following manner.

1. Analysis of NOI forecasts—The lender examines the estimates of NOI in terms of size, timing, duration and stability. Based upon his knowledge of the market in which the property is (or is to be) located, his forecasts of the future for this location and type of property and his past experience in lending on this type of property in the same or similar locations, he will establish the required *safety margin* for the loan.

2. Determination of mortgage constant—The previous analysis established the *duration* of the income stream or at least a range of years, say between 30 and 35. The lender also has established, again within a range, the interest rate that he must obtain on a current basis for long-term loans. Based upon this combination of term and interest rate, he can estimate an annual mortgage constant.

3. Mortgage loan amount—The first approximation of the loan amount can be calculated by dividing the ADS by the mortgage constant.

A numerical example of this process would be as follows.

NOI = $10,000

Lender requires 20% margin (ADS must be at least 80% of NOI)
Interest rate must be at least 8.5%
Term cannot exceed 20 to 25 years
ADS = $8,000 (80% × $10,000)
Mortgage constant = .097712 to .105671

Loan amount: $\dfrac{\$8,000}{.105671} = \$75,700$

to

$$\dfrac{\$8,000}{.097712} = \$81,870$$

Thus, the preliminary loan amount indicates an approximate range between $75,000 and $80,000. The most likely area of negotiation would be with the *term* of the loan.

4. Relation between loan to value and ADS to NOI—It is immediately apparent that there is direct relationship between the ratio of Loan/Value and ADS/NOI. The direct link between these two is the overall rate of capitalization. It is interesting to note that when the mortgage constant and the overall rate are *equal*, the ratios of Loan to Value and ADS to NOI are exactly equal.

Loan   .80 × .10 = .08
Equity .20 × .10 = .02
                    .10

$$\dfrac{\text{Loan } \$80,000}{\text{Value } \$100,000} = \dfrac{\$8,000 \text{ ADS}}{\$10,000 \text{ NOI}}$$

Analyzing before- and after-tax yields

In general, the typical problem of financing investment real estate may be analyzed on a before-tax basis without serious effect on the selection process of that structure which creates the highest equity yield within comparable levels of risk and duration. Depreciation provides the primary tax shield for ordinary income and, therefore, the method of financing may be analyzed before depreciation expense is considered in the calculation of tax liability.

Like most generalizations, however, this does not hold for all financing decisions. When possible, a complete after-tax analysis should be accomplished to ensure that all variables have been taken into account. For example, from the preceding examples illustrating various combinations of interest rate and amortization, it is clear that on a *before-tax* basis, an investor negotiating the specific terms of a *fixed mortgage constant* would always create the highest equity yield by negotiating the lowest interest rate acceptable to the lender. This is because within the context of a *given mortgage constant*, the before-tax cash flow is the same no matter what the interest rate is. Thus, the lower the interest rate, the greater the proportion of ADS allocated to principal reduction (equity buildup).

On an after-tax basis, however, the interest portion of ADS is charged off as a business expense and the higher the interest rate, the lower the tax liability. This relationship can be seen in the following.

Given: $80,000 Loan with monthly payments of $730.33
Alternative interest rates of 7% and 9%

EOY	Annual Interest Expense		Differential Expense	Tax Savings with 9% Loan According to Marginal Tax Rate		
	9%	7%		30%	50%	70%
1	$ 7,134	$ 5,496	$ 1,638	491	819	1,147
2	6,982	5,261	1,721	516	861	1,205
3	6,813	5,007	1,806	542	903	1,264
4	6,631	4,737	1,894	568	947	1,326
5	6,431	4,445	1,986	596	993	1,390
6	6,212	4,132	2,080	624	1,040	1,456
7	5,972	3,797	2,175	653	1,088	1,523
8	5,710	3,438	2,272	682	1,136	1,590
9	5,423	3,053	2,370	711	1,185	1,659
10	5,111	2,642	2,469	741	1,235	1,728
Total	$62,419	$42,008	$20,411			
Equity, EOY 10	$45,221	$65,632	$20,411			
Rate that *equates* EOY 10 differential equity with annual cash flows				26%+	15%+	8%+

This table indicates the relative trade-offs that occur with marginal tax rates of 30%, 50% and 70% respectively. If one selects the 9% loan and is subject to only a 30% tax on increment and investment earnings, he must be able to invest the *annual savings* through reduced income taxes at an after-tax rate of more than 26% in order for the savings to equal the difference in equity positions, $20,411, at the end of year 10. In contrast, if the investor is in a 70% tax bracket, he may well be better off selecting the 9% loan since he must only invest the differential cash flows at an after-tax rate above 8%.

As an example of the logic used here, suppose that an investor in the 70% marginal tax bracket selected the 9% loan. By doing so, he chose the annual tax savings over the $20,411 differential in equity buildup at the end of the tenth year. In essence, his 70% tax bracket provides a shield of 70% of $20,411 or $14,288. (Note that this is the arithmetic sum of the tax savings.) The real decision question becomes: Would I prefer a total of $14,288 received periodically over the ten-year period *or* $20,411 received in ten years? Thus the basic question is one of the time value of money. Suppose that our 70% investor could earn 10% after taxes on his money available for investment. If so, he could produce the following terminal value by the end of ten years.

EOY	Cash Available for Investment at 10% Through Tax Savings	Number of Years Invested at 10%	Future Values EOY 10
1	$1,147	9	$2,705
2	1,205	8	2,583
3	1,264	7	2,463
4	1,326	6	2,349
5	1,390	5	2,239
6	1,456	4	2,132
7	1,523	3	2,027
8	1,590	2	1,924
9	1,659	1	1,825
10	1,728	0	1,728
	$14,288		$21,975

Thus, the tax savings, if reinvested at 10%, will grow to an amount of $21,975, which is larger than the differential equity build-up of $20,411 achieved with the 7% loan.

Other financing calculations

Calculations with balloon payment mortgages

Generally speaking, mortgage payments include both interest and principal payments such that the original mortgage amount is completely repaid over the full term of the loan. Sometimes, however, the amortization schedule agreed upon by the borrower and lender provides for only partial reduction of the principal amount with a "balloon" payment of the remaining principal at the end of the term.

A popular and easy way of calculating the periodic payment under such a mortgage contract is to agree upon a *rate* and *term* but calculate the mortgage payment based upon a somewhat longer term.

Assume a 9% interest rate, 15 year term with monthly payments.

If a 20-year amortization schedule were agreed upon, the Annual Mortgage Constant would be as follows.

$.008997 \times 12 = .107964$

The percentage of original loan remaining (balloon payment) at the end of the term (15 years) is the following.

$$\frac{48.173373 \text{ (60 Month, 9\% Annuity Factor)}}{111.144953 \text{ (240 Month, 9\% Annuity Factor)}} = 43\%$$

Specific mortgage loan amount of $80,000
$80,000 \times .008997 \times 12 = \$8,637.12$ Annual Debt Service
$719.76 (Monthly Payment) × 48.173373 (60 months, 9% Annuity Factor) = $34,673.27
Balloon Payment

Calculating balloon payment Often during loan negotiations an amount that can be paid from NOI is specified by the borrower rather than utilizing a specific amortization schedule. For example, suppose that an $80,000 loan is desired by the mortgagor who indicates that he can pay a maximum of $650 per month. The

73

mortgagee is willing to lend at 9% for 15 years with monthly payments. If the loan were fully amortized over 15 years, the monthly payment would be as follows.

$80,000 × .010142 (180 months, 9% Amortization Factor) = $811.36

Thus it will be necessary to create a balloon payment loan if the mortgage loan is to be made. The size of the balloon payment at the end of fifteen years can be calculated as follows.

Present value of a 15-year annuity of $650 per month
Discounted at 9%:
98.593409 × $650 = $64.085.72
(180 months, 9% annuity factor)

Thus, of the $80,000 loan, $64,085.72 in the present is returned through the monthly payments: the difference, $15,914.28, is the *present value* of the remaining balance at the end of fifteen years. Therefore, the balance at EOY 15 is the following.

$15,914.28 × 3.838043 = $61,079.69
(180 months, 9% Future Value of 1)

Calculating periodic payment   A variation arises when the lender specifies the amount (or percentage of original loan) that is to be paid at the end of the term. For example, suppose that the lender requires that a balloon payment of $40,000 be made at the end of fifteen years on a 9%, $80,000 loan. To find the monthly payment, find the present value of $40,000 to be paid at EOY 15 when discounted by 9%, monthly.

$40,000 × .260549 = $10,421.96
(180 months, 9% reversion factor)

Subtracting the PV of $40,000 to be paid at EOY 15 ($10,421.96) from the original loan amount ($80,000), a difference of $69,578.04 is found. This amount must be amortized over fifteen years with monthly payments at 9%.

$69,578.04 × .010142 = $705.66
(180 months, 9% amortization factor)

Another way of viewing the process of partial amortization is to consider that only a portion of the loan is being amortized while the remainder is an "interest-only" loan. For example, the case of the balloon payment which was 50% of the original mortgage loan amount could be looked at as though it were two loans.

$40,000 interest-only loan; 9% with monthly payments

Plus

$40,000 9% monthly payment loan for 15 years

$$50\% \times .007500 = .003750$$
$$50\% \times .010142 = .005071$$

Weighted monthly amortization factor: .008821

     $80,000 × .008821 = $705.68 Monthly payment

Mortgage participation financing[1]

In 1967, a "lender's market" for mortgage funds was created by tight money market conditions which were part of a national effort to halt inflation. Since lenders held the clear upper hand during this period in their loan negotiations, they sought new ways to guard against inflation by not only increasing their yield through higher fixed interest rates on the loans but also by participating in a part of the anticipated gain or profit which had heretofore been reserved for the equity investor. One of the more interesting aspects of this lending innovation was the uniqueness of each contract, with over 40 "standard" formulas in use by lending institutions.

Forms of lender participation   Although there is a wide variety of contracts which provide the mortgage lender with some form or combination of forms of variable participation in the future benefits of the property, the interests can be classified in six basic forms.

1. Income participations—This type of participation grants the right of the lender to share in some part of the cash flow to the property for a specified period of time, generally the term of the loan. It takes on three major forms.

Percentage of gross income provides the lender with a fixed percentage of gross rental income for a specified period.

Percentage of gross income provides for a fixed percentage of the net income of the property.

Percentage of cash flow provides for a share of either before- or after-tax cash flow (NOI less Annual Debt Service).

2. Equity participation—This type of participation grants rights to the lender that may endure beyond the term of the loan and may represent a true equity share of the property. The equity participation may or may not involve any direct investment by the lender beyond the amount of the loan.

Percentage of equity reversion is the right to share in some future reversionary value such as that derived through refinancing or sale.

Percentage of equity interest is a means by which the right to share in all of the equity benefits is transferred to the lender.

Percentage of tax shelter is a means by which the lender acquires a right to use all or a part of the tax shelter associated with the mortgaged property.

Example of the analysis of lender participations   Assume a lending situation which involves a gross income participation where property has the following characteristics.[2]

---

[1] Much of this material and examples are from Dasso, Kinnard and Messner. *Valuation and Analysis of Interests in Participation Financial Properties.*

[2] *Ibid.*, pp. 21–22.

Gross Income: $200,000

NOI: $112,000

Mortgage Loan: Amount, $840,000
        Interest rate, 9%
        Term, 25 years with annual payments
        Annual debt service, $85,520

Forecast reversion: EOY 10, $1,000,000

Lender participation: 4% of gross income for 25 years
        Desired return on participation income, 10%

Equity investor: Desired yield, 12%
        Holding period of property, 10 years

In order to analye the impact of the 4% Gross Income participation, find the respective present values of each of the interests in the property, in this case the mortgagee and the mortgagor.

Mortgagee's Interest

Initial mortgage loan		$840,000
Present value of G. I. participation		
4% of Gross income	$ 8,000	
25 yr., 10% Annuity factor	9.07704	
		72,616
Investment value of mortgagee interest		$912,616
IRR to lender: 10.14%		

Mortgagor's Interest

Present value of cash flow to borrower		
Annual cash flow	$ 18,480	
10 yr., 12% Annuity factor	× 5.65022	
		$104,416
Present value of reversion to borrower		
Sale price, EOY 10	$1,000,000	
Mortgage balance, EOY 10	−689,350	
Cash proceeds, EOY 10	$ 310,650	
Less:		
Value of lender's interest	$ 8,000	
15 yr., 10% Annuity factor	× 7.60608	
	− 60,849	
Net cash proceeds, EOY 10	$ 249,801	
10 yr., 12% Reversion factor	× .32197	
	$ 80,428	
Investment value of mortgagor interest	$184,844	

Thus, the property has an Investment Value of $1,097,460 (the sum of the two interests in the property: $912,616 + $184,844). The lender has increased his yield from the simple mortgage interest rate of 9% to an overall yield of 10.14%. The investor's (borrower's) yield depends upon his original equity investment. If he invests exactly $184,844, his IRR is 12%.

Wrap-around mortgages

The wrap-around mortgage is simply a refinancing device in which one lender uses the relatively low interest rate on an existing mortgage loan of another lender to advantage by creating a new mortgage instrument which incorporates the original loan. The "wrap" lender utilizes financial leverage to increase his yield over the nominal rate of the new loan. This form of loan can also be seen in the situation of a land contract in which the owner/seller retains title until all (or a specified number) payments on the property have been made by the purchaser. In this situation, the seller may have or acquire a mortgage loan on the property that is below the rate being paid by the purchaser.

An example of this form of financing would be a situation where a lender is approached by a potential borrower who has a property with an existing mortgage loan. The existing loan was originally for $150,000 with a 7.5% interest rate and monthly payments for 25 years. The loan is presently five years old. The borrower wishes to refinance and the new lender offers to "wrap" the existing loan and advance a new wrap-around loan for $160,000 at 8.5% with monthly payments for 25 years. What is the rate of return on the new loan which wraps the existing loan?

First, calculate the present balance of the existing $7\frac{1}{2}$% loan.

Monthly debt service, 7.5% Loan
(300 Month amortization factor, 7.5%)
.007390 × $150,000 = $1.108.50

Mortgage balance, EOY 5
(240 Month annuity factor, 7.5%)
124.132131 × $1,108.50 = $137,600.47

Thus, the amount actually extended by the wrap lender is as follows.

$160,000.00
− 137,600.47
$ 22,399.53   Amount of cash loaned

This amount, $22,399.53, is then the initial investment that is made to obtain the future benefits of monthly debt service. The measure of this benefit is the following.

Monthly debt service, 8.5% Loan
(300 Month amortization factor, 8.5%)
.008052 × $160,000 = $1,288.32

For the first 240 months of the new mortgage, the following is received by the wrap lender.

$1,288.32   (8.5% Loan MDS)
− 1,108.50   (7.5% Loan MDS)
$ 179.82   Difference to wrap lender

In addition, the wrap lender receives the full $1,288.32 per month for the final 60 months of the loan.

IRR on new loan:

PV of 240 monthly payments of $179.82 at 11.75%
92.275858 × $179.82 = $16,593.04

Plus

PV of 60 monthly payments of $1,288.32 deferred 240 months at 11.75%
45.211388 × .096465 × $1,288.32 = $5,618.77

Together these future sums to be received have a present value of $22,211.81 when discounted at 11.75%. This is approximately equal to the original investment of $22,399.53. Thus, the IRR for the investment is approximately 11.75%.

Note that the appearance is that the loan rate through refinancing is increased by only one percentage point and that the new lender's yield is only 8.5% when, in fact, his yield is 11.75%.

Mortgage discount points

It is most common among mortgage lenders to require "discount points" on mortgage loans as a means of increasing their yield. A discount point is, by definition, one percent of the face value of the mortgage at the time it is granted. Obviously, by requiring the payment of discount points at the time the loan is granted, the lender decreases the amount he is lending without changing the flow of future debt service and thus increases his IRR on the loan.

Calculating the yield on discounted mortgages In order to determine the yield (rate paid by the borrower if the borrower pays the points *or* yield received by the lender) on a discounted mortgage, one has only to relate the actual amount loaned with the periodic mortgage payments.

Mortgage amount: $50,000
Terms: 7.5% for 25 years with monthly payments
Discount points: 5 (or an amount of $2,500)
Monthly payment: $369.50

First, calculate the amount actually loaned.

$50,000	Face amount of loan
2,500	Amount of discount
$47,500	Cash amount actually loaned

Next, relate this to the periodic payment.

$47.500 = 369.50×300 Month annuity factor

Therefore, $\dfrac{\$47,500}{\$369.50} = 128.552097$

Find a 300-month annuity factor that is approximately equal to this factor value.

%	300 Month Annuity Factor
8	129.564522
8.25	126.831103

Thus, the rate is just slightly above 8%

Note that this yield rate or IRR is applicable *only* if the mortgage is held to maturity and thus it represents the smallest possible yield that will be received by the lender. Suppose that the mortgage loan were paid off at the end of five years when a balance of $45,866.28 remained. The actual yield received by the lender would be calculated as though there were an investment of $47,500 which returned $369.50 per month for 60 months plus $45,866.28 at the end of the fifth year. Thus, we simply search for that rate which equates the sum of the present values of the future cash flows with the initial investment.

78

At 8.75% present values of the respective cash flows:

$45,866.28	Loan balance, EOY 5
.646674	Reversion factor, 60 months, 8.75%
$29,660.53	PV of 5th year loan balance

Plus

$ 369.50	Monthly payments for 300 months
48.456109	Annuity factor, 60 months, 8.75%
+$17,904.53	
$47,565.06	Approximately equal to $47,500

Thus, the yield is slightly over 8.75% *if* the loan is held for only five years. Because the monthly loan payments are based upon $50,000, the mortgage balance has an element of yield in it. In essence, the discount is additional interest spread over the entire life of the loan. If held to full term (maturity), the yield to the lender is slightly over 8% but if the loan is paid off early, the yield for the period held will be higher. In fact, the sooner the loan is paid off, the higher the yield to the lender. Imagine, if the loan were paid off seconds after being granted, an amount of $2,500 would have been earned for that brief period of time.

Calculating points to achieve yield   If the lender in this case wanted to achieve an 8.5 yield if the mortgage were held for the full term, he could calculate the necessary points in the following manner.

Determine the present value of the Monthly Debt Service payments when discounted at the desired yield rate of 8.5%.

$ 369.50	
124.188570	Annuity factor, 300 months, 8.5%
$ 45,887.68	Present value of monthly debt service

Clearly, if the lender invested $45,887.68 in return for 300 monthly payments of $369.50 his yield would be exactly 8.5%. Thus, the necessary discount to raise the 7.5% mortgage for 25 years to a full term yield of 8.5% is as follows.

$50,000.00	
−45,887.68	
$ 4,112.32	÷ $50,000 = 8.22% or 8.22 discount points

Section II

Impact of Federal Income Tax on Real Estate Investments

Chapter 7

The Tax Process

7

While neither the investor nor the real estate broker is expected to be an income tax expert, familiarity with the more general tax rules is essential for the purposes of determining motivation, comparison or consequences of an investment program. Such familiarity should also enable the broker or investor to read a tax report and understand its makeup and consequences.

Tax law background

Tax legislation is combined in one immense section of the Federal law called the Internal Revenue Code. This Code is revised from time to time by Congress; some revisions are extensive. In addition, Congress has created an administrative agency to collect the tax and interpret the tax law (the Internal Revenue Service, often referred to as "IRS"). IRS has issued elaborate Regulations and rulings interpreting the Internal Revenue Code. The Federal Courts also constantly review the Code, the Regulations and the rulings as applied to complaining taxpayers in literally thousands of cases and have at times upheld, upset or altered those rules by court opinions and decisions. As a result of an accumulation of more than half a century of legislation, administrative rulings and court opinions, a continuing and ever-changing mass of tax law has been developed. Although it takes full-time professional experts to research and interpret specific, complex situations, because the income tax is an escalating major cost of living item, it should be basically understood by every income-earning individual. Everyone has the legal right to minimize his tax bill by prudent management of his affairs within the framework of the rules.

Nature of taxable income

The tax law defines gross income as income from all sources. It is reported on forms and schedules provided by IRS and is reduced by deductions, adjustments and exemptions to arrive at a figure called "taxable income." To this figure is applied the applicable tax rate to determine tax liability. Certain credits, where allowable, reduce the calculated tax liability.

Following is a quick summary of various types of income and the progression from gross to taxable income for an individual. The total of the items is referred to as adjusted gross income, an intermediate step in calculating taxable income.

Income Sources	Minus Adjustments
Gross wages	Sick pay, moving expenses, business expenses
Dividends	$100 exclusion per person

Interest	State and municipal bond interest
Pensions, annuities	Formula adjustments
Rents, royalties	Depreciation, repairs, other expenses
Business	Costs of operation
Farm	Costs of operation
Sales and exchanges of property	Basis (cost of acquisition plus capital improvements and selling costs, minus depreciation), 50% of long-term capital gain, where applicable

Taxable income is obtained by deducting the following from adjusted gross income.

Itemized deductions for certain medical expenses, charitable contributions, interest expenses, taxes and other costs. (If deductions are not itemized, a flat standard deduction or low income allowance may be deducted. See page 86.)

Exemptions per taxpayer of $750. An additional $750 is allowed for each taxpayer who is over 65, each taxpayer who is blind and for each of the taxpayer's dependents. (For 1975, credits against the tax for taxpayer exemptions and dependents are also allowed. See page 87.)

Types of income

For Federal income tax purposes, taxpayers may have two types of taxable income, ordinary income and capital gains. As will be demonstrated later in this chapter, certain capital gains are taxed at much lower effective rates than is ordinary income.

There is a third type of income a taxpayer may have: tax-exempt income. This type is usually in the form of interest on bonds or other obligations of states, cities and other subdivisions of a state, commonly referred to as municipal bonds. It is also possible to have a gain or profit that is not recognized for tax purposes. That is to say that while the gain is there, at the moment it is realized, it is not taxable. That often occurs when there is an exchange of like-kind property, usually real estate. (Exchanges are gone into in depth beginning at page 195.)

In the determination of whether certain gains from the disposition of real estate are to be treated as capital gains or ordinary income, the status of the taxpayer relative to the property is a vital factor. If he is deemed to be an "investor," his gain will generally be a capital gain; however, if he is deemed to be a "dealer" in that property, his gain is ordinary income, i.e. income derived from the operation of his business.

Accounting methods

Taxable income is determined by reducing gross income by allowable deductions. However, there is a timing factor to be considered; that is, *when* income or expense arises. There are two common, recognized methods of accounting: the accrual method and the cash method.

The accrual method

This is considered the more accurate method; it matches the income and expense attributable to a period of time, regardless of when the income is actually received or the expense paid. In other words, income is reported when everything that has to be done to entitle the recipient to the income has occurred. Similarly, an expense is deductible when everything has been done that requires the payment. The fact that the payment date is to occur prior to or after all the other events is disregarded.

Examples

Brown is a landlord and is entitled to receive $1,000 a month for the premises he rents to Green. Rent is payable on the first day of the month for that month. Green is delinquent in his rent payment and pays the December 1974 rent in January 1975. If Brown is on the accrual basis, he must report the December rent in 1974 even though he received payment in 1975. Even if (in the unusual event) the December rent were actually payable in 1975, Brown would still have to report the December rent as 1974 income.

Brown, the landlord in the previous example, has fuel oil delivered to him in 1974. He receives a bill for $250. Under the terms of his agreement with the vendor, payment is not due until 1975. Brown pays for the oil in 1975. On the accrual basis, Brown deducts the $250 in 1974.

The accrual method can be used by any taxpayer. It is, however, required if inventories are a substantial income-producing factor in his business.

The cash method

This is a much simpler method to apply although it is not considered as scientifically accurate. It also permits greater flexibility in moving income and deductions from one year to another. Under this method, income is recognized and deductions are allowable when the actual payment takes place.

Examples

Going back to our first example, since Brown did not receive the December 1974 rent until 1975, as a cash basis taxpayer he reports that rent as income in 1975, when he receives it.

Brown gets the deduction for the fuel payment in 1975 when he paid for it.

Constructive receipt When the cash method is used, income may not be avoided merely by turning one's back to available income. Once payment is tendered or is available for the asking, the income is deemed to have been realized even though the actual payment has not been received. For example, when interest is credited to a savings bank account, it becomes income even though the amount is not withdrawn.

Once payment is tendered, it becomes income. Asking the payor to hold up on payment at that point is too late. However, it is permissible to arrange in advance when payment is to be due. For example, a broker can arrange before a closing that although title will close in December 1974, the seller will not pay him his commission until 1975. If this arrangement is made as a condition for the broker's representation of the seller prior to the sale, the income will become 1975 income if the broker is a cash-basis taxpayer. On the other hand, if the commission was to be paid at the closing and at that time the broker says, "hold onto the money until next year and then pay me," he has constructive receipt in 1974.

Choosing and changing accounting methods

A taxpayer may choose the accounting method he desires (subject to the limitation on inventories) on his first tax return for that business. Typically, individuals whose major (or sole) income is from wages and salaries use the cash method. Professionals (doctors, lawyers, accountants) and those in service businesses (real estate brokers, for example) use the cash method more often than not.

Once an accounting method has been chosen, the taxpayer must continue to use that method for that business unless he gets permission from the IRS to change. (When permission for change is granted, IRS generally requires certain adjustments and there may be additional tax to pay as a result. Often, the additional tax is permitted to be paid ratably over a 10-year period.)

Installment method

An exception to the cash and accrual method is the installment method. Under this method, gain on the sale of property is permitted to be reported ratably over the period of collection. This method applies when the sales price is to be paid over a period of more than one year. This is a very popular method for reporting gain on the sale of real estate. A complete discussion of the installment method and how to use it is on page 181.

Taxation of individual's ordinary income

Typically, an individual's ordinary income will arise from salary or wages if he is an employee; this includes the executive or the stockholder who is employed by his own corporation. If he is self-employed or a partner in a partnership, his ordinary income will, in effect, be the net profits from the operation.

Thus, we can say that the major source of an individual's ordinary income normally comes from his gainful occupation.

In addition, there are other types of ordinary income. Security income, dividends on stocks and interest on bonds or bank accounts are ordinary income. However, even a portion of security income may be tax exempt. The first $100 of each individual's dividend income is not taxable. If husband and wife each has dividend income, each can exclude the first $100 of dividends from his income. Should they hold stock in joint name, each is considered to own half for this purpose. Also, as previously mentioned, interest on municipal bonds is not taxable.

Royalty payments are ordinary income as are the taxable portions of annuity payments.

Real estate ownership can also create ordinary income. The ordinary income from investment real estate is the real estate taxable income; that is, gross income collected less depreciation, repairs and other expenses.

Because depreciation may exceed the total of the otherwise taxable income and the principal payments on the loan, it is possible to receive cash flow from the real estate and still have a net loss for tax purposes.

Examples

Gross rents collected		$130,000
Less: Depreciation	$40,000	
Repairs and maintenance	15,000	
Other expenses—interest, real estate taxes, management	85,000	140,000
Net loss		($10,000)

Although there was a tax loss, the owner of the property could still end up with cash in hand, where, for example, his cash outlay for principal payments (not deductible for tax purposes) was less than the deduction for depreciation (for which no cash outlay is required).

Assume in the preceding example that the owner paid $25,000 in mortgage principal payments during the year. His cash position would be as follows.

Gross rents collected		$130,000
Less: Cash outlays:		
Repairs and maintenance	$15,000	
Principal payment on mortgage	25,000	
Other expenses	85,000	125,000
Cash available to investor		$ 5,000

Thus, while he had a tax loss of $10,000, at the same time he has cash in hand of $5,000.

The tax loss of $10,000 is fully deductible. That is, it reduces the other ordinary taxable income the property owner may have. Thus, if his ordinary income from gainful employment dividends, interest, etc. totals $35,000 (after deductions and exemptions), his ordinary income will be reduced to $25,000 by applying the $10,000 taxable loss from the real estate investment.

Business income and farm income are reduced much the same way as rents. All necessary reasonable costs are deducted from the gross to get the net amount added to ordinary income.

Deductions and exemptions

In computing the tax of an individual, we must first reduce his ordinary income by allowable deductions and exemptions. We have already seen that in determining his ordinary income (or loss) from rental real estate, we reduce his gross operating income from the property by his operating expenses, interest expense of loans on the property (subject to limitations on page 139) and depreciation. But from the individual's total income (from gainful employment, securities and real estate, etc.) he may subtract personal deductions.

These are made up of charitable contributions, medical expenses, interest (other than interest already deducted in arriving at real estate taxable income), taxes (other than Federal income taxes and real estate taxes already deducted among the operating expenses of his real estate), casualty losses and other expenses related to investments or to the production of income. These are generally referred to as an individual's itemized deductions.

There is an alternative deduction, the standard deduction, that is available in lieu of the personal deductions. The standard deduction is taken when it exceeds the total of the personal deductions.

The standard deduction is a stated percentage of an individual's adjusted gross income. (Generally, his adjusted gross income is the total of salary or wages, net business income after business deductions, interest, dividends, royalties, annuities, taxable portion of capital gains and net taxable income from real estate.) The standard deduction is 15% of adjusted gross income but not more than $2,000.

There is also a minimum standard deduction called the low income allowance. The low income allowance is $1,300 ($650 for a married person filing separately). The primary purpose of this allowance is to remove those with low incomes from the tax rolls altogether. For example, a husband and wife are each entitled to a $750 exemption. The total of $1,500 plus the low income allowance of $1,300 permits them to have a total income of $2,800 without having to file a tax return.

For 1975 only, the standard deduction is 16% of adjusted gross income with a maximum of $2,600 for a married couple filing a joint return; $2,300 for a single person filing a separate return and $1,300 for each spouse when a married couple file separate returns. The low income allowance, for 1975 only, is $1,900 for a married couple filing a joint return; $1,600 for a single person filing a separate return and $950 for each spouse when a married couple file separate returns.

The standard deduction and the low income allowance are generally not of any significance to the real estate investor (and homeowner) whose itemized deductions, because of interest, real estate taxes and, often, state income and sales taxes, are likely to exceed the maximum standard deduction.

Once an individual determines the total of his personal deductions, he deducts that total or the larger of his standard deduction or low income allowance from his adjusted gross income.

In addition, the individual is entitled to a deduction for each exemption on his return. He gets one exemption for himself. If he files a joint return, he gets two, one for himself and one for his spouse. If either he or his spouse is blind, there is an extra exemption for each of them who is blind. If either he or his spouse is over 65, there is an extra exemption for each spouse over 65. In addition, there is a deduction for each dependent the taxpayer has. A dependent is someone who is closely related to the taxpayer (son, daughter, father, mother and other enumerated relatives) who receives more than half of his support from the taxpayer and whose gross income is less than $750. (A son or daughter who is either under 19 or a full-time student is permitted to have any amount of gross income and still be a dependent as long as the parent furnishes more than half of that child's support. In such a case, both parent and child may claim the exemption.) The amount of the deduction allowed for each exemption and each dependent is $750.

For 1975 only, in addition to the $750 deduction for each exemption and dependent, there is a $30 direct reduction of the computed tax by way of a tax credit for each exemption and dependent except for those exemptions allowed the taxpayer for blindness or being over age 65.

Computing the tax

After deducting the total of the personal deductions (or the standard deduction or the low income allowance) and the total of the deductions for exemptions and dependents from the individual's adjusted gross income, the tax can be computed. To the income that is left after deducting the personal deductions and exemptions (taxable income), the appropriate tax rate is applied.

The tax rates applied to the taxable income depend on the marital status of the taxpayer. The categories of taxpayers and the tax rate schedules they use (see page 89 for the rate schedule) are as follows.

Unmarried taxpayers not qualifying as heads of households	Schedule I
Married taxpayers filing joint returns and certain widows and widowers with dependent children	Schedule II
Married persons filing separate returns (and estates and trusts)	Schedule III
Unmarried taxpayers qualifying as heads of households	Schedule IV

The rates that apply to unmarried individuals who are not heads of households are about 20% greater than the rates that apply to joint returns. The rates on heads of households are about halfway between the rates on unmarried individuals who are not heads of households and the rates imposed on joint returns.

The rates range from a minimum of 14% to a maximum of 70% and, in each case, the total tax is a combination of all the graduated rates below the total amount reported as taxable income.

For example, assume that Jones, an unmarried individual, has a salary of $14,000 and security income of $3,600. That is a total of $17,600. He has personal deductions of $2,500 and is, of course, entitled to one exemption of $750. He deducts the $3,250 from the $17,600 to arrive at a taxable income of $14,350.

Since he is an unmarried individual who is not a head of a household, Jones' tax will be computed using Schedule I. Along the lefthand columns of this Schedule is a list of taxable brackets. One of these, the one into which Jones' income fits, is the "over $14,000 but not over $16,000" bracket. The tax listed is $3,210 plus 31% of the income in excess of $14,000. Since Jones' taxable income is $14,350, he has $350 of income in excess of $14,000; 31% of $350 is $108.50. To get the total tax, add the $3,210 tax on the $14,000 to the $108.50 tax on the $350 for a total tax of $3,318.50.

For 1975, Jones would reduce the computed tax by $30 (since he is entitled to one exemption). In the various examples and tax computations that follow, the $30-per-exemption credit is not taken into account because at this writing it is a temporary measure and for purposes of making comparisons and determining effective tax rates, it makes the examples unnecessarily complex. Generally, the amount of the credit will not be sufficiently significant to alter the comparative status of the examples.

Marginal and effective rates

In the example above, Jones paid a tax of $3,318.50. His total gross income (before deductions and exemptions) was $17,600. His total tax was approximately 19% of his gross income. In effect, he kept 81 cents, after taxes, out of each dollar of gross income he acquired that year. Thus, it can be said that his overall tax rate was 19%.

On the other hand, because of the bracket system of imposing tax, the last $350 of Jones' income was subject to a tax of 31%. This is his *marginal* rate, the rate at which the next dollar of additional income would be taxed. Often, you hear the expression, "he's in the 31% bracket." That's an expression of the marginal rate.

How, then, should a broker or investor look at tax rates?

Given a specific set of current facts, anyone who knows the tax rates can determine the exact tax. However, in most situations, we are dealing with comparisons and forecasts. We are determining the type and amount of income a property is

Schedule I

Single Taxpayers not Qualifying as Heads of Households

If the taxable income is: The tax is:

Not over $500....14% of the amount on line 48.

Over—	But not over—		of excess over—
$500	$1,000	$70+15%	$500
$1,000	$1,500	$145+16%	$1,000
$1,500	$2,000	$225+17%	$1,500
$2,000	$4,000	$310+19%	$2,000
$4,000	$6,000	$690+21%	$4,000
$6,000	$8,000	$1,110+24%	$6,000
$8,000	$10,000	$1,590+25%	$8,000
$10,000	$12,000	$2,090+27%	$10,000
$12,000	$14,000	$2,630+29%	$12,000
$14,000	$16,000	$3,210+31%	$14,000
$16,000	$18,000	$3,830+34%	$16,000
$18,000	$20,000	$4,510+36%	$18,000
$20,000	$22,000	$5,230+38%	$20,000
$22,000	$26,000	$5,990+40%	$22,000
$26,000	$32,000	$7,590+45%	$26,000
$32,000	$38,000	$10,290+50%	$32,000
$38,000	$44,000	$13,290+55%	$38,000
$44,000	$50,000	$16,590+60%	$44,000
$50,000	$60,000	$20,190+62%	$50,000
$60,000	$70,000	$26,390+64%	$60,000
$70,000	$80,000	$32,790+66%	$70,000
$80,000	$90,000	$39,390+68%	$80,000
$90,000	$100,000	$46,190+69%	$90,000
$100,000	....	$53,090+70%	$100,000

Schedule II

Married Taxpayers Filing Joint Returns and Certain Widows and Widowers

If the taxable income is: The tax is:

Not over $1,000....14% of the amount on line 48.

Over—	But not over—		of excess over—
$1,000	$2,000	$140+15%	$1,000
$2,000	$3,000	$290+16%	$2,000
$3,000	$4,000	$450+17%	$3,000
$4,000	$8,000	$620+19%	$4,000
$8,000	$12,000	$1,380+22%	$8,000
$12,000	$16,000	$2,260+25%	$12,000
$16,000	$20,000	$3,260+28%	$16,000
$20,000	$24,000	$4,380+32%	$20,000
$24,000	$28,000	$5,660+36%	$24,000
$28,000	$32,000	$7,100+39%	$28,000
$32,000	$36,000	$8,660+42%	$32,000
$36,000	$40,000	$10,340+45%	$36,000
$40,000	$44,000	$12,140+48%	$40,000
$44,000	$52,000	$14,060+50%	$44,000
$52,000	$64,000	$18,060+53%	$52,000
$64,000	$76,000	$24,420+55%	$64,000
$76,000	$88,000	$31,020+58%	$76,000
$88,000	$100,000	$37,980+60%	$88,000
$100,000	$120,000	$45,180+62%	$100,000
$120,000	$140,000	$57,580+64%	$120,000
$140,000	$160,000	$70,380+66%	$140,000
$160,000	$180,000	$83,580+68%	$160,000
$180,000	$200,000	$97,180+69%	$180,000
$200,000	....	$110,980+70%	$200,000

Schedule III

Married Taxpayers Filing Separate Returns

If the taxable income is: The tax is:

Not over $500....14% of the amount on line 48.

Over—	But not over—		of excess over—
$500	$1,000	$70+15%	$500
$1,000	$1,500	$145+16%	$1,000
$1,500	$2,000	$225+17%	$1,500
$2,000	$4,000	$310+19%	$2,000
$4,000	$6,000	$690+22%	$4,000
$6,000	$8,000	$1,130+25%	$6,000
$8,000	$10,000	$1,630+28%	$8,000
$10,000	$12,000	$2,190+32%	$10,000
$12,000	$14,000	$2,830+36%	$12,000
$14,000	$16,000	$3,550+39%	$14,000
$16,000	$18,000	$4,330+42%	$16,000
$18,000	$20,000	$5,170+45%	$18,000
$20,000	$22,000	$6,070+48%	$20,000
$22,000	$26,000	$7,030+50%	$22,000
$26,000	$32,000	$9,030+53%	$26,000
$32,000	$38,000	$12,210+55%	$32,000
$38,000	$44,000	$15,510+58%	$38,000
$44,000	$50,000	$18,990+60%	$44,000
$50,000	$60,000	$22,590+62%	$50,000
$60,000	$70,000	$28,790+64%	$60,000
$70,000	$80,000	$35,190+66%	$70,000
$80,000	$90,000	$41,790+68%	$80,000
$90,000	$100,000	$48,590+69%	$90,000
$100,000	....	$55,490+70%	$100,000

Schedule IV

Unmarried Taxpayers Who Qualify as Heads of Households

If the taxable income is: The tax is:

Not over $1,000....14% of the amount on line 48.

Over—	But not over—		of excess over—
$1,000	$2,000	$140+16%	$1,000
$2,000	$4,000	$300+18%	$2,000
$4,000	$6,000	$660+19%	$4,000
$6,000	$8,000	$1,040+22%	$6,000
$8,000	$10,000	$1,480+23%	$8,000
$10,000	$12,000	$1,940+25%	$10,000
$12,000	$14,000	$2,440+27%	$12,000
$14,000	$16,000	$2,980+28%	$14,000
$16,000	$18,000	$3,540+31%	$16,000
$18,000	$20,000	$4,160+32%	$18,000
$20,000	$22,000	$4,800+35%	$20,000
$22,000	$24,000	$5,500+36%	$22,000
$24,000	$26,000	$6,220+38%	$24,000
$26,000	$28,000	$6,980+41%	$26,000
$28,000	$32,000	$7,800+42%	$28,000
$32,000	$36,000	$9,480+45%	$32,000
$36,000	$38,000	$11,280+48%	$36,000
$38,000	$40,000	$12,240+51%	$38,000
$40,000	$44,000	$13,260+52%	$40,000
$44,000	$50,000	$15,340+55%	$44,000
$50,000	$52,000	$18,640+56%	$50,000
$52,000	$64,000	$19,760+58%	$52,000
$64,000	$70,000	$26,720+59%	$64,000
$70,000	$76,000	$30,260+61%	$70,000
$76,000	$80,000	$33,920+62%	$76,000
$80,000	$88,000	$36,400+63%	$80,000
$88,000	$100,000	$41,440+64%	$88,000
$100,000	$120,000	$49,120+66%	$100,000
$120,000	$140,000	$62,320+67%	$120,000
$140,000	$160,000	$75,720+68%	$140,000
$160,000	$180,000	$89,320+69%	$160,000
$180,000	....	$103,120+70%	$180,000

expected to produce. Exact tax computations reflect specious accuracy; all of the other figures with which we are dealing are estimates. Thus, we can rely on marginal rates.

For example, assume that an investor has an amount of income which would cause his next dollar of income to be taxed at 39%. We can use that marginal rate in determining the tax effect on future income arising from the investment under consideration. It is only a guess but it is based on the best information currently available.

In using marginal rates for projections, it should be remembered that the rate applies to a "slice" or "bracket" of income. For example, on a joint return, the 39% rate applies to a $4,000 slice of taxable income (taxable income in excess of $32,000 but not in excess of $36,000). If the income segment involved in the projection exceeds that $4,000, it may be necessary to apply more than one marginal rate to the projected income.

One more point should be made regarding the forecasting of the income tax impact on projected income. All assumptions (tax rates, applicability of certain tax rules, etc.) can be based only on the tax law in effect when the forecast is made. That is the best information available at the time. However, tax laws are frequently revised. Consequently, periodic updating of prior forecasts becomes a necessity.

Taxation of individuals' capital gains

Up until this point, we have been concerned with the tax impact on ordinary income. However, capital gains get a special tax break.

Capital gains result from the sale or exchange of capital assets or assets which, for tax purposes, are treated as capital assets.

For the most part, property held for investment (by someone who is not a dealer in that type of property) is a capital asset. So, stocks, bonds and vacant land may be capital assets. Similarly, other personal use items not held for sale in business, such as a personal residence or personal car, are capital assets.

There is a special rule for assets used in a business. Non-inventory depreciable assets and land held for more than six months and used in the business produce a capital gain when sold at a gain and ordinary loss when sold at a loss. These are referred to as Section 1231 assets. Property held for production of income, such as a rental apartment, is a Section 1231 asset. Factory buildings, warehouses and machines used in a business are all Section 1231 assets.

Real estate held by dealers, i.e. held for sale to customers in the ordinary course of business, is neither a capital nor a Section 1231 asset. Gain or loss on a sale or exchange would result in ordinary income or loss. See page 172.

Depreciation recapture and capital gains

When a Section 1231 asset is sold or exchanged, some "depreciation recapture" may result. It is only the gain remaining after deducting the depreciation recapture that is treated as a Section 1231 gain. The portion of the gain that is considered to be depreciation recapture is taxed as ordinary income. (When and how depreciation recapture arises and how to compute it is explained on page 175.)

Computing Section 1231 gains and losses

It was stated previously that Section 1231 gains receive capital gain treatment and Section 1231 losses are treated as ordinary losses. In a broad sense that is the tax rule. However, it needs some modification. Actually, all the Section 1231 gains and losses that occur in one year are first aggregated to arrive at a *net* Section 1231 gain or loss. Then, if the net figure is a gain, it is treated as a capital gain; if the net result is a loss, it is treated as an ordinary loss. Thus, Section 1231 losses first offset Section 1231 gains before any net loss is applied against ordinary income.

Calculating long- and short-term capital gains and losses

The favorable rates that apply to capital gains apply only to net long-term capital gains. Long-term gains arise from the sale or exchange of property held more than six months. (All items that qualify for Section 1231 treatment must also have been held for more than six months and in the case of livestock, two years.) Gains or losses from the sale or exchange of capital assets held six months or less are short-term gains or losses. Gains or losses on Section 1231 property held less than six months are treated as ordinary income or losses.

Determining long- and short-term gains and losses   In determining the net long- and short-term gains or losses for the year, short-term capital gains are aggregated with short-term losses and long-term gains are aggregated with long-term losses.

If both categories end up with gains, the short-term gains are treated as ordinary income and the long-term gains get the special capital gains treatment.

If both categories end up with losses, the rules for capital losses (different rules for corporations and individuals) apply. These rules are spelled out later in this chapter.

If one category ends up with a gain and the other with a loss, the gain and loss must be aggregated to arrive at a net long-term or short-term gain or loss. The net figure is then given the treatment described in the preceding two paragraphs for a net gain or loss of that nature. Of course, if all the transactions fall into only one category, the net gain or loss in that category gets the treatment previously described for that category.

Examples

Some examples are required to more fully explain the foregoing principles regarding the calculation of long- and short-term capital gains and losses.

1. Assume the following facts concerning the following sales of capital assets.

Purchase Date	Sales Date	Cost or Basis	Sales Price	Long-Term Gains (Loss)	Short-Term Gains (Loss)
4/4/74	3/9/75	$10,000	$15,000	$5,000	
7/14/74	1/14/75	4,000	8,000		$4,000
2/14/75	6/8/75	5,000	4,000		(1,000)
9/9/74	3/10/75	20,000	17,000	(3,000)	
		Totals		$2,000	$3,000

Since both categories end up with gains, the $2,000 long-term capital gain gets the special capital gain treatment, while the $3,000 short-term gain is added to ordinary income.

2. Assume the following facts concerning the following sales of capital assets.

Purchase Date	Sales Date	Cost or Basis	Sales Price	Long-Term Gain (Loss)	Short-Term Gain (Loss)
3/11/70	1/2/75	$10,000	$40,000	$30,000	
8/8/74	1/18/75	15,000	20,000		$5,000
2/4/74	9/19/75	20,000	16,000	(4,000)	
6/6/75	12/6/75	16,000	9,000		(7,000)
		Totals		$26,000	($2,000)
				(2,000) ←	
				$24,000	

In this case, one category (long-term) ended up with a gain, while the other (short-term) ended up with a loss. Therefore, the two results have to be aggregated, resulting in a long-term capital gain of $24,000. This gain is eligible for the special long-term capital gain treatment.)

3. The facts are.

Purchase Date	Sales Date	Cost or Basis	Sales Price	Long-Term Gain (Loss)	Short-Term Gain (Loss)
3/11/75	7/9/75	$10,000	$14,000		$4,000
6/16/74	9/1/75	40,000	45,000	$5,000	
5/6/75	10/10/75	10,000	2,000		(8,000)
4/8/75	11/4/75	16,000	10,000	(6,000)	
		Totals		($1,000)	($4,000)

Here, we have a loss in both categories. The capital loss treatment explained later in this chapter applies.

4. Assume the following facts.

Purchase Date	Sales Date	Cost or Basis	Sales Price	Long-Term Gain (Loss)	Short-Term Gain (Loss)
3/12/68	1/4/75	$ 4,000	$ 8,000	$4,000	
4/5/74	2/4/75	18,000	16,000	(2,000)	
3/12/75	4/14/75	3,000	6,000		$3,000
5/6/75	9/9/75	20,000	12,000		(8,000)
		Totals		$2,000	($5,000)
				→	2,000
					($3,000)

Since we have a net gain in one category (long-term) and a net loss in the other (short-term), the two results must be aggregated giving a net result of a net short-term loss of $3,000. The capital loss treatment explained later in this chapter applies.

At this point, let us consider the effect of Section 1231 transactions. Assume the following results from three Section 1231 transactions in 1975.

Transaction		Gain (Loss)
#1		$10,000
#2		(16,000)
#3		20,000
	Net Result	$14,000

Since the result is a gain, the gain is treated as a long-term capital gain. Therefore, we would include this gain as a long-term capital gain in making our calculations of net long- or short-term capital gains. In other words, this $14,000 gain would be listed as a long-term capital gain along with any other capital gains and losses we may have had for the year when we set up our calculation (in the same manner as in the prior examples). For instance, if in addition to the facts listed in Example 4, we also had the $14,000 Section 1231 gain computed in this example, we would get the following results.

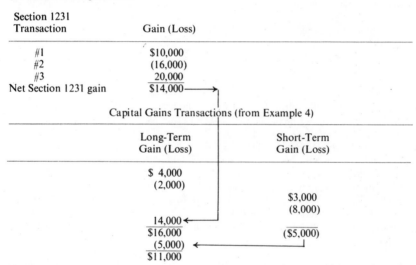

Section 1231 Transaction	Gain (Loss)
#1	$10,000
#2	(16,000)
#3	20,000
Net Section 1231 gain	$14,000 ──────→

Capital Gains Transactions (from Example 4)

Long-Term Gain (Loss)	Short-Term Gain (Loss)
$ 4,000	
(2,000)	
	$3,000
	(8,000)
14,000 ←	
$16,000	($5,000)
(5,000) ←	
$11,000	

If the aggregate of the Section 1231 transaction had been a loss, the loss would be a direct deduction against ordinary income and have no effect on any of the other capital gain or capital loss transactions for the year.

Taxation of short-term capital gains

If, as a result of the calculations, the individual taxpayer ends up with a short-term capital gain, that gain is added to ordinary income. Short-term gains are not added to ordinary income until *after* all of the aggregation of capital gains and losses are first made (as in Examples 1–4). These short-term gains must first be offset against short-term and possibly long-term losses before being added to ordinary income.

Long-term capital gain treatment for individuals

There are two methods by which long-term capital gains can be taxed: the regular method and the alternative tax method. The taxpayer chooses the method which results in the least amount of tax.

Regular method Under this method, one-half of the total net long-term gain is added to ordinary income. The tax is then computed on the resulting total. The effect of this method is to tax the long-term capital gain at one-half the rate of ordinary income.

Example

Smith has $25,000 of salary income and $5,000 of deductions and exemptions. He also sold a property for $80,000 for which he had an adjusted basis of $60,000. The property was held for more than six months and resulted in a $20,000 long-term capital gain. Smith files a joint return.

Here is how Smith's tax is calculated, using the ordinary method of taxing long-term capital gains.

Salary income	$25,000
One-half of $20,000 long-term capital gain	10,000
Total	35,000
Less: Deductions and exemptions	5,000
Taxable income	$30,000

Tax computation (using Schedule II for joint returns):

Taxable income	$30,000		
Tax on	28,000	is	$ 7,100
Tax (39%) on excess over $28,000 or	2,000	is	780
Total Tax			$ 7,880

Note that if the full capital gain had to be included in ordinary income, Smith's taxable income would have been $40,000 and the tax would have been $12,140. If Smith had no capital gain at all, his taxable income would have been $20,000 and the tax would have been $4,380. If $4,380 is subtracted from $12,140, the result is $7,760. That would be the tax on the $20,000 gain on the sale of the property if the capital gain rules did not apply. If we subtract $4,380 from $7,880 (the total tax computed by including only half the capital gain in ordinary income) we get $3,500. That is the tax required on the capital gain computed by using the regular method for reporting long-term capital gains. Thus, it is apparent that long-term capital gains receive a substantial tax break. In this case there is a saving of $4,260 in taxes.

Alternative tax method of taxing long-term capital gains Instead of using the regular method (including one-half the net long-term capital gains in ordinary income), the taxpayer may use the alternative tax method when it results in less tax. Under this method, he first computes tax on his taxable income without including any long-term capital gains. Then he adds 25% of the net long-term capital gains to the tax computed on the ordinary income. The sum of these is his total tax.

The idea behind the alternative tax is to prevent the tax on net long-term capital gains from being more than 25%. But under the regular method, the gains may be taxed at less than 25% if the taxpayer's other income does not put him in too high a tax bracket. In this case, the regular method of taxing capital gains will be used. But if the regular method results in a tax on capital gains of more than 25%, the alternative method is used.

There is a limit on the use of the 25% alternative tax. It applies only to long-term capital gains of up to $50,000 ($25,000 for a married taxpayer filing a separate return).

The following example shows how to apply the 25% alternative tax rule when the total net long-term capital gains for the year do not exceed $50,000.

Brown, who files a joint return, has ordinary income of $58,000 and deductions and exemptions totalling $5,000. In addition, he has a long-term capital gain of $8,000.

Total tax if he uses the regular method of taxing long-term capital gain.

Ordinary income			$58,000
Half the $8,000 long-term capital gain			4,000
Total			62,000
Less: Deductions and exemptions			5,000
Taxable income			$57,000

Tax computation (Schedule II):			
Taxable income	$57,000		
Tax on	52,000	is	$18,060
Tax (53%) on excess over $52,000	5,000	is	2,650
Total Tax			$20,710

Total tax if he uses the alternative tax method of taxing long-term capital gains.

Ordinary income			$58,000
Less: Deductions and exemptions			5,000
Taxable ordinary income			$53,000

Tax computation (Schedule II):			
Taxable ordinary income	$53,000		
Tax on	52,000	is	$18,060
Tax (53%) on excess over $52,000 or	$ 1,000	is	530
Total tax on ordinary income			18,590
Add: 25% of $8,000 long-term capital gain			2,000
Total Tax			$20,590

Consequently, Brown will use the alternative tax method for determining the tax on his long-term capital gain because it saves $120 in taxes.

Total tax using regular method of taxing long-term capital gains	$20,710
Total tax using the alternative tax method of taxing long-term capital gains	20,590
Tax saved by using the alternative tax method	$ 120

If we look at the tax rate schedules the reason for the lower tax by the alternative method becomes clear. Brown's marginal rate was 53%. (In computing his tax on ordinary income, the amount in excess of $52,000 was taxable at 53%.) If we add half the capital gains to that ordinary income (which we would do if we use the regular method), we would be subjecting half the capital gain to a 53% tax. That is the same as subjecting the entire capital gain to a $26\frac{1}{2}\%$ tax. Since $26\frac{1}{2}\%$ is obviously more than the 25% tax to which the capital gain would be subject using the alternative method, the latter method produces the lower tax.

Thus, if the ordinary income is high enough to raise the marginal rate above 50%, it is less expensive to use the alternative tax. While this may be useful as a general rule of thumb, there are situations when the marginal rate is less than 50% and yet the alternative tax would produce a lower overall tax. This happens when the capital gain is very substantial in relation to the ordinary income so that even though only half the gain is added to the ordinary income, much of the gain is subject to tax rates in excess of 50%. This indicates that in close cases it is always safer to calculate the tax both ways, by the regular and the alternative method, and then choose the one that produces the lower tax.

The alternative tax applies only to so much of long-term capital gains not in excess of $50,000. If the total of the net long-term capital gains is more than $50,000 (and it is desirable to apply the alternative tax to the first $50,000 of net long-term capital gain) the following computation has to be made.

1. Compute the tax on the ordinary income.

2. Add 25% of the first $50,000 of long-term capital gain.

3.a. Compute the tax on the total of ordinary income plus half the *total* net long-term capital gain.
b. Compute the tax on the total of ordinary income plus $25,000 (which is half the capital gain to which the 25% rate was applied).
c. Subtract the tax computed in (b) from the tax computed in (a).

The total tax for the year is the total of Steps 1, 2 and 3.

This computation taxes the first $50,000 of capital gain at 25%. The excess over $50,000 is included in ordinary income at half the amount of the capital gain (just as when the tax on long-term capital gains is calculated under the regular method). However, when half the long-term capital gains in excess of $50,000 is added to ordinary income, for the purposes of determining the ordinary income tax rate that will apply to that excess, it is added to the ordinary income level that would have been achieved if half of the $50,000 capital gain (to which the 25% alternative tax applied) had also been added to ordinary income.

Example

In 1975, Brown (who files a joint return) has ordinary income, after deductions and exemptions, of $65,000. He also has net long-term capital gains of $70,000. The following form, which incorporates Steps 1, 2 and 3, can be used to determine Brown's taxable income.

Step 1

1. Ordinary income	$65,000	
2. Calculate tax on amount in Line 1		$24,970

Step 2

3. 25% of first $50,000 of long-term capital gain	12,500

4. Ordinary income	$ 65,000		
5. ½ of total long-term capital gain	35,000		
6. Total of L. 4+L. 5	$100,000		
7. Calculate tax on amount on L. 6		45,180	
8. Ordinary income	$ 65,000		
9. Add $25,000 (½ of first $50,000 of long-term			
capital gain)	25,000		
10. Total of L. 8+L. 9	$ 90,000		
11. Calculate tax on amount on L. 10		39,180	
12. Subtract L. 11 from L. 7			6,000
13. Total tax (L. 2+L. 3+L. 12)			$43,470

Treatment of capital losses for individuals

Net capital losses (both short- and long-term) may be used to offset ordinary income up to $1,000. The losses remaining are then carried over to the following year and used as long- or short-term losses in that year. There is no limit on the number of years an individual may carry over a loss. But there is a difference between how a long-term loss and a short-term loss is used to offset the $1,000 of ordinary income. (Of course, if ordinary income is less than $1,000, the maximum amount that a capital loss may offset is the amount of the ordinary income.)

In applying capital losses as offsets against ordinary income, $2 of long-term loss must be used to offset $1 of ordinary income. Short-term losses offset ordinary income on a dollar-for-dollar basis. If a taxpayer has both short- and long-term losses, short-term losses are applied first in offsetting ordinary income. If the short-term losses are insufficient to offset $1,000 of ordinary income (or the total of ordinary income if that total does not exceed $1,000) then long-term losses (on a two-for-one basis) are applied.

The following examples illustrate these rules.

1. In 1975, Green has a long-term capital gain of $1,000 and a short-term capital loss of $4,000. After netting the two, he has a net short-term loss of $3,000. His ordinary income is $12,000. He applies $1,000 of his short-term loss to reduce his ordinary income to $11,000 and carries over $2,000 as a short-term capital loss to 1976.

2. In 1975, Green has the same $12,000 ordinary income but has a short-term gain of $1,000 and a long-term loss of $4,000. Now he has a net long-term loss of $3,000. In this case he has to use $2,000 of the net long-term loss of $3,000 to offset $1,000 of ordinary income, reducing his ordinary income to $11,000. He has $1,000 of long-term capital loss left which is carried over to 1976 as a long-term capital loss.

3. In 1975, Green has ordinary income of $12,000, a short-term loss of $1,200 and a long-term loss of $400. He applies $1,000 of his short-term loss to reduce his ordinary income to $11,000. He carries over to 1976 a short-term loss of $200 and a long-term loss of $400.

4. In 1975, Green has ordinary income of $12,000, a short-term loss of $400 and a long-term loss of $1,600. He applies the $400 short-term loss to offset $400 of ordinary income. He has to use $1,200 of his long-term loss to offset $600 of ordinary income, thus offsetting a total of $1,000 of ordinary income. He has $400 of long-term capital loss to carry over to 1976.

Special tax computations for individuals

There are additional aspects to the computation of the income tax for individuals: two tax relief provisions and one additional tax.

One of the relief provisions is a limitation on the tax rate that can apply to earned income. That limit is 50%.

The second relief provision is called income averaging. Whenever the current year's income is considerably greater than the prior four years' average income, there is a special way of computing the tax on the current year's income which is intended to have the effect of averaging the current year's income with the prior four years and arrive at a tax that would have applied if the income had been earned ratably instead of being bunched into one year.

The other special tax computation deals with the minimum tax on tax preferences. This is an additional tax that may apply when the taxpayer has a considerable amount of what is deemed to be "tax preference" income.

Special tax limit on earned income

Although the highest tax rate applicable to individuals is 70%, the highest rate on earned income is 50%.

The following example illustrates the mechanics of determining the tax by applying the earned income limitation.

Jones, who files a joint return, has total taxable income in 1975 of $90,000. Of this amount, $67,000 is earned taxable income. To compute his tax, he follows these steps.

1. He determines his total taxable income. That is given in this example as $90,000.

2. He determines how much of that taxable income is earned taxable income. For the purposes of this example, we are given the amount of $67,000. (How earned taxable income is computed is explained later.)

3. He determines the highest dollar of income (in the tax rate schedule that applies to him) that is taxable at not more than 50%. Here are the amounts that apply.

Single individuals (Schedule I)	$38,000
Joint returns (Schedule II)	52,000
Head of household (Schedule IV)	38,000

Since Jones files a joint return, the $52,000 figure applies to him.

4. Jones subtracts the $52,000 determined in Step 3 from the total earned taxable income (Step 1) of $67,000 in order to find that amount of earned taxable income that would have been subject to a rate higher than 50% were it not for this earned income limitation in the law. Subtracting $52,000 from $67,000 leaves $15,000.

5. To determine the total tax on the $67,000 of earned income under the 50% limitation, Jones first finds the tax on $52,000 (since he knows that no part of that is taxable at more than 50%). The tax on $52,000 (from Schedule II) is $18,060. To this he adds 50% of the remaining $15,000 (since this is the highest rate applying to earned income) or $7,500. That gives a total tax on the $67,000 of $25,560.

6. Jones has accounted for the tax on $67,000 of the $90,000 taxable income. He now has to determine the tax on the remaining $23,000 of taxable income. That income is taxable at the rates that would have applied had the first $67,000 of income been taxable at the regular rates instead of the special rates that apply to earned income. To determine the tax on the $23,000, the following calculation is made.

Tax on $90,000 of taxable income (without any special limitations)	$39,180
Less: Tax on $67,000 of taxable income (without any special limitations)	26,070
Tax on the $23,000 of income not qualifying as earned income	$13,110

7. The total tax on the $90,000 of taxable income determined by applying the 50% limitation on earned income is thus the total of the tax determined in Steps 5 and 6 as follows.

Tax on $67,000 or earned income (from Step 5)	$25,560
Tax on $23,000 of income that did not qualify as earned income (from Step 6)	13,110
Total tax on $90,000 taxable income	$38,670

As can be seen in Step 6, the tax on $90,000, if there were no earned income limitation, would be $39,180. The total tax computed (with the 50% limitation) is $38,670. So, by using the earned income limitation, $510 in taxes was saved.

What is earned taxable income? As the above example illustrates, earned taxable income is subject to a maximum tax of 50%. But it is the earned *taxable* income that is subject to that limitation. Since taxable income (as explained previously) is what is left after deducting personal expenses (or the standard deduction) and exemptions, the law requires that the earned income portion of the total adjusted gross income bear part of these expenses. In other words, if adjusted gross income consisted of $70,000 earned income and $30,000 other ordinary income and personal deductions and exemptions amounted to $25,000, the tax law insists that the $25,000 be allocated ratably against both parts of the adjusted gross income. The $30,000 unearned income not subject to the 50% limitation may not be reduced by the entire $25,000 of deductions and exemptions.

Consequently, the tax law requires the following procedures.

1. Determine the gross amount of earned income. Earned income includes wages, salaries, professional fees and any other compensation for personal services. Individuals engaged in unincorporated businesses in which both services and capital are material income-producing factors treat 30% of their profits as earned income.

2. The gross amount of earned income is then reduced by business expenses, travel expenses while away from home, outside salesmen's expenses and transportation expenses. The result is net earned income.

3. The net earned income is then divided by the adjusted gross income to determine what percentage of adjusted gross income constitutes net earned income.

4. The percentage is then applied to the total taxable income to find earned taxable income. (If the taxpayer has tax preference income in excess of $30,000, that excess is subtracted from the total taxable income before applying the percentage in Step 3. Tax preference income is explained on page 101.)

Once earned taxable income is determined the total tax can be computed (applying the 50% tax rate limitation to the earned taxable income) as described in the example involving Mr. Jones.

In the earlier example, in which Jones' tax was computed by applying the 50% maximum tax on earnings, it was stated that his total taxable income was $90,000 and his total earned taxable income was $67,000. In arriving at those figures, let us assume that the following facts were true.

1. Total earned income	$76,000	
2. Total other income	25,000	
3. Total gross income		$101,000
4. Deductions allowed for determining adjusted gross income		7,000
5. Adjusted gross income		$ 94,000
6. Total earned income (line 1)		$ 76,000
7. Less business expenses included in line 4		6,000
8. Net earned income		$ 70,000

Since net earned income (line 8) is 74.4% of adjusted gross income (line 5), 74.4% of the total taxable income of $90,000 or $67,000 is treated as earned taxable income.

Income averaging

The tax law recognizes that some taxpayers may have unusually high incomes in some years and that since the tax is computed on an annual basis, this can result in unfairness. For example, one individual has taxable income of $25,000 a year for five years. Another's taxable income is $10,000 a year for four years and $85,000 in the fifth year. Each has $125,000 of income over the five-year period, yet their total tax bills for the five-year period will be substantially different.

Assuming each files a joint return, the man with $25,000-a-year taxable income will have an annual tax of $6,020 or a total for the five years of $30,100. The other individual will have an annual tax in the first four years (on $10,000 annual taxable income) of $1,820. In the fifth year, his tax on $85,000 will come to $36,240. His five-year total will be $43,520 or $13,420 more than the first taxpayer. The reason for this great disparity results from the high tax brackets into which the large fifth-year income is raised.

Income averaging is intended to give some tax relief to the second individual. In essence, under income averaging, if the current year's taxable income exceeds the prior four years' average taxable income by more than 120%, that excess over the 120% (if it is at least $3,000) is taxed at an overall rate that would apply to one-fifth of the excess.

Income averaging is a special method to compute the *current* year's taxes. Prior years' taxes are not recalculated. The income averaging procedure is as follows.

1. Determine the tax on that portion of the current year's taxable income that is equal to 120% of the prior four years' average taxable income.

2. Determine the portion of the current year's taxable income that exceeds 120% of the prior four years' average taxable income. This is referred to as excess income. Divide this amount by five.

3. Determine what the tax on this one-fifth of the excess income would be if this one-fifth were added to 120% of the prior four years' average income.

4. Multiply by five the tax computed in Step 3.

5. Add the tax determined in Step 1 to the tax determined in Step 4. That is the total tax due for the current year.

Reverting to the two individuals referred to at the outset of this discussion, how would our second individual fare with income averaging in the fifth year? Without income averaging, his tax on $85,000 of taxable income (on a joint return) was $36,240.

Applying the five-step procedure, the tax, by applying income averaging, amounts to $23,940 (a saving of $12,300 in taxes).

1. Our individual's average taxable income for the prior four years was $10,000. 120% of that amount is $12,000. The tax on $12,000 is $2,260.

2. $12,000 (120% of the prior four-year average taxable income) is subtracted from the $85,000 total taxable income of the fifth year. The remaining $73,000 (the excess income) is divided by 5, giving a resulting figure of $14,600.

3. The $14,600 is added to the $12,000, giving a combined amount of $26,600. The tax computed on this amount is $6,596. This is the tax that results when one-fifth of the excess income is added to 120% of the prior four year's average income. The tax of $2,260 (computed in Step 1) is subtracted from the $6,596 in order to determine what portion of this amount is attributable to the addition of one-fifth of the excess income to the 120% of the prior four-year average taxable income. Thus, it is determined that $4,336 is attributable to the one-fifth of the excess income.

4. Since the entire excess income is to be taxed at the rate that applies to one-fifth of that excess when added to 120% of the prior four-year average income, the $4,336 determined in Step 4 is multiplied by five, resulting in a tax of $21,680.

5. In Step 1, the tax on $12,000 (or 120% of the prior four-year average taxable income) was determined. In step 4, the tax on the excess $73,000 was determined. Hence, the total tax for the year is as follows.

Tax from Step 1	$ 2,260
plus	
Tax from Step 4	21,680
Total tax	$23,940

Minimum tax for tax preferences

The Tax Reform Act of 1969 introduced a new concept into the tax law: the minimum tax. This is a tax, *in addition to the regular income tax*, on certain items called "tax preferences." The idea here is to tax special tax benefits available to some taxpayers.

The tax is a flat 10% of the preference items in excess of the total of $30,000 plus the amount of the regular income tax paid on the income. So, if the tax preference items do not exceed that total, there is no tax on tax preferences. Tax preferences that must be totalled (and from which total is subtracted $30,000 plus the income tax) include the following.

Accelerated depreciation on real property   The excess of the depreciation deducted over the amount that would have been deductible had the straight line method of depreciation been used constitutes a tax preference. Similarly, the excess of the amounts deducted under special five-year amortization of certain rehabilitation expenses over the straight line rate is also a tax preference.

Accelerated depreciation on personal property   This is the same rule that applies to real property *but only if* the personal property is leased out on a net lease.

One-half of long-term capital gains   It makes no difference whether the taxpayer uses the regular or alternative method for determining the tax on long-term capital gains; one-half of the net long-term capital gains is a tax preference.

Percentage depletion   To the extent that the amount deducted as percentage depletion exceeds the basis of the property, the excess is a tax preference.

Amortization of certified pollution facilities and railroad rolling stock   These items are subject to special quick amortization write-offs. To the extent the deduction allowed exceeds the depreciation deduction otherwise allowable, the excess is a tax preference.

Stock options   The excess of the market value of stock received by an employee in exercising a restricted or qualified stock option over the price he pays for the stock is a tax preference.

Reserves for bad debts of banks and financial institutions   These taxpayers calculate bad debt reserves under a formula. If the reserves they thus set up exceed what their experience indicates the reserves should be, the excess is a tax preference.

The following example illustrates the operation of the minimum tax on tax preferences. Arthur Nelson has taxable income of $94,000, is married and files a joint return. Among his items of income and deductions for the year were the following.

Long-term capital gains	$100,000
Depreciation deducted on real estate under the 200% declining balance method	72,000
Straight line depreciation on the same real estate	30,000

First, Nelson's tax is computed without regard to tax preferences. From Schedule II the tax on $94,000 on a joint return is determined to be $41,580. The tax preferences are then listed.

Half of long-term capital gains	$50,000	
Excess of accelerated depreciation over straight line on the real estate	42,000	
Total tax preferences		$92,000
Less: Statutory exemption	$30,000	
Income tax	41,580	71,580
Amount subject to minimum tax on tax preferences		20,420
Tax on Tax Preferences (10%)		$ 2,042

The $2,042 is added to the regular tax of $41,580, giving a total tax for the year of $43,622.

Taxation of partnerships

Partnerships and other joint, unincorporated ownership forms (which, for tax purposes, are treated as partnerships) are not separate taxable entities. The partners, be they individuals, corporations or other entities, report their shares of the partnership's ordinary income or loss and capital gains and losses on their own tax returns, subject to the rules that govern their preparation.

Partnership income or loss passes directly to the partners. While most tax elections, e.g. installment sale treatment, must be made by the partnership rather than by its partners, it is not a taxpaying entity. Types of income and deductions which have a special tax significance retain their special characters as they pass through the partnership conduit. Consider the following illustration.

David, Melissa, Michael and Jeffery form a real estate partnership. At the end of 1975, their partnership records disclose the following items of income and expenses.

Rental income	$25,000
Tax exempt interest income from municipal bonds	10,000
Operating expenses (before depreciation)	17,000
Depreciation:	
Bonus "first year" (see page 165)	2,000
Regular	5,000
Charitable contributions	1,000

On their personal income tax returns, each of the partners will report his share of the income and special items of the partnership. Actual distribution of funds is not required from the partnership to the partners; each partner is taxed on his *distributive* share of the profits or losses and special items (the share he is entitled to) for the partnership taxable year that ends within his taxable year. The partnership will file an income tax return, an information return and will pay no tax. The tax returns of the four individual partners will reflect the following items of taxable income and deduction.

			Partnership	Each 25% Partner
Tax exempt income			$10,000	$2,500
Rent income		$25,000		
Operating expense	$17,000			
Depreciation regular	5,000			
		$22,000		
Net rent income			3,000	750 income
Bonus depreciation			2,000	500 deduction
Contributions			1,000	250 deduction

An examination of the foregoing example indicates that each partner shares in the profits and losses of the partnership as well as in certain special items. Thus, tax free income passes through to each partner as tax free income. Each partner must report his own share of the partnership's charitable contributions.

Since each partner picks up his share of the partnership's income or loss, the effect that depreciation has on the profit picture is reflected on each partner's own tax return. If, for example, the partnership in the illustration had depreciation deductions of $10,000, it would have had a net loss from real estate operations of $2,000 and each partner would have reported a $500 loss on his own tax return. Any spendable income that the partnership earned could be distributed to the partners without causing any additional tax to them.

The first year "bonus" depreciation is divided among the partners in their profit and loss-sharing ratio. Each partner then can deduct on his own return bonus depreciation up to the maximum allowed for an individual ($2,000 on a separate return: $4,000 on a joint return).

Limited partnerships

The discussion thus far concerning partnerships has dealt with the general partnership. The tax rules for limited partnerships are similar to the general partnership tax rules.

While a partner is taxed on his portion of the gain from the partnership, the amount of loss which he is permitted to deduct is limited to his basis for his partnership interest (that is the total amount he has placed at risk of the business plus his share of partnership earnings and minus partnership losses allocable to him and earnings which he withdrew from the partnership).

In addition, each partner may add to his basis his share of the partnership liabilities. This, of course, increases the basis against which he may deduct losses.

For a general partner this rule presents no problem. Since he has unlimited liability, his share of all partnership liabilities increases his basis. The limited partner, however, does not have unlimited liability; his liability is limited to his investment. Thus, conceptually, he has no share in the partnership's liabilities.

This limitation on a limited partner's ability to deduct his share of partnership losses beyond his basis of his contribution would be a great deterrent to real estate syndications. However, IRS has agreed that if a liability is a non-recourse loan (i.e. the creditor can look only to the property mortgaged and not to the partnership in general in the event of default) then the liability is not a partnership liability but a liability of *all* the partners including the limited partners. So, each limited partner may increase his basis by his share of the non-recourse liabilities of the partnership. (This concept is explained in the Appendix beginning on page 302.)

Income tax aspects of corporate ownership

The income tax rules applying to corporations differ in many respects from the rules applying to individuals. The corporation is a separate *legal* and *taxpaying* entity. It pays income taxes on its ordinary income at the rate of 22% on the first $25,000 and 48% on income in excess of $25,000.

For taxable years ending after 1974 and before 1976, only, the following rates apply to corporate ordinary income: 20% on the first $25,000; 22% on the second $25,000; 48% on excess over $50,000. Since this rate structure (at this writing) is very temporary, all calculations hereafter are based on the 22%–48% structure rather than on this temporary rate structure.

If a real estate corporation has losses, created very often by virtue of large deductions for depreciation, these tax losses may *not* be utilized by the individual owners of the corporation on their own income tax returns. If such property was owned directly by the individuals, they would be entitled to use the excess real estate deductions to reduce their taxable income from other sources.

Even though the corporation's losses are not available to its stockholders, a corporation having income tax losses and cash flow available might be able to make cash distributions to its shareholders that would not be taxable to them. These distributions would not be taxable at all to the extent that they did not exceed the shareholders' bases for their corporate stock. The rule is that a corporation which has *neither* current nor accumulated earnings and profits (a tax concept related to but not exactly the same as taxable income) may make distributions to its shareholders which will not be taxed as dividends. Such distributions are treated as a return of capital and, therefore, are not taxable at all to the extent that they reimburse the corporate shareholder for his investment in the stock of the corporation. Distributions received which exceed the tax basis for the stock are taxable but as capital gains.

In determining a corporation's earnings and profits, for corporations' taxable years beginning after June 30, 1972, only straight line depreciation will be allowed. This does not mean that accelerated depreciation will not be allowed to be used to determine the taxable income of the corporation; it will be allowed to be used if the corporation is eligible to use it. But straight line will have to be used to find out how much earnings and profits the corporation has in order to determine how distributions to the stockholders are to be taxed. This means that while a corporation may have a loss due to accelerated depreciation, it may still have earnings and profits for determining whether a distribution to its stockholders is to be taxed as a dividend rather than a return of capital investment (or capital gain where the basis for the stockholder's stock has already been recovered via prior distributions).

Should the real estate corporation realize taxable profits, however, any distribution of such after-tax profits to the shareholders as dividends will be taxed again. That is, these earnings would be taxed first to the corporation and then again to the individuals.

Example

X Corporation has taxable income of $10,000. Its tax on that amount is $2,200. It distributes the remaining $7,800 to Mr. A, its sole shareholder, as a dividend. Mr. A must include the $7,800 in his own taxable income and pay a second tax.

To some extent this second tax can be avoided by the payment of salaries to the corporation's owners provided such owners actually perform services and their compensation is reasonable. This payment reduces the income upon which the corporation pays taxes, thus removing these salaries from one layer of taxation and, to that extent, results in a single tax on that salary income.

Example

In the preceding example, in which X Corporation had taxable income of $10,000, if Mr. A had performed services for the corporation and he were to receive a salary of $10,000 (or if his salary were increased by $10,000), the corporation would have no taxable income since it would get a $10,000 deduction for salaries paid. It would pay no tax but would distribute the entire $10,000 to Mr. A as salary. He would include the $10,000 in his own taxable income.

In this connection, it is important to recognize that it may not be desirable for Mr. A to be taxed on an additional $10,000 if he is already in a high personal income tax bracket. It may be more desirable to have the corporation pay the tax and make no distribution of dividends to its shareholders. This raises a different tax problem.

If, even after the deduction of reasonable salaries to the shareholder-employees, the corporation still has taxable profits which it desires to shelter from double taxation by refusing to pay dividends, it may face another corporate tax. Such excess accumulation of earnings, beyond the reasonable needs of the business and in excess of $150,000, which are accumulated to avoid the tax on the shareholders are subject to an additional tax. (For taxable years beginning before December 31, 1974, the $150,000 minimum credit for reasonable business needs was $100,000.) This is an annual tax at the rate of $27\frac{1}{2}\%$ of the first $100,000 and $38\frac{1}{2}\%$ on any excess of earnings beyond $100,000 unreasonably accumulated during the year. It is called an accumulated earnings tax.

Example

X Corporation has accumulated earnings of $175,000 on January 1, 1975. During 1975 it earns $50,000 *after all taxes* including federal income taxes.

Unless it can show a reasonable business need for the $225,000 accumulation of earnings or the lack of a purpose to avoid income tax to shareholders, the corporation will be subject to an additional tax of $13,750; $27\frac{1}{2}\%$ of $50,000. If X Corporation pays a dividend of $50,000 to its shareholders this tax will not be imposed. (The preceding is a simplified version of a very complicated subject. For purposes of illustration certain technical adjustments have been omitted.)

Multiple corporations

Because there is a 22% tax on the first $25,000 of corporate ordinary income and a 48% tax on amounts in excess of $25,000, it is obviously a tax advantage to have several corporations each with its own $25,000 income segment taxable at the lower rate than to have only one corporation with only one $25,000 segment subject to the 22% rate. Hence, many corporate enterprises are set up as multiple corporations.

Congress has moved to curb this practice by providing in substance that where five or fewer persons own more than one corporation, the corporate group as a whole is allowed only one $25,000 segment of income at the 22% rate.

Taxation of corporate capital gains

The starting point for corporations is the same as for individuals.

Short-term, long-term and Section 1231 gains and losses are determined in the same manner as for individuals (see page 91).

Net Section 1231 gains are included in long-term capital gains and *net* Section 1231 losses are deducted from ordinary income.

Long-term gains and losses are aggregated separately, short-term gains and losses are aggregated separately and the results in the two categories are aggregated if one is a gain and the other is a loss.

The final results are net short-term and/or long-term gains and losses in the same manner as computed for an individual.

Corporate net short-term capital gains These are added to ordinary income in the same manner as for individuals.

Corporate net long-term capital gains These are treated in one of two ways (the corporation chooses the method that results in the lower tax).

1. The *full amount* of the net long-term capital gains is added to ordinary income and taxed at ordinary income rates.

2. The corporate *alternative tax* is used. A flat 30% rate is applied to the net long-term capital gains. This tax is then added to the corporate tax computed on the ordinary income alone.

To understand the significance of the two methods, it must be remembered that the corporate tax on ordinary income is 22% on the first $25,000 of ordinary income and 48% on all ordinary income in excess of $25,000. Since the alternative tax on corporate long-term capital gains is a flat 30%, the alternative way saves taxes only when the 48% rate would apply to the capital gains were they added to ordinary income. Stated conversely, the alternative tax would not be used when the capital gains, if converted to ordinary income, would be subject only to the 22% tax. If, by adding long-term capital gains to ordinary income, part would be taxed at 22% and part at 48%, it is necessary to calculate the tax both ways to determine whether or not it is advisable to use the alternative tax. It is important to note that it is not permissible to add part of the long-term capital gain to the ordinary income and apply the alternative tax to the other part. The entire long-term capital gain must either be added to ordinary income or be subjected to the alternative tax.

Examples

1. White Corporation has $10,000 ordinary income and $5,000 long-term capital gain. It will obviously add the long-term capital gain to its ordinary income since, in that way, the long-term gains will be subject to a tax of only 22% (the total income, ordinary and capital gain, is not more than $25,000).

2. Black Corporation has $100,000 of ordinary income and $20,000 of long-term capital gain. It will obviously apply the alternative (30%) tax to the $20,000 capital gain. If it added that gain to its ordinary income, that gain would be subject to a 48% tax.

3. Grey Corporation has ordinary income of $15,000 and long-term capital gains of $40,000. Although there is room for an additional $10,000 of ordinary income at 22%, if the $40,000 capital gain is added to the ordinary income, $30,000 of that income will be subject to a 48% tax. It will be cheaper to use the alternative tax.

If the ordinary income approach is used

Ordinary income	$15,000
Long-term capital gain	40,000
Total	$55,000

Tax on $25,000 (22%)	$ 5,500
Tax on 30,000 (48%)	14,400
Tax on $55,000	$19,900

If the alternative tax is used

Tax on $15,000 ordinary income (22%)	$ 3,300
Tax on 40,000 capital gain (30%)	12,000
Tax on $55,000	$15,300

107

Corporate net capital losses   Whether the corporation ends up with a net long-term loss, a net short-term loss or both, it cannot deduct any part of that loss against ordinary income of any year.

Net capital losses become carrybacks and carryovers in the form of *short-term* capital losses (regardless of whether they arose as long- or short-term). The loss may be carried back three years and forward five in the following manner.

For example, if the loss arose in 1974, it would first be carried back to 1971. It is then determined whether, if that loss arose as a short-term capital loss in 1971, the corporation's taxable income would have been different. (If the corporation had net capital gains, long- or short-term in 1971, the short-term loss carried back to that year would affect that year's taxable income since part or all of those gains would be offset by the loss. If it had no net long- or short-term capital gains in 1971, the short-term capital loss carried back to 1971 would have no effect on 1971 taxable income.) If the loss carried back to 1971 *does* reduce the 1971 tax, the tax-payer corporation is entitled to a refund.

If the corporation is unable to use all of the carryback loss in 1971, the portion not used is then carried to 1972 and the procedure used for 1971 is repeated.

To the extent the loss is not used in 1972, it is carried to 1973 and again the procedure is repeated.

If there is still an unused capital loss carryback after applying it to the prior three years, it becomes a carryforward to the succeeding five years. Thus, continuing our example, the unused loss would be available as a short-term capital loss in 1975. If there were not enough capital gains in 1975 to absorb the entire carry-forward loss, the balance would be carried to 1976 as a short-term capital loss and then to 1977, 1978 and 1979, if necessary. After 1979, if the loss had not been absorbed by offsetting capital gains, if would no longer be available to the corporation for any purpose.

Corporate dispositions

Once the corporate form has been chosen as the form of ownership, not only are there tax problems during ownership (e.g. non-availability of corporate losses to offset individual income) additional tax problems also arise at the time it is decided to dispose of the property.

If the corporation sells the property, the gain or loss will be taxed to it, the corporate entity. What happens to the after-tax profits on the sale that remain in the corporation? They could be subject to a second tax if distributed to the shareholders. However, some tax relief provisions are available to those who have taken the proper steps to qualify for special corporate liquidations. In other cases, by way of corporate reorganization, tax may be deferred (as in the case of an exchange of like-kind properties) and a shareholder's investment diversified. Again, it is necessary to know the rules and make preparations to qualify. The rules and strategies involved in using corporate liquidations and reorganizations are set forth in the Appendix on page 312.

Chapter 8

Acquisitions

8

When an investment in real estate is made, a major decision involves the form of ownership.

If the property is being acquired by a single investor, he may take the property in his own name, as sole owner or jointly with his spouse. Or, he may decide it would be better to have the property owned by a corporation even though he owns all the corporate stock.

Where more than one person will own the property, it may be held in partnership, joint tenancy, tenancy in common or in a corporation. It is also possible to hold property in a trust.

When more than one form of ownership is available, which one should an investor choose? The answer is not simple. It depends on the investor's immediate and long-term goals, his personal current tax position and his expected tax position in the future (plus good guesses about the state of the tax law and the economy in the future). No intelligent decision can be made, however, without an understanding of the meaning of the various forms of ownership and the tax consequences of each.

Another important factor in the acquisition of property is the establishment of basis. This is the starting point for the calculation of the important depreciation deductions and the determination of gain or loss on ultimate disposition of property. Establishing basis depends on the application of the appropriate rule (drawn from a complex network of different rules applicable to different forms of acquisition). The second part of this chapter devotes itself to explanations of the rules of basis and their ramifications.

Forms and nature of ownership

The basic forms of ownership have been alluded to in a previous chapter (see page 22). Following is a summary of the various forms of *rights* of ownership.

Rights Conveyed

Form of Ownership	Extent	Duration
Fee Simple	All	Infinite
Lease	Defined in terms of agreement	Terms of years, generally
Easement	Specified by agreement, usage or State law	Infinite or specified
Life estate	Defined by agreement	For a specified life

At this point, the nature of the *owner*, rather than the nature of his ownership interest, will be considered.

Individual ownership

Individual ownership refers to the situation in which a person owns property in his or her own name. The danger of unlimited liability is often a deterrent to the use of this form of ownership. Where feasible, insurance may reduce or eliminate this risk. The factors which often tip the scales in favor of individual ownership are the income tax rules and available flexibility with respect to freedom of action by the individual in making decisions regarding the acquisition, management and disposition of his investment. However, an individual may have only a limited amount of capital at his disposal for use in any particular venture. For this reason, one of the other forms of ownership, which makes greater sums of capital available, is often preferred.

From a tax viewpoint, an advantage of individual ownership of real property which is held for investment or income-producing purposes is the availability of substantial depreciation deductions which can be used to offset the owner's taxable income from other sources.

Example

Miss A is unmarried and has net taxable income after deductions and exemptions of $50,000 in 1975. Her income tax bill on this amount is $20,190. If she were to invest in a property which showed a tax loss of $30,000 due to large depreciation deductions, her taxable income would be reduced to $20,000. Thus, her tax would be only $5,230; a saving and an increase in available cash flow of $14,960.

It is important to note that in the above example, it would not be necessary for Miss A to invest $30,000 in cash to produce a tax loss of that amount. As noted in the discussion dealing with basis for depreciation, basis includes any mortgages on the property. So, if an investor could buy a building for $20,000 cash and $80,000 debt, his basis for depreciation of the building would still be $100,000.

Of course, if Miss A had created a corporation, even if she were its sole owner, and the corporation had purchased the property, the tax loss would not be available for use on her personal return. She would have saved no personal income tax for that year.

Joint ownership

Joint ownership is a type of concurrent ownership of property by several persons. It may be with or without a right of survivorship. Each joint owner possesses an undivided interest in the whole property.

There are several types of joint ownership. A tenancy in common is one which does not involve any rights of survivorship. Upon the death of one of the co-owners, his heirs or his estate becomes the owner of his share.

In a joint tenancy there *is* the right of survivorship. Upon the death of one of these co-owners, his share passes to the other co-owner or owners. Sometimes this is referred to as a "joint tenancy with right of survivorship." Generally, no probate proceedings are required to effectuate the transfer to the surviving joint owners. Where a joint tenancy exists between spouses, it is often called a "tenancy by the entirety."

Who is entitled to the income from property held in some form of joint ownership depends upon the provisions of law in the state where the property is located.

Thus, under some forms of joint ownership between husband and wife, the husband is entitled to all of the income earned by the property. In other states, income from joint property is divided equally.

As in the case of individual ownership, the profits or losses of the jointly-owned property pass directly to the owners according to the state rules for picking up income or losses.

Tenancy in common is often preferred to a formal partnership because each owner picks up his income or loss directly without regard to his co-owners. Each owner can make his own tax elections (e.g. accounting method, reinvestment of involuntary conversion proceeds). In a partnership, the partnership files an information return in which each partner's share of income and losses is revealed. If one partner's tax return is examined (perhaps because of nonpartnership items on his individual tax return), the other partners may find that their returns will be examined too. With tenants in common, this result is less likely.

A problem arises, however, when the jointly-owned property is, in effect, a business (e.g. ownership of rental property that involves more than passive ownership as where the co-owners also manage the property). In that case, although the legal form of ownership is a tenancy in common or a joint tenancy, for tax purposes, the owners will be treated as partners and a partnership tax return will be required.

Since joint ownership is so similar to ownership by a partnership, many of the advantages and disadvantages are identical. However, those forms of joint ownership which involve rights of survivorship present the additional advantage of avoiding probate on the death of one of the co-venturers. At death, the decedent's interest passes automatically with no need for court proceedings.

One disadvantage of this form of joint ownership is that upon the death of one of the joint owners, unless it can be clearly shown that he did not supply all the consideration for the purchase of the assets, IRS will include the *entire* value of the jointly-held assets in the *taxable* estate for Federal Estate Tax purposes of the first joint owner to die. Subsequently, when the next joint owner dies, the entire value of the assets may again be included in *his* taxable estate. (How this tax rule affects the basis of the property in the hands of the surviving joint tenant is explained on page 121.)

Community property

Under the laws of some states, property owned by married individuals is deemed to be property of both of them. Generally, property owned by them prior to their marriage is separate property and property acquired after the marriage is community property. Laws of the states applying this type of ownership vary and will not be discussed in detail in this book. It is important for the real estate broker to know and be able to explain to clients how the community property laws are applied, if they are applied, in his state.

Federal income taxation of property held in this form of ownership, as in the case of other types of joint ownership, is dependent upon the rules of state law as to who is entitled to the income and liable for the expenses.

Partnerships

Partnerships have become a very important form of ownership of real estate with the advent of the wide use of syndications.

The partnership form of ownership permits the passing through of losses and income directly to the partners. Furthermore, the use of limited partnership limits the investors' liabilities much in the same manner as the liabilities of corporate shareholders are limited. The use of non-recourse loans to the partnership increases the limited partners' bases for their investments far beyond the amounts of their actual cash investments.

The rules pertaining to limited partnerships are very complex especially in view of recent IRS actions taken to curb what the Government sees as abuses in this area. A comprehensive analysis of limited partnerships will be found in the Appendix, beginning on page 302. What follows is a brief discussion of the partnership form of ownership.

Partnerships include all sorts of *unincorporated* businesses owned by more than one individual or entity. (In most states, corporations and other partnerships may also be partners in a partnership.)

Among the reasons for use of the partnership form of owning investments is the increased availability of capital and skills that arises from an association of more than one individual. A group of investors may be able to purchase a larger piece of property than a single investor and have available a wider range of business skills including managerial and financial talent.

On the other hand, it may be difficult to arrive at a consensus in making decisions for the group investment. Unless one member is given authority to act for the group, it may be hamstrung in efforts to act quickly to take advantage of rapidly changing business or market conditions.

Partnerships terminate at the death of a partner in absence of special arrangements to the contrary. Heirs and successors are usually entitled to an accounting for benefits and results but have no claim on specific partnership assets.

Partner's capital contributions As a general rule, no gain or loss is recognized by either the partner or the partnership on contributions of either cash or property. The basis of the partner's interest in the partnership is the amount of money contributed plus that partner's adjusted basis in the property transferred. In a similar manner, the partnership assumes the partner's basis in the property transferred.

In order to prevent inequities between partners from arising when appreciated property with a low tax basis is contributed to the partnership, the tax law permits the partnership agreement to provide for special allocations of depreciation, depletion or gain or loss with respect to the property among the partners.

A problem frequently arises with regard to the formation of a real estate partnership when a promoter-developer receives a partnership capital interest in exchange for services. The Regulations take the position that the promoter-developer has received ordinary income to the extent of the fair market value of his services. This result might be avoided if the promoter-developer receives a partnership profits interest (the right to share in future partnership income), rather than a capital interest. In this manner, the tax would be postponed until he actually shares in the partnership income. However, the Tax Court and the Seventh Circuit Court have held that the promoter-developer will be taxed on the value of the income interest *upon receipt* if the profit interest has a determinable market value. (In this case, the promoter sold his interest three weeks after he got it, so the value was easily established.)

To the extent that an acquired interest in partnership capital results in taxable income, that partner's basis is increased by the amount of such income.

Partnership structure Limitation of liability and income tax consequences are determined by the nature of the partnership. A general partnership is one in which all partners share in profits or losses. There is no limitation of liability; partnership liabilities to the extent they cannot be satisfied out of partnership assets become claims against the individual partners. For income tax purposes, treatment is similar to the individual form of ownership. The partnership files an income tax return which is merely an information return. It pays no federal income tax. All of the income and deductions of a partnership flow through to the income tax returns of those who are partners.

A disadvantage of both the individual and general partnership form is the lack of limited liability afforded by these forms. That is, each of the general partners places not only his partnership investment, but all his other business investments and his personal assets as well, at the risk of the partnership venture. Each may be legally responsible for the business actions of *all* of the other partners in their conduct of the partnership business.

Another form of partnership is the limited partnership. It is made up of both limited and general partners. The limited partnership must have at least one general partner. It is the general partner or partners who usually conduct the business of the limited partnership. (A limited partner may not participate in active management without risking identification and liability as a general partner.) Each limited partner's liability is limited to the amount he has invested. Claims against the partnership which exceed partnership assets may be collected from the general partners only, not from the limited partners.

Possibly the greatest advantage of the limited partnership is that it enables larger amounts of capital to be invested than a single investor could raise on his own and yet it provides limited liability for the bulk of its investors without the formalities and often onerous tax burdens of the corporate form.

Disadvantages of both the general and limited partnerships may arise when their size becomes too great for efficient operation. Further, some complications may arise with respect to the transferability of the interests of retiring and deceased partners.

Syndicates

A syndicate is a loosely used term which describes any sort of combination of investors. It may be set up in the form of a corporation, a general partnership or a limited partnership.

Trusts

A trust is another type of legal arrangement sometimes used as a vehicle to hold property. It is not itself a legal entity; the trust *itself* does not own property. Rather, the trustee, sometimes called the fiduciary, is the legal owner of all trust property. He holds it for the benefit of someone else. That someone else is called the beneficiary. The person who sets up the trust arrangement by giving the property to the trustee to hold in trust is the grantor, settlor or creator.

Every trust must have one or more beneficiaries. They may get income from the trust and sometimes deductions. A beneficiary can have an income interest or a remainder interest in the trust property. If he has an income interest, he has a right to some or all of the trust's income as it is earned. If he has a remainder interest, then he has a right to receive trust property at the termination of the trust.

Trusts are often used to separate burdens of management from the benefits of ownership. For example, if it is desired to make a gift of income-producing real estate to someone who would not be capable or qualified to manage it (or to hire competent management) and to decide if, and when, the property should be sold or exchanged, the gift might be made to someone whose business acumen is respected by the donor, *in trust*, for the benefit of the intended beneficiary. The trustee will manage, or hire someone to manage, the property and make decisions about changing investments, while the beneficiary will receive the net income after expenses.

Some trusts are created by will, as testamentary bequests; others are created by written instruments or deeds during the lifetime of the grantor, as *intervivos* (or lifetime) gifts. An advantage of the trust as a gift vehicle is that it can be used as an arrangement for testamentary disposition of assets yet be set into operation during the life of the grantor. Thus, he can view, during his lifetime, the operation of his testamentary plan. If he has retained the right to revoke or to change the trust, he may alter his testamentary plan if its operation does not work out as he had anticipated.

Since the powers of the trustee are set forth in the trust instrument and in the law of a particular state, the trust form is sometimes a little cumbersome in its operation. As with a corporation which may act only via its authorized officers, persons dealing with a trustee should always be sure that he is authorized to perform whatever acts he purports to be within the scope of his authority. Consequently, copies of the trust instrument may often be required.

Federal income taxation of trusts is a somewhat complex topic. Very briefly, it may be said that the income of a trust is sometimes taxed to the trustee; that is, he pays the tax from the funds he holds in trust and not from his own personal funds. Sometimes it is taxed to the beneficiary and sometimes part of the trust income is taxed to the beneficiary and part to the trustee. In some instances trust income may even be taxed to the grantor. The determining factors are the terms of the trust instrument and sometimes local law. If the grantor gives property to a trustee but retains too much control over the property, then trust income will be taxed to him as though he still owned the property.

When the trust instrument requires all the income to be distributed to the beneficiary, then that beneficiary will usually be taxed on all the trust's income, even if he has not actually received it. If, however, the trustee has discretion to distribute income to the beneficiary or hold it in the trust, the beneficiary is taxed only on the amount he actually receives and the trustee pays the tax on the income that is retained. However, on subsequent distribution of the income on which the trust was taxed, an additional tax may have to be paid by the beneficiary. This is called the throw-back rule. Under this rule, if the trust paid less tax on the income it retained than the beneficiary would have paid had the income been distributed instead of retained, the difference in tax is paid upon ultimate distribution of the retained income.

Depreciation on property held by a trustee is generally allocated among the beneficiaries and the trustee in the same proportion in which the income is allocated. If local law or the trust instrument provides that the trustee must set aside a reserve for depreciation, then the depreciation deduction is allocated to the trustee to the extent of trust income he retains. These principles are illustrated as follows.

1. A sets up a trust wherein T is the trustee and B is the beneficiary. According to the trust instrument, all of the trust income is required to be distributed to B each year. In 1975, trust income consists of rent income of $7,000. Deductible expenses before depreciation amount to $4,000 and depreciation amounts to $1,000.

Here, the net income before depreciation is $3,000; $7,000 income minus $4,000 expenses. B is entitled to receive this $3,000. Were it not for the special rule allocating the depreciation deduction to the person getting the income that would be it. B would have to pay on $3,000 and the deduction for depreciation would go to the trustee since he is the legal owner of the property. Since the trustee has no income, the deduction would be wasted. Applying the special rule requires the allocation of all the depreciation deduction to the one getting the income. Therefore, B is required to pay tax on only $2,000; $3,000 net income less $1,000 depreciation deductions. T, as trustee, has zero taxable income and pays no tax.

2. If, using the same facts in the preceding illustration, T had been required by the trust instrument or by local law to set aside $1,000 as a reserve for depreciation, then B would only be entitled to receive $2,000; $3,000 income less $1,000 set aside for depreciation. B would pay tax on that $2,000. T, as trustee, would have $1,000 of income allocated to him and also $1,000 of depreciation expense, for a net result of zero taxable income and no tax due.

3. If the trust instrument had given T the right to withhold or distribute income to B in his own discretion and local law imposed no requirement as to a reserve for depreciation, then the results for tax purposes would depend on how much, if any, of the trust income was actually distributed to B. If T distributed half of the net income to B then B would be entitled to half the depreciation deduction. The final result using the facts of the example above would be that the $2,000 would be taxable: one-half (or $1,000) to B and the other one-half (or $1,000) to T.

Corporate ownership

A corporation is a legal entity chartered by a state. (Each state has its own procedual rules that must be followed to create a corporation.) The corporation is a fictional person with certain unusual attributes such as unlimited life. It is particularly suited for use when large amounts of capital are required or desirable. It enables centralized management to direct the investments of numerous owners called shareholders. The owners elect a Board of Directors. This Board is responsible for the overall policy decisions of the corporation. It, in turn, elects officers who are in charge of the corporation's everyday activities.

Corporate form is also available for small groups of owners, even one owner. Because it is a legal person, the corporation is often used to shield its owners from the dangers of business liabilities or reversals.

Example

X Corporation is owned solely by individual A. Mr. A buys an old house at 2 Main Street in his own name. X Corporation buys the house next door at 4 Main Street. Some children injure themselves on the broken steps leading up to both houses.

The children who were injured on the steps leading to 2 Main, owned by Mr. A, can sue him for all he's worth. That includes assets he owns personally as well as **115** all his investments in business, other corporations, etc. The children injured on the steps of 4 Main, owned by the corporation, can only sue the corporation for all of *its* assets. They cannot get any of Mr. A's other assets (unless he was personally negligent). They can't touch his other assets, neither his personal assets nor his other business assets, *even though he is the sole owner of X Corporation.*

This attribute of limited liability, the risking of only those assets held by the corporation and not the shareholders' other assets, is the most frequently cited reason for using a corporation to hold property. For example, should the income from a parcel of real estate diminish so that its expenses exceed its income, the mortgage holder may not recover from the individual stockholders of the corporation, unless, of course, they have given personal guarantees of payment.

The fact that the stockholders are often called upon to personally guarantee the debts of a corporation should not be overlooked, however. Many times, for example, a corporation is formed upon advice to "limit liability." Yet, under practical circumstances, the stockholders must personally endorse the notes. As a result, the limitation of liability is not really available and the formation of the corporation may have deprived the individuals of the tax losses that would have been available to them to offset their personal income or may result in double taxation.

It should also be remembered that the limitation of liability may be accomplished by means other than incorporating. One holding property as an individual may arrange for the mortgage debt to apply only to property mortgaged and not to any of his personal or other business assets. Similarly, he may take out liability insurance to cover possible injuries to people caused by defects in the premises. However, the cost of insurance might be prohibitive, as in a run-down or slum area.

Another aspect of the corporate form is its continuity. The life of a corporation may be perpetual or for a fixed term. Death of one or more shareholders does not require that corporate activity be stilled. Corporate life goes on with the estate of the deceased or his beneficiaries as shareholders.

Another advantage is that management can be vested in representatives of the owners who may usually operate without unanimous consent, thus permitting widely split ownership (including minors) without making management decisions cumbersome or impractical.

Subchapter S corporations   Certain corporations may take on a special status for tax purposes. Provisions for this special status are found in Subchapter S of the Internal Revenue Code. These corporations have all of the non-tax aspects of regular corporations but if certain requirements are met, their income may escape taxation at the corporate level. Instead, the profits and losses are passed through to the stockholders who then report their proportionate shares of the corporate profits or losses on their own individual tax returns.

A Subchapter S Corporation may not have more than 10 stockholders and may have only one class of stock. Stockholders must be individuals or estates of deceased individuals (Trusts, corporations or partnerships may not own stock in Subchapter S corporations.) The corporation must elect Subchapter S status and that election must be consented to by all its stockholders. However, a Subchapter S Corporation may not have more than 20% of its gross receipts from royalties, rents, dividends, interest, annunities and capital gains from the sale or exchange of stock or securities. Since most real estate operations involve the receipt of rents that exceed 20% of gross receipts, Subchapter S status is generally not available to real estate corporations. However, when substantial services are also rendered to the tenant, such as the services given at a hotel, motel, trailer court, public swimming pool, etc., the rents received will not disqualify the corporation from Subchapter S status. In those cases Subchapter S may be available.

Operating safeguards   Because a corporation is a fictional legal entity, it can act only through *authorized* human beings. When dealing with a corporation, it is vital to be sure that the humans who are representing the corporation have the *authority* to act for the corporation. Only then can the corporation be legally bound.

Thus, it is necessary that documents ostensibly signed in behalf of the corporation bear the proper signatures, those authorized by its Board of Directors. It is wise to obtain a copy of the authorization by the Board of Directors for the officers or other representatives of the corporation to sign or enter into the transaction. And, of course, any documents to which the corporation is a party should bear the corporate seal.

Summary of forms of ownership

The foregoing discussion has considered the various forms of entities which may be owners of real estate in some detail. Following, in tabular form, is a summary of the types of ownership entities and their various legal and tax attributes.

Types of Owners

Owner	Limited Liability	Authorized To Act	Taxable Status	Ownership Transferability
Corporation	Yes	Officers, employees & agents	Pays tax	Easily assigned, sold or divided
Subchapter S Corporations	Yes	Officers, employees & agents	Conduit	Easily assigned, sold or divided
Individual	No	Himself, agents & employees	Pays tax	Easily assigned or sold but less divisible (spouse may have to join)
General Partnership	No	Partners, agents & employees	Conduit	Partners must join or authorize.
Limited Partnership	No—for general partners	General partners, agents & employees	Conduit	General partners must join or authorize; no inchoate interest in spouse
	Yes—for limited partners			Limited partnership interest easily assigned or sold; no inchoate interest in spouse
Trusts	Yes	Trustee, agents & employees	May pay tax, be a conduit, or be a combination of both	Assignment or sale may be prohibited or at best difficult
Joint Ownership	No	Joint owners, agents & employees	Conduit (each owner pays tax on his share)	Easily assigned or sold; may require spouse to join

How to determine basis of property

Basis is a tax term that describes a taxpayer's investment in property. It is an important term to the real estate investor and broker because, for income tax purposes, it is an essential ingredient in determining gain or loss on the sale or exchange of property and the amount of depreciation deductions allowable.

The concept of basis may be illustrated in terms of a simple example. If property is bought for $10,000 and later sold for $20,000, it would appear offhand that the seller has realized a $10,000 gain because the selling price exceeded his cost by $10,000. But is this necessarily so?

The seller may have made improvements to the property after he acquired it. The improvements increased his investment in the property. Furthermore, he probably deducted depreciation during the time he held the property. These deductions reduced his investment in the property since they were recoveries of his investment. Consequently, the seller's original cost should be "adjusted" before it is compared to the selling price in order to compute gain or loss on the transaction.

And what was that original cost? If all that he paid to acquire the property was $10,000 in cash, it is quite clear that his original cost was $10,000. However, he might have given a mortgage, or assumed or took subject to one, in connection with the acquisition of the property. Or, perhaps, he didn't "buy" the property at all; he may have received it as a gift, inherited it or acquired it in an exchange for other property.

Since all of these various possibilities have to be taken into account, instead of "cost" the tax law refers to "basis" and "adjusted basis."

Basis is the starting point: its determination depends upon how the property was acquired. (Various methods of acquisition and the method of determining basis in each case are examined later in this chapter.)

Once basis at time of acquisition is determined, subsequent events may require the basis to be adjusted upward or downward. (After detailing the methods of determining basis at time of acquisition, the various adjustments are set forth.)

After the basis has been adjusted as required, the result is the adjusted basis. It is the adjusted basis that is then used in determining gain or loss on the sale or exchange of property and for the purpose of computing depreciation.

Allocation of basis

Before considering the various rules concerning the basis in each type of acquisition, it should be borne in mind that the basis determined for the entire property acquired may have to be allocated over a number of component parts of the property acquired. In the allocation, it is necessary to determine the portion of the basis applicable to the land and the portion applicable to improvements. Because the improvements might have different useful lives, further allocation among improvements may be necessary. The building might have a 50-year useful life whereas the furniture might have a five-year life.

It is possible for a purchase contract to specify how much is being paid for the land and how much for each of the improvements. These figures are usually accepted for income tax purposes if they were arrived at by unrelated parties in an "arm's-length" transaction. If, however, the sale is between related parties, such an allocation in the contract may be given less credence.

In the absence of a bona fide allocation in the contract, an allocation must be made on the basis of relative market values. Land and improvement values may be determined by competent appraisals made by appraisers or contractors.

Example

A parcel consisting of land and building is purchased for a total of $100,000. An MAI appraiser estimates the allocation of the purchase price in proportion to the relative market values of the land and building. The appraisal indicates that 80% of the value of the parcel is due to the value of the building. Therefore, $80,000 of the total $100,000 purchase price will be allocated to the building and will be subject to depreciation. The remaining $20,000 will be allocated to the land and will not be subject to depreciation.

In the absence of fair market value appraisals, it is possible to allocate between land and improvements based on the relative assessed values of land and building for real estate ad valorem tax purposes. This procedure is one of the methods frequently used.

Example

An individual buys a parcel consisting of land and a building. He pays $100,000 for the parcel; the purchase contract contains no allocation of price between land and building. Assessed values of the land and building are $10,000 and $40,000 respectively on the real estate tax bills. One acceptable method of allocation is to use the relationship of assessed values. So, in this situation, the ratio of the value of the land to the entire value of the parcel is 20%; $10,000/$50,000. The ratio of building to the whole is 80%; $40,000/$50,000. Therefore, in allocating basis to the building for the purpose of computing depreciation deductions, $80,000, 80% of $100,000, will be allocated to the building. $20,000 of the $100,000 purchase price will be allocated to the land.

Basis of purchased property

It is clear that if property is purchased for $50,000, the basis of that property is $50,000. It makes no difference whether the buyer pays all cash or meets part of the purchase obligation by giving a mortgage or by assuming (or taking subject to) an existing mortgage. The basis is still $50,000.

Examples

1. The purchase price of a parcel is $50,000. There is an existing mortgage on the property of $20,000. The buyer pays $30,000 cash and assumes the existing mortgage. The buyer's basis is $50,000.

2. Same as above but the buyer pays only $20,000 in cash and, in addition to assuming the $20,000 existing mortgage, he also gives the seller a second mortgage of $10,000. His basis is still $50,000.

3. Same as above but there is no existing mortgage on the property. The buyer secures a $30,000 mortgage from a bank using the mortgage proceeds plus $20,000 of his own funds to make the purchase. Again, his basis is $50,000.

Note that if the buyer pays a fee to secure the mortgage, that fee is not deductible for tax purposes. Nor can he add the fee to the basis of the property he is acquiring. **119** says the IRS. However, assuming that the property is either income-producing or business property, he can deduct the fee by amortizing it over the life of the mortgage. So, for example, if he paid a $300 fee to secure a 15-year mortgage, he can deduct $20 per year.

Property can be purchased with other than cash or a mortgage. For example, other property, a car, boat, diamond ring, stocks or bonds, might be used as part payment. The fair market values of these properties used to make the purchase are part of the purchase price. If, however, the basis for property the buyer uses as part of the purchase price is less than that property's market value, the difference between basis and market value will be treated as a gain realized by the buyer.

Example

Williams buys land for $35,000. He pays for it by transferring to the seller stock in AT&T that has a market value of $35,000. Williams basis for the land he has acquired is $35,000. However, if Williams' basis for the AT&T stock was $20,000, he will have realized a $15,000 gain on the transaction.

Exchanges

Note that in the above example, Williams gave up stock in part payment for the property he acquired. Suppose, however, he exchanged "like-kind" property, for example, land held for investment or an apartment building held for investment. In that case, even though the basis of the land he gave up was less than the market value of the building he received, the gain would not be taxable if he received nothing else but the building.

When property is exchanged for other like-kind property, there may be no immediate tax consequences (that is, the transaction may be tax free). In such cases, the basis of the property received is computed by reference to the basis of the property given up. But because the net debt against the property may change (as in the case in which mortgage on the property given up is larger or smaller than the mortgage on the property received) and because cash or other unlike kind property may be given or received to equalize the equities of the properties given up and received in the exchange, the basis of the property acquired may be higher or lower than the basis of the property given up. Furthermore, the allocation of basis between land and building on the acquired property may be made in proportions other than the proportions applied to the property given up.

A complete discussion of the effect of exchanges on basis begins on page 204.

Basis of inherited property

The basis of the property to the one inheriting is the market value at the date of death of the person from whom he is inheriting it.

An estate required to file a Federal Estate Tax Return, one in which the total value of the estate property exceeds $60,000 may, however, choose an alternate valuation date to value the property in the estate. Instead of using the date-of-death values, it may elect to use values six months after date of death. (However, if property is *sold* or *distributed* to the beneficiaries *during* the six months after death and the alternate valuation date is chosen, the alternate valuation date for the sold or distributed property is the date of sale or distribution.) If the alternate valuation date is used, the basis of the property inherited becomes the value on the alternate valuation date, the value at which it was included in the Federal Estate Tax Return.

When values have *increased* during the six months after death, the estate may elect the higher alternate valuation date value in order to increase the basis of the property to those who will receive it (and thereby increase furture depreciation deductions if the property is depreciable as well as reduce any subsequent gain or increase any subsequent loss when the property is sold). If the values have *decreased* during the six months after death, the estate may still elect to use the alternate valuation date value for estate tax purposes in order to reduce the amount of the estate tax. The choice is generally made after comparing the estate tax bracket with the income tax brackets of those who will receive the property. Generally, the valuation date chosen is the one that will save the most taxes overall.

Examples

1. Green dies, leaving in his estate property for which he had an adjusted basis of $20,000. Value of the property at the date of Green's death was $50,000. Six months after Green's death the value of the property was $60,000.

If, on the estate tax return the date-of-death value is used, the estate's basis for the property is $50,000.

However, if on the estate tax return the value six months after death is used, the estate's basis is $60,000. (If the value six months after Green's death had been $45,000 and the alternate valuation date were used, the estate's basis would have been $45,000.)

2. Wilson dies, leaving in his estate property for which he had an adjusted basis of $10,000 and which had a date-of-death value of $20,000. Six months after Wilson's death, the property has a value of $30,000. But Wilson's entire gross estate amounted to $40,000. Because a Federal Estate Tax Return was not required (since the total estate was less than $60,000), the alternate valuation date is not available. Hence, the estate's basis for the property is $20,000.

Basis of jointly-held property

When two or more people hold property jointly, they may be holding the property as tenants in common or joint tenants.

Tenants in common If property was held by the parties involved as tenants in common, each has his own interest in the property and his own basis. If one of the tenants in common should die, the basis of his interest to whoever inherits it is determined by the basis rules concerning inherited property (discussed previously).

Joint tenancy When property is held in joint tenancy, usually, upon the death of one of the joint tenants, his interest in the property automatically passes to the surviving joint tenant or tenants. For example, if property is held by husband and wife as joint tenants (in many states, this type of ownership is referred to an tenancy by the entirety), when the husband dies, his interest automatically passes to wife; she ends up owning the entire property.

How does the wife figure her basis after the husband's death? The answer depends upon several factors: who paid for the property and what the state law provides with respect to allocation of income from property held jointly by husband and wife.

The rules in this case can best be explained by a series of examples.

1. Assume husband and wife, using funds belonging to both half of the funds

belonged independently to each, bought land in joint tenancy at a cost of $10,000 in 1965. In 1967, they built an improvement on the land (again from joint funds) at a cost of $60,000. They added another improvement in 1972 at a cost of $12,000. The husband died on January 1, 1975.

Depreciation claimed on the $60,000 improvement for three years amounted to $7,500. Depreciation on the $12,000 improvement for the two years totalled $1,200. The market value of the property at the husband's death was $180,000.

The Federal Estate Tax rules require that the full value of the jointly-held property must be included in the estate of the first joint tenant to die except to the extent that it can be shown that the surviving joint tenant contributed from his own funds to acquisition of the jointly-held property. In this example, it was assumed that the wife actually contributed half the cost of the property and the improvements from her own independent funds. So, only half the value of the property or $90,000 is included in the husband's estate. The wife's basis for the entire property after her husband's death, on the premise that she owned one-half from the beginning and inherited the other half, is computed as follows.

Cost of land	$ 10,000
Cost of 1971 improvement	60,000
Cost of 1972 improvement	12,000
Total cost	82,000
Depreciation allowed	8,700
Adjusted basis of property at time of husband's death in 1975	$ 73,300
Wife's basis for half interest ($\frac{1}{2}$ of $73,300)	36,650
Value of husband's half interest included in his estate	90,000
Basis of property to wife after husband's death on entire property	$126,650

2. Assume the same facts as in Example 1 with this one exception: husband paid for everything with his own funds although he took title to the property in the joint names of himself and his wife as tenants by the entirety. Assume further that under state law income from the property would be allocated equally between husband and wife.

In these circumstances, when the husband dies *the entire* $180,000 value of the property would be included in his estate. Hence, the wife's basis for the property would then become $180,000 less one-half the depreciation allowed on the property during the husband's life. So, the wife's basis for the property after her husband's death becomes $175,650 ($180,000 minus $4,350, which is half the $8,700 depreciation previously deducted).

The date-of-death value has to be reduced by half the depreciation because the wife was entitled to half the income from the property during her husband's lifetime. Hence, she should be charged with half the depreciation deduction allowable in computing her basis.

3. Assume the same facts as in Example 2 except that under state law, during the husband's life, all of the income was allocated to him.

In that case, the entire $180,000 value at the date of death included in his estate becomes the wife's basis for the property after her husband's death.

Community property Suppose property is held by husband and wife in a community property state and constitutes community property so that each spouse is deemed to own half the property.

When the husband dies, half the property will be included in his estate. Nevertheless, the date-of-death value of the entire property will become the wife's basis for the property after her husband's death (assuming, of course, that she inherits the husband's half of the property).

Using the figures in our examples, upon the husband's death and the wife's inheriting his half of the community property, her basis for the property will be $180,000.

Life estates

Sometimes an individual acquires a life estate in a piece of property. For example, when Brown died, he left an apartment house he owned to his wife for her life and at her death the property was to go to his son. During her life, Mrs. Brown has a life estate in the property. On her death the property automatically goes to her son.

During her life, Mrs. Brown is entitled to collect the rents from the property. In computing her net taxable income from the property she is, of course, entitled to take a deduction for depreciation. How does she compute her basis for depreciation?

The tax law provides that Mrs. Brown's basis is the basis she would use if she owned the property outright. For example, if the property, when included in Brown's estate had a value of $100,000, that $100,000 becomes Mrs. Brown's basis. If $80,000 of that $100,000 is allocable to the building, she uses $80,000 as her basis for figuring her depreciation. On Mrs. Brown's death, her son gets the property outright. What's his basis for the property?

The son's basis is the basis remaining to Mrs. Brown after deducting the depreciation she took during her lifetime.

If Mrs. Brown sells her life interest, she has to use a zero basis for determining gain. Hence, everything she receives is gain. If, however, Mrs. Brown's son joins with Mrs. Brown in the sale, so that the purchaser is acquiring the entire property and not only Mrs. Brown's life interest, then the remaining basis of the property (i.e. the original basis to Mrs. Brown minus the depreciation deductions she took) is divided between Mrs. Brown and her son according to factors in the Government table (based on Mrs. Brown's life expectancy). Mrs. Brown and her son each figures her and his gain or loss using the basis assigned to each from the table and comparing that with the portion of the total sales price received by each.

What about the purchaser? If he has purchased Mrs. Brown's life estate only, he is entitled to keep the property only so long as Mrs. Brown lives. In that case, he can take the entire cost of the life estate and deduct that cost over the life expectancy of Mrs. Brown. In other words, he divides the cost of the entire property to him by the number of years Mrs. Brown is expected to live and deducts that amount each year. (If he paid $100,000 for the property and Mrs. Brown's life expectancy is 10 years, he deducts $10,000 a year for 10 years. If Mrs. Brown dies before he has fully deducted the $100,000, he deducts the remaining amount of the cost in the year Mrs. Brown dies. If she lives longer than 10 years, he gets no further deductions after he has recovered his $100,000 cost.)

123

Basis of property received as a gift

When property is received as a gift, the general rule is that the donee (the one who receives the gift) has as his basis for the property received the adjusted basis to the donor of the property at the time of the gift. If the donor has to pay a gift tax on the gift, the donee adds to his basis the amount of the gift tax. However, in no case can the donee's basis be increased beyond the market value of the property at the time of the gift by adding the gift tax to the donor's adjusted basis.

Example

Father has an adjusted basis for a property of $25,000. The market value of the property is $30,000. Father makes a gift of the property to his son and pays a gift tax of $2,000. His son's basis of the property is $25,000 (father's adjusted basis) plus the $2,000 gift tax or a total of $27,000.

If the gift tax had been $6,000, the son's basis would be $30,000. Although the total of the father's basis plus the gift tax is $31,000, the son's basis cannot be increased above the market value at the time of the gift as a result of adding the gift tax to the donor's basis.

Property sold at a loss   A special basis rule applies if the donee sells the property received as a gift at a loss.

If at the time of the gift the market value of the property was higher than the donor's adjusted basis, the general rule explained above applies.

Green makes a gift of land to his daughter. Green's basis was $10,000. Fair market value of the property at the time of the gift was $12,000. No gift tax was payable. Green's daughter subsequently sold the land for $8,000. Her basis is $10,000 (donor's basis, i.e. the general rule) and her loss is $2,000.

If at the time of the gift the market value is less than the donor's basis, the donee's basis for the purpose of computing the loss is the lower of the two values.

Brown makes a gift of land to his brother. Brown's basis for the land is $20,000. Fair market value of the land at the time of the gift is $18,000. No gift tax is due. Later, the brother sells the land for $15,000. Although the general rule is that the donee takes the donor's basis, the exception to the rule applies here. Since the market value was less than the donor's basis at the time of the gift and the gift property was subsequently sold at a loss, the donee takes as his basis the lower value, the market value of $18,000. Hence, his loss on the sale at $15,000 is $3,000.

In some cases the special basis rule creates a situation in which neither gain nor loss can be computed on the subsequent sale and so no gain or loss is reported.

Smith makes a gift of land to his mother. The fair market value at the time of the gift is $5,000; Smith's basis is $10,000. No gift tax is due. Smith's mother later sells the land for $7,000. If Smith's mother used the donor's basis ($10,000) as her basis, there would be a loss of $3,000. But when there is a loss and at the time of the gift the fair market value is less than the donor's basis, the donee is supposed to use the fair market value as her basis. But if Smith's mother uses the fair market value of $5,000 as her basis, the subsequent sale results in a $2,000 gain.

And basis for gain is always the donor's basis. Hence, in a case like this neither gain nor loss can be computed. So, Smith's mother has no gain or loss to report on the sale at $7,000.

Basis of property received for services rendered

If the one who is rendering the services is paid with property instead of with cash, the market value of the property received is ordinary income to the recipient since that is his compensation for his services. The same fair market value of his services becomes the basis for his property received.

Example

A real estate broker receives his fee in property rather than cash. He is entitled to a $5,000 commission and receives a parcel of land worth $5,000. He has commission income of $5,000 and the basis of the land to him is $5,000.

Suppose, instead of receiving land worth $5,000, he receives improved property worth $25,000 subject to a mortgage of $20,000. He still has $5,000 of income since his compensation income is the net value of the property received. But his basis for the property is $25,000. The situation is the equivalent to a purchase by the broker of a parcel for $25,000 by using his $5,000 fee and financing the balance with a mortgage.

Basis of property acquired through foreclosure or other repossession

When the seller receives a purchase money mortgage as part of the purchase price, he may subsequently repossess the property on default of the buyer. He then must determine whether he has realized a gain or loss on the repossession by applying special tax rules that apply to repossessions.

The tax rules differ, depending upon whether the property repossessed is real estate or personal property.

Repossession of real property   When the seller repossesses the property in full or partial satisfaction of the purchase money mortgage, the tax rules provide that no loss may be recognized for tax purposes on the transaction and that gain, if any, will be taxed only to a limited extent. (Losses are not recognized in these situations probably on the theory that the seller really has not lost anything since he has his property back.)

On the other hand, he may have a gain. This would be the case if he received some money (and possibly also some other property such as marketable securities) and then got his property back, too. For income tax purposes, he has realized a gain equal to the amount of the cash and the other property received less that portion of the gain on the original transaction that he has already reported.

Example

Barton sold a parcel of real estate which had a basis of $15,000 for $25,000. He received $5,000 cash and a purchase money mortgage for $20,000 bearing 9% interest, payable $4,000 annually commencing the next year. The following year he received the $4,000 payment (plus interest) but the year after that the buyer defaulted and Burton repossessed the property.

Assuming that Barton had elected the installment method of reporting (discussed on page 181) the tax treatment would be as follows.

Total cash received ($5,000 + $4,000)	$9,000
Reduced by gain previously reported	
Gross profit = $10,000 ($25,000 minus $15,000)	
Gross profit % = 40% ($10,000/$25,000)	
40% of $9,000 collected	3,600
Gain on repossession	$5,400

Had the installment method not been used and if the entire $10,000 gain had been reported in the year of sale, there would have been no gain on Barton's repossession.

But this is not the complete story. There is another tax rule which applies in some cases to limit the gain on repossession. This limitation is the amount of gain on the original sale of the property reduced by the total of the gain already reported and the cost of repossession.

On the same facts as the preceding illustration and assuming that costs of repossession amount to $1,200, the limitation on gain would be computed this way.

Original gain		$10,000
($25,000 sales price less $15,000 adjusted basis)		
Reduced by		
Gain previously reported	$3,600	
Repossession costs	1,200	4,800
Limitation		$ 5,200

Under the facts in the illustration, the limitation would apply to reduce the gain of $5,400 to $5,200.

Tax basis of repossessed real estate   The basis of the repossessed property is the basis of the unpaid obligation plus the sum of any gain required to be recognized by the rules above and the costs (if any) of repossession. This rule applies even if there is no gain and even if there is a loss which cannot be deducted for tax purposes. Its effect in situations where there is a non-recognized loss on repossession is to add that loss to basis.

Continuing the illustration to compute the basis of the property repossessed, we find the following.

Face value of the unpaid notes	$16,000
Less: Unreported gain 40% of $16,000	6,400
Basis of unpaid notes	9,600
Plus: Gain on repossession	5,200
Repossession costs	1,200
Basis of repossessed property	$16,000

Had the installment method not been used and the entire $10,000 gain been reported in the year of sale, the loss on repossession would have been $1,000 ($9,000 total cash received minus $10,000 gain already reported). While this $1,000 loss would not be deductible under the rules relating to repossessions of real estate, it would, in effect, be added to the basis of the property by the application of the previous rule. The computation would be as follows.

Face value of notes (Same as basis of unpaid notes)	$16,000
Plus: Repossession costs	1,200
Basis of repossessed property	$17,200

Notice that the new basis of the property can be said to consist of the following items.

Original basis		$15,000
Loss on repossession (not recognized):		
Gain taxed on sale	$10,000	
Less: Cash received	9,000	1,000
Repossession costs		1,200
New basis of repossessed property		$17,200

Situations involving principal residence All of the rules discussed before regarding repossessed real estate may not apply if the realty consists of the seller's principal residence. The law provides that when the principal residence is sold and all or part of the gain is not recognized either under the special rule for persons aged 65 or the special rule involving reinvestment of the proceeds in a new residence within prescribed time, then if the seller resells the repossessed residence within one year of repossession, all the rules discussed previously will not apply. In those cases, the resale is treated as part of the original sale, ignoring the repossession. However, if the resale is not made within the year following repossession, then all of the rules with respect to gains on repossessions and new basis with respect thereto will apply.

Basis of repossessed personal property The owner of realty will also, in connection with his real estate, often sell personal property such as furniture within his building. Rules regarding repossessions of such property differ from those involving real estate.

The market value of the property repossessed becomes the basis of that property after repossession because gain or loss is recognized to the seller on the repossession at the time of the repossession.

Gain or loss is the difference between the market value of the property retaken and the seller's basis for the notes cancelled or adjusted, when necessary, for other amounts realized or other costs incurred in connection with the repossession. As in the case of real property discussed above, the seller's basis of defaulted notes is their face minus any unreported profit with respect to them.

Example

In connection with the sale of his hotel, Green also sells the furniture for $15,000. His adjusted basis for the furniture at the time of the sale was $10,000. He received $3,000 in the year of the sale and a note for $12,000, payable $1,000 per month, with 8% interest, beginning in the year following the sale. Green reports the gain using the installment method since he did not receive more than 30% of the sales price in the year of sale. (Since his profit on the sale is $5,000 or $33\frac{1}{3}\%$ of the selling price, he will report $33\frac{1}{3}\%$ of each collection of cash as gain at the time he collects it.)

After making three payments, the buyer defaulted and Green repossessed the furniture. Fair market value of the furniture at the time of the repossession was $14,000 and expense of repossession was $1,000. Green computes his gain on repossession as follows.

Market value of the repossessed furniture		$14,000
Basis of buyer's notes:		
Original face amount	$12,000	
Less: Three payments made	3,000	
Face value of unpaid notes	$ 9,000	
Less: Unrealized profit (33⅓% of $9,000)	3,000	
Basis of unpaid notes		6,000
Gain on repossession		8,000
Less: Repossession costs		1,000
Taxable gain on repossession		$ 7,000

If the installment method of reporting had not been used and the entire gain or loss on the sale was reported in the year of sale, the basis of the notes or other obligations would be their face amount (unless a lesser amount was taken into account in computing gain in the year of sale under the deferred payment sale rules; see page 189).

Example

Assume that in the previous example the entire gain was reported in the year of sale. That gain was $5,000 and the basis of the unpaid notes was $12,000, their face amount. Subsequently, $3,000 of notes were paid off. So, at the time of repossession, the remaining unpaid notes had a face amount (and a basis) of $9,000. Since the fair market value of the repossessed furniture was $14,000, there was a gain on the repossession of $4,000, computed as follows.

Market value of repossessed furniture		$14,000
Less: Basis of unpaid notes (equal to face)	$9,000	
Repossession costs	1,000	10,000
Gain on repossession		$ 4,000

In either of the two examples, the basis of the repossessed furniture would be $14,000, its market value at time of repossession.

Nature of the gain on repossession If the original sale was reported as an installment sale, any gain or recognized loss on the repossession of either real property or personal property (under the rules spelled out above) is treated the same way as the gain on the installment sale was treated. That means if the sale resulted in capital gain under the installment method, the gain on the repossession is also a capital gain. But note this about depreciation recapture: as explained on page 188, if part of the gain on a transaction reported as an installment sale constitutes depreciation recapture, gains realized in the year of sale and subsequent years are first allocated to depreciation recapture. Remaining gain realized is then treated as capital gain. Hence, if prior to the repossession not all of the depreciation recapture had yet been reported, gain on the repossession would first be applied to the recapture and then any remaining gain would be taxable as capital gain.

Example

Gain on an installment sale was $15,000, of which $5,000 was depreciation recapture and $10,000 was capital gain. After $4,000 of the gain was reported under the installment method, the seller repossessed the property. Gain realized on the repossession was $6,000. Since only $4,000 of the $5,000 depreciation recapture had previously been reported, $1,000 of the $6,000 gain on the repossession is treated as depreciation recapture and the remaining $5,000 gain is treated as capital gain.

If the original sale was not an installment sale, the gain on repossession is treated as a redemption of the notes held by the seller. This results in ordinary income unless the notes or other obligations held by the seller are corporate obligations. In that case, the gain is capital gain. No depreciation recapture problem arises in this case because the entire gain was originally reported in the year of sale. Hence, any depreciation recapture was reported at that time.

Basis of property foreclosed by third party mortgagees

When money is borrowed from someone other than the seller of property and a mortgage or other pledge is given, the creditor is sometimes called a third party mortgagee. Rules with respect to defaults on such obligations are similar to those of reposessions of personal property.

When mortgaged or pledged property is sold and the net proceeds are less than the amount of the debt, the difference, to the extent it is uncollectible, is deductible as a bad debt loss by the mortgagee. Business bad debts are fully deductible as ordinary losses; however, non-business bad debts are treated as short-term capital losses.

The buyer of such property at a foreclosure sale, if he is not the creditor, has a basis for the property equal to the amount he pays.

Example

Shaw holds a $25,000 mortgage note which is in default. A foreclosure sale is held at which Smith buys the property for $15,000. Expenses of the sale amount to $1,000. The results are as follows: Shaw has a bad debt loss of $11,000 because that is the difference between his basis for the note ($25,000) and the net proceeds ($15,000 less $1,000) he received. Smith has a basis of $15,000 for the property because that is what he paid for it.

When the person buying the property at the foreclosure sale is also the creditor, it is possible for another gain or loss to occur. That is because the buying in of the property with the defaulted obligation is considered a taxable transaction. Therefore, if the value of the property differs from the creditor's basis for his notes, he will have a gain or a loss. His basis for the property will be its market value at the time he acquired it.

Example

If, in the preceding illustration, Shaw had bid in the foreclosure sale and had purchased the property for $10,000 (assuming that its fair market value was still $15,000) he would have had a loss on the note of $16,000; $25,000 less net proceeds of $9,000. He also would have had a capital gain of $5,000 on the exchange of note for property, market value of the property less the $10,000 bid price.

Conversely, if he had bid in the property at $20,000, $5,000 in excess of its fair market value, he would have a loss on the note of $6,000 ($25,000 less net proceeds of $19,000) and a capital loss of the $5,000 excess on the exchange. Whether this is long- or short-term depends on the holding period of the mortgage note.

Finally, if he had bought in the property at $15,000, its fair market value, his bad debt loss on the note, as in the case when the property was bought by Smith, would be $11,000 and he would have no gain on the exchange.

His basis for the property would be $15,000, its fair market value, in all three cases.

Note that the usual presumption is that the bid price is the fair market value. The Treasury Regulations make that assumption unless overcome by clear evidence to the contrary. Furthermore, the Uniform Commercial Code which applies in most states requires that bids be made in good faith and hence presumes that the bid price is the fair market value. Hence, there would be very few situations where there could be a difference between the price at which the property was bid in and its fair market value. Consequently, the first two situations in the example are not very likely to occur.

Basis of property after involuntary conversions

Sometimes property is converted from one kind to another against the wishes of its owner. Such a conversion occurs when property is condemned by a governmental authority and replaced by cash or state bonds. Similarly, such an event takes place when a natural disaster, e.g. fire, storm, destroys property and it is replaced with cash by an insurance company. When such an event occurs, a gain may result. That is, the proceeds received exceed the basis of the property destroyed.

When there is a gain as a result of an involuntary conversion, the taxpayer has the option of postponing the taxability of such gain. To achieve such a postponement of taxation, the taxpayer must (within a specified time) purchase replacement property which costs as much as or more than the net proceeds received from the conversion. The replacement has to occur by the end of the second year after the year in which any part of the gain is realized. Thus, for example, if any part of the gain is realized *any time during* 1974, the replacement has to occur by the end of 1976. If a longer period is needed to make the replacement, IRS has the authority to extend the period on the request of the taxpayer.

If the replacement property costs less than the net proceeds received from the involuntary conversion, the gain is taxed to the extent of the unexpended portion.

Example

Long's factory is condemned by the state and he was awarded $160,000 for the property for which he had a basis of $150,000. Therefore, he realized a $10,000 gain from the condemnation. If he purchases another factory for $160,000 or more within the specified replacement period, he may elect to postpone the tax on his gain. If his new factory cost only $158,000, he would be required to pay tax on $2,000, the part of the gain not reinvested in the new factory.

Note that the *cost* of the new property must equal the proceeds of the involuntary conversion to avoid the tax on the gain on the conversion. However, cost does not necessarily mean cash. Hence, while a $150,000 cash award on condemnation might have been received, taxable gain is avoided if $150,000 is reinvested in the proper property within the required time even if, for example, $20,000 cash is paid and a mortgage of $130,000 is given.

The replacement property has to be property similar or related in service and use to the property which it replaces. That means, says IRS, that it must be functionally the same as the property it replaces; it must serve the same use. *There is a big exception to this rule for real estate, however.*

This exception applies when real property used in a trade or business or held for production of income or for investment is involuntarily converted as a result of its seizure, requisition, condemnation or sale under threat thereof. (This exception would therefore not apply where the involuntary conversion is a result of a fire loss.)

When the exception applies, the replacement property can be any other real property used in the taxpayer's trade or business or held for the production of income or for investment. In other words, it makes no difference that the replacement property is not similar or related in service or use to the property converted. It doesn't matter whether the property that was given up or the property that was acquired is improved or unimproved real property.

Basis of replacement property When replacement property is acquired and an election to have the tax on the gain on the involuntary conversion of the old property postponed is made, the basis of the new (replacement) property must be reduced by the amount of gain which has not been taxed.

Example

In the prior example, assume Long invests $162,000 in a new factory property within the required time. He elects not to report any part of the gain since he has reinvested at least the entire $160,000 proceeds. His basis for his new factory is $152,000, computed as follows.

Amount paid for new factory	$162,000
Less: Gain realized on condemnation that was not reported for tax purposes	10,000
Basis of new factory	$152,000

If Long had invested only $156,000 in the new factory, he would have been taxed on $4,000 of the $10,000 gain on the condemnation. $6,000 of the $10,000 gain would be non-taxable. He has to reduce the nontaxable portion of the gain by the $4,000 difference between the $160,000 proceeds from the condemnation and the $156,000 reinvested in the new factory. In that case, the basis of his new factory would be $150,000, computed as follows.

Amount paid for new factory	$156,000
Less: Gain realized on condemnation but not reported for tax purposes	6,000
Basis of new factory	$150,000

Basis of property acquired through exercise of options

Often, prior to the acquisition of real property, the buyer first obtains an option. For example, he may pay $1,000 for a three-month option to acquire a property at $15,000. Within the three months, he exercises his option, paying the $15,000 for the property. His basis of the property acquired is $16,000; the $15,000 purchase price plus the $1,000 he paid for the option.

If he lets the three-month period expire without exercising the option, he has a $1,000 loss. The nature of the loss is the same as the kind of loss he would have had had he sold the property (on which he had the option) at a loss.

Basis if converted from personal residence to income-producing property

If property has not been used in a trade, business or has not been held for the production of income, such as a former residence which is being converted into rental property, there is a different rule for basis computation. In that case the basis for computing depreciation is the lower of (1) the property's adjusted basis or (2) the market value of the property. Both of these factors should be determined at the date of the conversion to income-producing status.

Example

Felix bought his personal residence in 1967 for $39,000. In 1975 he moves to an apartment and rents his house to Finch. In 1975, at the time of the rental, the house is worth only $30,000. Felix's basis for it is still the $39,000 that he paid; there have been no adjustments. (He was not permitted to deduct depreciation on a personal residence.)

For the purpose of computing depreciation to reduce Felix's taxable rental income reportable on his 1975 Federal income tax return, the basis to be used for the entire property is $30,000, the lower figure. (An allocation must then be made between land and improvements.)

Adjustments to basis

After the initial, unadjusted basis is determined under the rules set forth previously, necessary adjustments are made to the basis to arrive at adjusted basis. Adjustments can take the form of additions to as well as reductions of the initial, unadjusted basis.

Additions to basis

The cost of improvements to the property increases the basis. As a rule of thumb, and that is IRS' position, improvements and betterments that have a useful life of more than one year are added to basis.

Capital improvements must be distinguished from repairs and operating expenses. Repairs and operating costs, as well as improvements with a useful life of one year or less, are current deductions and have no effect on basis at all. (See page 136 for a discussion of repairs vs. capital improvements.)

Capitalized carrying charges, interest and taxes The tax law provides owners of certain type of real estate the option to deduct or capitalize interest, taxes and carrying charges. If the owner elects to capitalize these items, he adds them to his basis. If he elects to deduct them, then, of course, these items have no effect on basis.

There are two categories of property to which the option of capitalizing or deducting is permitted.

The election to capitalize annual real estate taxes, mortgage interest and deductible carrying charges on unimproved and unproductive real property is effective only for the year for which the election is made. A new election may be made each year as long as the property remains unimproved and unproductive.

Example

Smith owns land. The land is both unimproved and unproductive for two years. The third year the land is leased to a department store which uses it as a parking lot. Smith could elect in either or both of the first two years to capitalize taxes, interest and carrying charges. However, in the third year, he could not elect to capitalize those expenses because the property was no longer unproductive that year.

Someone who is engaged in the development of real estate or in the construction of an improvement to real estate may elect to capitalize interest on a loan, carrying charges and taxes incurred in connection with the development or improvement which would otherwise be deductible. (Taxes include Federal Unemployment

Insurance taxes and Social Security taxes on the wages of the employees engaged in the development or construction work as well as state and local taxes.) These expenses may be capitalized whether the property is improved or unimproved or productive or unproductive but only for such expenses paid or incurred up to the time the development or improvement is completed. Any or all of the taxes or carrying charges for each development or construction project may be capitalized. But once an election is made to capitalize a particular type of tax or carrying charge for a particular project, that type of expenditure must continue to be capitalized until the project is completed.

On the sale of property, real estate taxes for the current real property tax year are apportioned between seller and buyer. To the extent that the buyer pays taxes allocable to the seller and other prior years' taxes that had been assessed on the property while owned by the seller, they are added to the purchaser's basis of the property.

Purchase commissions, legal fees for the cost of perfecting or defending title to the property and the cost of title insurance are all items the cost of which are added to the basis of the property.

When property is sold, the cost of selling it (e.g. brokers' commissions) reduce the gain on the sale or increase the loss. The expenses of sale are not separate deductions against ordinary income (unless the seller is a dealer). Normally, it makes no difference whether the expenses of sale are added to the seller's basis or deducted from the sales price in arriving at the gain; in either case, the result is the same.

Selling price: $100,000
Selling expenses: $6,000
Basis: $64,000

The gain is $30,000. This can be arrived at by reducing the selling price to $94,000 and then subtracting the basis of $64,000; or, it can be arrived at by adding the $6,000 selling costs to the $64,000 basis and subtracting the resulting $70,000 from the $100,000 selling price.

IRS takes the position that the costs of sale are subtracted from the selling price. When an installment sale is made, however, there is one instance when adding the costs of selling the property to the basis may be advantageous to the taxpayer. That occurs when the existing mortgage on the property exceeds the seller's basis. That excess is treated as an amount received by the seller in the year of sale (if amounts received in the year of sale exceed 30% of the selling price, installment reporting is not available for tax purposes). Hence, if the selling costs are able to be added to basis, the gap between the mortgage amount and the basis is narrowed and there is less of an excess to be treated as an amount received in the year of sale. One court has supported the taxpayer's position that selling costs are to be added to the seller's basis. However, IRS refuses to go along with this decision. (Installment sales and the impact of the treatment of selling expenses are dealt with in detail on page 184.)

Reductions of basis

Depreciation The major item that reduces basis is the depreciation allowed or allowable during the time the property was held. Thus, if for some reason the property owner deducts less depreciation than the amount he is allowed to deduct under his method of depreciation, his basis must still be reduced by the amount of the depreciation that was allowable. (The first-year "bonus" depreciation allowed on personal property, see page 165, must also be deducted from basis). Conversely, if the owner deducted more depreciation than he was entitled to deduct under his method, or under an improper method, his basis is reduced by the actual depreciation deducted (as long as the depreciation deducted reduced his tax liability in the year it was deducted).

Reduction of basis when there is a partial divestiture of property   When property is acquired, it is necessary to make an allocation of basis between land and building. But subsequently, suppose part of the land is sold. Or, perhaps, part is taken by condemnation. How is the basis of the land allocated between the part that is disposed of and the part that is retained? The Treasury Regulations are not too helpful in this area. They require that an equitable apportionment be made.

If the property was bought on a "square foot" basis to begin with or for a single purpose and each part of the land has the same value as each other part, a square foot approach can be used in determining the basis of the portion disposed of and the portion retained. For example, if 20,000 square feet of land are bought for $20,000 and a building is erected on half the land at a cost of $100,000, and immediately the other half of the land is sold, all other things being equal, the basis of the land sold would be $10,000 (half the basis of the total land) and the basis of the other half of the property would be $110,000 (the $10,000 basis of the remaining land plus the $100,000 cost of the building).

However, all things are not always equal and a portion of the property (due to favorable frontage, for example, or lack of access to the other portion of the land) may be worth more or less than another portion of the property. In that case, allocation of the basis to the various portions of the land in relation to their relative market values would be in order.

In one tax case, for example, a 10-acre tract of land was acquired for the purpose of developing a shopping center. Later the plans fell through and a portion of the land was sold. IRS argued that the basis should be allocated to the land on a square foot basis because the entire land was acquired for a single purpose to erect a shopping center. However, the portion of the land sold, considerably less than 40% of the total acreage, was determined by the court to be the most valuable portion of the land due to the fact it fronted on two busy streets (it was a corner plot) and was worth about 40% of the total value of the land. Hence, 40% of the basis was allocated to the portion of the land sold. Subsequently, IRS announced that it would go along with that decision.

Undivided interests   If the owner of a tract of land sells an undivided interest in the entire land, rather than the sale of a specific portion of it, he allocates to the property sold the same portion of the basis that he has given up in terms of the undivided interest. So, if land cost Smith $100,000 and he sells Jones a 25% undivided interest in the entire tract, Smith will allocate $25,000 (25% of the basis of the entire tract to him) to the interest he sold to Jones. Consequently, if Jones paid $40,000 for his 25% undivided interest, Smith would have a $15,000 gain.

Parcels acquired at different times   If several parcels of land are acquired at different times at different prices, although they are contiguous and thus form one tract of land, the basis for each parcel is kept track of separately. Upon subsequent disposition, gain or loss on the parcel disposed of is computed separately by comparing the basis for that parcel with the portion of the sales price allocated to that

134   parcel.

Casualty losses If property was partially destroyed by fire, storm or other casualty, the owner may have been entitled to a casualty loss deduction. The casualty loss is the difference between the value of the property immediately before and after the casualty (but not more than the adjusted basis at the time of the casualty) reduced by any insurance recovery. (For individuals, the first $100 of the casualty loss is not deductible.) The amount of the insurance proceeds received plus any casualty loss deducted reduce the basis of the property.

Example

Stevens owned land and building used in his business for which he had originally paid $40,000, having allocated $35,000 to the building and $5,000 to the land. After it was purchased, Stevens built an addition to the building at a cost of $10,000. On October 1, 1975, the building was completely destroyed by fire. Up to the time of the fire Stevens had been allowed depreciation deductions totalling $23,000. Stevens sold what salvage he could recover for $1,300 and collected $19,700 insurance. He also deducted a $1,000 casualty loss on his 1975 tax return. He spent $19,000 of the insurance proceeds to restore the building. The restoration was completed by the end of 1975. The adjusted basis of his property on January 1, 1976, is computed as follows.

		Land	Building
Original cost of property		$5,000	$35,000
Addition to building			10,000
			45,000
Less: Depreciation			23,000
Basis before casualty		5,000	22,000
Less:			
Casualty loss deduction	$ 1,000		
Insurance proceeds	19,700		
Salvage proceeds	1,300		22,000
Basis after casualty		5,000	none
Add: Cost of restoring building			$19,000
Basis on January 1, 1976		$5,000	$19,000

Easements If the property owner receives payments for the grant of an easement on the property, the amount received for the easement reduces the basis of the property.

Chapter 9

Operations

As has been previously discussed, the investor's return from an investment in real estate consists both of the income produced from operating the property and the profit on its ultimate disposition. In both instances, however, there are income tax consequences with which to reckon. These consequences, of course, affect the net return on the investment.

In this chapter, we will be concerned with the impact of the tax rules on the income from operations of real estate, basically, the investor's return in terms of rental income and the impact of the tax rules on the cash flow from the property.

Nature of income from operations

Typically, the real estate investor receives a current return from his property in the form of rent. This rent is ordinary income. However, rental income is income from a trade or business and only the net income (after deducting ordinary and necessary business expenses) is subject to taxation. It is possible that after deducting all of the ordinary and necessary business expenses from the gross rental income the result will be a taxable loss. As explained previously, such a loss can be used by the investor to reduce his other taxable income.

Deductible items

What are the ordinary and necessary business expenses that the real estate owner may deduct in reducing gross rental income to net taxable income (or loss)?

Utility costs, management and maintenance salaries and wages, real estate taxes, repair and maintenance costs, interest and depreciation are the major items of deductions.

The items of repairs and maintenance, interest and depreciation require more detailed examination and are analyzed later in this chapter. It should also be mentioned that in some instances, interest, taxes and carrying charges may be capitalized (at the taxpayer's election) and thus are not deductible as current expenses but become part of basis (see page 132).

Cash flow

Any examination of the tax aspects of real estate operations must necessarily become involved in a consideration of the cash flow from the investment. At the end of this chapter there are several illustrations of how the application of the tax laws to the income from operations affects the investor's cash flow.

Repairs or improvements

Sometimes, it is difficult to distinguish between a repair and a capital improvement. There are probably over 1,000 tax cases on this subject. Typically, the courts and IRS say that each case must be decided on the basis of its own particular facts and circumstances, a statement that offers no practical guide to anyone trying to distinguish between a repair and an improvement.

As a general rule it can be said that an improvement is either *an addition* to the property (with a useful life of more than one year) or is something that *prolongs* the useful life of the property. A repair is something more in the way of maintenance, the effect of which merely maintains but does not increase the useful life of the property.

The Revenue Act of 1971 contained the provisions of a Regulation that IRS issued at the same time it made the ADR (Asset Depreciation Range) system of useful lives available (see page 144). Under this Regulation, if a taxpayer elects ADR he can also elect (if he wishes) to use the percentage repair allowance rule. This rule is intended to take some of the controversy out of the repair vs. improvement question. Under this rule a percentage repair allowance is published for each class of assets in the guidelines. This is a percentage of the average unadjusted basis of the taxpayer's assets in that guideline class. Expenditures up to that amount are allowed as repairs; excess expenditures are treated as capital additions. Certain items that are clearly capital additions do not get that treatment. Nor can the taxpayer make it a policy to buy old, worn-out items and then claim a deduction for the expenditures to bring them up to working condition.

Note that unless the ADR rules are adopted for a particular year, the percentage approach is not available. The percentage approach is only useful in situations where expenditures are made for hybrid items, part expense and part improvement. If it is clearly expense, a deduction is available without electing to use the percentage method. If it is clearly an improvement, the percentage method cannot be used.

It should be further noted that the ADR rules are not particularly attractive for real estate and are not likely to be used for buildings and other structures (see page 145). Consequently, the percentage approach is rarely a significant factor in solving the repair-improvement dilemma in real estate situations.

The interest deduction

A major item of deduction for most real estate investors is interest expense. The general rule is that all interest paid on any indebtedness is deductible, whether the interest cost is related to an indebtedness incurred in business or income-seeking transaction or a personal debt. One major exception is interest paid or incurred to acquire or carry securities the interest income of which is tax exempt. For example, if an indebtedness is incurred to buy or carry municipal bonds (the interest income of which is exempt from federal income taxes), the interest paid on such indebtedness is not tax deductible.

Although the general rule is that interest is deductible, there are two problem areas that affect the deductibility of interest. One concerns the prepayment of interest. The other involves the rules governing excess investment interest, under which a portion of the interest expense may not be deductible currently.

Prepaid interest

There was a time when as much as five years' interest paid in advance by a cash basis taxpayer was allowed as a current deduction. In recent years IRS has taken the position that not more than one year's interest paid in advance can be taken as a current deduction. But IRS has gone further than that. It has successfully argued in the Tax Court that *no* part of prepaid interest may be deducted currently by a cash basis taxpayer if allowing the interest deduction would materially distort the taxpayer's income.

To illustrate when IRS might successfully prevent the deduction of *any* prepaid interest, it is instructive to examine the facts of the Tax Court case which disallowed the prepaid interest as a deduction.

The taxpayer borrowed $5,000,000 three days before the end of the year. Of this, $1,000,000 was added to his bank account and mingled with other funds. The following day he caused the bank (the lender) to debit his account for $377,000 which represented one year's interest on the loans. IRS denied 362/365ths of the interest paid as a deduction (the portion representing prepaid interest for the following year).

IRS argued that the taxpayer, in substance, received the discounted amount of the loan, i.e. the loan minus the interest that was almost immediately prepaid. Interest on a discounted loan is not deductible until the loan is repaid.

The Tax Court rejected this argument saying that the total loan proceeds received were co-mingled with the taxpayer's other funds and then he paid the interest. And, in addition, the taxpayer had sufficient other funds with which to make the prepaid interest payment. Thus, the Tax Court concluded, "we hold petitioner to have prepaid, in cash, interest on certain loans. Accordingly section 163(a) will permit petitioner an interest expense deduction for the taxable year 1969 [the year prepayment was made]." *Nevertheless, the Court proceeded to disallow the deduction.*

The Court said that IRS, relying on section 446 of the Internal Revenue Code, could disallow all but 3/365ths of the deduction on the grounds that the balance of the deduction would materially distort the taxpayer's income. Hence, even though the prepaid interest was "deductible" it turned out not to be.

When does prepaid interest materially distort a taxpayer's income? In *Rev. Rul. 68–643*, IRS announced that the deduction of prepaid interest may not result in a clear reflection of income for the taxable year of payment. Some of the factors to be considered in determining whether the deduction for prepaid interest created a material distortion of income, said IRS, include the following.

The amount of income in the taxable year of payment
The income of previous taxable years
The amount of the prepaid interest
The reason for prepayment
The existence of a varying rate of interest over the term of the loans

The Tax Court, in this case, concluded that the prepayment would distort the taxpayer's income in the year of payment because of the following.

1. Taxpayer realized a long-term capital gain in the year of payment of $968,000, an amount far in excess of his gross income in the two prior years.

2. The prepayment of $377,000 of interest on December 30, 1969, was based on loans he made one day earlier in the amount of some $5,000,000.

3. The taxpayer conceded that his motivation for borrowing the $5,000,000 was the deduction he would receive for the prepaid interest.

Obviously, in light of the IRS position and the Tax Court decision, a cash basis taxpayer cannot assume that in every case prepayment of up to one year's interest will automatically be allowed as a deduction. An examination should be made to determine whether factors such as those listed by IRS are present to give credence to an argument that the deduction materially distorts the taxpayer's income.

Excess investment interest

Part of an individual's interest expense (the rule does not apply to corporations) may be disallowed as a current interest deduction if it constitutes excess investment interest.

Generally excess investment interest is that interest expense that exceeds income from investments. (The rules for determining excess investment interest are very complex and technical and are analyzed in greater detail later in this section. At this point reference is made to the general rule in order to describe how and when the disallowance of part of the excess interest expense is applied.)

How the disallowance rule works The best way to explain how much, if any, of current interest expense is disallowed as a current deduction is to proceed step-by-step through an example.

Assume that in 1975 a taxpayer has the following.

Investment interest expense of	$62,000
Net investment income of	11,000
Net long-term capital gains of	10,000

The following steps are necessary to determine how much, if any, of the $62,000 interest expense is not deductible in the current year.

1. Subtract $25,000 from investment interest expense. The $25,000 is a flat allowance provided for in the law. If the $25,000 is sufficient to absorb the entire amount of the investment interest expense, the entire amount of the investment interest expense is then currently deductible and no further calculations are required. In this case, subtracting the $25,000 from the $62,000 investment interest expense leaves a balance of $37,000 so Step 2 must be taken.

2. Subtract from the balance remaining in Step 1 the amount of the net investment income. (As indicated later, if the total of specified expenses attributable to the property exceeds the gross rental from the property, the excess is added to the net investment income.) Again, if this subtraction eliminates the entire balance brought over from Step 1, the entire investment interest expense is currently deductible. In this case, subtracting the $11,000 net investment income from the $37,000 balance brought over from Step 1 leaves a balance of $26,000. So it is necessary to proceed to Step 3.

3. Subtract from the balance brought over from Step 2 the net long-term capital gain (or so much of that net gain as is necessary to eliminate the remaining balance brought over from Step 2). Again, if the balance brought over from Step 2 is entirely eliminated, the full amount of the investment interest expense for the year is currently deductible. In this case, subtracting the long-term capital gains or $10,000 from the $26,000 balance brought over from Step 2 leaves a balance of $16,000. So we must do Step 4.

4. One-half of the balance remaining in Step 3 is the amount of interest expense

139

that is not allowed to be deducted currently as an interest expense. Since the balance in Step 3 was $16,000, half of that, or $8,000, is not allowed as an interest expense in 1975.

Of the total interest expense of $62,000, $8,000 is not allowed as a deduction in 1975. But that $8,000 may be carried over to be deducted in a future year (as will be explained).

Capital gains used to save the interest deduction   In Step 3 of the preceding example, $10,000 of long-term capital gains was used to offset excess interest expense and thus preserve $10,000 of the interest deduction. However this procedure exacts a cost from the taxpayer. To the extent that capital gains are used to preserve the interest deduction, that amount of capital gains ceases to be treated as capital gains and must be reported as ordinary income. By converting capital gains to ordinary income, however, the amount of tax preferences is reduced by one-half of the amount converted (since one-half of long-term capital gains constitutes items of tax preferences; see page 102).

In view of the fact that applying capital gains to offset excess investment interest converts capital gains to ordinary income, it is important to follow the steps in the example in the order indicated. Thus, the $25,000 statutory allowance and the amount of the net investment income are first applied to preserve the interest deduction. It is only if there is excess interest remaining after applying those two amounts that capital gains need be applied.

Carrying over the disallowed interest   If part of investment interest is disallowed as a deduction, it is not necessarily lost forever. It becomes a carryover that may be deducted as interest expense in a following year. There are statutory limitations on the amount of the carryover that may be used as a current deduction in the year of carryover. These limitations are best illustrated.

In 1975 (continuing the previous example), $8,000 of the taxpayer's interest expense was disallowed as a deduction. In 1976, he has net investment income of $30,000 and investment interest expense of $45,000 as well as net long-term capital gains of $2,000.

To find the portion of the $8,000 carryover that is deductible in 1976, the taxpayer first adds his 1976 net investment income of $30,000 to a statutory amount of $25,000 to arrive at a total of $55,000. From this total he subtracts the larger of a statutory $25,000 or his actual 1976 investment interest expense. In this case the larger amount is $45,000. Hence, the $45,000 is subtracted from the $55,000, giving a difference of $10,000. One-half of that $10,000 or $5,000 is the maximum amount of the carryover currently deductible.

Since the carryover from 1975 was $8,000 and only $5,000 is deductible in 1976, $3,000 remains as a carryover to the following year, with one additional limitation. In 1976, the taxpayer had a $2,000 long-term capital gain. The $3,000 carryover must be reduced by half the long-term capital gain (again, in effect, converting long-term capital gain to ordinary income). Hence, the carryover to 1977 is reduced to $2,000.

What is excess investment interest?   In the foregoing discussion excess investment interest was defined very generally. However, since the concept of excess investment interest is an arbitrary concept created by statute, it is necessary to understand the technical definition of the term. It is to the technically-defined excess investment interest that the rules detailed previously concerning the possible disallowance of the interest deduction apply.

Excess investment interest is the amount by which individual investment interest expense exceeds the total of (1) *net* investment income and (2) the excess of certain expenses attributable to the property over the gross rent from the property.

First, then, investment interest expense must be determined. The statute says that investment interest expense means "interest paid or accrued on indebtedness incurred or continued to purchase or carry property *held for investment*" (emphasis added). Specifically excluded from investment interest expense is interest on indebtedness incurred or continued in the construction of property to be used in a trade or business.

Will interest paid on a mortgage on rental property *not* subject to a net lease fall into the investment interest category? It would seem not, for the following reasons.

1. Traditionally over the years property held for rental income has been considered "trade or business" property by IRS and not investment property. Gains and losses from the sale of this property have been considered Section 1231 gains and losses by the Governement (see page 90).

2. There is a special provision dealing with property subject to a net lease and specifically treating that property as investment property.

When property is subject to a net lease that was entered into after October 9, 1969, the property is treated as held for investment rather than used in a trade or business. In other words, interest expense in connection with the purchase or carrying of that property *is* investment interest expense.

The law spells out two situations in which it is deemed that a net lease exists.

1. The lessor is guaranteed a specified return or he is guaranteed, in whole or part, against loss of income.

2. Ordinary and necessary expenses allowed under Section 162 of the Internal Revenue Code in connection with the property are less than 15% of the rental income from the property. The expenses included here are reasonable salaries, travel expense while away from home, contributions to the Federal National Mortgage Association in excess of the value of the stock received and certain expenses to lobby against legislation of direct interest to the taxpayer. If any of the other expenses otherwise allowed to be included are reimbursed to the landlord by the tenant, then the landlord may *not* include those expenses in determining whether his expenses exceed 15% of rental income.

As can be seen, very few of these items, other than salaries, would apply to the owner of real estate. Other expenses such as interest, taxes and depreciation are not included in Section 162; they are allowed by other sections of the Code and do not enter into the calculation here. Hence, in most net lease situations, and in some situations which are not net leases in the conventional sense, it would probably be difficult to meet the 15% requirement and the interest *would* be investment interest expense.

What happens when there is more than one lease on a single parcel of property (for example, a shopping center may have separate leases with each of its tenants)?

For the purposes of determining if there is a net lease, the law allows the taxpayer to elect to combine all the leases and treat them as one. This is a taxpayer election; it does not happen automatically.

Special modifications of the net lease rule—The law provides two special modifications concerning net leases.

1. Expenses in excess of gross rentals—As indicated, expenses such as interest, real estate and personal property taxes, legal and accounting fees in connection with computing taxes or other costs incurred by an investor for the production or collection of income or management, conservation or maintenance of his property are *not* deductible in determining whether the 15% rule is met to avoid net lease treatment. However, if the total of these expenses when added to the expenses allowed in determining whether the 15% net lease test is met exceeds the gross rental from the property, the excess expenses are added to the taxpayer's investment income. Since it is only the interest expenses that *exceed* investment income that is subject to possible disallowance as a tax deduction, adding those expenses to the investment income reduces the excess investment interest.

2. Real property in use for more than five years—If real property has been in use for more than five years, the taxpayer can elect to exempt that property from net lease treatment. In other words, even though there is a net lease on that property, the taxpayer can treat the property as not held for investment and thus the interest paid in connection with that property will not be treated as investment interest. Note that the taxpayer has to elect to have the property treated as non-investment property; it does not happen automatically.

Once the amount of the investment interest expense has been determined, it is reduced by the total of net investment income for the year plus specified expenses in excess of rental income from the property. Only to the extent that the investment interest expense exceeds that total is there excess investment interest.

Net investment income is investment income reduced by investment expenses. Investment income is made up of interest, dividends, rents, royalties, net short-term capital gains from investment property and depreciation recapture from property that is not a capital asset or a Section 1231 asset. None of this income can be trade or business income. Thus, rent would be investment income probably only in the "net lease" situations described previously in connection with investment interest expense. (Note that if an election is made to treat property subject to a net lease on non-net lease property because it has been in use for more than five years, the rental income from that property would not be investment income. Thus, this factor must be taken into consideration before making the election.)

Investment expenses are real and personal property taxes, bad debts, depreciation, amortizable bond premiums, expenses for production of income on investment property and depletion. Of course, these expenses have to be directly connected with the production of investment income. The depreciation allowed in this calculation is straight line depreciation only and the depletion allowed is cost depletion only.

In summary, the following is how to find excess investment interest.

1. Determine total investment interest expense.

2. Subtract investment expenses from investment income and add total expenses in excess of gross rental, which gives net investment income.

3. Subtract the amount in item 2 from the amount in item 1.

Depreciation deductions for real property

From a tax viewpoint, depreciation is a cost allocation concept. The cost or, more accurately, the adjusted basis of the property, is allocated over the years of its useful life. The allocation to each year constitutes a tax deduction for that year as a proper charge against the income earned by the property that year.

Put simply, if the basis allocable to a rent-producing property is $75,000 and the property is expected to last 25 years (after which time it is estimated the building will be worthless), it could seem reasonable that 1/25 of the basis or $3,000 be allocated as an expense to each of the 25 years. (As will be pointed out later in this chapter, while a portion of the adjusted basis is apportioned to each year, it does not necessarily have to be done on a straight line basis; that is, by use of accelerated methods, a greater portion of the basis is allocated to earlier years of ownership and a lesser amount to the later years.)

The availability of the depreciation deduction sets real estate apart from many other forms of investment. The deduction does not depend on a cash outlay. Yet it reduces the taxable income arising from the investment and thereby can generate a cash flow by reducing taxes that otherwise would have had to be paid. Examples of the cash flow application are set forth at the end of this chapter.

How to compute depreciation

These steps must be followed to properly calculate depreciation.

1. Determination of adjusted basis of property
2. Allocation of basis to land and depreciable improvements
3. Estimation of useful life of depreciable improvements
4. Selection of depreciation method
5. Construction of deprecation schedule

Determining and allocating adjusted basis of property

In Chapter Eight, the determination of adjusted basis for each type of acquisition was explained. It is worth reemphasizing that basis includes the entire investment in the property, including the portion that is supported by loans. Thus, if property is purchased for $100,000, with the buyer paying $10,000 in cash and using mortgage money (either assuming or taking subject to an existing mortgage, acquiring new financing or a combination of both) to supply the remaining $90,000 of the purchase price, nevertheless his basis is $100,000. And depreciation deductions are calculated in terms of the portion of the $100,000 allocable to the depreciable portion of the property.

Allocation of basis in determining depreciation deductions is required because land is not a depreciable asset and real property structures and personal property acquired in the same purchase are likely to have different useful lives. Consequently, the amount of the annual depreciation deduction available to the property owner will depend on how much of the total basis of the acquired property is allocable to each depreciable asset within the overall property acquired. Methods and techniques for allocating basis are discussed in the previous chapter on page 118.

Estimating useful life

Just as the basis of the depreciable item helps determine the amount of the annual depreciation deduction, so does the property's useful life. As explained earlier, depreciation, from a tax and accounting viewpoint, is a cost allocation concept. The cost (i.e. basis) is allocated over the useful life of the property. The shorter the useful life, the larger the annual deductions; the longer the useful life, the smaller the annual deductions. In this setting, as might be expected, controversy often arises between taxpayers and IRS as to the proper useful life to be employed in determining the depreciation deductions for a particular property.

IRS Regulations define *useful life* as "the period over which the asset may reasonably be expected to be useful to the taxpayer in his trade or business or in the production of his income." Note that it is the useful life "to the taxpayer" that counts and not the actual physical remaining useful life. Thus, if the taxpayer can show that he is likely to retain a piece of property for 25 years (even though its remaining physical life is 40 years), he would be entitled to use 25 years as the useful life in computing his depreciation deductions. (Of course, if the taxpayer intends to keep the property for a considerably shorter period of time than its remaining physical useful life, there may be a considerable salvage value to be taken into account. The effect of salvage value on depreciation deductions is explained on page 161.)

But how is this period determined? Generally, reference is made to experience with similar property taking into account conditons as they are at the time of acquisition and as they are likely to be in the future. Many factors must be considered in arriving at this time period. Among them are the following: wear and tear from natural causes; policies as to repairs, replacements and renewals; obsolescence, both technological and economic; climatic and other local conditions.

IRS guidelines and the ADR system   To try to limit controversy about useful lives, IRS has issued guidelines for various classes of assets. These guidelines are not required to be used; a taxpayer can use any useful life he is able to justify.

As far as real property is concerned, the guidelines used by IRS for buildings and other structures are generally considered to be unrealistically long by real estate professionals and are not generally used. To the extent the IRS guidelines are used by taxpayers, they are generally used in connection with personalty: machinery, equipment, furniture and fixtures.

The Asset Depreciation Range (ADR), which was tacked onto the guidelines by Congress in the Revenue Act of 1971, makes the use of the guidelines more attractive than ever before in the case of personalty.

Under ADR, each year, if the guideline lives are adopted for all depreciable assets acquired that year, the taxpayer may elect a useful life for each class of assets acquired that ranges from 20% below to 20% above the guideline lives. (Of course, taxpayers interested in maximum depreciation deductions currently will elect useful lives 20% shorter than the guideline lives.)

The difficulty with the ADR rules for real estate owners was that Congress required that all assets acquired in one year use ADR or none of them acquired that year use ADR. And *all depreciable assets* included buildings and other structures. So, if a taxpayer acquired a machine and a building in the same year, he could use the ADR approach for his machine only if he used it for his building as well. As previously indicated, the IRS guideline lives for buildings, even after reducing them by 20%, were considered much too long by real estate people (they were generally able to justify shorter useful lives based on all the facts and circumstances in their cases).

Congress took note of the objections of real estate owners; when it enacted ADR, it postponed the requirement that real estate had to be included in the ADR approach if the real estate was acquired in the same year as other assets for which the ADR approach was desired. The postponement ran to the end of 1973 or until the Treasury issued revised guidelines for buildings and other structures, whichever occurred first.

1973 came and went and IRS did not revise its guidelines for real estate. So, in the last days of 1974, Congress passed legislation continuing the postponement of the requirement for including real estate in ADR calculations. The postponement is to continue until IRS issues revised useful life guidelines for real estate. Thus, until such revised guidelines are issued, a taxpayer who acquires both real estate and personalty in the same year may use ADR for the personalty without being required to apply it to the real estate.

Following are guidelines for land improvements and buildings as issued by IRS before the revision referred to by Congress.

IRS Guidelines for Depreciation

Group	Life Years	Percentage
One: Assets used by business in general		
Land improvements*		
Buildings**		
Apartments	40	2.5
Banks	50	2.0
Dwellings	45	2.222
Factories	45	2.222
Garages	45	2.222
Grain Elevators	60	1.667
Hotels	40	2.5
Loft Buildings	50	2.0
Machine Shops	45	2.222
Office Buildings	45	2.222
Stores	50	2.0
Theaters	40	2.5
Warehouses	60	1.667
Two: Class 1(d), Farm buildings	25	4.0
Three: Class 17(d), Gasoline service stations	16	6.25

*Includes land improvements such as paved surfaces, sidewalks, canals, waterways, drainage facilities and sewers, wharves, bridges, all fences except farm fences, landscaping, shrubbery and similar improvements; agricultural and improvements not classified as soil and water conservation expenditures under the Internal Revenue Code of 1954; radio and television transmitting towers. Excludes land improvements which are the major asset of a business such as cemeteries or golf courses. The depreciable life of such land improvements shall be determined according to the particular facts and circumstances. Excludes land improvements of electric, gas, steam and water utilities; telephone and telegraph companies; and pipeline, water and rail carriers; these improvements are covered under Group Four. Excludes dry docks, ski slopes and related

145

property and swimming pools, the depreciable lives of which shall be determined on the particular facts, circumstances and buildings.

**Includes the structural shell of the building and all integral parts thereof; equipment which services normal heating, plumbing, air conditioning, fire prevention and power requirements and equipment such as elevators and escalators. Excludes special-purpose structures which are an integral part of the production process and which, under normal practice, are replaced contemporaneously with the equipment which they house, support or serve. Non-industrial and general-purpose industrial buildings, such as warehouses, storage facilities, general factory buildings and commercial buildings are not special-purpose structures. Special-purpose structures shall be classified with the equipment which they house, support or serve and their depreciable lives determined by reference to the appropriate guidelines for the particular industries.

The depreciable lives of buildings which are not special-purpose structures nor included in the types of buildings listed shall be determined according to the facts and circumstances.

Includes additions, capitalized remodeling costs, components and partitions, both permanent and semi-permanent.

Choosing the useful life of the property   As was previously indicated, the IRS guidelines need not be followed if there is evidence of a different (generally shorter) useful life.

It should be remembered that the guidelines are for new property. If the property acquired was previously used (i.e. the taxpayer is not the first user), the guidelines do not apply.

Second, evidence for shorter useful life can be based on the quality of construction, economic obsolescence or other pertinent data. Revenue agents are apt to rely on the guidelines for new property but then can often be convinced that shorter lives are applicable. In some situations, it may be necessary to go to court to win.

In summary, while no hard, fast yardstick can be established, the guidelines need not be accepted without question. Setting forth the facts, often with the help of expert appraisers, can justify a faster write-off than the guidelines call for. Also keep in mind that Congress has indefinitely postponed the application of ADR to real property (see page 145) in recognition of the inadequacy of the guidelines as they pertain to real estate improvements.

Component and composite methods

In calculating annual depreciation deductions, the basis of the property is allocated over the property's useful life. However, in the case of real estate improvements, the questions of "what basis" and "what useful life" may arise in terms of whether a composite or component method of depreciation is being used.

When the *component method* of depreciation is used, separate age lives are assigned to each of the various parts of the building, i.e. the foundation, roof, plumbing, electrical system, etc. and each is depreciated on a separate schedule.

Under the *composite method*, the depreciation rate used each year represents the average rate that the entire improvement is wasting. Although the foundation,

146

roof, painting, electrical and plumbing systems all wear out at different rates, one average rate is estimated.

An apartment building is constructed for $100,000. A breakdown of the cost produces the following analysis.

Shell of building	$ 40,000
Roof	5,000
Elevator	10,000
Plumbing	15,000
Electrical	15,000
Heating	7,500
Air conditioning	7,500
Total	$100,000

Each of the above categories of asset within the building may have a different useful life; the shell may be expected to last for 40 years; the roof for 10 years; etc.

By using the component method, and calculating separately the annual depreciation deduction for each component, it may be possible to arrive at a higher total annual depreciation deduction (in the earlier years of ownership) than would result were the composite method employed.

Consider the apartment building of the previous illustration.

Item	Cost	Life	S/L %	S/L Depreciation
Shell of bldg	$ 40,000	40 yrs.	$2\frac{1}{2}$	$1,000
Roof	5,000	10	10	500
Elevator	10,000	$12\frac{1}{2}$	8	800
Plumbing	15,000	$12\frac{1}{2}$	8	1,200
Electrical	15,000	10	10	1,500
Heating	7,500	10	10	750
Air conditioning	7,500	$12\frac{1}{2}$	8	600
	$100,000			$6,350

Using the straight line method of depreciation for each component, the total depreciation deduction for one year equals $6,350. This indicates an average rate of 6.35%. But what would be the result if depreciation were computed on the entire $100,000 as one amount? Theoretically, it should be the same.

To be $6,350, the rate applied against the $100,000 cost would have to be 6.35%; this would mean a life of about 16 years. Without the component breakdown, it might be difficult to support an estimated life of 16 years. If a Revenue Agent required the use of $33\frac{1}{3}$ years or a composite rate of 3% the annual straight line depreciation would be only $3,000.

A taxpayer is permitted to use either the composite or component method with respect to any class of assets. However, he may not use both with respect to the same class of asset. So, for example, when the government's guideline lives are used, since they are composite lives, a taxpayer may not also use component depreciation with respect to an item included within his building.

When component depreciation may be used At first, IRS resisted the use of component depreication for real estate improvements. Subsequently, it conceded that **147** it could be used for new structures because, in that case, it was not difficult to determine the cost of each component. However, for a long time, IRS continued to resist the use of component depreciation for used structures. Finally, it conceded on that point as well as long as the taxpayer can establish the cost of each component (which probably requires a professional appraisal).

It should be noted that the method of depreciation used for each component is governed by the rules applying to real estate as a whole. Hence, for example, if the property acquired is used commercial property, only straight line depreciation may be used for each component. On the other hand, if it is residential new property, 200% declining balance may be used for each component. (The available depreciation methods for real estate are set forth on page 150.)

Methods of computing depreciation

After basis and useful life have been determined, it is necessary to decide upon a depreciation method before the depreciation deduction for any year can be computed.

As has been indicated previously, the depreciation deduction process is an allocation of basis over the asset's useful life. But the depreciation method used determines how that allocation will be made.

An equal allocation to each year, straight line, reflects but one philosophy of how depreciation occurs. Other theories assign greater proportions of the basis to earlier years, with corresponding lesser portions to the later years. The straight line method assumes that the property to be depreciated is wearing out at an equal rate each year. The accelerated methods make the assumption that during the earlier years the improvements wear out faster than in the later years.

The method used most often, because it is the simplest, is called the straight line method. It divides the cost to be recovered *evenly* among the income-producing years.

Example

Alan buys a two story building for $20,000. He expects to be able to rent the building to a business firm for a 10-year period, after which the building will be worthless. Using straight line depreciation, the $20,000 basis is divided by the 10-year life and $2,000 of this basis is allocated to each of the 10 years.

Salvage value Often, even though a building may no longer be suited for the purposes for which it was intended, it is still able to be used for some other purpose. For example, at the end of 10 years, Alan (in the previous example) might be able to sell his building to Jones for $4,000. If he can do so, he should not be permitted to deduct his entire $20,000 basis as depreciation.

The solution to this problem is the rule which Alan must use to estimate, at the time he computes his first depreciation amount, what he will be able to salvage from his investment when its useful life has ended. This is called "salvage value" and must be subtracted from the cost to be allocated over the period of useful life.

Example

Alan buys a two-story building for $20,000. He expects to realize income from the building for a 20-year period, after which he expects to be able to sell the building for $4,000.

He will use $800 as straight line annual depreciation computed as follows. First, Alan reduces his adjusted basis by the estimated salvage value. Then he divides the remaining amount by the number of years of expected life. This would be $20,000 minus $4,000 or $16,000 divided by 20 years. This results in straight line depreciation of $800 per year.

Thus, we see that an investor may recover part of his investment through depreciation and part of it by selling the asset when he is finished with it.

Under *accelerated* depreciation methods, the taxpayer is allowed to spread out his depreciation deductions over the useful life of the property in an uneven fashion; that is, unlike the straight line method, the amount deducted each year is different from the amount deducted in any other year. The total amount deductible, however, may not in any case exceed the adjusted basis of the property minus the salvage value.

Under the accelerated methods, the depreciation deductions in the early years of ownership are greater than the deductions allowed under the straight line method; while the deductions in the later years are lower than those allowed by straight line depreciation. The theory justifying this approach to depreciation deductions is that many assets depreciate more rapidly in their early lives.

The accelerated depreciation methods to be explained in the following pages are the 200% (or double) declining balance method, the 150% declining balance method, the 125% declining balance method and the sum-of-the-years-digits method. As will be explained later, under the tax law, there are restrictions concerning the use of these methods; all of these methods are not necessarily available in each situation.

After each of the depreciation methods is explained, they will be compared with each other. Finally, those situations when a change of method is desirable and will be permitted by IRS are explored.

Before getting into a detailed explanation of the various depreciation methods, one additional fact should be made clear. At this point, we are considering the accounting and tax depreciation methods of allocating adjusted basis (net of salvage value) over the expected useful life of the property. The depreciation so computed is not necessarily the same as the physical depreciation of the property. Thus, if a building has an original cost of $100,000 and tax depreciation deductions reduce its adjusted basis to $70,000, this does not mean that the building is actually worth $30,000 less than it was worth when the owner purchased it. It might be worth more or even less than $70,000.

Straight line method

As described, the basis of the property less its estimated salvage value is allocated equally over the estimated useful life of the property. Thus, the depreciation deduction for a given year may be calculated by dividing the adjusted basis of the property at the beginning of the taxable year, less its estimated salvage value, by the remaining useful life of the property at that time. This may also be expressed in terms of a fraction, decimal or percentage.

Example

Jackson builds a garage for $6,000. He expects to rent it for four years and then to sell it for $2,000.

The basis, $6,000, less its estimated salvage value, $2,000, is $4,000. Dividing this by its useful life of four years results in annual depreciation of $1,000. Expressed as a percentage, this is 25% of the depreciable base ($4,000) each year. Jackson's depreciation position may be expressed in tabular form.

Year #	Annual Depreciation	Accumulated Depreciation
1	$1,000	$1,000
2	1,000	2,000
3	1,000	3,000
4	1,000	4,000

Straight line percentage is computed by dividing one by the number of estimated life years and converting the decimal fraction to a percentage. For example, if the estimated life is four years, the percentage is 25%. One divided by four is a decimal fraction of .25 which equals that percentage. If the estimated life is 20 years, the percentage is 5%. One divided by 20 equals .05 which is 5%.

Declining balance method

Under the straight line method, a constant amount is deductible each year. This is so because the straight line percentage is applied to the adjusted basis (less salvage value) at the time of the acquisition. So, in the example, after the $6,000 adjusted basis was reduced by the $2,000 salvage value, the 25% rate was applied each year to the same $4,000 figure resulting in a uniform $1,000 depreciation deduction each year.

With the declining balance method, the appropriate percentage is determined and that percentage is applied each year to the remaining adjusted basis, *without reduction for salvage value*, computed at the beginning of each year. This continues until the basis is reduced to salvage value. Depreciation is never permitted to reduce the basis of an asset below its estimated salvage value.

So, for example, if the appropriate percentage to use under the declining balance method was 10% and the adjusted basis at the beginning of the first year was $100,000, the first year's depreciation deduction would be $10,000 (10% of $100,000). But for the second year, the adjusted basis will have been reduced to $90,000 and the second year's depreciation deduction would be $9,000 (10% of $90,000). The $9,000 deduction will then reduce the adjusted basis to $81,000 and the third year's deduction would be $8,100. And so on each succeeding year until the adjusted basis is reduced to the estimated salvage value.

Declining balance rates For Federal income tax purposes three different maximum declining balance rates are permitted. These are 125%, 150% and 200% of the straight line rate. The applicable rate depends on the nature of the property, its useful life, whether acquired new or used and when it was acquired.

The three rates are maximum rates. Anyone eligible to use 150% declining balance can use any rate of declining balance *up to* 150%, 140% for example. As a practical matter, however, taxpayers will always use the maximum allowed.

When are the three declining balance rates applicable?

200% declining balance depreciation   This rate applies to the following categories.

1. All new (i.e. the first user) personal property with a life of three years or more. The kind of property referred to here includes (for a real estate investor) such items as furniture, refrigerators, window air conditioners and other items not considered real estate.

2. All real estate acquired *new* before July 25, 1969, having a useful life of at least three years. This also applies to property the construction, reconstruction or erection of which began before July 25, 1969. If there was a binding contract entered into before July 25, 1969, for the construction, reconstruction, erection or permanent financing of the property, that property, too, is eligible for 200% declining balance depreciation.

Property eligible for 200% declining balance depreciation before the July 25, 1969, date and which used the 200% declining balance method can continue to do so after that date.

3. Residential rental property acquired new after July 24, 1969. (Of course, property acquired new prior to July 25, 1969, would have been eligible to use the 200% declining balance method anyhow). To qualify for residential rental property, 80% of the gross income from the building must be rental income from dwelling units. (For this purpose, the rental value of space occupied by the owner can be included.) This 80% calculation is a year-by-year calculation; so the owner may be eligible to use 200% declining balance in some years and not in others. (This is more fully explained on page 153.)

150% declining balance depreciation   This rate applies to the following groups.

1. All used personal property with a life of three years or more

2. All used real estate acquired before July 25, 1969. This also applies to used real estate acquired after July 24, 1969, if, on July 24, 1969, there was in existence a binding written contract for the acquisition or permanent financing of that property.

As a result of this provision, no declining balance depreciation of any kind can be taken on used non-residential rental property acquired after July 24, 1969. Certain residential rental property is eligible for a lesser declining balance rate, as is explained in the next category.

3. New residential rental property that does not meet the 80% test

4. New commercial property

125% declining balance depreciation   This rate is applicable to used residential rental property acquired after July 24, 1969, if the property at the time of acquisition has a useful life of 20 years or more. Residential rental property has the same 80%-of-gross-income test as is applied in the case of new residential property eligible for 200% declining balance depreciation.

Applying the 125%, 150% or 200% declining balance methods   In applying the declining balance method of depreciation, it is first necessary to determine the straight line rate. This is merely the percentage arrived at by dividing the useful life into one (e.g. 20 year useful life; straight line rate, 1 divided by 20 is 5%.)

Once the straight line rate is determined, it is multiplied by the applicable per-   **151** centage, 125%, 150% or 200%. The result is the declining balance method rate. (For example, if the straight line rate is 4%, the 125%-method rate would be 5%; the 150%-method rate would be 6%; and the 200%-method rate would be 8%.) The declining balance rate is then applied to the full adjusted basis (*not reduced by salvage*) to determine the depreciation the first year. In each succeeding year, the same percentage is applied but to the *reduced* basis (the starting basis minus depreciation deductions already taken).

It is important to note that, while salvage value is not deducted from adjusted basis in the early years of the declining balance method of depreciation, once the basis of the property has been depreciated down to the salvage value, further depreciation deductions are not permitted.

The following three examples, using the same useful lives and the same cost figures, illustrate how the 125%, 150% and 200% declining balance depreciation methods operate. A useful life of five years was chosen, even though (especially in the case of new property) a five-year life is quite short and very rare. By using a five-year life, for illustrative purposes only, the complete depreciation picture for the property can be conveniently presented in concise form, both in terms of the procedure of calculating the depreciation deduction under each of the declining balance methods and for the purposes of comparing the results of each method.

For detailed presentations of the annual and accumulated depreciation for varying useful lives under all of the most commonly used depreciation methods, see the tables in the Appendix on page 294.

Examples

1. 125% Declining Balance Depreciation

Brown acquires land and building for $25,000 in 1975 of which $20,000 is allocable to the building. This is used residential rental property. Hence it is eligible for the 125% declining balance depreciation method.

Note that in order to be eligible for 125% declining balance depreciation the property must have a useful life of 20 years or more. For the purposes of illustrating the computations and for comparison with the other declining balance methods only, we are using a 5-year life in this example.

If the useful life of the building is five years, the straight line rate is 20% (5 divided into 1 gives 0.20 or 20%). 125% of the 20% rate is 25%. So, Brown will use the 25% rate in computing depreciation deductions as follows.

	Adjusted Basis	Depreciation Deductions Claimed
First Year		
Adjusted Basis	$20,000	
Depreciation (25% of adjusted basis of $20,000)	5,000	$ 5,000
Second Year		
Adjusted Basis	15,000	
Depreciation (25% of adjusted basis of $15,000)	3,750	3,750

Third Year		
Adjusted Basis	11,250	
Depreciation (25% of adjusted basis of $11,250	2,812	2,812
Fourth Year		
Adjusted Basis	8,438	
Depreciation (25% of adjusted basis of $8,438)	2,109	2,109
Fifth Year		
Adjusted Basis	6,329	
Depreciation (25% of adjusted basis of $6,329)	1,582	1,582
Remaining basis not recovered by depreciation after five-year life	$ 4,747	
Accumulated depreciation deducted over five-year life		$15,253

2. 150% Declining Balance Depreciation

Using the same figures as in the previous example, we will assume that Brown's 1975 investment of $25,000 ($20,000 allocable to the building) is in a brand new structure which he rents out for warehouse space. The maximum declining balance rate to which he is entitled is the 150% rate. Since the straight line rate is 20%, the 150% declining balance rate is 30% and the annual depreciation deductions will be computed as follows.

	Adjusted Basis	Depreciation Deductions Claimed
First Year		
Adjusted Basis	$20,000	
Depreciation (30% of adjusted basis of $20,000)	6,000	$6,000
Second Year		
Adjusted Basis	14,000	
Depreciation (30% of adjusted basis of $14,000)	4,200	4,200
Third Year		
Adjusted Basis	9,800	
Depreciation (30% of adjusted basis of $9,800)	2,940	2,940
Fourth Year		
Adjusted Basis	6,860	
Depreciation (30% of adjusted basis of $6,860)	2,058	2,058
Fifth Year		
Adjusted Basis	4,802	
Depreciation (30% of adjusted basis of $4,802)	1,441	1,441
Remaining basis not recovered by depreciation after five-year life	$ 3,361	
Accumulated depreciation deducted over five-year life		$16,639

3. 200% Declining Balance Depreciation

Taking the same figures, let us assume that the property acquired by Brown was new in use to him and qualified as residential rental property. So he was eligible to use 200% declining balance depreciation. Since the straight line rate for a five-year **153** life is 20%, the rate under the 200% declining balance depreciation method is 40%. Depreciation would be calculated as follows.

	Adjusted Basis	Depreciation Deductions Claimed
First Year		
Adjusted Basis	$20,000	
Depreciation (40% of adjusted basis of $20,000)	8,000	$ 8,000
Second Year		
Adjusted Basis	12,000	
Depreciation (40% of adjusted basis $12,000)	4,800	4,800
Third Year		
Adjusted Basis	7,200	
Depreciation (40% of adjusted basis of $7,200)	2,880	2,880
Fourth Year		
Adjusted Basis	4,320	
Depreciation (40% of adjusted basis of $4,320)	1,728	1,728
Fifth Year		
Adjusted Basis	2,592	
Depreciation (40% of adjusted basis of $2,592)	1,037	1,037
Remaining basis not recovered by depreciation after five-year life	$1,555	
Accumulated depreciation deducted over five-year life		$18,445

Factors to keep in mind about declining balance depreciation   Each year the same percentage is applied to the declined balance. Thus, in the example dealing with 150% declining balance depreciation the 30% rate is applied in the second year to $14,000. This $14,000 is the adjusted basis of the property after reducing the original cost basis by the $6,000 depreciation deducted in the first year. Similarly, the 30% rate in the third year is applied to $9,800 (the basis remaining after reducing the second year's adjusted basis of $14,000 by the $4,200 depreciation deducted in the second year). This process is repeated each year. Were straight line depreciation used, the 20% straight line rate would have been applied to the same amount of basis each year. Thus, if salvage value were $4,000, the original basis of $20,000 would have been reduced by the $4,000 and the 20% rate would be applied each year to $16,000, giving a uniform depreciation deduction in each of the five years of $3,200.

Under the declining balance method, whether it is the 125%, 150% or the 200% method, the entire basis might not be recovered. At the end of the five-year useful life, there was still $3,361 of basis not recovered under the 150% method. But, it is important to note that although salvage value is not taken into consideration in making the calculations, depreciation may no longer be deducted once the salvage value is reached. Consequently, it would have been necessary to reduce the depreciation deduction in the fifth year had the salvage value been estimated at more than $3,361.

In the example, if at the time of acquistion, salvage had been estimated at $4,000, then in the fifth year the depreciation deduction would have been limited to $802. This would have brought the adjusted basis at the beginning of the year

($4,802) down to the salvage value of $4,000 at the end of the year. If 200% declining balance had been used, the $4,000 salvage value figure would have been reached in the fourth year, limiting the depreciation deduction in the fourth year to $320.

While the deductions in the early years are greater under declining balance depreciation than under straight line depreciation, in later years the opposite is the case. If the straight line method were used and salvage value were $4,000, the annual depreciation deduction in each of the five years would have been $3,200. ($20,000 adjusted basis minus salvage value of $4,000 leaves $16,000; 20% of $16,000 is $3,200.) In the first two years of using either of the declining balance depreciation methods, the deductions far exceeded $3,200. Thereafter, however, the deductions fell below what the straight line method would have produced. Under either the declining balance or straight line method, the total depreciation deducted over the useful life of the building would have been the same. But under the declining balance method, the larger deductions were concentrated into the early years of life.

Because the depreciation deductions under the declining balance method *do decline* in later years, at some point in time it becomes advisable to switch to straight line depreciation. See page 164.

Sum-of-the-years-digits method

Another method of accelerated depreciation is the sum-of-the-years-digits method. This is sometimes abbreviated SYD, SOD or SOYD.

For property acquired after July 24, 1969, this method has very limited application. It is only available in those cases in which the 200% declining balance method of depreciation is available (see page 150).

Under this method, the depreciable base (adjusted basis reduced by salvage value) is multiplied by a different fraction each year. The numerator of the fraction is the number of years of remaining useful life at the beginning of that year. The denominator remains constant; it is the sum of all of the years' digits of the estimated useful life of the asset.

Example

An asset is determined to have a four-year useful life. In using the sum-of-the-years-digits method, the fractions to be used would be as follows.

First year: Numerator is number of years of remaining useful life or 4. Denominator is sum of all the years' digits of the estimated useful life; $4+3+2+1=10$. Therefore, the fraction for the first year will be 4/10.

Second year: Numerator is number of years of remaining useful life or 3. Denominator remains constant, same as last year or 10. Therefore the fraction for the second year will be 3/10.

Third year: Using the same procedure this will be 2/10.

Fourth year: 1/10.

155

Expressed in tabular form, we see the symmetry of this method.

Year #	Fraction	Percentage
1	4/10	40%
2	3/10	30%
3	2/10	20%
4	1/10	10%
Total	10/10	100%

SYD formula   To save time and effort, mathematicians have developed a formula to determine what the denominator will be without having to add all of the numbers. This is particularly useful when dealing with a comparatively long life, e.g. 30 or 45 years. Here's the formula.

Multiply the number of numbers by the sum of: one plus the last number.
Divide the result by two.

Expressed mathematically this is: $\dfrac{N(N + 1)}{2}$

N = the number of numbers and also the last number.

Example

In the case of a ten-year life, this would be the result.

$$\frac{N(N + 1)}{2} = \frac{10(10 + 1)}{2} = \frac{10(11)}{2} = 5(11) = 55.$$

In the case of a 45-year life, the formula would be used as follows.

$$\frac{N(N + 1)}{2} = \frac{45(45 + 1)}{2} = \frac{45(46)}{2} = 45(23) = 1{,}035.$$

Sum-of-the-years-digits method   Let us revert to our example illustrating the declining balance depreciation. In that example, Brown acquired a property for $25,000, $20,000 of which was allocable to a building with a useful life of five years. Here is how Brown would calculate his depreciation each year under the sum-of-the-years-digits method.

First, Brown finds the sum of the years digits by applying the formula.

$$\frac{N(N + 1)}{2} = \frac{5(5 + 1)}{2} = \frac{5(6)}{2} = \frac{30}{2} = 15$$

Therefore, the demoninator of the fraction will be 15.

The fraction each year will be applied to the adjusted basis at the beginning of the useful life *less salvage value*. Assuming a salvage value of $4,000, the fraction each year will be applied to $16,000 (the $20,000 adjusted basis at the time the property was acquired less the $4,000 salvage value).

The following table summarizes the total depreciation picture for the five-year useful life.

Year	Adjusted Basis Less Salvage	Fraction	Annual Depreciation Deduction	Total Depreciation (Cumulative)
1	$16,000	5/15	$5,333.33	$ 5,333.33
2	16,000	4/15	4,266.67	9,600.00
3	16,000	3/15	3,200.00	12,800.00
4	16,000	2/15	2,133.33	14,933.33
5	16,000	1/15	1,066.67	16,000.00

Note that just as in the case of the declining balance methods of depreciation, the depreciation deductions in the *earlier* years exceed the $3,200 per year deduction that would be allowable under the straight line method. In the latter years, straight line depreciation deductions will exceed the deductions allowed under the sum-of-the-years-digits method.

Special rules for residential rental property

As previously indicated, new residential rental property is eligible for 200% declining balance depreciation and used residential rental property with a useful life of 20 years or more is eligible for 125% declining balance depreciation.

Residential rental property requires that 80% of the gross income from the building must be rental income from dwelling units. For this purpose, the rental value of the space occupied by the owner is treated as rental income from dwelling units.

If in some years the 80% test is met and in other years is not, the accelerated depreciation may be used in the years the test is met and other permissible methods used in the years it is not met. Switching methods of depreciation from year to year in these circumstances is not considered a change of accounting method and does not require permission from the Commissioner of Internal Revenue.

Example

On January 1, 1975, a residential rental property is acquired. $100,000 of the purchase price is allocated to the building. The building has a remaining useful life of 25 years.

The rent for 1975 from the building is as follows.

Two stores on the ground floor	$ 5,000
Rental value of owner's apartment	2,400
Rent from remaining apartments	18,000
Total gross rentals	$25,400

The rent for 1976 is as follows.

Two stores	$ 6,000
Rental value of owner's apartment	2,400
Rental from remaining apartments	18,000
Total gross rentals	$26,400

The total received from rental of dwelling units in each of the two years is $20,400 (the $18,000 received from rental of the apartments other than the owner's apartment plus the rental value of the owner's apartment).

157

In 1975, the gross rentals were $25,400. 80% of that figure is $20,320. Hence the 80% test is met. Thus, if the building were new property, the owner can use either the 200% declining balance method or the sum-of-the-years-digits method of depreciation. If it is used property, he can use 125% declining balance depreciation.

In 1976, the gross rentals were $26,400. 80% of that figure is $21,120. In this case the 80% test is not met. Hence, if the property is new, the owner must use either 150% declining balance or straight line depreciation. If the property is used, he has to use straight line.

The application of the 80% rule makes it necessary to determine the useful lives to be used each time there is a shift to or from an accelerated depreciation method when the 80% test is met or failed. IRS' Regulations set forth the following rules.

When switching to a declining balance method   (This occurs, for example, when originally the 80% test was not met and the straight line method was adopted.) The original useful life of the property (i.e. its useful life at the time of acquisition) must be used in determining the depreciation rate at the time of the switch to declining balance.

When switching to the straight line method   (This occurs when, after using a declining balance or sum-of-the-years method, the 80% test is failed and the straight line method must be used.) At the switch to straight line, the remaining useful life at the time of the switch (minus salvage value) must be used in calculating depreciation deductions.

When switching to the sum-of-the-years-digits method   (This occurs when either 150% declining balance or straight line depreciation was used because the 80% test was not met and a switchover to sum-of-the-years-digits is desired when the 80% test is subsequently met.) The remaining useful life (minus salvage value) is used to calculate sum-of-the-years-digits.

Examples

1. In 1970, Wilson acquired a used apartment house which then had a 25-year useful life. Because he could not meet the 80% test, he used straight line depreciation. In 1975, he meets the 80% test and wishes to switch to 125% declining balance depreciation. When he acquired the property, the straight line rate was 4% (1 divided by 25 = .04 or 4%). Hence the declining balance rate at 125% of 4% is 5%. It is this 5% rate that Wilson applies to the remaining basis of the property in 1975 when he switches from straight line to 125% declining balance. (He is not permitted to compute his 125% rate based on the remaining useful life at the time of the switchover. That is, he may not compute a new straight line rate of 5% (remaining life of 20 years divided into 1 = .05) and use a 125% rate of 6.25%.

2. Assume that in 1970, when Wilson acquired his property, it met the 80% test and he used 125% declining balance depreciation. Since the property had a 25-year useful life, he used a 5% rate for declining balance purposes. In 1975, it ceases to meet the 80% test and he must use straight line depreciation. At this point, the property has a remaining useful life of 20 years. Wilson must reduce his remaining basis by estimated salvage value and calculate his straight line depreciation deductions using a 20-year life.

3. In 1974, Green constructs a building having a cost of $100,000, a 40-year useful life and a salvage value of $10,000. It does not meet the 80% test. So, Green uses 150% declining balance depreciation. The straight line rate is 2.5% (1 divided by 40 = .025); so the 150% declining balance rate is 3.75%. His deduction for depreciation is 3.75% of $100,000 or $3,750.

In 1975, the 80% test is met and Green decided to use sum-of-the-years-digits. At that time its remaining useful life is 39 years, his basis is $96,250 and the salvage value is $10,000. The sum of the digits 1 through 39 equals 780. 39/780 = .05. Hence, Green's deduction for depreciation for 1975 is 5% of $86,250 ($96,250 remaining basis minus $10,000 salvage) or $4,312.50.

In 1976, the 80% test is not met and Green reverts to the 150% declining balance method. His adjusted basis is now $91,937.50 (the $96,250 at the beginning of 1975 minus the $4,312.50 deducted in 1975). His depreciation deduction for 1976 is 3.75% of $91,937.50 or $3,447.66.

Five-year depreciation for rehabilitation of low-income rental housing

To encourage the rehabilitation of low-income rental housing, the 1969 Tax Reform Act has a special rapid depreciation provision for rehabilitation expenses. These expenses can be written off over a 60-month period under the straight line method without salvage value.

To qualify for the rapid write-off, the following requirements concerning the rehabilitation expense must be met.

1. The expenditure has to take place after July 24, 1969, and before January 1, 1976.

2. The total amount of rehabilitation expense spent on one dwelling unit (defined below) cannot exceed $15,000.

3. The special write-off applies only if expenses for the rehabilitation of a dwelling unit in two consecutive years (including the taxable year) exceeds $3,000.

What are rehabilitation expenditures? These are amounts spent in connection with the rehabilitation of an existing building for low-income rental housing. They have to be for property additions or improvements to the property with a useful life of five years or more. They do not include the cost of the building or an interest (e.g. lease) in the building.

What is low-income rental housing? It is a building in which the dwelling units are rented to families and individuals of low or moderate income. The Commissioner of Internal Revenue will determine which buildings qualify, using as his guide the Housing and Urban Development Act of 1968.

What is a dwelling unit? It is a house or an apartment used to provide living accommodations in a building or structure. *It is not* a unit in a hotel, motel, inn or other establishment in which more than half the units are used on a transient basis.

How the $3,000–$15,000 limit works   Assume the following amounts are spent on rehabilitation expenditures on one dwelling unit in the years indicated.

1971	$1,000
1972	1,500
1973	4,000
1974	6,000
1975	5,000

The 1971 expenditure is not eligible for the 60-month write-off because, when combined with the 1972 expenditure, the more-than-$3,000 requirement is not met.

The 1972 expenditure is eligible for the 60-month write-off because, when added to the 1973 expenditure, the more-than-$3,000 requirement is met.

1973 and 1974 are eligible for the 60-month write-off because each, on its own, meets the more-than-$3,000 requirement.

In 1975, of the $5,000 expended, only $3,500 is eligible for the 60-month write-off. This is so because the previous expenditures eligible for the special write-off (i.e. the $1,500 of 1972, the $4,000 of 1973 and the $6,000 of 1974) already total $11,500. Since not more than $15,000 of expenditures are eligible for the special write-off on one dwelling unit, there is only room for another $3,500 to bring the total up to $15,000. (Note that the $1,000 of 1971 that was not eligible for the special 60-month write-off is not counted in totalling up the $15,000.)

What happens to the $1,000 expended in 1971 and the excess $1,500 expended in 1975? They are not eligible for the 60-month write-off. But these expenses are recoverable via depreciation under the method and useful life that applies to the property without taking into account this special 60-month write-off provision.

Note that amortization in excess of straight line depreciation may be subject to depreciation recapture on disposition of the property; see page 178.

Amortizing child-care and on-the-job-training facilities expenditures

Section 188 was added to the tax law by the 1971 Revenue Act. It provides for a 60-month write-off (on a straight line basis) of capital expenditures to construct, reconstruct or rehabilitate Section 188 property. The 60-month period begins to run in the month the property is placed in service. The amortization deductions are allowed in lieu of depreciation. The taxpayer must elect the special write-off; otherwise the usual depreciation rules apply.

What is Section 188 property?   The special fast write-off is available for Section 188 property. That property consists of tangible property (both real and personal) which qualifies as a facility for on-the-job training for employees or prospective employees or a child care center facility primarily for children of employees.

Section 188 property must be property which is of a character subject to depreciation (although the 60-month amortization, rather than depreciation deductions, is claimed). Furthermore, the 60-month amortization tax break is not available if the property is located outside the United States.

Negative aspects of the 60-month write-off   If the special 60-month write-off is elected, the following negative factors should be noted.

1. The investment credit is not available in connection with that property.

2. On sale or other disposition, the amortization deductions are subject to depreciation recapture. See page 180.

3. The excess of the amortization deduction over the depreciation deduction otherwise available (including accelerated depreciation that could have been claimed) is treated as a tax preference item.

Effective dates   The 60-month write-off provision applies only to expenditures made after December 31, 1971, and before January 1, 1977.

Salvage value and demolition

Salvage value represents an amount estimated to be realizable when the asset is no longer useful to the owner and is to be retired from service. It is an educated guess, made at the time the asset is acquired or more usually at the time the first depreciation deduction is computed, as to how much of the investor's cost will be recovered when he disposes of his asset.

Example

Empire Manufacturing erects a new plant at a cost of $100,000. It plans to use that plant for 20 years; the building has a 50 year life. At the end of 20 years, the company expects to be able to sell the plant for $60,000. Salvage value in this example is the $60,000 that Empire expects to be able to receive when the plant will no longer be used by the company.

Salvage value, then, may be a large portion of original cost. It may also be only a small fraction of original cost or even zero. The determination depends upon the owner's policies, whether he disposes of assets still in good condition or whether he uses them until they are no more than junk.

It is most important to remember that it is the *owner's* replacement policy and not the asset's inherent life which is the determining factor. So in the illustration, $60,000 and 20 years were used rather than the estimated value of the building at the end of 50 years.

Demolition of property   It is possible that the owner will not dispose of the building or other improvement at the end of its useful life but will have it demolished and erect a new building or improvement. In that case a set of special rules apply.

1. If, at the time the owner bought the parcel upon which the building is situated, his sole intention was not to use the building at all but to demolish it (in order to erect another building, for example), he may not deduct *any* depreciation on the old building. The cost of the old building plus the cost of tearing it down are all deemed part of the cost of the land upon which the new structure will be situated.

2. The taxpayer acquiring the property may intend to demolish it at the time of acquisition but it may be several years after acquisition before he is able to do so. In the meantime, he may continue to rent the premises to tenants. In such case, IRS concedes that he is entitled to deduct depreciation during the time he earns rent from the property. However, the portion of the purchase price that may be allocated to the building (constituting the basis for depreciation) cannot exceed the present value (that is, the value at the time of acquisition) of the right to receive rentals from the building for the period of its expected use as rental property. If,

instead of renting the property to others, the buyer intends to use the property in his own trade or business for a limited time prior to demolition, he, too, may allocate a portion of the purchase price to depreciable building. This amount is based on the present value of rentals that could be realized on that property if it were rented.

Example

In January 1975, Grey purchased land and a building for $60,000 with the intention of demolishing the building. In April, 1975, Grey concludes that he will be unable to start constructing the proposed new building for a period of more than three years. Accordingly, on June 1, 1975, he leases the building to Green for a three-year period at an annual rent of $1,200. Grey intends to demolish the building at the end of the three-year lease. In these circumstances, Grey may allocate a portion of the $60,000 basis of the acquired property to the building to be depreciated over the three-year period. The allocable portion is the present value of the right to receive the total of $3,600 rent over three years. (This amount is determined by applying an appropriate interest rate to determine the discounted value of the rental payments over the three-year period.) Assuming that the value so determined is $2,850, Grey may use $2,850 as the depreciable basis of his building. Assuming Grey has a taxable year ending May 31, for the taxable year ending May 31, 1976, he may deduct $950 ($\frac{1}{3}$ of the $2,850 basis). If after two years, Green moves, the lease is terminated and Grey demolishes the building he can deduct the remaining, undepreciated $950 of basis at that time.

3. If at the time of acquisition the buyer has no present intention of demolishing the building but later determines that it should be demolished, he is entitled to deduct his unrecovered basis of the building at the time of demolition. In addition, he may also deduct the costs of demolishing it in the year of demolition.

Depreciation in the year assets are sold at a gain   The importance of determining salvage value of a building at the time of acquisition does not relate only to the computation of depreciation deductions. It is also relevant in the computation of capital gains on the sale of the depreciable property.

The IRS has for years used the salvage value concept to disallow depreciation deductions in the year that depreciable property is sold if the adjusted basis at the beginning of the year was less than the selling price. The theory was that the selling price was the salvage value and since, by the time the tax return for the year of sale was due, the taxpayer knew the salvage value (i.e. the sales price) and could not depreciate below it.

Example

Smith's adjusted basis for his 20-year-old building on January 1 was $25,000. On October 30 of the same year, he sold the building for $30,000. Depreciation for the 10-month period (under the depreciation method used by Smith) would be $2,000. Smith reduced his basis by the $2,000 by taking a depreciation deduction of $2,000 and then reported a capital gain of $7,000. Under the Government's theory, Smith would get no depreciation deduction, his basis would remain $25,000 and his capital gain would be $5,000.

Taxpayers and their representatives argued vociferously against this Government position and it finally took a decision of the Supreme Court of the United States to settle the conflict. That Court ruled that there is nothing in the law which disallows depreciation deductions in the year an asset is sold. However, the Court did note that useful lives or salvage values may be redetermined when it becomes apparent that they have been miscalculated. Its opinion went so far as to state that: "the fact of sale of an asset at an amount greater than its depreciated basis may be evidence of such a miscalculation."

So, the Government changed its point of attack. Now instead of trying to disallow depreciation in the year an asset is sold, as a matter of law, when it is sold for more than its adjusted basis at the beginning of the year, the attempt is made to show that the estimated salvage value was too low. The Government's position is even stronger when the taxpayer has failed to set up any salvage at the time of acquisition. If he did set up reasonable salvage, mere changes in price levels or inflation, for example, will not justify changing the salvage value.

Since depreciation may *not reduce* the adjusted basis of an asset *below estimated salvage value*, it is important to be able to substantiate the accuracy of the calculation of the estimated salvage value at the time it is made. Otherwise, the investor runs the risk of having an Internal Revenue Agent successfully contend (often with the benefit of hindsight) that the amount allocated to salvage was incorrect.

To some extent, the disallowance of depreciation in the year of sale is academic where the depreication recapture rules (see page 175) apply. If depreciation recapture applies, the portion of the gain attributable to recaptured depreciation is taxable as ordinary income anyhow. Capital gain that would be reduced by disallowing depreciation in the year of sale would also be reduced if the year-of-sale depreciation were allowed and then immediately became subject to recapture. However, because the depreciation recapture rules as they apply to real estate never (except where the parcel is held less than a year) recapture *all* of the depreciation deducted (and may recapture none as where only straight-line depreciation was used), the Government's new approach to the disallowance of year-of-sale depreciation by claiming that the taxpayer used too low a salvage value is still of importance to owners of real estate.

Example

Smith's adjusted basis for his building on January 1, 1975, was $25,000. On October 30, 1975, after owning the building for six years, he sold it for $30,000. Assume that depreciation for the 10-month period would be $2,000 and that $1,500 would be subject to recapture.

In this case, although Smith may be entitled to a depreciation deduction of $2,000 which would reduce his adjusted basis to $23,000 and result in a gain on the sale of $7,000, $1,500 of that $7,000 gain on the sale will be reportable as ordinary income. To the extent of that $1,500, Smith has obtained no advantage; he has an ordinary deduction for depreciation and he has ordinary income on the sale. However, as to the remaining $500, he *has* received a benefit. He has an ordinary depreciation deduction and a capital gain. A disallowance of the entire depreciation deduction in the year of sale by IRS claiming erroneous salvage value, if sustained, could create ordinary income *in addition* to the ordinary income created by the depreciation recapture rules.

Comparison of methods

The tables in the Appendix, beginning on page 294, provide a basis for a quick comparison of methods. They also serve an additional function of permitting a quick, approximate computation of depreciation for the purposes of planning transactions (where a fairly close approximation, rather than a precise dollar amount, may very well do).

Depreciation allowed or allowable

During the period that property is held for production of income or used in a trade or business, depreciation reduces basis in an amount equal to the greater of the depreciation *allowed or allowable* according to the depreciation method used by the taxpayer.

Thus, if for some reason the property owner actually deducts less depreciation than the amount he is *allowed* to deduct under his method of depreciation, his basis must still be reduced by the amount of the depreciation that was allowable. (The first-year "bonus" depreciation that is available on personal property, see page 165, reduces basis only if it is actually deducted.)

Conversely, if a taxpayer has deducted more depreciation than he was entitled to deduct under his method or because he has used an improper method, his basis is reduced by the actual amount of depreciation he has deducted (so long as the depreciation he deducted reduced his tax liability in the year it was deducted).

Change of depreciation method

May a taxpayer change from one depreciation method to another at will or does he need permission?

Changes without permission   A change to straight line from the declining balance or sum-of-the-digits method may be made at any time without permission. There is a point when it becomes advantageous to switch from declining balance to straight line. The switchover points are indicated in depreciation tables in the Appendix (page 294). It should be borne in mind, however, that in switching to straight line, salvage value must be taken into account in calculating the straight line depreciation deductions thereafter.

As is explained on page 157, it may be necessary to switch back and forth between higher and lower percentages of declining balance or between declining balance and straight line when residential rental property is involved. These switches are freely made without permission from IRS.

Changes with permission   All depreciation changes not mentioned previously may be made only after securing permission from IRS.

Depreciation of personal property

Many acquisitions of real property include personal property as well. A hotel includes furniture, kitchen equipment and other types of personal property. An apartment house may include window air conditioners, movable refrigerators and so forth.

As has been indicated previously, because of the different useful lives and other rules that apply to personal property, allocation of basis on acquisition of a combination of real and personal property to the various types of property acquired is a necessity.

The applicability of the various accelerated depreciation methods to personal property has also been previously explained (see page 150).

At this point, several other depreciation aspects peculiar to personal property will be examined. These deal with first-year "bonus" depreciation, special salvage value rules and the investment credit.

First year "bonus" depreciation

Tangible personal property acquired by purchase which has a useful life of six years or more and is subject to depreciation may, if the taxpayer elects, be subject to an additional deduction for depreciation of 20% of its cost in the first year such asset is placed in service by the taxpayer. However, there is a dollar limitation on this so called "bonus." Only property costing a total of $10,000 each year, $20,000 for a married couple filing a joint return, may be subject to this election.

Example

Alex purchases new window air conditioning units for installation in his motel cabins at a total cost of $25,000. In the year he puts them into service, he may elect to deduct an additional $2,000, 20% of the $10,000 limitation, as depreciation expense on his tax return. This is in addition to the depreciation he computes using one of the methods described earlier in this chapter. If he is married and files a joint return, he may deduct $4,000 instead of $2,000 as "bonus" depreciation.

This additional depreciation deduction which is allowed in the first year of an asset's use, like the regular depreciation deductions, also reduces adjusted basis. So if Alex files a joint return and his regular depreciation is computed on a 10% straight line basis (ignoring salvage value for the moment), his depreciation deduction for the first year would be computed as follows.

Bonus depreciation (20% of $10,000 basis is $2,000 but since he files a joint return, he may take 20% of $20,000)		$4,000
Basis of air conditioners	$25,000	
Less: Bonus depreciation	4,000	
Adjusted basis	21,000	
Regular depreciation (10% of adjusted basis—ignoring any salvage value for the purpose of this example)		2,100
Total depreciation deductible in first year		$6,100

In each subsequent year, Alex will deduct $2,100 as his regular depreciation deduction.

Salvage value of personal property

Depreciable personal property which has a useful life of three years or more is subject to another special benefit. When computing depreciation on such property, a taxpayer has the option of ignoring salvage value for an amount up to 10% of the basis of the property. This means that in those cases where salvage value is estimated to be 10% or less of the basis of such property, salvage value may be *ignored completely*. Where salvage exceeds 10% of basis, only 10% may be ignored.

Example

Simon buys some window air conditioners for his motel at a cost of $3,000. Their estimated life is 4 years and estimated salvage value is $500. He elects to use the straight line method of depreciation, giving him a rate of 25%. His computations are as follows.

Basis for depreciation		$3,000
Less: Salvage value	$500	
Special 10% reduction	300	
Net reduction for salvage value		200
Amount to be depreciated over 4 years		$2,800
Annual depreciation @ 25%		$ 700

165

Investment credit

With respect to investments in tangible personal property for which depreciation is allowable, a *reduction* in tax, known as the investment credit, is permitted. It is restricted to personal property but includes elevators and escalators and does not include buildings and their structural components.

Even as to personal property, the investment credit does not apply to property used in connection with the furnishing of permanent lodging, e.g. window air conditioners in an apartment house. But it does apply to coin-operated vending machines and coin-operated washing machines and dryers. It also applies to non-lodging commercial facilities located in an apartment house; for example if the facilities are available to non-tenants, e.g. personal property in a store located in an apartment building. The credit also applies to property used in connection with lodgings made available by a hotel or motel where the predominant portion of the accommodations is used by transients.

The investment credit provides for a reduction in tax of 7% of the qualified investment which depends in part on the life of the asset.

Note that the 7% investment credit has been increased to 10% for property acquired and put into service by the taxpayer beginning January 22, 1975, through December 31, 1976. Thereafter, the rate reverts to 7%. Thus, in the discussion which follows, wherever the 7% figure is used, the 10% amount should be substituted for property put into use during the period from January 22, 1975, through December 31, 1976.

Rules with regard to the lives of the assets subject to the investment credit are as follows.

Life (in years)		Portion of investment
At least	But less than	which qualifies
0	3	None
3	5	1/3
5	7	2/3
7 or more		All

Example

Bill purchases a motel used primarily for transients. $30,000 of the purchase price is allocated to furniture and fixtures with an estimated life of six years. His tax liability prior to computation of the investment credit is $8,000.

Since the estimated life is six years, only ⅔ of the investment qualifies. Therefore, the 7% credit is computed on $20,000, ⅔ of $30,000. His tax of $8,000 is reduced by $1,400, 7% of $20,000, and therefore, his tax liability is $6,600.

If Bill were to dispose of this equipment prior to the expiration of the estimated useful life on which the credit is based, he might have to return part or all of the investment credit to the government. At the time he disposes of the property he has to determine what the investment credit would have been at the time of acquisition if the useful life used in the calculation of the credit had been the *actual* period of time he held the property (rather than the time he *estimated* he would hold the property).

Thus, if Bill disposed of the equipment after holding it five years and two months, he would not have to return any part of the investment credit. Had he used a useful life of five years and two months at the time he calculated the investment credit he would have come up with the same amount of credit as he did by using the estimated useful life of six years. In either case, the credit would be based on $\frac{2}{3}$ of the qualified investment.

Suppose, however, that Bill disposed of the equipment after holding it only four years. Had he used a four-year life in calculating the investment credit at the time he acquired the property, only $\frac{1}{3}$ of the investment or $10,000 would have qualified for the 7% credit. Hence, his credit would have been only $700. Since Bill reduced his tax bill in the year of acquisition by $1,400 (because he assumed he was going to hold the equipment for six years), in the year of disposition he has to return $700 of that tax saving to the government. He therefore adds $700 to the tax he owes for the year of disposition.

In addition, there are certain other restrictions which apply to this area of the law. If the purchased property is *used* (rather than property of which the taxpayer is the first user), a maximum of only $50,000 of property per year qualified for the investment credit. (For taxable years beginning *after* 1974 and *before* 1977, e.g. calendar years 1975 and 1976, the $50,000 limit is increased to $100,000.) Furthermore, the amount of investment credit is limited depending on the amount of the tax. If the tax is $25,000 or less, the credit is limited to the amount of tax. If the tax exceeds $25,000, then the credit is limited to $25,000 plus 50% of the excess. When these limitations cause some of the credit to go unused, there are provisions for carrying the credit back and forward to other taxable years.

Comparison of effect of different depreciation methods

This example will give an indication of how the depreciation taken will be affected by the methods selected.

Property value	$110,000	
Land value	10,000	
Depreciable improvement	$100,000	Future useful life: 25 years

Component Breakdown of Improvements

		Life	Percent	
10% roof	$10,000	20 yrs.	5	$ 500
5% heating	5,000	25	4	200
5% wiring	5,000	25	4	200
10% air conditioning	10,000	10	10	1,000
10% plumbing	10,000	25	4	400
20% store front	20,000	10	10	2,000
30% shell	30,000	40	$2\frac{1}{2}$	750
10% carpeting, flooring and lighting fixtures	10,000	10	10	1,000

167

Assuming the property to be eligible for all methods, the result for the first year is as follows.

Depreciation Taken

	Composite	Component
Straight Line	$4,000	$ 6,050
125% DB	5,000	7,562
150% DB	6,000	9,075
200% DB	8,000	12,100
Sum-of-the-year's-digits	7,690	11,631

Further, assuming that the property has a net operating income of 8% or $8,800 and the property were free and clear, the net taxable income resulting from the various depreciation schedules for the first year of ownership would be.

Net Taxable Income

Method	Composite	Component
Straight Line	$4,800	$1,750
125% DB	3,800	1,238
150% DB	2,800	(275)
200% DB	800	(3,300)
Sum-of-the-year's-digits	1,110	(2,831)

It can be readily seen that the taxable income depends, in part, on the method of depreciation selected. Since, within limits, the selection of the depreciation method is somewhat within the control of the investor, he then has some control over the amount of taxes he must pay on his real estate income. In fact, by selecting a schedule and method that results in a tax loss, the investor not only will pay no income tax on his real estate income but in addition, he can offset the real estate loss against his other earnings. This, then, will reduce his income tax liability on his regular income.

True loss in value of the property by physical depreciation could be greater than, equal to or less than the income tax depreciation deductions claimed by the taxpayer.

When the situation occurs in which physical depreciation is accruing more rapidly than the income tax depreciation deductions claimed, the taxpayer is in effect not accumulating sufficient reserve for replacements. Sooner or later he will realize that what he thought was earnings was really a return of his own capital.

It also follows that if the physical deterioration, functional or economic obsolescence is the same as the amount of depreciation deducted for tax purposes, the taxpayer is merely recovering an amount equal to the amount the asset is wasting.

However, when the depreciation deducted exceeds the actual physical depreciation in a property, the depreciation tax deduction results in tax-free income to the extent the income tax depreciation deductions exceed the actual physical depreciation.

Further, when the depreciation schedule provides a higher depreciation deduction than actually occurs in the early years and in conjunction with this the property is favorably affected by inflation and growth, the investor has even greater benefits in tax-free income.

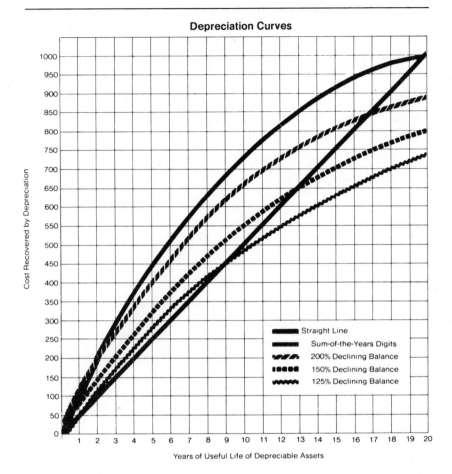

Depreciation Curves

Cost Recovered by Depreciation

Years of Useful Life of Depreciable Assets

Legend:
- Straight Line
- Sum-of-the-Years Digits
- 200% Declining Balance
- 150% Declining Balance
- 125% Declining Balance

Cash flow

Real estate investors commonly examine their investment results in terms of cash flow, e.g. how much actual cash (often referred to as "spendable dollars") is available to them after taxes from their investment. They are not content merely with the bookkeeping result of net profit or loss from the operation.

The major reason for a difference between net operating income (or loss) and cash flow stems from the interaction of the depreciation deduction and the principal payments made on any mortgages on the property. Depreciation reduces net taxable income from the property but requires no outlay of cash. On the other hand, principal payments require an outlay of cash but are not deductible for tax purposes. Further, a net taxable loss from operations reduces the property owner's other taxable income and thereby reduces the cash outlay required for income taxes.

169

To illustrate the interaction of the factors just discussed and their impacts on cash flow, let us consider the following three examples. (The figures used are somewhat arbitrary and are used merely to illustrate the principles involved.)

1. Assume that in 1975, Brown's rental property produces $100,000 of gross rents. He has operating expenses of $60,000, mortgage interest of $9,000, principal payments of $10,000, real estate taxes of $12,000 and a depreciation deduction of $15,000.

His taxable income from the property would be computed as follows.

Rental income		$100,000
Operating expenses	$60,000	
Mortgage interest	9,000	
Real estate taxes	12,000	
Depreciation	15,000	96,000
Taxable income		$ 4,000

His cash flow from the property, however, would be computed as follows.

Rental income		$100,000
Operating expenses	$60,000	
Mortgage interest	9,000	
Real estate taxes	12,000	
Principal payments	10,000	91,000
Cash flow before taxes		9,000
Less: tax on $4,000 taxable income (assuming a 40% marginal rate)		1,600
Cash flow after taxes		$ 7,400

The $3,400 excess of cash flow over taxable income is accounted for as follows.

Excess of depreciation over principal payments	$5,000
Less: income tax on taxable income	1,600
Difference between cash flow and taxable income	$3,400

2. Even though the result of operations is a taxable loss, it is still possible to have a positive cash flow from the property.

Assume the same facts as in Example 1 except that the depreciation deduction is $22,000 instead of $15,000. Taxable income (loss) would be computed as follows.

Rental income		$100,000
Operating expenses	$60,000	
Mortgage interest	9,000	
Real estate taxes	12,000	
Depreciation	22,000	103,000
Taxable loss		($ 3,000)

Cash flow from the property would be computed as follows.

Rental income		$100,000
Operating expenses	$60,000	
Real estate taxes	12,000	
Mortgage interest	9,000	
Principal payments	10,000	91,000
Cash flow before taxes		9,000
Plus: income taxes saved by applying $3,000 loss to owner's other income (assuming 40% marginal rate)		1,200
Cash flow after taxes		$ 10,200

The $13,200 difference between the net taxable loss from operations of the property and the cash flow after taxes is accounted for as follows.

Excess of depreciation over principal payments	$12,000
Income tax savings generated by loss from operations	1,200
Difference between cash flow and taxable loss	$13,200

3. It is of course possible to have a negative cash flow, i.e. the investor has to add cash from his pocket to the operations. This will generally result when the amount of the principal payments during the year exceed the depreciation deductions.

Assume the same facts as in the first example except that the depreciation deduction is $10,000 while the principal payments are $20,000. Taxable income would be calculated as follows.

Rental income		$100,000
Operating expenses	$60,000	
Mortgage interest	9,000	
Real estate taxes	12,000	
Depreciation	10,000	91,000
Taxable income		$ 9,000

Cash flow from the property would be calculated as follows.

Rental income		$100,000
Operating expenses	$60,000	
Mortgage interest	9,000	
Real estate taxes	12,000	
Principal payments	20,000	101,000
Cash outflow		(1,000)
Tax on taxable income (40% marginal rate)		(3,600)
Negative cash flow after taxes		($ 4,600)

The $13,600 difference between the taxable income of $9,000 and the negative outflow of cash of $4,600 is accounted for as follows.

Excess of principal payments over depreciation deductions	$10,000
Tax on taxable income from operations	3,600
Difference between taxable income and negative cash flow	$13,600

Chapter 10

Dispositions

10

Whenever property is sold or exchanged for cash, obligations or other property, gain or loss is realized.

Gain or loss is the difference between the basis of the property given up and the amount or value received. The gain is reduced (or the loss increased) by the cost of the transaction (e.g. brokers' commissions).

The gain or loss realized is not always immediately taxable or deductible. Like-kind exchanges, for example, have the effect of deferring the gain or loss. (The topic of tax-deferred exchanges is discussed in the next chapter.) In addition, it is possible, via the use of the installment method, to spread the taxation of the gain over the period during which the sales price is collected.

Unless the seller is a dealer, gain on the sale of real estate generally results in a capital gain. More accurately, it is usually a Section 1231 gain. (The tax treatment of these types of gains is explained in detail on page 91.) Furthermore, even though, conceptually, the gain qualifies for capital gain treatment, part or all of the gain may be treated as ordinary income if the rules for recapture of depreciation apply.

In this chapter the questions of who is a dealer, how to use installment and other deferred sales and when and how depreciation recapture rules apply are explored in detail. In addition, other methods of disposition such as sales and leasebacks, involuntary conversions, demolition, charitable contributions and other gifts and corporate liquidations and reorganizations are examined for their tax consequences.

Dealer or investor

Whether a seller is a dealer or investor makes no difference in the economic sense. These are tax terms and in taxation they make a huge difference. That difference involves the treatment of gain on sale as ordinary income when realized by a dealer or as capital gain (i.e. a Section 1231 gain in most cases) when realized by an investor. This difference, as pointed out in the discussion beginning at page 90, may often mean the difference of many tax dollars. For individuals and trusts the maximum tax rate for ordinary income can be as much as 70% as compared to a maximum of 25% for capital gains of up to $50,000.

Expressed briefly, gain on the sale of real property will be treated as ordinary income when the property was "held by the taxpayer primarily for sale to customers in the ordinary course of his trade or business." The definition of the word "primarily" is so elusive that it took a decision of the United States Supreme Court to settle the controversy between taxpayers and the Government. In that case, the Supreme Court held that the word "primarily" means "of first importance" or "principally." It does not mean merely a "substantial" purpose.

Therefore, with respect to each parcel of property, a taxpayer must make the determination (and be able to support it if his tax return is examined by the IRS) as to whether it is being held principally as (1) an investment, (2) as property used in his trade or business or (3) as property held for sale in the ordinary course of his trade or business. Generally, the first two categories yield capital gain if sold at a profit; the third yields ordinary income. More precisely, the tax treatment for real estate is as follows.

1. Non-income producing investment property (such as non-productive land) when sold at a gain will yield capital gain. When such property is sold at a loss, the result is capital loss, which, as explained on page 97, is of limited value.

2. Property used in the trade or business of a taxpayer and held for more than six months is called Section 1231 property. (Included in this category is property held for rental purposes.) All gains (other than those representing recapture of depreciation discussed on page 175) and losses from such property for the taxable year are combined. As explained on page 91, if the net result is profit, it is taxed as a capital gain; if the net result is a loss, it is taxed as an ordinary loss.

3. Property held for sale to customers in the ordinary course of trade or business yields ordinary income or ordinary loss. It is this type of property that is designated as dealer property.

Factors indicating dealer status

In some cases, the taxpayer is obviously a dealer, e.g. a developer of a tract of residential properties which he sells individually to separate buyers. In other cases, he is clearly an investor, e.g. he buys one rental property, holds it for a number of years for the investment return and subsequently sells it, never previously having made a similar sale.

The difficulty arises in the "grey area" as when someone who claims he is an investor is involved in numerous sales transactions.

The issue is considered to be a factual one; each case is considered on its own merits. However, there are certain factors which are usually examined in cases such as these to decide whether property is being held for sale in the ordinary course of business. No one of them is all-important and the relative degree of importance of each factor varies with the individual case. Of course, if a taxpayer declares (by advertising or some such means) that he is in the business of buying and selling real estate and he sells one of the parcels he holds as part of the inventory of properties he has for sale, he would be hard-pressed later to claim that he was really holding that parcel for investment purposes and not as a dealer in real estate. But that is the extreme case.

Quite often, the taxpayer is not in the real estate business on a full-time basis. He may be a doctor, a lawyer, a police chief, etc. In these cases it is often difficult to determine the principal purpose for holding the real estate.

Following are some of the factors that would tend to cause one to be classified as a dealer.

He has a real estate license and lists his occupation as "real estate dealer" on his income tax returns.

He belongs to various real estate dealer organizations.

He makes frequent, quick turnover transactions.

His business stationery, advertising and publicity releases all refer to him as a real estate dealer.

He employs a staff of salespeople to solicit offers from purchasers.

He develops property by making substantial improvements and subdividing; then he advertises it for sale.

He receives a large part of his total income from the sale of real estate.

He spends most of his working time on real estate purchase and sales activities.

His purpose at the time of acquisition and/or sale is for quick resale.

All of these factors and more must be examined in *each case* with respect to *each property* sold in order to determine the proper income tax treatment. Thus, for example, if a taxpayer in the business of renting real property decides to liquidate, the sale of the rental property would be the sale of property used in the trade or business and hence, any gain would be a Section 1231 gain taxable as a capital gain. However, by the same token, if that taxpayer then engaged in such a large degree of activity, subdividing, improving, sales promotion, etc., his status might be converted to dealer status; that is, holding the property for sale in the ordinary course of business.

Dealer as an investor

It is possible for a real estate dealer to hold some of his property for use in his trade or business or for investment purposes and not for sale to customers in the ordinary course of his business. A real estate dealer or broker who owns the building in which his office is located is holding that building for use in his business and not for sale to customers in the ordinary course of his business. If he were to decide to move his office and he sold that building, the gain would be treated as a Section 1231 gain.

Since a dealer may also be an investor, it is important that some designation be made, not only in the taxpayer's mind but tangibly on paper and by action, to indicate which property he is holding for investment or for use in his trade or business.

Example

Roberts is a real estate dealer. He buys and sells real estate in the ordinary course of business.

When he buys real estate for his own investment and not for sale to customers in the ordinary course of business, he segregates the purchase on his books of account. His financial records have separate accounts for (1) his inventory property; (2) his investment property and (3) the building in which his office is located, his business property.

Depreciation recapture

When depreciable property is sold at a gain, the likelihood is that part of the gain is attributable to the fact that depreciation deductions were taken which reduced the basis of the property.

For example, if depreciable property is purchased for $100,000 and depreciation deductions totalling $40,000 are taken over a period of years, the adjusted basis of the property becomes $60,000. A subsequent sale of the property at $100,000 (same as the original purchase price) results in a $40,000 gain. In this case, the entire gain arises from the fact that $40,000 of depreciation was deducted. If the property were sold for $110,000, the resulting gain would be $50,000 of which $40,000 would be due to the fact that the depreciation deductions were taken.

The idea behind depreciation recapture is to prevent converting an ordinary deduction (depreciation deductions reduce ordinary income) into a capital gain when the amount of the previously-deducted depreciation is recovered in the sales price.

Consequently, the depreciation recapture rules are designed to treat so much of the gain on the sale as is attributable to the recapture of depreciation deductions by the seller as ordinary income. The depreciation recapture rules accomplish this result in the case of the sale of depreciable personal property (e.g. furniture, machinery, etc.). In the case of depreciable real property, the tax law does not attempt to treat all of the gain attributable to depreciation deductions as ordinary income. Instead, it treats only so much of the gain as is attributable to *excess depreciation* as ordinary income. *Excess depreciation* is the total amount of the depreciation deducted that exceeds the total of the depreciation deductions that would have been available had the straight line method of depreciation been used. (And in some situations, less than the full amount of the excess depreciation is recaptured as ordinary income.)

Depreciation recapture on disposition of personalty

The concept underlying depreciation recapture is more easily demonstrated by the rules affecting personalty than those dealing with real property. Hence, we will examine the personal property rules first.

Section 1245, enacted in 1962, provides for a recapture of all depreciation deducted after 1961 that is reflected in the gain on the sale or other disposition of the personalty (that is, movable depreciable property such as furniture, machinery, etc.). Depreciation deducted prior to 1962 does not enter into the calculation of Section 1245 depreciation recapture. Thus, if the depreciation deducted after 1961 is equal to or less than the gain on the sale, the portion of the gain equal to the depreciation deducted is treated as ordinary income. The balance of the gain (if any) is Section 1231 gain. If the gain is less than the depreciation deducted, the entire gain is ordinary income. If there is a loss on the sale, Section 1245 recapture does not enter into the picture. (Note that depreciation recapture under Section 1245 also applies to depreciation deducted on elevators and escalators after June 30, 1963.)

Example

Smith sells furniture and fixtures used in his hotel. His adjusted basis for the items sold is $15,000. Depreciation claimed after 1961 on these items totalled $4,000. Tax treatment of the gain or loss on the transaction, for each of the sales prices indicated, is as follows.

Sales price is $17,000; gain is $2,000. Since the depreciation total after 1961 is $4,000, the entire gain of $2,000 is treated as ordinary income.

Sales price is $19,000; gain is $4,000, exactly equal to the depreciation deducted since 1961. Hence, the entire gain of $4,000 is treated as ordinary income.

Sales price is $21,000; gain is $6,000. This is greater than the total depreciation deducted since 1961. In this case, $4,000 of the gain is treated as ordinary income and $2,000 as a Section 1231 gain.

Sales price is $12,000; since there is a loss of $3,000, depreciation recapture rules do not apply. The loss is a Section 1231 loss.

Depreciation recapture on disposition of real property

Section 1250 provides generally for a recapture (as ordinary income) of only part of the depreciation deducted after 1963 and reflected in the gain on the sale or other disposition of depreciable real estate. This section (except with regard to property held for not more than one year) is designed to recapture *part or all* of the depreciation deducted in excess of the depreciation allowed under the straight line method. The percentage of the excess depreciation that may be recaptured in some cases is progressively reduced as the taxpayer's holding period for his property is increased.

The total excess of the depreciation deducted over the amount deductible under the straight line method is referred to as "excess depreciation." The portion of the excess depreciation that is subject to recapture is referred to as the "applicable amount."

The applicable amount depends on a number of factors.

The holding period of the property
The depreciation method used
How much depreciation was deducted
    After 1969
    After 1963 and before 1970
    Before 1964
Whether the property qualified for special uses

Straight line depreciation used   If only straight line depreciation has been used for the real property being sold or disposed of, there cannot be any depreciation recapture under Section 1250 as long as the property was held for more than one year.

Property held not more than one year   If the property being sold or otherwise disposed of has been held for one year or less, all of the depreciation deducted, regardless of the depreciation method used, becomes subject to recapture. (This is essentially the same procedure used to recapture depreciation on personalty under Section 1245 as explained above.) Of course, if the gain is less than the depreciation deducted, only the amount of the gain is treated as ordinary income.

Property held more than one year   When the property has been held for more than one year, the *maximum* amount of depreciation that can be recaptured is the excess depreciation.

In determining the applicable amount of the excess depreciation that may be recaptured, the depreciation deducted and the amount of straight line depreciation have to be determined for three different periods of time.

Depreciation deducted before 1964; this amount does not enter the picture since the excess depreciation attributed to that period is not subject to recapture.

Depreciation deducted after 1963 and before 1970.

Depreciation deducted after 1969.

The first step is to determine gain on the disposition in the usual manner, as if there were no depreciation recapture provision in the law. This gain is then compared with the applicable amount of excess depreciation for the period after 1969. If the gain is equal to or less than the applicable amount for the post-1969 period, the entire gain is ordinary income. If the gain exceeds the applicable amount, it is then necessary to compare the remaining gain to the applicable amount that pertains to the period after 1963 and before 1970. If the remaining gain is equal to or less than the applicable amount for the years 1964–1969, the entire gain is ordinary income. If the remaining gain exceeds the applicable amount for the 1964–1969 period, the excess gain is Section 1231 gain. All of the rest of the gain is ordinary income.

Examples

1. Gain on the sale of real property in 1975 is $60,000. Applicable amount of excess depreciation is as follows.

Period after 1969 is $62,000

Period after 1963 and before 1970 is $160,000.

Since the applicable amount of excess depreciation after 1969 is more than the entire gain on the sale, the entire gain is treated as ordinary income. There is no need to refer to the applicable amount of excess depreciation for the period before 1970.

2. Assume all the facts in Example 1 except that the gain on the sale was $100,000. First the $62,000 applicable amount of excess depreciation for the period after 1969 is applied. That still leaves $38,000 of gain not recaptured. Then, the applicable amount of excess depreciation for the period after 1963 and before 1970 is applied. Since that is more than the remaining $38,000 of gain, the entire gain of $100,000 is treated as ordinary income.

3. Assume the same facts as in Example 1 except that the gain on the sale was $250,000. First the $62,000 applicable amount of excess depreciation is applied against the $250,000 gain, leaving $188,000 gain. Next the $160,000 applicable amount of excess depreciation is applied, leaving $28,000 of gain. Hence, of the $250,000 gain, $222,000 is treated as ordinary income (depreciation recapture) and $28,000 is treated as Section 1231 gain.

Of course, the figures used in the examples were arbitrary, merely to illustrate how the applicable amounts of excess depreciation are applied against the gain to determine what portion of the gain is ordinary income and what portion is Section 1231 gain.

Determining the applicable amount of excess depreciation

As indicated, it is not the entire excess depreciation that is necessarily compared to the gain to determine the amount of depreciation recapture. It is the *applicable amount* of that excess. And there are different rules for excess depreciation arising after 1969 and excess depreciation arising after 1963 and before 1970.

Applicable amount of excess depreciation arising after 1969   Unless one of the following two exceptions is met, the applicable amount of the excess depreciation *is the total excess depreciation.*

Exception 1 applies to property disposed of pursuant to a written contract which was binding on July 24, 1969 and at all times thereafter; and property constructed, reconstructed or acquired before January 1, 1975, which qualifies as a low-income housing project financed under Section 221(d)(3) or 236 of the National Housing Act or under similar state-sponsored financing.

Exception 2 applies to residential rental property (see page 157 for a definition of this type of property) unless that property also qualifies for Exception 1 because it is more favorable. Exception 2 also applies to depreciation deductions for rehabilitation expenses described on page 159.

When Exception 1 applies, excess depreciation after 1969 is first calculated in the usual way. Then the number of whole months in the holding period of the property is determined (a fraction of a month is disregarded). The number of months in the holding period is subtracted from 120. The resulting number is converted into a percentage. It is this percentage of the excess depreciation that becomes the applicable amount. Thus, if the holding period is 40 months, 80% of the excess depreciation becomes the applicable amount (120 minus 40 = 80, which is converted to 80%). Under this exception, if the holding period is 20 months or less, the full amount of the excess depreciation will be recaptured since subtracting not more than 20 from 120 will result in a figure of 100% or more (however, never more than 100% of excess depreciation can be recaptured). On the other hand, if the holding period is 120 months (i.e. 10 years) or more, there will be no depreciation recapture since subtracting 120 or more from 120 will result in a figure of 0%.

When Exception 2 applies, the same approach is used as under Exception 1. However, the holding period in full months is subtracted from 200 (instead of 120). Under this approach if the holding period is 100 months or less, the full excess depreciation becomes the applicable amount (since subtracting 100 or less from 200 will result in 100% or more; but not more than 100% is used). That means that the applicable amount is 100% of the excess depreciation if the holding period does not exceed eight years and four months. On the other hand, once the holding period reaches 16 years and eight months (i.e. 200 months), there is no depreciation recapture at all because the applicable amount is 0% of the excess depreciation.

Applicable amount of the excess depreciation arising after 1963 and before 1970
The rule is the same as in Exception 1: the number of full months in the holding period is subtracted from 120 with the resulting figure converted to a percentage and applied against the excess depreciation to find the applicable amount. Note, however, that the *full holding period* (measured in full months) of the property is used including the holding period beginning before 1964 and extending beyond 1969. However, the percentage determined is applied only to the excess depreciation for the period that began after 1963 and ended before 1970.

There is one exception to the holding period rule. If property is acquired in a tax-deferred exchange (see page 195), the property starts a new holding period beginning the day following the exchange. This new holding period applies for depreciation recapture purposes only.

Example

Assume that on January 1, 1966, Jones acquired an office building for $100,000. (For the purpose of the example, we will assume that the entire $100,000 is the basis of the building. In this example, we will not concern ourselves with the portion of the purchase or sales prices allocable to the land.) On January 1, 1975, he sold the building for $80,000.

When he acquired the building it had a useful life of 30 years and he was eligible to use 200% declining balance depreciation, which he used.

His accumulated depreciation at the time of sale may be analyzed as follows.

	200% Declining Balance	Straight line (assuming zero salvage value)
1/1/66 through 12/31/69	$24,116	$13,333
1/1/70 through 1/1/75	22,140	16,667
Totals	$46,256	$30,000

(Note that since the property was not held prior to 1964, there is no need to determine what portion of the total depreciation deducted is allocable to that period.)

The total excess depreciation for the entire holding period is $16,256. However, as will be seen, the applicable amount will be less than that amount.

Step 1. Calculate the gain in the usual manner, assuming no improvements were made during the holding period and sales commission of $4,000 was paid by Jones. Since his original basis was $100,000 and the total depreciation deducted was $46,256, Jones' basis at the time of sale was $53,744.

Sales price		$80,000
Less: Basis	$53,744	
Sales commission	4,000	57,744
Gain		$22,256

Step 2. Calculate excess depreciation for period after 1969.

Depreciation deducted	$22,140
Straight line for that period	16,667
Excess depreciation	$ 5,473

Since neither Exception 1 nor 2 applies, the full $5,473 is the excess depreciation for the period after 1969. Hence, at least $5,473 of the gain of $22,256 is to be treated as ordinary income arising from depreciation recapture.

It is then necessary to determine whether any portion of the remaining gain (i.e. $22,256 minus $5,473 or $16,783) must also be treated as ordinary income. To do that, we must determine the applicable amount for the period prior to 1970.

Step 3. Calculate the applicable amount for the period after 1963 and before 1970. (Here only the years 1966 through 1969 are involved.)

Depreciation deducted	$24,116
Straight line for that period	13,333
Excess depreciation	$10,783

The property has been held for 108 full months. Consequently 108 is subtracted from 120. The remaining figure of 12 becomes 12%. Applying 12% to the excess depreciation of $10,783 gives an applicable amount of $1,294. Hence, of the remaining gain of $16,783, $1,294 is treated as ordinary income arising from depreciation recapture. The results of Steps 1–3 are summarized as follows.

Gain on the sale		$22,256
Applicable amount of excess depreciation:		
After 1969	$5,473	
After 1963 and before 1970	1,294	6,767
Gain remaining after depreciation recapture		$15,489

Hence, of the $22,256 gain, $6,767 is reported as ordinary income and $15,489 is treated as a Section 1231 gain. This is so even though the total excess depreciation was $16,256 and the total depreciation deducted was $46,256. (Were this personal property, the entire gain of $22,256 would be taxed as ordinary income because the total gain was less than the total depreciation deducted.)

Special rule for child-care and on-the-job-training facilities

As explained on page 160, a special 60-month write-off is available for these facilities (instead of the usual depreciation rules). But as was also pointed out, there is depreciation recapture on the disposition of these facilities.

Even though real property may be involved, the depreciation recapture rules that apply are those that apply to personal property (as explained on page 175). That is, *all* of the write-off taken (not only the amount in excess of straight line) is subject to recapture.

The amount of amortization deducted is compared to the amount of the gain on the disposition. If the amortization deducted is equal to or greater than the gain, the entire gain is ordinary income. If the gain exceeds the amortization deducted, the gain equal to the amortization is ordinary income and the excess gain is a Section 1231 gain.

Tax-free exchanges and depreciation recapture

As is explained beginning at page 195, it is possible to have a so-called tax-free exchange of property of a like-kind without *any* gain being recognized for tax purposes. In other cases, while the *entire* gain may not be recognized for tax purposes, *part* of the gain may be taxable. That occurs when "other property" than like-kind is received in the exchange. Often that "other property" is cash.

In the case of an exchange of personal property, the amount of the depreciation deducted since 1961 (or after June, 1963, for elevators and escalators) is compared to the portion of the gain that is taxable in the exchange. In other words the recognized portion of the gain is treated as total gain.

The maximum amount of depreciation recapture on real property that can be taxable as ordinary income when there is this type of exchange is the larger of the two amounts determined under the following rules.

1. The amount equal to the portion of the gain on the exchange that is taxable under the exchange rules (see page 199).

2. The excess of (a) the potential depreciation recapture on the exchange (computed as though a sale were made for cash) over (b) the fair market value of the depreciable real property received in the exchange. The purpose of this rule is to permit IRS to impose the real estate recapture rules when a good portion of the property being received in exchange is not depreciable real property and hence will not be subject to depreciation recapture in the future.

Similar rules are applied where property is replaced after an involuntary conversion (see page 130) or after the sale of and reinvestment in a qualified low-income housing project (see page 159).

Installment sales

It is quite common for real estate to be sold using an installment sale. That is, the buyer pays the purchase price over a number of years. Commonly, the purchaser will be paying part of the purchase price via mortgage principal payments.

Of course, if the mortgages are being held by banks or other lending institutions, the seller will receive all that he is going to in the year of the sale. Then, the entire gain on the sale will be reportable by him for tax purposes in the year of sale.

Examples

Seller has an adjusted basis for his property of $70,000. He sells it for $100,000 resulting in a $30,000 gain. The buyer pays the $100,000 price by paying $40,000 of his own cash and securing a mortgage on the property for $60,000 from a bank. In this case, the seller gets the full $100,000 at the time of the sale and buyer ends up owing the bank the $60,000. So, the seller reports the full gain in the year of sale. As far as he is concerned the sale is not an installment sale. The buyer is paying installments by way of mortgage principal payments but to the bank and not the seller.

In other cases, however, the installment payments are made to the seller.

In the preceding case, if instead of borrowing $60,000 from the bank, the seller pays $40,000 in cash and gives the seller a purchase money mortgage of $60,000, the seller will collect the $60,000 balance of the sales price over the term of the mortgage. Here, the seller considers the transaction an installment sale.

Another variation of this transaction might shape up as follows. Seller sells for $100,000 but there is an existing mortgage of $25,000 on the property. The buyer pays the $100,000 by paying $40,000 cash, taking subject to the $25,000 mortgage and giving the seller a second mortgage of $35,000. Here, too, part of the sales price will be paid to the seller over a number of years, the term of the second mortgage. Again, there is an installment sale as far as the seller is concerned.

When there is an installment sale, the gain on the transaction is calculated in the usual way. That is, the seller's adjusted basis is subtracted from the sales price to determine the gain. And if the gain qualifies as a capital gain, it is taxed as such. But since the seller will not get all his money in the year of sale, he would like to avoid paying the tax on the full gain in that year. He would like to spread the tax burden over the period during which he will collect the portion of the selling price he has not received in the year of the sale. The tax law permits this spreadout by allowing the seller to elect the installment method of reporting the gain *if certain technical rules are met.*

The 30% rule

The major rule for installment sale reporting is the 30% rule. Simply stated, it says that if the seller wants to report his gain using the installment method, he must not receive more than 30% of the sales price in the year of sale.

The 30% rule appears to be very simple at first glance but it needs some elaboration and explanation. Before getting into that, it should be pointed out that the 30% rule applies to so-called "casual" sales, sales by those who are not in the business of making such sales. In other words it does not apply to real estate dealers. A dealer *can* use the installment method, too, for reporting his ordinary income on installment sales. But he must adopt that method for reporting all his installment sales and may not change to another method without permission from the Commissioner of Internal Revenue. The "casual" seller, however, if he meets the 30% test as to any one sale, can use the installment reporting method for that sale even though he may decide not to report another sale using the installment method and although that other sale also qualifies under the 30% rule. In other words, the seller can decide as to each "casual" sale that qualifies whether he wants to report it as an installment sale or not. He is not bound by his prior action as to what he does concerning a later sale.

How the 30% rule works   The sum of payments received by the seller in the year of sale is compared to the total sales price (including any mortgages which the buyer assumes or takes subject to). If the payments received in the year of sale do not exceed 30% of the sales price, the sale qualifies for installment reporting.

Payments in year of sale

In order to have an installment sale, the seller will have to receive evidences of indebtedness from the buyer. Usually, this takes the form of a mortgage but it doesn't have to. Notes or other evidences of indebtedness of the buyer do not have to be secured by the property sold. However, if the buyer gives a demand note, the tax law makes it clear that the note will be treated as cash received in the year of sale rather than as evidence of indebtedness. So, the amount of the demand note will be counted as cash received in the year of sale in determining whether the 30% test was met.

If a corporate buyer gives a registered note or bond or one with coupons attached, that, too, will be treated as cash received in the year of sale if it is readily tradable on a securities market. Similarly, any other corporate obligation designed to be readily tradable on a securities market will be treated as cash.

There is often a problem in determining how much the seller received in the year of sale. Obviously, the amount paid by the buyer at the time of the closing of the sale (plus any deposits previously paid to the seller) are payments in the year of sale. Also to be included in the year of sale are payments on the purchase money mortgage made to the seller during the year of sale.

Example

White sells a building in April, 1975, for $100,000. At the closing he receives $25,000 in cash from the buyer plus a mortgage for $75,000. Mortgage payments are due every three months. On July 1 and October 1, 1975, White receives principal and interest payments on the mortgage. The total payments on principal amount to $6,500. This $6,500 must be added to the $25,000 received at the time of sale, giving a total of $31,500 in payments received by the seller in the year of sale. Since $31,500 exceeds 30% of the $100,000 selling price, the transaction does not qualify for installment sale reporting.

Indirect payments have presented a problem. For example, what happens if the buyer (in the year of sale) pays liens, taxes or other expenses relating to the property acquired that were existing obligations at the time the property was transferred to the buyer. At one time, IRS held that such payments by the buyer to third parties during the year of sale were to be treated as payments to the seller in the year of sale in determining whether the 30% rule was met. Subsequently, IRS changed its mind. Such payments do not constitute payments in the year of sale unless the sales contract directs that such amounts be paid out of the purchase price.

This IRS position also clears up the question of how to treat mortgage principal payments made to the third parties by the buyer in the year of sale. For example, if the buyer acquires the property subject to an existing mortgage and makes a mortgage principal payment to the mortgagee during the year of sale, at least one court case implied that the mortgage principal payment should be included in the amount of payments received by the seller in the year of sale for the 30% test. IRS now makes it clear that such payment is not included in the payments of the seller in the year of sale *unless* the mortgage was put on the property in the year of sale in order to get around the 30% rule.

Effects of mortgages on payments in the year of sale

Normally, the fact that the buyer is taking subject to or assuming an existing mortgage on the property does not create any problems. The takeover of the mortgage is not considered payment in the year of sale except when the amount of the mortgage exceeds the seller's basis for the property being sold.

Mortgage exceeds basis   If the seller's adjusted basis for the property he sells is less than the mortgage the buyer takes over, the excess mortgage amount is considered payment received by the seller in the year of sale.

Example

Seller bought a piece of property some years ago for $40,000. His adjusted basis, because of depreciation deductions he has taken, has been reduced to $20,000. However, the property has appreciated very considerably in value, so he was able to place a mortgage of $35,000 on it. He now sells the property for $60,000. The buyer pays $5,000 cash in the year of sale, assumes the $35,000 mortgage and gives the seller a purchase money second mortgage of $20,000. The seller wishes to report his gain of $40,000 ($60,000 sales price minus $20,000 adjusted basis) using the installment method. Since he has received only $5,000 cash in the year of sale, he believes he is well within the 30% rule (since 30% of $60,000 is $18,000). But the $35,000 mortgage assumed by the buyer exceeds the seller's basis for the property by $15,000. This $15,000 is considered payment received in the year of sale. When this $15,000 is added to the $5,000 cash received by the seller in the year of sale, the $20,000 total exceeds the $18,000 maximum permitted to be received. Hence, the seller will not be permitted to use the installment method of reporting.

It should be borne in mind that the excess mortgage rule applies to existing mortgages and not to purchase money mortgages that arise as part of the sales transaction, e.g. the mortgage the seller takes back as security for the portion of the purchase price that the buyer is to pay in the future.

183

Selling expenses   It is clear that selling expenses reduce the profit or increase the loss of the seller who is not a dealer; they are not separate deductions against ordinary income. However, in some installment sales situations it can become important whether, in arriving at the profit on the sale, the selling costs are added to basis or merely subtracted from the sales price. Numerically, the result is the same whichever method is used.

For example, if the sales price is $100,000; basis without regard to selling costs, $50,000; and selling costs, $5,000, the profit on the sale is $45,000. This result can be arrived at by subtracting the selling costs from the sales price, to arrive at $95,000, and then subtracting the $50,000 basis. It can also be arrived at by adding the selling costs to the basis, for a total of $55,000, and then subtracting the new basis of $55,000 from the $100,000 sales price. Normally, it makes no difference which approach is used; the result is the same.

Where, however, existing mortgages exceed the seller's basis (before taking selling costs into account), adding the selling costs to the basis reduces the difference between the mortgage and basis. It is this difference, it will be recalled, that is treated as payment in the year of sale when applying the 30% rule to an installment sale.

The importance of the proper treatment of selling costs was graphically illustrated in a recent case. The seller's basis (before selling costs) was $100,000. The sales price was $430,000. The buyer paid $80,000 in cash in the year of sale, assumed a $160,000 existing mortgage and gave a note for the balance of $190,000. IRS argued that installment reporting was not available because the seller received $140,000 in the year of sale, the $80,000 cash plus the $60,000 by which the mortgage exceeded the seller's basis, which was more than 30% of the $430,000 selling price (30% of $430,000 is $129,000). The seller insisted that the selling costs of $25,000 should be added to his basis. In that case the excess of morgage over basis would be $35,000. Adding the $80,000 cash to the $35,000 excess mortgage would produce a total of $115,000, well below the 30% mark of $129,000.

The Tax Court sided with IRS. However, on appeal, the Court of Appeals for the Ninth Circuit overturned the Tax Court decision and agreed that the taxpayer could add the selling costs to his basis and was thus eligible to report the sale as an installment sale. Subsequently, IRS announced that it would not follow the Ninth Circuit's decision in future cases.

Taxpayers faced with this problem are still on the horns of a dilemma. If they wish to rely on the Ninth Circuit decision, they can be quite certain that they will have to litigate because IRS has made it clear it will not follow that decision. And taxpayers have no assurance (if they are not located in the area within the jurisdiction of the Ninth Circuit) that other courts will follow the decision of the Ninth Circuit. If a taxpayer loses his litigation, then the installment reporting he relied on will be invalid and the entire gain will be taxable in the year of sale. Obviously, the safer course to pursue, at least until further litigation resolves this issue more clearly, is to avoid relying on the addition of selling costs to basis as a means of meeting the 30% test.

Imputed interest

Normally, if the buyer gives a mortgage to evidence the unpaid portion of the purchase price (or takes subject to or assumes a mortgage), presumably a fair interest rate will be paid. As long as the interest paid on the installment debt is at least 4% simple interest, no problem arises as to the reporting of installment sales.

(The principal payments are considered receipts of part of the sales price and the interest is taxed to the seller as ordinary income.)

A problem can arise when a sale is made calling for installment payments but not calling for interest or calling for interest of less than 4%. This is not the usual case in real estate sales but was once a method employed to avoid having ordinary income from interest. (The price was adjusted to concede something to the buyer in exchange for denying him interest deductions and the seller reported the entire gain as capital gain.)

Today if interest is not called for (or, if less than 4% simple interest is called for), interest will be imputed at 5%. That is, using Government tables, each installment payment will be "discounted back" to the date of sale and the difference will be considered interest.

For example, an installment payment received in April 1975 amounts to $1,000. The sale was made in April 1973, 24 months previously. No interest was set forth in the installment contract. Under the Government tables, $1,000 discounted (at 5%) for 24 months makes the value of that $1,000 at the time of the sale in 1973 about $906. Hence, $94 of the $1,000 is treated as interest income.

The problem with the imputed interest rule as it applies to installment sales is that it reduces the sales price. In the example, the $1,000 installment due in 1975 (which was part of the computed sales price at the time of the sale in 1973) was reduced to $906. That reduced the total sales price in 1973 by $94, too. What was done with that one $1,000 installment must be done with every installment. As a result the entire sales price may be reduced considerably. And if it is, the payments received in the year of sale may suddenly become more than 30% of the revised sales price and prevent the use of the installment method of reporting.

As a result of the imputed interest rule, it has become imperative to have the install-ment contract call for interest. As explained, the present position of the IRS is that if the contract calls for at least 4% simple interest, the imputed interest rules will not be applied. (Congress has given IRS the power to alter the lowest accept-able interest rate from time to time. Since the inception of the imputed interest rule, IRS has used the 4% simple interest figure.)

Note: as this book goes to press, IRS has announced that it proposes to raise the 4% to 6% for transactions entered into on or after July 24, 1975. Similarly where no interest (or insufficient interest) is called for, IRS proposes to raise the 5% rate to 7%.

How to report gain under the installment method

The prior discussion dealt with the qualifications for installment reporting. Once a sale qualifies for installment reporting, how is the gain reported? (Note that installment reporting applies to gains only; losses may not be spread over a number of years via installment reporting.)

Installment reporting of gains requires the following steps.

1. Determine the gain in the usual manner as if the installment method were not being used.

2. Determine the contract price. The contract price is the sales price reduced by mortgages (or other indebtedness) assumed (or taken subject to) by the buyer and *payable to third parties.*

3. Divide the gain (determined in Step 1) by the contract price (determined in Step 2) to determine the percentage of the contract price that the gain equals.

4. In each year in which payment is received from the buyer (the year of sale and subsequent years) multiply the amount received by the percentage determined in Step 3. This procedure determines the amount of the gain to be reported in each year.

The following two examples illustrate installment reporting. The first example illustrates a situation in which there are no existing mortgages on the property; the second deals with a case where there is an existing mortgage.

Examples

1. Smith sells a parcel of land that cost her $20,000 for $50,000. The land is un-encumbered. The buyer pays $10,000 in the year of sale and will pay $5,000 a year for the next eight years (plus $7\frac{1}{2}\%$ interest on the unpaid balance). Smith pays a broker a commission of $2,500 for bringing about the sale. Smith wants to report the sale using the installment method. Since the payments received in the year of sale ($10,000) do not exceed 30% of the $50,000 selling price, she may do so according to the following procedure.

Sales price		$50,000
Less: Commission	$ 2,500	
Adjusted basis	20,000	
Total		22,500
Gain on sale		$27,500

The contract price is the same as the sales price because there is no indebtedness taken over by the buyer payable to third parties. Hence, the contract price is $50,000.

The gain is 55% of the contract price ($27,500 divided by $50,000).

In the year of sale, $10,000 was received by the seller. Therefore, 55% of the $10,000 or $5,500 is reported as gain in that year.

In each subsequent year, $5,000 will be received by the seller. So, in each of those years, the seller will report a gain of $2,750 (55% of $5,000). In each of these years, the seller will also receive interest payments. The interest will be reported separately as ordinary income.

2. Brown sells land and building for $100,000. His adjusted basis for the property at the time of the sale is $59,600. He pays a sales commission of $5,000. Terms of the sale are.

Cash paid at time of sale	$25,000
Existing mortgage on property assumed by buyer	40,000
Second mortgage given to seller (purchase money mortgage)	35,000
Total	$100,000

The second mortgage is to be paid in seven equal annual installments of principal plus 8% interest.

Brown may elect to report the transaction as an installment sale because payments received in the year of sale ($25,000) do not exceed 30% of the $100,000 sales price. (Since the $40,000 mortgage assumed by the buyer does not exceed Brown's basis for the property sold, no part of that mortgage is treated as payment received in the year of sale.)

Here is how Brown determines the portion of the gain reportable each year under the installment method of reporting.

The gain on the sale is $35,400, determined as follows.

Sales price		$100,000
Less: Adjusted basis	$59,600	
Sales commissions	5,000	
		64,600
Gain		$ 35,400

The contract price is $60,000, determined as follows.

Sales price	$100,000
Less: Mortgage assumed by buyer payable to third party	40,000
Contract price	$ 60,000

The gain is 59% of the contract price ($35,400 divided by $60,000).

In the year of sale, Brown received payments totalling $25,000. He reports 59% of the $25,000 or $14,750 as gain in the year of sale.

In each of the succeeding seven years, Brown will receive $5,000 as principal payment on the $35,000 second mortgage. Each year, Brown will report as gain on the sale $2,950 (59% of $5,000). The interest received each year will be reported separately as ordinary income.

Recapitulation Including the year of sale, Brown is to receive total payments of $60,000. (The remaining $40,000 of the sales price will be paid by the buyer to the mortgagee under the mortgage assumed by the buyer.) His total gain is $35,400. Under the installment method of reporting here is how the gain is reported over the years of collection.

Year	Payment Received	Taxable Gain
1	$25,000	$14,750
2	5,000	2,950
3	5,000	2,950
4	5,000	2,950
5	5,000	2,950
6	5,000	2,950
7	5,000	2,950
8	5,000	2,950
Totals	$60,000	$35,400

How installment sales gains are taxed

We have seen how to determine the gain on an installment sale and how to spread the gain over the years of collection. But does the fact that installment sale reporting is used affect the nature of the gain: that is, if the gain, but for installment sale reporting, would have been a long-term capital gain, are the gains reported in the subsequent years treated as capital gains?

The answer is yes. The nature of the gain is determined at the time of the sale. If under the rules previously discussed, the gain is a long-term capital gain, in each year that a part of the gain is reported that portion of the gain is treated as a long-term capital gain.

187

What happens if part of the gain is subject to depreciation recapture? As explained beginning at page 175, where there is depreciation recapture, part of the gain on the sale may be taxed as ordinary income.

To explain the treatment of depreciation recapture when the installment method is used, refer back to Example 2. The gain on the sale Brown reported was $35,400. Let us assume that of that gain, $15,000 was depreciation recapture. That means that $15,000 of the gain will be taxable as ordinary income and $20,400 will be taxable as capital gain.

Government Regulations provide that where the gain is reported using the installment method, the first amounts of gain reportable are all attributed to the depreciation recapture. After the depreciation recapture has been accounted for, the balance of the gain can be reported as capital gain.

So in Example 2, since $14,750 of gain is reported in the year of sale and that is less than the total $15,000 of depreciation recapture, the entire $14,750 would be reported as ordinary income in the year of sale. In the second year, $2,950 of the gain is reportable. Since $250 of the $15,000 depreciation recapture is still to be reported, $250 of the $2,950 gain will be reported as ordinary income in the second year and the remaining $2,700 of gain will be reportable as long-term capital gain. In the third through the eighth years, the full $2,950 gain reported each year will be reported as long-term capital gain because the entire depreciation recapture will have been accounted for in previous years.

Advantages of installment reporting

The tax cost of the gain is matched to the collections. In other words, the taxpayer does not have to pay out cash in the form of taxes before actually receiving the payments in which his gain is included.

The time value of money is demonstrated. To the extent that the taxpayer can defer the payment of the tax, he has the use of the tax money at no interest cost for the period of deferral.

To the extent that the gain is spread over a number of years, it may be subject to lower marginal tax rates than if the entire gain were reported in one year. This is obviously true to the extent the gain is reportable as ordinary income (i.e. depreciation recapture). It may also be true as to the capital gains.

If the taxpayer uses the regular method of reporting capital gains, one-half of the gain is included in ordinary income. By spreading the gain over a number of years, the amount of the gain included each year may be subject to lower marginal rates than the marginal that would apply if the entire gain were included in one year.

If the taxpayer may use the alternative tax, only a maximum of $50,000 in one year is subject to the flat 25% alternative tax. If the gain is very substantial, spreading the gain over a number of years may entitle the entire gain to be taxed at the 25% rate whereas including the entire gain in income in one year may bring the $50,000 ceiling into play, causing the gain in excess of $50,000 to be taxed at rates higher than 25%.

One-half of the long-term capital gains reported each year become items of tax preference (see page 102). To the extent that the total of the items of tax preference in one year exceed the sum of the tax for that year plus $30,000, the excess is subject to a 10% tax. By spreading the gain over a number of years, the amount added to the items of tax preference is spread over those years and reduces the probability of the 10% tax.

Deferred payment sales

Although the most common method of deferring the tax on sales in which payment is deferred is the installment sale, there are other methods available when the installment method is not (as when the 30% test cannot be met).

The income tax Regulations permit sellers of real estate, as an alternative to the accrual method of accounting, to include in the year of sale as proceeds from the sale the cash or other consideration received plus the market value of any evidences of indebtedness received (generally mortgage notes). Thus, if the market value of these notes, etc. is less than their face amounts, the difference is deferred until collection.

Example

Assume that the taxpayer sells his property for $100,000, receiving $40,000 in cash in the year of sale plus mortgage notes totalling $60,000. His adjusted basis and selling costs amount to $70,000. His gain is $30,000.

Because he has received more than 30% of the selling price in the year of sale, he cannot use the installment sale method of reporting. However, assume that the fair market value of the mortgage notes is only $50,000 (that is what he could get for them if he tried to sell them). In that case, the seller may take into account in the year of sale the actual value of the notes instead of their face value. This has the effect of treating the sales price as only $90,000 ($40,000 cash plus $50,000 value of the notes) and reducing the taxable gain in the year of sale to $20,000.

Assume that the $60,000 face amount of the notes is to be paid to the seller at the rate of $6,000 a year for 10 years. In each year subsequent to the year of sale, as the seller receives the $6,000 due that year, he will have $1,000 of gain (since he had only included $5,000 of each $6,000 face amount of notes in his income in the year of sale).

Under the deferred payment sales method, the deferred part of the gain may have to be reported as ordinary income. This may occur even though, had the entire gain been reported in the year of sale, the entire gain would have been capital gain.

In the illustration, the $20,000 gain reported in the year of sale would be reported as a capital gain if it was from the sale of a capital or Section 1231 asset. But the $1,000 gain on collection of the notes in each of the succeeding taxable years would have to be reported as ordinary income if the buyer, whose notes they were, was an individual. If the buyer were a corporation or a government (or political subdivision) then the $1,000 gains in the 10 years following the year of sale would also be reported as capital gains.

Sale for a "bare contractual promise"

When a deferred payment sale is made, the buyer's obligations received have an ascertainable value, even though that value is less than the face amount of the obligations. In the example, we assumed that the obligations received that had a face amount of $60,000 had a market value of $50,000. But that was a certain value, $50,000. In that case, the value of the notes was added to the cash received to arrive at the total sales price. In other words, there had occurred what is called a "closed" transaction. The gain computed was the difference between the value **189** of what was received less the adjusted basis of the property sold. If more than the value taken into account in determining the gain in the year of sale was subsequently received, that extra amount was considered ordinary income (except in the case of a corporate obligation).

But suppose it is impossible to value the buyer's obligations. In the jargon of the tax fraternity, suppose the buyer's promise to pay has an "unascertainable value." In that case, the disposition of the property has occurred in an "open" transaction. In that case, the amount of gain or, sometimes, even the existence of a gain cannot be determined in the year of sale. The rule for an open transaction is that cash payments are applied to reduce basis. After basis is recovered, anything received is gain. And if the gain (were it all realized in the year of the sale) would be a capital gain, all gain realized, as it is realized over a period of years as collections in excess of basis come in, is treated as capital gain.

Example

Brown sells property for $100,000 which has an adjusted basis to him of $60,000. Had he received the entire $100,000 in the year of sale, he would have had a $40,000 long-term capital gain. However, he only received $50,000 in the year of sale and $10,000 a year during the next five years. Assume that the buyer's promise to pay the $50,000 over the succeeding five years has no ascertainable value.

In the year of sale, Brown would report no gain. He would merely treat the $50,000 received as a return of his basis.

In the following year, Brown receives $10,000. This, too, would be treated as a recovery of his basis. At this point, Brown will have recovered his entire $60,000 basis.

In each of the following four years, Brown receives $10,000. In each of those four years, he would report a long-term capital gain of $10,000.

When does the buyer's promise to pay have an unascertainable value? The IRS takes the position that the case is rare indeed when the buyer's promise to pay has an unascertainable value. However, several courts have held that a bare contractual promise to pay by an individual buyer of real estate (i.e. no negotiable notes or mortgages are given by the buyer) has an unascertainable value. (If the buyer's contract could be discounted at a bank, for example, it still would have an ascertainable value.) As could be expected, IRS has announced that it will not follow these court decisions. Hence, the use of this approach of reporting the gain on a sale where an individual buyer merely agrees contractually to pay the balance may require litigation to sustain the taxpayer's position.

Sale and leaseback

A sale and leaseback describes a transaction in which the owner of the property sells the property and immediately leases it back from the new owner. Consequently, during the term of the lease, the seller-lessee's physical relationship to the property remains unchanged.

A sale and leaseback transaction is often looked upon as a financing transaction. In other words, it is often a substitute for refinancing by the owner via a new mortgage. There is one major difference between a sale-leaseback and a mortgage: at the end of the lease term the former owner (now lessee) loses possession of the property; in the case of a mortgage, he retains the property. Consequently, the residual value of the property (the value at the end of the lease term) is an important factor in comparing the economic results of sales-leasebacks and mortgages.

In this section we are primarily concerned with the tax consequences to the seller-lessee. The tax consequences, of course, weigh heavily in calculating the net financial results of the transaction.

Tax consequences

Two distinct transactions are involved.

Upon the sale, the seller realizes gain or loss in the same manner as upon any other sale. The tax consequences are the same as for any other sale; possible Section 1231 gain or loss, possible depreciation recapture.

Upon becoming a lessee, the former owner pays rent for the occupancy rights to the property. Normally, rent is a fully deductible expense for tax purposes, assuming that the property is used in the lessee's trade or business (including the business of holding the property for rent to others).

The foregoing are the general tax rules that apply to a sale-leaseback. There are, however, a number of problems that can arise which may modify these rules.

Lease term for 30 years or more　If the lease term is for 30 years or more, IRS says the lease itself is property of a like-kind to other real estate. Hence, the sale-leaseback is to be treated as a tax-deferred exchange. Since, in a sale-leaseback, the seller usually receives cash, if the result of the sale-leaseback is a gain, even if it is deemed to be a like-kind exchange, the gain would be taxable to the extent of the cash received.

The difficulty arises if the sale portion of the sale-leaseback results in a loss. In that case, if the IRS view prevails and a 30-year lease is treated as like-kind property, the loss would not be recognized for tax purposes.

The courts have sustained the IRS view in some cases and the safer approach (when there is a loss) is to use a lease term of less than 30 years. In this respect, it should also be noted that a shorter lease term with a renewal term that is not realistic (either in length of time or greatly reduced rent) may cause the IRS to attempt to combine the lease terms for the purposes of its 30-year rule.

Repurchase option　As has been pointed out, one of the unfavorable aspects of the sale-leaseback (from the seller's viewpoint) is that, as lessee, he loses the property at the end of the lease term.

To overcome that objection to the sale-leaseback, the seller may be given an option to reacquire the property at the termination of the lease. The difficulty with this arrangement, from a tax viewpoint, is that it may upset the treatment of the lease as a lease. If, for example, the seller-lessee may reacquire the property at the end of the lease term for a nominal payment, IRS will likely contend that the arrangement was not a lease from the outset but that it was merely a financing arrangement similar to a mortgage. In that case, the rental deductions the lessee expected each year would be disallowed. Instead, the lessee would be allowed that portion of his "rent" payments that represented a reasonable interest rate on borrowed money as a deduction. He would, in that case, also be entitled to depreciation deductions (since he would be considered the owner of the property).

To avoid having the lease treated as a loan, any repurchase option contained in the arrangement must call for a purchase price that can be sustained as representing the fair market value of the property at the time the lease expires. A repurchase price to be determined by professional appraisers at the time of the repurchase is probably one satisfactory approach. Other reasonable approaches that would result in an equivalent of an arm's-length purchase price at the end of the lease term may be used.

"Tax arithmetic" of leasebacks

Owners of property are entitled to depreciation deductions and deductions for interest paid. Lessees are entitled to tax deductions for rent paid.

The owner of property, finding that his depreciation deductions are declining (e.g. where he uses accelerated depreciation methods), recognizing that the portion of his' basis allocable to the underlying land is non-depreciable for tax purposes and yet aware of the fact that the value of his property has increased looks to convert that appreciation into cash for use in his business or for further investment. If he sells the property, he realizes the appreciation but loses the use of the property (which he may need in his business; a factory or warehouse, for example). If he refinances, he may not be able to borrow as much as he can realize on the sale. A sale-leaseback may give him the best of both possible worlds (however, the loss of the property at the end of the lease term should not be overlooked).

In comparing the refinancing via a mortgage and a sale-leaseback in terms of tax consequences, it is simple enough to make after-tax cash comparisons.

The sale-leaseback Assuming that the sale is made at a gain, the seller will have a cash amount equal to the sales price minus selling costs and the tax on the gain. The "cost" of this after-tax cash is the net cash outlay of the rental payments over the term of the lease. Since the rent payments constitute tax deductions, the net cash outlay is the difference between the rent called for in the lease and tax saved by the deductibility of the rent (the amount of the rent multiplied by the taxpayer's marginal rate).

The total after-tax outlay for rent over the lease term will likely exceed the net after-tax cash realized on the sale. Thus, in that sense, the sale-leaseback is financing. However, the additional cost of after-tax cash on the sale is the loss of the property at the end of the lease term.

One other point to be made regarding the sale-leaseback is that without the sale-leaseback, the owner's depreciation deductions are limited in total to his basis in the improvements (land is non-depreciable). After the sale and leaseback, he has realized the proceeds from the sale of both the land and improvements and is paying rent on both. To that extent, he has converted the non-depreciable land into an investment amortizable over the life of the lease.

Mortgage financing If instead of selling and leasing back, the owner seeks to refinance, he needs to obtain a loan that is equal to the after-tax proceeds of the sale (in the sale-leaseback) to have the same cash availability at that point.

Assuming that the mortgage term is as long as the lease term, the after-tax cash outlay over the same period in repaying the loan may be compared with the after-tax cash outlay for the rents.

In determining the after-tax cash outlay, it is recognized that principal payments on the loan are not tax deductible. However, the interest payments are deductible for income tax purposes thereby reducing the effective cash outlay for the interest. Furthermore, when the mortgage financing route is used, the borrower continues to own the property and is, therefore, entitled to depreciation deductions. These deductions do not require a cash outlay but reduce taxable income and the cash required for tax payments. Hence, in determining the total cash outlay over the mortgage term (in order to compare it with the total net cash outlay over the lease term were a sale-leaseback employed), it is proper to subtract from the total of the principal and interest payments to be made over that period the tax savings arising from the deductibility of both the interest payments and the depreciation on the property.

Other dispositions of property

In addition to the more conventional types of disposition of property, there are a number of less usual types of disposition which have special tax consequences.

Involuntary conversions

A disposition of property can arise involuntarily, as when property is condemned by a governmental body or when property is destroyed by fire or other casualty. Gain or loss may then arise. The condemnation award or insurance proceeds are compared to the basis of the property converted to determine the gain or loss. Typically, the gain or loss is treated in the same manner for tax purposes as would the gain or loss on the sale of the property. Tax on the gain may be deferred, however, if reinvestment in similar property is made to a sufficient extent and within a prescribed time. The rules for tax deferral when there is an involuntary conversion are detailed on page 130.

Demolition

Existing structures may be demolished to make room for other structures. The tax treatment of the loss resulting from the demolition depends on the owner's intentions at the time the property was acquired. If there was no intent to demolish at the time of acquisition, subsequent demolition results in an ordinary loss for tax purposes. If there was an intent to demolish at the time of acquisition, all "losses" resulting from demolition become part of the basis of the land. Further details on the tax treatment of demolitions will be found on page 161.

Gifts and charitable contributions

One method of disposing of property is to give it away. A gift may be made to a family member as part of an estate plan or it may be contributed to a charitable organization. There are many tax factors involved in either type of disposition; estate and income taxes may be saved and capital gains may be avoided.

The planning methods and tax consequences of these types of dispositions are examined in detail in two special appendices devoted to this topic. See pages 321 and 326.

Corporate liquidations and reorganizations

Because a corporation is an entity separate from its shareholders (the owners), a disposition of corporate property may create a double tax in the process of getting the sales proceeds into the hands of the shareholders. This double tax may be avoided in some instances by employing one of several methods of liquidating the corporation. (In some cases, although one of the two taxes is avoided, it may not be possible to use installment sale reporting.) In other cases, it may be possible to avoid all taxes and convert the shareholders' equity in the corporation into equity in a larger corporation with more diversified holding (somewhat equivalent to a tax-deferred exchange) by going through a corporate reorganization.

The liquidation and reorganization routes require compliance with a number of technical tax rules (as well as compliance with the requisite state corporation laws). The tax advantages and pitfalls of liquidations and reorganizations and descriptions of the various tax rules that must be met are set forth in a special appendix. See page 312.

Chapter 11

Exchanges

11

Exchanging real estate, rather than selling it outright and reinvesting the proceeds, generally stems from two different motivations.

First, exchanging properties is a method of marketing real estate when a sale does not appear to be possible because of a number of reasons, including the following.

Buyers with cash are not available.

A sale on "terms" does not give the seller sufficient funds with which to acquire another property.

The seller will not price his property realistically so that it will attract a purchaser.

Second, and probably the most important motivating force for exchanging property, is the available income tax deferral. That is, the capital gains tax that would normally be paid on the gain from the sale may be postponed or even avoided in full or in part.

The following example dramatically illustrates why the tax deferral is such an important motivation for an exchange.

Assume Wilson, a married man filing a joint return, has a property with a market value of $100,000. His adjusted basis for the property is $10,000. In 1975, if he sold the property for $100,000 cash, he would have a capital gain of $90,000. The capital gains tax on $90,000 (assuming Wilson's ordinary taxable income is $52,000) is about $26,000. Hence, he would only have $74,000 to reinvest ($100,000 sales price minus $26,000 tax.)

Were he to exchange, he would receive property worth $100,000 and so could have the full $100,000 of the value of his present property reinvested. Thus, a tax-free exchange would preserve $26,000 of his capital. Assuming a 10% capitalization rate on his investment, the $26,000 would produce $2,600 per year of ordinary income. Consequently a tax deferral for ten years, for example, would build up a gain for the investor of $52,000, the $26,000 of capital preserved via the tax-free exchange plus the $26,000 return on that investment (at 10% per year).

The balance of this chapter is devoted to a discussion of exchanges in terms of the second motivating factor, i.e. tax deferral.

Before discussing the rules of tax deferral in detail, it is important to keep in mind that the sale at a taxable gain coupled with a reinvestment in another property has the effect of stepping up basis. In an exchange, however, essentially (subject to adjustments discussed later) the basis of the property given up becomes the basis of the property acquired. Consequently, a question presents itself: is the property owner better off selling, paying a capital gains tax and reinvesting to get a higher basis and larger depreciation deductions in the future or will he fare better by avoiding current taxation via a tax-deferred exchange and forego larger depreciation deductions in the future?

The tax dollars saved currently by going through a tax deferred exchange rather than realizing a capital gain could easily be calculated. This amount could then be compared to the total of the discounted values of the future tax savings that would arise from additional depreciation deductions that would be available had there been a sale and reinvestment in property with a higher adjusted basis.

There cannot be one pat answer to the question of exchanging or selling and re-investing. Differing results with the same properties could be obtained by tax-payers with different marginal tax rates. Hence, individual calculations should be made.

Since the current values of future tax savings are, at best, a good guess (future tax rates can change or the taxpayer's other income streams may be altered thus in-creasing or decreasing his marginal rate), many investors prefer the "bird in the hand" of a current tax saving via a tax-deferred exchange. Be that as it may, the value of future tax savings via larger depreciation deductions (when basis is stepped up through a sale and reinvestment) is mentioned here so that at least it may be considered among all of the other factors in determining whether to ex-change or sell outright.

Whenever a decision to exchange is made, it is then important to follow the rules set forth in the balance of this chapter.

Tax law requirements for tax-deferred exchanges

Section 1031 of the Internal Revenue Code provides that when certain property is exchanged for other property, some or all of the gain which is *realized* economi-cally may not have to be *recognized* for tax purposes.

Example

Davidson has a property which is worth $100,000. His adjusted basis for that property is only $40,000. If he sells that property for its value, he will *realize* a gain of $60,000. If he sells for cash, that gain will also be *recognized* for tax purposes: he would have to pay tax on a gain of $60,000. If, instead, he exchanged it for another property worth $100,000, he would still realize a gain of $60,000 but that gain would not be recognized for tax purposes; that is, he would pay no tax be-cause of that transaction.

This example illustrates the difference between gain which is *realized* and that which is *recognized*. "Realized" is an economic concept, how much gain actually resulted from the transaction. "Recognized" is a tax concept, how much gain (if any) is taxable.

Section 1031 provides that no gain or loss is to be recognized, i.e. taxed, if certain business or investment property is exchanged solely for property of a like-kind which is also to be held for use in business or as an investment. To the extent that the exchange is not *solely* for like-kind property, some of the gain might be recognized; the balance of the gain may still be deferred. A more thorough discus-

sion of these terms and some detailed illustrations are presented.

It is important to note that the provisions of Section 1031 are not discretionary with the taxpayer or with the government. *If a transaction fits within the statutory requirements, no gain or loss is recognized.*

It should be made clear that when a transaction is described as tax-free in this discussion, it does not necessarily mean that the gain escapes taxation completely. What is meant is that the tax on the gain is deferred or postponed. Since the appreciation in the original property is not recognized for tax purposes, it does not increase the basis of the new property.

Example

A owns a parcel of land with a market value of $50,000 and a basis of $10,000. He exchanges it for another piece of land which is also worth $50,000. A's basis for the new land acquired is $10,000, the same as his basis for the land he gave up. There is no tax on this exchange. But if some years later A should sell the second parcel of land for $50,000, he would have a $40,000 recognized gain *at that time*. Consequently, the effect of Section 1031 on that exchange was to defer the $40,000 taxable gain until the subsequent disposition; it did not eliminate the gain forever.

Of course, a tax deferral is very valuable. As was illustrated in a prior example (where the tax of $26,000 was deferred), the deferral permitted the accumulation of an additional $26,000 of income over a 10-year period. Looking at it another way whenever a tax can be deferred, in effect, money is borrowed from the U.S. Treasury without interest. (And, should an individual die without having disposed of the property in a taxable transaction, that deferred income tax will never have to be paid. When property is inherited, the basis to the heirs is the market value of that property on the date of the owner's death; see page 120.)

Elements required for Section 1031 exchange

In order to qualify for non-recognition of gain or loss on an exchange under this section, certain elements must be present.

1. Both the property received and the property given up must be held either for productive use in a trade or business or for investment. Specifically excluded from the kinds of property that are benefitted by this section are stock in trade or other property primarily held for sale (inventory), stocks, bonds, notes, choses in action, certificates of trust or beneficial interest or any other securities or evidences of indebtedness or interests.

2. To qualify, both properties must be of a *like-kind* to each other, that is, the nature or character of both properties must be alike.

3. Finally, the properties must be *exchanged* for each other.

Property used in a trade or business   Property held for productive use in a trade or business means precisely what it says. Thus it may include any kind of property which is used in the taxpayer's trade or business, e.g. machinery, office equipment, automobiles, factory buildings and land on which the building is situated. Property held for rental purposes, an apartment house or office building, is property used in a trade or business.

Held for investment   This is property held for appreciation in value (and for the income therefrom) and not held for resale or in business. Since rental property (which is held for income) is defined as trade or business property, in terms of real estate, property held for investment is generally limited to vacant land. However, since property used in a trade or business also qualifies for a Section 1031 exchange, the distinction between trade or business property and investment property has no particular significance in terms of tax-free exchanges of real estate.

Like-kind This concept relates to the nature of the property rather than its grade or quality. Improved real estate is considered to be of the same nature as unimproved real estate. They are both of a like-kind. The fact of improvement or unimprovement relates only to the grade or quality of the property and not to its kind or class. For this purpose, real estate is considered to be the same kind of property as a leasehold for real estate if the leasehold has 30 years or more to run.

Property used in a trade or business may be exchanged for other property used in a trade or business or may be exchanged for investment property. Similarly, property held for investment may be exchanged for other investment property or may be exchanged for property used in a trade or business.

The following exchanges are illustrations of like-kind properties permitted to be exchanged: city real estate for a ranch or farm; a truck for a truck; a vacant lot for land and building; and a leasehold for real estate with 30 or more years to run for a parcel of real estate owned outright.

The fact that a taxpayer *pays* cash or some other type of non-qualifying type of property in addition to the property he gives up as part of the exchange will not destroy the tax-free nature of the transaction. It is only the *receipt* of such non-qualifying property which may cause all or part of the transaction to be taxable.

Requirement of exchange To enable the gain to be deferred under Section 1031, the property must be exchanged. Care must be taken to avoid a sale and a purchase when an exchange is intended.

For example, in one court case, Development Company wanted to buy some farmland from Rancher. Rancher did not want to sell but would exchange if Development could find suitable property for Rancher. Such property was found. The plan was for Development Company to purchase the new property and then exchange it with Rancher for the property that Development wanted to buy from him. In order to avoid duplication in transfer deeds and possibly some real estate transfer tax, the new property that Development had purchased was transferred directly to Rancher instead of first to Development and then to Rancher. The court held the transaction to be a sale by Rancher of his property, not an exchange. A tax-free transaction was thus converted into a taxable one. The form of the transaction governed.

Disqualification from Section 1031

At this point it is advisable to examine more closely those attributes of a transaction which will disqualify it from non-recognition treatment of Section 1031.

First is the nature of the property *received* in exchange for that given up. If the property received is not the same kind as that given up, the transaction will not qualify under Section 1031. If the property received is totally cash, notes, stocks, bonds, inventory or any of the other kinds of property referred to on page 197 which are specifically excluded from the beneficial treatment accorded by the section, the transaction will not qualify.

The exclusion of inventory-type property prevents a real estate dealer from exchanging any of his *real estate inventory* under the umbrella of Section 1031. (For a detailed discussion of when one is deemed to be a real estate dealer and when a dealer may be holding property for investment rather than as inventory see page 172.)

Both the property received as well as that given up must have been held either (1) for productive use in a trade or business or (2) for investment. Thus, property which is held for personal use, such as an automobile or a yacht, does not qualify. Similarly if the property received is immediately resold or exchanged, an inference is created that the property received is not acquired for investment or for use in business but for the purpose of resale. This could destroy the tax-free nature of the transaction.

So, too, when the property received is not the same kind as that given up, the exchange will not qualify. Thus if investment real estate is exchanged for factory machinery, the exchange would not qualify because real estate is not the same kind of property as factory machinery which is personal property.

Computation of indicated gain

As has been shown above, the presence of unlike property in the exchange may cause some gain to be taxed. Before the amount of gain that will be taxed can be determined, it is necessary to compute the amount of gain *realized* on the exchange. Another term used for "realized" gain is "indicated" gain. Both mean the amount of gain that the property owner would have had if the property was sold rather than exchanged.

Example

Simon has a parcel which has an adjusted basis to him of $6,000 and a fair market value of $10,000. If he were to sell it for cash, his realized gain would be $4,000.

Market value (cash received)	$10,000
Adjusted basis	6,000
Realized (indicated) gain	$ 4,000

If Mr. Simon had exchanged his parcel for another one which also had a fair market value of $10,000, the computation and the result would be precisely the same. So the indicated gain may be computed by taking the difference between the adjusted basis of the property transferred and its fair market value. This is so because the total of what is received in exchange (net equity in real estate, cash, other property, etc.) will normally have a market value equal to the total of what is given up.

Effect of receipt of unlike property

It is a rare situation when two or more properties being exchanged will have identical equities. Before the exchange is made the equities must be balanced.

The equity in a property is its market value less any encumbrances on it. Thus if property A has a market value of $50,000 and first mortgage of $10,000 on it, the equity in that property is $40,000. If property B has a market value of $150,000 with a mortgage of $110,000, it, too, has an equity of $40,000. Thus on the basis of equal equities, these two properties can be exchanged even-up; each side is giving up $40,000 of equity and receiving $40,000 of equity. **199**

Suppose we have this set of facts, however: Stone owns a property with a market value of $100,000, subject to a mortgage of $40,000. His equity is therefore $60,000. Brown's property has a market value of $80,000, subject to a mortgage of $40,000, giving him an equity of $40,000. Obviously, in this case, Stone and Brown cannot make an even exchange; the equities first must be balanced.

Brown might pay Stone $20,000 in cash *in addition* to exchanging the buildings to balance the equities. Or he might give Stone other property, a boat, a car or other property totaling in value $20,000.

Brown might give Stone promissory notes totaling $20,000. It might be in the form of a mortgage on the property Brown is acquiring from Stone in exchange.

Stone might put an additional encumbrance on his property before the exchange, borrowing another $20,000 on a second mortgage on his property, and then transferring the property to Brown subject to mortgages totaling $60,000 and thereby reducing the equity in his property to $40,000 before the exchange.

In all of these situations, the process of balancing the equities brings about a situation in which either something in addition to the exchange property passes from one party to the other or one party is relieved of a greater amount of loan on the property he is giving up than the amount of loan to which the property he is acquiring is subject. It is the presence of cash, other property or net loan relief that can produce a partial (or total) taxable gain in an exchange which is subject to Section 1031.

If, under the circumstances mentioned, some of the property received qualifies for the non-recognition treatment and some does not, realized gain will be recognized, taxed, only to the extent of the value of the unlike property. There are, generally speaking, three kinds of unlike property: cash, other unlike property (called "boot") and net mortgage (loan) relief.

The mortgage debt attached to the property given up, which the former owner will now not have to pay, is considered to be unlike property. However, a special rule applies when the former owner takes his new property also subject to a mortgage. In that case, the unlike property received is deemed to be only the *net* loan relief; the two mortgages are netted and unlike property is considered to have been received only to the extent the mortgage on the property given up exceeds the mortgage on the property received. These rules apply regardless of whether the mortgage is assumed or the property received is merely taken subject to the mortgage with no personal liability assumed; it makes no difference.

Example

Assume Arthur and Baker wish to exchange their properties. Prior to the exchange, the pertinent facts concerning each property are as follows.

Arthur		Baker
$50,000	Market value	$70,000
30,000	Mortgages on property	40,000
20,000	Equity	30,000

Since Baker's equity is greater than Arthur's by $10,000 on the exchange, Arthur will also pay Baker $10,000 cash. Each will acquire the other's property subject to mortgages on the properties. On the exchange, Baker will be relieved of a

$40,000 mortgage and acquire a property subject to a $30,000 mortgage. So he will have net loan relief of $10,000. In addition, he will receive $10,000 cash. Hence, he will have received $20,000 of unlike property. Arthur will have an *increased* loan and will *pay* $10,000 cash. Hence, he will not have received any unlike property.

There can be situations in which one party to the exchange has net loan relief but also pays cash. In that case, he may reduce the net loan relief by the cash paid in determining the net unlike property received. On the other hand, if he *receives* cash and also assumes a greater loan than he gives up, he *may not* reduce the amount of cash received by the increase in his loan burden. Hence, the full amount of the cash received will be treated as unlike property in determining the amount of the recognized gain.

Effect of transaction costs   Transaction costs, brokerage commissions paid on the transfers, excise taxes on deeds, etc. are considered reductions of the proceeds of the sale and thereby reduce the indicated gain. They then become part of the basis of the property acquired in the exchange.

IRS has ruled that cash paid for transaction costs is to be treated as cash paid in the exchange transaction. Therefore, the IRS ruling provides that the transaction cost paid in cash reduces any cash received in the exchange in calculating the amount of unlike property received. Presumably, the same logic allows for the reduction of net loan relief by the amount of the transaction costs paid in cash in determining the amount of unlike property received in the exchange.

Examples of application of exchange rules

The following examples illustrate the tax effects of exchanges, including the calculation of the recognized gain and the treatment of the giving and receiving of unlike property.

Dr. Brown owns an apartment house which has an adjusted basis of $100,000 and a market value of $220,000 but is subject to a mortgage of $80,000. Prof. Smith also owns an apartment house. His apartment house has an adjusted basis of $175,000, a market value of $250,000 and is subject to a mortgage of $150,000. Dr. Brown exchanges his apartment house for Prof. Smith's apartment house and $40,000 cash. Each apartment house was exchanged subject to the mortgage on it. Dr. Brown's realized or indicated gain would be computed as follows.

Received

Value of Prof. Smith's apartment house	$250,000
Cash	40,000
Mortgage on property given up	80,000
Total received	$370,000

Given up

Adjusted basis of old building	$100,000	
Transaction costs	16,500	
Mortgage on property received	150,000	
Total given up		266,500
Gain realized (indicated gain)		$103,500

A quick way to calculate the indicated gain is as follows.

Market value of Brown's property		$220,000
Less: Adjusted basis of his property	$100,000	
Transaction costs	16,500	116,500
Indicated gain		$103,500

A similar computation would apply to Prof. Smith.

Received

Value of Dr. Brown's property	$220,000
Mortgage on property given up	150,000
Total received	$370,000

Given up

Adjusted basis of old building	$175,000	
Transaction costs	19,000	
Cash paid to Dr. Brown	40,000	
Mortgage on property received	80,000	
Total given up		314,000
Gain realized (indicated gain)		$ 56,000

Here, too, the indicated gain for Prof. Smith can be calculated as follows.

Market value of Prof. Smith's property		$250,000
Less: Adjusted basis of his property	$175,000	
Transaction costs	19,000	194,000
Indicated gain		$ 56,000

Calculations of recognized gain Dr. Brown received $40,000 in cash. He surrendered a property with an $80,000 mortgage but acquired a property subject to a mortgage of $150,000. Hence, he had no net loan relief. Thus the only unlike property he received was the $40,000 cash. But he paid $16,500 in transaction costs, which reduces the cash received by that amount. His net unlike property received was $23,500. Since the $23,500 is less than his indicated gain of $103,500 he has a recognized (i.e. taxable) gain of $23,500.

Prof. Smith gave up property subject to a mortgage of $150,000. He acquired property subject to an $80,000 mortgage. Hence he had a loan relief of $70,000. However, he paid out in cash $40,000 to Dr. Brown and $19,000 in transaction costs. This total of $59,000, when subtracted from the $70,000 net loan relief, gives him net unlike property received of $11,000. Thus of his indicated gain of $56,000, $11,000 is recognized gain.

Losses in a Section 1031 exchange

If a transaction qualifies fully under Section 1031, that is if there is a like-kind exchange of qualifying property with no unlike property, then neither gain nor *loss* is recognized. Presence of unlike property *received* may cause some gain to be recognized but will never cause the recognition of loss.

Examples

Green exchanges his apartment house having a basis of $16,000 and a market value of $12,000 for an apartment house having a $10,000 market value plus $2,000 cash. Although Green has an indicated loss of $4,000, no part of that loss is deductible.

If, however, unlike property is *transferred*, it is possible for the transferor to realize and to deduct his loss on the unlike property that he is transferring.

Phillips exchanges investment real estate plus stock for another piece of real estate to be held for investment. The real estate given up has an adjusted basis of $10,000 and a market value of $11,000. The stock given up has a basis of $4,000 and a market value of $2,000. The real estate received has a fair market value of $13,000.

Phillips is deemed to have received a $2,000 portion of the new real estate in exchange for the stock he gave up because that is its fair market value at the time of the exchange. A loss of $2,000 is recognized on the transfer of the stock by Phillips. No gain or loss is recognized on the transfer of the real estate because that was an exchange completely within the provisions of Section 1031; no unlike property was *received* by Phillips.

Multiple exchange

It is often difficult to find two persons who are willing to exchange parcels of real estate with each other. Very often one of them will be willing to take the parcel owned by the second but the second has no desire to receive the parcel owned by the first. In such cases, sometimes a third parcel can be found which the second individual may be willing to take. Then a three-way exchange may be executed.

For Federal income tax purposes, such an exchange will still satisfy the requirements of Section 1031. Each owner will compute his realized and recognized gain in the same manner as described previously. The mechanics of the exchange may be performed as follows.

A, B, and C each hold parcels of real estate for investment purposes. They agree to exchange lots with any difference in acreage to be made up for at the rate of $100 per acre.

In the exchange, C acquires the lot owned by B, B acquires the lot owned by A and A acquires the lot owned by C. The position of the Treasury Department, expressed in *Rev. Rul. 57–244*, is that the transaction constitutes exchanges within the scope of Section 1031 and gain, if any, is recognized only to the extent of the cash received.

Note the importance of this ruling is that for Section 1031 to apply, it is *not* necessary to receive the property in an exchange from the person to whom the property is being transferred. As is demonstrated in the example, although A transferred his lot to B, he acquired the lot owned by C. In other words, only three deeds were needed to carry out the transaction: A gave the deed to his land to B, B gave the deed to his land to C and C gave the deed to his land to A.

There may be a practical difficulty with the three-way exchange as described here: the difficulty of documentation. Not all exchanges are "text book" exchanges with all of the parties to the entire multiple exchange sitting around one table. The multiplicity of the exchange is usually developed by the broker who, after analyzing a number of different situations, is able to put together a multiple exchange for

203

the benefit of all of the parties concerned. Consequently, a round-robin deeding of property, as described in the preceding paragraph, may not always be practical. (And where it is practical, it may be a good idea to have all the parties sign a document indicating that an exchange took place as described so that on a future tax examination, any one of the three parties can document the entire transaction.)

An alternative to the use of only three deeds, where for practical reasons not all the parties are available to do the direct deeding as would be required, is to follow a procedure such as this. (1) A deeds his property to B and B deeds his property to A. (2) B then deeds the property he acquired from A to C and C deeds his property to B. This arrangement clearly indicates that exchanges were made. The difficulty with this type of arrangement is that B will not have a tax-free exchange on his acquisition of A's property because he has not acquired it for use in his trade or business or for investment (he has acquired it for the purpose of exchanging it). Of course, if B wants to "cash out," i.e. really sell his property, it makes no difference to him because he expected to have a taxable transaction. However, if he, too, wants a tax-free exchange, in order to follow the deeding procedure described in this paragraph, a fourth party (probably the broker) would have to get involved. He would act as a conduit; the various parties would transfer properties to him and he would exchange with the other parties. Thus, A, B and C would deed their properties to D (the broker); D would then deed the A property to C, the B property to A and the C property to B.

Items which affect basis in an exchange

As pointed out, the reason there is really only a tax deferral as a result of an exchange is that, generally, basis of the old property carries over to the new. Adjustments have to be made, however, for the unlike property that passed in the exchange, the payment of transaction costs and the recognition of some gain in many cases. Just how is the adjusted basis of the property acquired in an exchange computed?

If the gain on a transaction escapes recognition for tax purposes, the tax result is often that the new piece of property, the property received, will be penalized by having a basis that is less than its fair market value by the amount of non-recognized or non-taxed gain. Conversely, to maintain the symmetry of the tax concepts, any loss which is not recognized will have the effect of increasing the basis of the property received.

Before the basis of the property received can be calculated, certain items of information must be known. These items and their effects on the basis of the property acquired are considered in the following.

First, we need to know the adjusted basis of the property which is being transferred, that is, the basis of the old property at the time of the exchange (including addition of transaction costs paid). To that amount add the amount of cash paid, the market value of any unlike property transferred, the amount of the mortgage on the new property received and the amount of any gain which is recognized on the transaction because of unlike property received. From the total of all those items will be subtracted the amounts of loans on the property which is being given up, cash received and the fair market value of any unlike property which is received. A tabular form of the computation appears in the following excerpt from the Exchange Basis Adjustment form of the REALTORS® National Marketing Institute (RNMI).

Transfer of Basis

18	Adjusted Basis (L2) Plus (L3)*											
19	Plus: New Loans (L11)											
20	Plus: Cash or Boot Paid (L9)											
21	Plus: Recognized Gain (L17)											
22	Total Additions											
23	Less Old Loans (L10)											
24	Less: Cash or Boot Received (L8)											
25	NEW ADJUSTED BASIS											

* Basis of property given up plus transaction costs.

Technique of adjusting basis in an exchange

At this point it is appropriate to see how this computation works with actual numbers. We will use the Dr. Brown and Prof. Smith exchange on page 201 in computing the gain realized and the gain recognized. Thus we will round out the picture by showing how the realized and recognized gains with the adjustments to the basis of the property acquired in a Section 1031 exchange.

Dr. Brown would have a basis of $170,000 for the property he received. The computation of his new basis is as follows.

Transfer of Basis

18	Adjusted Basis (L2) Plus (L3)*	116 500								
19	Plus: New Loans (L11)	150 000								
20	Plus: Cash or Boot Paid (L9)									
21	Plus: Recognized Gain (L17)	23 500								
22	Total Additions	290 000								
23	Less Old Loans (L10)	80 000								
24	Less: Cash or Bbot Received (L8)	40 000								
25	NEW ADJUSTED BASIS	170 000								

* Basis of property given up plus transaction costs.

A similar computation would be made to determine the basis that the property, formerly held by Dr. Brown, now held by Prof. Smith would have to him. His computation would be as follows.

Transfer of Basis

18	Adjusted Basis (L2) Plus (L3)*	194 000								
19	Plus: New Loans (L11)	80 000								
20	Plus: Cash or Boot Paid (L9)	40 000								
21	Plus: Recognized Gain (L17)	11 000								
22	Total Additions	325 000								
23	Less Old Loans (L10)	150 000								
24	Less: Cash or Boot Received (L8)									
25	NEW ADJUSTED BASIS	175 000								

* Basis of property given up plus transaction costs.

If we now examine the situation after the new basis computations have been made, we can see the net effect of what has happened. Dr. Brown acquired an apartment house with a value of $250,000. In the process he benefited from a non-recognized gain of $80,000. Remember that only $23,500 gain was recognized out of his total realized (indicated) gain of $103,500. Therefore, the basis for his new property is $170,000, which is the same as the value of the property acquired ($250,000) minus the portion of the gain that was not recognized ($80,000).

Similarly, Prof. Smith acquired an apartment house with a market value of $220,000. His non-recognized gain was $45,000 ($56,000 indicated gain minus $11,000 recognized gain). His basis for the property acquired ($175,000) is equal to the value of the property acquired ($220,000) less the non-recognized gain ($45,000).

From this it should become apparent that the penalty for the benefit of being able to defer gain is a decrease in basis below the market value of the parcel received by the amount of the gain which is deferred.

Increases in basis for depreciation

It may be noticed from the example that it is possible for basis to be built up, actually increased, as a result of an exchange. Dr. Brown started with a parcel having an adjusted basis of $100,000. When he was finished he had a parcel, of greater value, with a basis of $170,000. That increase of $70,000 was due largely to the increase in mortgage liability attributable to his new parcel.

Thus, it is possible to increase the basis of a property which is subject to depreciation and thereby gain the advantage of additional depreciation deductions reducing taxable income without the expenditure of cash. What can be accomplished by this method is an increase in the leverage factor and the value of his investment.

Example

Green owns a property with a market value of $100,000 which has a mortgage of $20,000 and an adjusted basis of $45,000. He holds that parcel for the production of rental income; therefore it is property used in a trade or business. He exchanges it for another rental building which is worth $150,000 and has a mortgage of $70,000. The equity in each building is therefore $80,000.

Green has a tax-free exchange under Section 1031. No gain is recognized because he has received no cash, no other property and no net mortgage relief. But what about his basis for the property received? It is as follows.

Basis of property given up	$ 45,000
Add: Amount of loan on property received	70,000
Total	$115,000
Subtract: Loan on property given up	20,000
Basis of property received	$ 95,000

(Transaction costs have been omitted to simplify the example.)

As indicated, Green had increased the value of the property he holds from a $100,000 parcel to a $150,000 parcel. He has also increased his basis for depreciation from $45,000 to $95,000. And he hasn't paid out any cash.

Allocation of basis between land and buildings Another possibility for increasing the basis of property subject to the allowance for depreciation arises from the requirement that basis be allocated between land (which is not depreciable) and building (which is depreciable). This is discussed in detail on page 118.

This principle can be applied to a common situation where the adjusted basis of a building has been reduced because of depreciation deductions to such a point that it is far below the basis for the land and the relative market values are such that the building is worth considerably more than the land. When two such situations exist, an exchange of the properties can result in a dramatic increase in the basis for depreciation of both buildings.

Assume that Smith and Green each owns land and buildings having a value in excess of basis, as follows.

	Adjusted Basis	Market Value	
		$	%
Smith			
Land	$40,000	$ 40,000	$33\frac{1}{3}$
Building	10,000	80,000	$66\frac{2}{3}$
	$50,000	$120,000	100%
Green			
Land	$30,000	$ 30,000	25
Building	30,000	90,000	75
	$60,000	$120,000	100%

If Green and Smith should exchange properties, here are the tax results (ignoring transaction costs).

Smith's basis for the total property acquired from Green would be $50,000. But he can allocate that basis between the acquired land and building according to their relative market values. Since 75% of the fair market value of the property acquired from Green is attributable to the building, Smith can allocate $37,500 of his $50,000 basis to the building and the remaining $12,500 to the land. Hence, as a result of the exchange, Smith has boosted his basis for depreciable property from $10,000 to $37,500 and stepped down his basis for land from $40,000 to $12,500.

On acquiring Smith's property, Green would use $60,000 as his basis for that property, the same basis he had for the property he exchanged. But he, too, would allocate that basis between land and building according to relative fair market values. Hence, he would allocate $\frac{2}{3}$ of his $60,000 basis or $40,000 to the building and the remaining $\frac{1}{3}$ or $20,000 to the land. So he, too, will have increased his basis for depreciable property from $30,000 to $40,000.

Hence Green and Smith *both* get stepped up bases for their building and increased depreciation deductions as a result of the exchange.

Depreciation recapture and the Section 1031 exchange

As has been explained, beginning on page 175, part or all of the gain on the sale or exchange of depreciable property may be treated as the recapture of previously-deducted depreciation and taxed as ordinary income. How does this depreciation recapture rule affect exchanges made under Section 1031 when part or all of the gain is not recognized for tax purposes?

If the property is personal property (e.g. furniture, equipment, etc. not part of the real estate), Section 1245 provides that the amount of the depreciation deducted after 1961 (or after June 1963, for elevators and escalators) is compared to the portion of the gain that is taxable in the exchange. In other words, for purposes of depreciation recapture, the *recognized* portion of the gain is treated as the total gain. That amount is the maximum amount that is subject to depreciation recapture.

In the case of real property, Section 1250 applies. It provides that although depreciation recapture can convert capital gain into ordinary income on the sale of real estate, ordinary income from depreciation recapture can be avoided in a Section 1031 exchange. Ordinary income is recognized on the exchange due to depreciation recapture *only if*

1. there is some recognized gain on the exchange due to the receipt of unlike property; or

2. the amount of Section 1250 gain that would have been recognized had this been an outright sale rather than exchange exceeds the market value of Section 1250 property (depreciable real estate) received in the exchange.

If neither (1) nor (2) is true, there is no ordinary income due to depreciation recapture on the exchange. If either (1) or (2) is true, the maximum amount of ordinary income due to depreciation recapture on the exchange is the amount computed in (1) or (2). If both (1) *and* (2) are true, the larger amount is taxable.

Similar rules are applied when property is replaced after an involuntary conversion (see page 130) or after the sale of and reinvestment in a qualified low-income housing project (see page 210).

Allocation of basis   After the exchange, if any ordinary income due to depreciation recapture has been avoided under the above rules, basis of all the property acquired in the exchange is first computed in the usual way. Then, an allocation of the basis must be made.

First, basis is allocated between Section 1250 property and other property received in the exchange. For example, if land and building were acquired, the land is not Section 1250 property while the building is. The total basis is allocated in proportion to the properties' fair market values. But the fair market value of the Section 1250 property is reduced by the amount of ordinary income avoided on the exchange because the Section 1250 rules did not apply under the provisions explained.

Example

Brown exchanges his land and building for Spencer's land and building. This is a tax-free exchange in which no gain or loss is recognized. Had this been a taxable transaction, Brown would have realized $10,000 of ordinary income under the Section 1250 depreciation recapture rules. Since no unlike property was received in the exchange, item (1) above does not apply. Since the market value of the building received is greater than the $10,000 of ordinary income from depreciation recapture that would have resulted in a taxable transaction, item (2) does not apply. Hence, there is no ordinary income from depreciation recapture recognized on this transaction.

Assume that Brown's basis for the total property he acquired, under the usual rules for computing basis in a tax-free exchange, is $42,000. Assume, too, that the market value of the building is $70,000 and the market value of the land is $30,000.

The $42,000 basis must be allocated to building and land. To do this, reduce the market value of the building (the Section 1250 property) by the $10,000 that would have constituted ordinary income from depreciation recapture if the transaction had been fully taxable. Thus the market value of the building becomes $60,000 and market value of the land remains $30,000. Since $60,000 is $\frac{2}{3}$ of the total market value of $90,000, $\frac{2}{3}$ of the $42,000 basis or $28,000 is allocated to the building and $\frac{1}{3}$ or $14,000 to the land.

Suppose instead of getting one building in the exchange, there were two, whose total value was $70,000, with the remaining $30,000 market value attributable to the land on which they stand. The $28,000 basis for buildings (calculated previously) must be allocated between the two buildings in relation to their market values. But here the market values of the buildings are not reduced by the ordinary income from depreciation recapture that was avoided on the exchange. Thus, assume the $70,000 market value is allocable $40,000 to Building 1 and $30,000 to Building 2. In that case $\frac{4}{7}$ of the $28,000 basis allocable to the Section 1250 properties or $16,000 is allocable to Building 1; and $\frac{3}{7}$ or $12,000 is allocable to Building 2.

What happens to the ordinary income from depreciation recapture that was avoided on the tax-free exchange? It carries over to the new properties as excess depreciation. In the example above, if only one building was acquired, the full $10,000 is allocated to the building. If two buildings were acquired, the allocation is made in proportion to the bases of the two buildings, i.e. $\frac{4}{7}$ of $10,000 or $5,715 to Building 1; and $\frac{3}{7}$ of $10,000 or $4,285 to Building 2.

Suppose $5,000 of the $10,000 ordinary income due to excess depreciation arose before 1970. (Under the rules applying to the depreciation recapture for that period, the total excess depreciation is reduced by one percent for each month in excess of 20 that the property was held; see page 178). Assume the property is held two more years and sold at a gain of $50,000. During the two years the property was held, 125% declining balance depreciation was used (because the property acquired was residential rental property; see page 151). The total depreciation deducted in those two years was $4,095, while straight line depreciation for the two years would have totalled $3,360. Hence there was excess depreciation for the two years of $735.

Since the property sold was acquired in a tax-free exchange, for *depreciation recapture purposes only* it is necessary to use a holding period commencing with the acquisition of the property. Hence, here, we use two years. Consequently, the depreciation recapture (ordinary income) portion of the $50,000 gain is calculated as follows.

Excess depreciation since the acquisition of the exchanged property (the total excess is used since, although the property is residential rental property, its holding period is only 24 months, far less than 100 months; see page 178)	$ 735
$5,000 of depreciation recapture after 1969 (carried over from prior property)	5,000
$5,000 of depreciation recapture prior to 1970 (carried over from prior property) reduced by 4% because property was held 24 months (using new holding period)	4,800
Portion of $50,000 gain subject to ordinary income treatment due to depreciation recapture	$10,535

Non-recognition of gain on sale of low-income housing

The tax law permits the owner of a qualified low-income housing project to sell the project to the tenants or to a cooperative for the benefit of the tenants and avoid the tax on the gain. To do so, he has to reinvest the proceeds of the sale in another qualified low-income housing project within a specified time.

A qualified housing project is a rental or cooperative housing project for lower income families which (1) has a mortgage insured under Sections 221(d)(3) or 236 of the National Housing Act and (2) under the National Housing Act has a limited rate of return to the owner and limited rentals or occupancy charges.

How the tax is avoided

The net amount realized on the sale to the tenants or their cooperative organization has to be reinvested in another qualified housing project, either by purchase, construction or reconstruction, within the reinvestment period. The reinvestment period is the period beginning one year before the disposition and ending the end of the taxable year following the year in which any part of the gain on the disposition is realized. So, if a disposition takes place on February 16, 1974, and gain is realized at that time, the reinvestment period begins February 16, 1973 and ends December 31, 1975. The Commissioner of Internal Revenue can extend the reinvestment period on application of the taxpayer.

How much of the gain is not recognized for tax purposes?

Compare the cost of the property in which the reinvestment was made with the net amount realized on the disposition of the old property. If the cost of the reinvestment property is at least equal to the net amount realized, no gain is recognized. If the cost of the reinvestment property is less than the net amount realized, the difference is recognized as gain. (Of course, in no event can more than the total gain be recognized.)

How much is the net amount realized?

It is the total amount realized minus the expenses incurred which are directly connected with the disposition and any taxes (other than income taxes) connected with the disposition. So if the seller realized $100,000 and paid a $5,000 sales commission and $2,000 of local taxes connected with the disposition, the net amount realized would be $93,000.

What is the basis of the new property?

It is its cost minus any gain that was not recognized on the disposition.

Example

Stern, on October 7, 1974, disposed of a qualified housing project to its tenants for $200,000. He has sales commissions and other costs of $10,000. The net amount he realized is $190,000. He has a basis of $140,000. So his realized gain is $50,000. On December 11, 1975, he acquires a qualified housing project for $210,000. He can elect to avoid taxation on the $50,000 gain on his disposition of the housing project on October 7, 1974. His basis for the December 11, 1975, acquisition is his $210,000 cost minus the $50,000 non-recognized gain or $160,000. If he had invested only $160,000 in the new property, he would have had a recognized gain of $30,000 ($190,000 net amount realized minus the $160,000 reinvested). His basis would be $160,000 cost minus the $20,000 non-recognized gain or $140,000.

Depreciation recapture If there would have been ordinary income due to depreciation recapture on the disposition of the qualified housing project, all or part of that ordinary income can be avoided by making the reinvestment within the prescribed period. Rules similar to those applying to tax-free exchanges apply (see page 207). So if no gain is recognized on the transaction and the amount of the ordinary income that would have been recaptured if the special rules did not apply is not more than the cost of the Section 1250 property acquired, no part of the ordinary income due to recapture is taxable. If some gain is recognized, the amount of ordinary income that can be taxable is not more than the amount of the recognized gain. (If, however, the amount of the ordinary income due to recapture is more than the cost of the Section 1250 property acquired and if that difference is more than the gain recognized, the amount of that difference is treated as ordinary income at the time of the disposition.)

Allocation of basis The basis of the newly-acquired property (computed as described) has to be allocated according to a formula when ordinary income due to recapture is avoided due to the special rules that apply to reinvestment in qualified low-income housing.

The basis is first allocated to Section 1250 property (i.e. buildings) acquired the cost of which does not exceed the net amount realized from the sale of Section 1250 property (minus any gain recognized). The amount of basis allocable to that Section 1250 property is the cost of that property minus any gain not recognized. Any remaining basis is allocated to non-Section 1250 property (i.e. land) acquired up to the amount of the cost of the land minus any gain not recognized. Any basis remaining is allocated to any additional Section 1250 property acquired.

What happens to the ordinary income due to recapture that was not taxed because the seller reinvested the amount realized and did not have a recognized gain? It is allocated to the Section 1250 property acquired in the same manner as the allocation is made when there is a tax-free exchange (see page 209). But note that unlike the case of a tax-free exchange, the holding period of the Section 1250 property acquired includes the holding period of the old property sold. This is especially significant in this case because if the reinvestment takes place before January 1, 1975, there is no depreciation recapture at all if the total holding period is 10 years or more. (See page 178).

Section III

Case Problems in Real Estate Brokerage Applications

Section III

Introduction

The previous sections of this book have been devoted to the presentation of a framework of real estate investment analysis. Much attention has been given to the methods of calculating rate of return for use in comparing all forms of investments. Income tax impact on real estate investments has been given consideration in order that the cash flow analysis can be calculated in an after-tax situation.

The real estate investment broker's role is to combine into a meaningful investment proposal his knowledge of properties, client, investment analysis and income tax regulations.

To assist the real estate investment broker in this task, the Commercial-Investment Council of the REALTORS® National Marketing Institute of the National Association of REALTORS has developed several standard forms. Their purpose is to ease and simplify the accumulation and evaluation of data necessary to understand a particular investment property.

The forms address themselves to the major problem of real estate investment analysis, namely: defining or estimating the future income stream and measuring the stream by discounting it to a present value or measuring its rate in terms of an investment amount.

Some of the most widely used forms are presented in this section.

Annual Property Operating Data
Cash Flow Analysis
Internal Rate of Return Worksheet
Exchange Recapitulation
Exchange Basis Adjustment

The purpose of this section is to provide illustrative case studies of a limited number of important brokerage applications. This is by no means an exhaustive presentation but is intended to serve only as a foundation for the broker who will use the fundamentals presented in solving his specific brokerage or counselling problems. The potential for other applications is unlimited.

Chapter 12

After-Tax Investment Analysis

12

The effective investment broker understands that clients can make decisions most readily when they understand their alternatives. As has been discussed, the most comparable unit of measurement in real estate investment analysis is the yield calculation known as the Internal Rate of Return (IRR).

Three steps are required to make the IRR calculation.

Define the projected income from the investment.

Define the initial cost (investment) to acquire the income.

Discount the projected income stream at such a rate that the sum of the discounted cash flows equals the initial investment.

Before the real estate investment broker can determine the Internal Rate of Return from a real estate investment, based on a given down payment, he must first define the projected income stream of cash flows.

Because the broker is concerned with after-income tax cash flows, the two types of income must be further defined as follows.

The net annual income from the investment after deducting income tax
The net sale proceeds after marketing costs and income taxes are deducted

Before the broker can calculate the after-tax cash flows, it is necessary that he develop the components of the cash flows before income tax. This is possible only by analyzing the income potential of the real estate as illustrated in Chapter 5 on page 60. Investment analysis therefore consists of the following steps.

Property analysis before taxes
Cash flow analysis after taxes
   Annual income
Resale proceeds
Calculation of internal rate of return

The purpose of this case study is twofold. First it will illustrate the steps necessary to make a complete after-tax investment analysis; secondly it will demonstrate how some of the forms mentioned in the Introduction to this section are used to assist in the analysis.

The Annual Property Operating Data form will be used to begin the analysis by showing how to do the following.

Gather information from the owner (Owner's Statement).

Develop a complete operating statement of the property (Broker's Reconstructed Statement).

Estimate both the present owner's position and a potential client's position in the property annually before income taxes.

Owners statement

As previously discussed, the first step in the process of property analysis is obtaining all possible financial and physical data about the property from the owner and his records. The Annual Property Operating Data form acts as a checklist in the gathering of financial data. It must be emphasized that the broker is obtaining information at this stage and not evaluating, interpreting or analyzing it.

Broker's reconstructed statement

To test the validity of the income information submitted by the owner, the broker reconstructs a new operating statement based upon the owner's statement and other market data.

This reconstructed statement is a broker's task and is accomplished on another Annual Property form. The broker is interested in developing an operating statement that will more closely reflect what the property might be expected to do for the next full calendar year. It is important to understand that the time frame of the projected statement is for the next full calendar year.

When the Broker's Reconstructed Statement is completed, it is possible that not one single item of expense or income will be the same as shown for any previous year. This statement, when contrasted with the Owner's Statement, should more closely reflect the income that the building can be expected to produce in the next full calendar year.

In the event the investment broker expects any adjustments to income or expenses or outlays for capital items to take place in the future, these are not indicated in the first year's annual operating statement but rather estimated as income or expense in the year in which they are expected to occur.

Finally, the Broker's Reconstructed Statement can be used to project before-tax cash flows to various parties. The owner's position indicates the annual cash flow to the present owner based on the net operating income as estimated in the Broker's Reconstructed Statement, less the annual debt service on his existing encumbrances and before income tax. The client position indicates the potential annual cash flow to a new purchaser under new financing necessary to acquire the property (also before income taxes).

Illustrative case

The following hypothetical situation will be used to demonstrate the use of the Annual Property Operating Data form for an Owner's Statement and a Broker's Reconstructed Statement as well as providing the data for the final investment analysis.

At a recent service club meeting Bill Broker met John Seller. During the course of the evening Seller indicated to Broker that he had an apartment house for sale. Broker made an appointment to see the apartment the following week and after the inspection the owner indicated he wanted $365,000 for the property. He also gave the following information to Mr. Broker.

Rents collected in the previous year	$55,000
Expenses:	
Taxes	$ 4,200
Insurance	1,500
Utilities	2,000
Supplies	100
Maintenance	500

He also indicated there was an existing mortgage on the property of approximately $160,000, payable to $1650 per month, including interest at 6%. Broker told Seller that he wanted to analyze the property and would get back to him.

Owner's statement Upon return to his office, Bill Broker began his analysis of the property by preparing an Owner's Statement. He systematically entered information supplied by the owner. His job was to make the entries without attempting to analyze, verify or evaluate the information at this stage. Fig. 1 shows the completed Owner's Statement. Note the indicated cash flow before income taxes of $26,900.

At this point, two things should be noted; first the form provides a standard form for recording data from the owner. As a checklist, it shows what information is lacking. Second, the broker gets an overall look at the property income stream from a quantity standpoint. The owner's reported income of $55,000 and expense of $8,300 indicates that the property produces $46,700 before debt service. Reported expenses are 15% of reported income. If this is a low expense ratio for the type of property, perhaps further investigation of the expenses is needed. Is the income too high or the expenses too low? The cash flow of 13% on equity is good but is it too good? It's apparent that the broker should delve deeper to better understand the property. His next step is to develop the Broker's Reconstructed Statement.

Broker's reconstructed statement

Up to this point, the broker has just organized the owner's own figures in an orderly manner and produced some key income and expense figures. However, there is no assurance that these numbers are close or realistic.

The next step is to determine the validity of the information supplied by the owner and then to estimate as closely as possible the future income stream that the property will produce. The information that was submitted by the owner reflects his previous year's operation. Last year's results may or may not be an indication of the future income. Consequently an analysis must be made of the potential income of the property in terms of quantity, quality and durability, since the purchaser is buying future, not historic, income. The Broker's Reconstructed Statement is designed to analyze the future potential of the quantity of income.

It should be apparent that a projected operating statement is more valid for a shorter term than for a longer one. That is, the possibility of projecting a valid income and expense statement for next year is greater than a projection of income fifteen years from now. The time frame for the Broker's Reconstructed Statement is the next calendar year.

General Information

Another Annual Property Operating Data form is used and its purpose is indicated as Broker's Reconstructed Statement.

Fig. 1

Annual Property Operating Data

Purpose _Owner's Statement_
Name _John Seller_
Location _16752 SW Cedar Way_
Type of Property _24-Unit Apartment_

Date _____

Price $ _365,000_
Loans $ _160,000_
Equity $ _205,000_

Assessed/Appraised Values

Land	$_____	____%
Improvement	$_____	____%
Personal Property	$_____	____%
Total	$_____	100 %

Adjusted Basis as of _____ $_____

FINANCING

	Balance	Payment	Period	Interest	Term
Existing $				%	
1st $	_160,000_	_1650_	_Mo_	6 %	
2nd $				%	
3rd $				%	
Potential					
1st $				%	
2nd $				%	

		%	2	3	Comments
1	GROSS SCHEDULED RENTAL INCOME				
2	Plus: Other Income				
3	TOTAL GROSS INCOME				
4	Less: Vacancy and Credit Losses				
5	GROSS OPERATING INCOME			55000	
6	Less: Operating Expenses				
7	Accounting and Legal				
8	Advertising, Licenses and Permits				
9	Property Insurance		1500		
10	Property Management				
11	Payroll - Resident Management				
12	Other				
13	Taxes-Workmen's Compensation				
14	Personal Property Taxes				
15	Real Estate Taxes		4200		
16	Repairs and Maintenance		500		
17	Services - Elevator				
18	Janitorial				
19	Lawn				
20	Pool				
21	Rubbish				
22	Other				
23	Supplies		100		
24	Utilities - Electricity		2000		
25	Gas and Oil				
26	Sewer and Water				
27	Telephone				
28	Other				
29	Miscellaneous				
30					
31	TOTAL OPERATING EXPENSES			8300	15% (low?)
32	NET OPERATING INCOME			46700	
33	Less: Total Annual Debt Service			19800	
34	CASH FLOW BEFORE TAXES			26900	15% Down Payment

From the Assessor's Office the assessed value of land improvements was found and entered. (The percentage of the improvement to value enables the broker to estimate the improvement value and to calculate annual depreciation from that amount.) The broker also obtained a verbal estimate from a lender as to their opinion of a new loan amount in terms of a new loan. These figures are entered under potential financing. From the seller's account, it was determined that the owner's adjusted basis (depreciated value or book value) was $195,000, which is entered beside the adjustment basis

Annual Property Operating Data

Purpose **Broker's Reconstructed Statement**
Name **John Seller**
Location **16752 SW Cedar Way**
Type of Property **24-Unit Apartment**

Date _____

Price $ _____
Loans $ _____
Equity $ _____

Assessed/Appraised Values

Land	$ 15,200	21.5 %
Improvement	$ 54,280	76.8 %
Personal Property	$ 1,130	1.7 %
Total	$ 70,610	100 %

Adjusted Basis as of **12/31/7-** $ **195,000**

FINANCING

Balance	Payment	Period	Interest	Term
Existing $			%	
1st $ 160,000	1,650	Mo	6 %	
2nd $			%	
3rd $			%	
Potential				
1st $ 270,000	2174.11	Mo	8.5 %	25 Yr
2nd $			%	

Operating statement

To test the validity of the information submitted by the owner, the broker reconstructs a new operating statement (next full calendar year) based on the owner's statement and other market data (Fig. 2). The first item entered is gross scheduled rental income. This is the income that the property will produce the coming year if rented at market or economic rents 100% of the time. To estimate scheduled gross income, it is necessary to know what typical rentals in the neighborhood are for the type of apartment owned by the sellers. Studies may have to be made to determine unit rents or square foot rent or rent on a cubic foot per room or per apartment basis. In this case, rentals were estimated as follows.

12 one-bedroom units at $200 per apartment	$2,400 monthly	
12 two-bedroom units at $240 per apartment	2,880 monthly	
Per month	$5,280	
Per year	$63,360	

The property had leased washer and dryer and after investigation, the broker estimated $50 per month income from this source.

Broker studies also indicated that vacancies and credit losses are estimated at 6% of scheduled gross rents or $3,840. This is deducted from the total gross income resulting in a gross operating income of $60,120.

Next an analysis of operating expenses was made. The broker developed estimates of these expenses based on his experience with this type of property and by asking questions of persons who had better information than he. His investigation and knowledge produced the following estimates.

1. Accounting and Legal (line 7)—$220 based on past experience with managing properties of this size

2. Advertising, Licensing and Permits—$120 based on past experience with this property

3. Property Insurance—$1,600 obtained from broker's insurance agent who recommended typical coverage

4. Property Management—$3,600; typical professional property management for this type of building is 6% with managing office paying all advertising costs

5. Resident Manager—$4,200 investigation indicated the resident manager could be obtained for $110 a month plus a two-bedroom apartment

219

Although the seller now acts as resident manager and property manager, these costs must be reflected as expenses of the property. A new owner may not wish to be so actively involved.

6. Personal Property taxes are estimated at $200.

Although seller reported $4,200 for the previous year, broker determined that a new school bond levy will go in effect next year and raise the taxes to approximately $6,800.

7. Repairs and Maintenance—$2,400

The property is in good repair and broker's contact with property manager indicates $100 per apartment per year should provide an adequate coverage (about 4% of the gross operating income).

8. Lawn—broker estimates $50 a month will handle this

9. Rubbish—$240

10. Supplies—$290 was based on an estimate of $1 per month per unit

11. Utilities—$2,880; tenants pay for electricity, heating, cooling, and hot water. Past experience and records with the utility company indicate that $10 per month per unit will cover the cost of house electricity, washer, dryer, etc.

12. Miscellaneous Expenses estimated at $500 per year

Total operating expenses came to $23,650 which is 39% of gross operating income. Broker finds that 38 to 40% is a typical expense ratio for properties of this type which helps him confirm that his reconstructed statement has greater validity than the owner's statement. After deducting the seller's annual debt service, there is a cash flow from the property to the owners of $16,670 or 8% on the $205,000 equity. It should be pointed out that the owner's statement indicates a cash flow of $26,900. This discrepancy was probably caused by not accounting for all costs and not differentiating between property income and the management income the owner paid himself. The completed Broker's Reconstructed Statement is shown in Fig. 2.

Fig. 2

Annual Property Operating Data

Purpose _Broker's Reconstructed Statement_ Date _____

Name _John Seller_

Location _16752 SW Cedar Way_

Type of Property _24-unit Apartment_

Price $ _____

Loans $ _____

Equity $ _____

Assessed/Appraised Values

Land	$ 15,200	21.5 %
Improvement	$ 54,280	76.8 %
Personal Property	$ 1,130	1.7 %
Total	$ 70,610	100 %

Adjusted Basis as of _____ $ _____

FINANCING

	Balance	Payment	Period	Interest	Term
Existing $				%	
1st $	160,000	1,650	Mo	6 %	
2nd $				%	
3rd $				%	
Potential					
1st $	270,000	226,583	Mo	9 %	25 Yr
2nd $				%	

		%	2	3	Comments
1	GROSS SCHEDULED RENTAL INCOME			63 360	12 @ $200 ; 12 @ $240
2	Plus: Other Income _laundry_			600	$50 mo
3	TOTAL GROSS INCOME			63 960	
4	Less: Vacancy and Credit Losses	6		3 840	
5	GROSS OPERATING INCOME			60 120	
6	Less: Operating Expenses				
7	Accounting and Legal		220		
8	Advertising, Licenses and Permits		120		
9	Property Insurance		1 600		
10	Property Management	6	3 600		inc. Advertising
11	Payroll - Resident Management		4 200		2 Br. Apt. + $110 mo.
12	Other				
13	Taxes-Workmen's Compensation				
14	Personal Property Taxes		200		
15	Real Estate Taxes		6 800		
16	Repairs and Maintenance	4	2 400		$100 /unit /Yr.
17	Services - Elevator				
18	Janitorial				
19	Lawn		600		$50 /mo.
20	Pool				
21	Rubbish		240		$20 /mo.
22	Other				
23	Supplies		290		$1 /mo. /unit
24	Utilities - Electricity		2 880		$10 /mo. /Apt.
25	Gas and Oil				
26	Sewer and Water				
27	Telephone				
28	Other				
29	Miscellaneous		500		
30					
31	TOTAL OPERATING EXPENSES			23 650	39%
32	NET OPERATING INCOME			36 470	
33	Less: Total Annual Debt Service			19 800	
34	CASH FLOW BEFORE TAXES			16 670	8%

The development of the Broker's Reconstructed Statement was to estimate, as best as possible, the next full calendar year's income that the property would produce. But the property does not produce income for itself; it produces income for an owner. It is the investment broker's role to understand how that income benefits the present owner or a prospective owner.

The Annual Property Operating Data form can be used to see how a new owner (Potential Client) under new financing would fare. Fig. 3 takes the data as developed in the Broker's Reconstructed Statement and changes the debt service to that required by the potential loan. Note that the first year cash flow before taxes is $9,280 for a new owner after making the down payment necessary to the maximum new loan.

Cash flow analysis

The Broker's Reconstructed Statement for a potential client becomes the basis for an investment analysis and the Cash Flow Analysis form helps in the process.

Before going through the steps of such an analysis, it is necessary to point out the purpose, the limitations and assumptions of a cash flow analysis.

Purpose

The cash flow analysis is a projection of an investor's cash flow after income tax from the real estate under study. The cash flows derive from annual operations and resale proceeds. The study period is usually done over a typical real estate investment holding period, 10 to 15 years. Although some believe this period is too long, studies indicate the yield increases with the holding period up to about 12 to 14 years. Our example will be for 15 years. In real life, each investor theoretically evaluates all his investments periodically. He will switch investments (sell one he has to acquire another) only if the prospects of the new one appear to have greater potential yield than the one which he is disposing.

Limitations and assumptions necessary

No person can accurately predict the exact annual operating statement or the resale price but one can make projections based on certain assumptions. Therefore the mathematics of the projections are valid if we recognize the limitations of our ability to project. We have said that the Broker's Reconstructed Operating Statement is the best estimate for the next full calendar year's operation. Projections based on these numbers must be done cautiously. If it is felt that over the study period the net operating income will increase or decrease, the "next year's operating statement" can be adjusted accordingly. Projections can also show outlays for further capital costs (carpets, major repairs, etc.) at some particular time during this study period. Reserves are to be set aside each year for these purposes thereby reducing annual cash flows. As an alternative, no funds need be set aside but capital expenditures can be made from cash flows of the year of the improvement (and even by additional capital at that time) thereby creating a negative cash flow in the year that the improvement is added.

As the projection may be made on any basis, it is imperative that each cash flow analysis be evaluated not only in terms of the final resulting numbers but also by the assumptions under which the study was made. This also pertains to the resale price. The resale price can be indicated the same as the purchase price or higher or lower. When the projected investment is evaluated, the broker must question how reasonable the assumptions are.

Fig. 3

Annual Property Operating Data

Purpose **Broker's Reconstructed Statement**
Name **Potential Client**
Date _____

Location _____
Type of Property **24-Unit Apt.**

Price $ **365,000**
Loans $ **270,000**
Equity $ **95,000**

Assessed/Appraised Values

Land	$_____	_____ %
Improvement	$_____	_____ %
Personal Property	$_____	_____ %
Total	$_____	100 %

Adjusted Basis as of _____ $ _____

FINANCING

	Balance	Payment	Period	Interest	Term
Existing $				%	
1st $				%	
2nd $				%	
3rd $				%	
Potential					
1st $ **270,000**		**2,265.87**	**Mo.**	**9** %	**25 Yr.**
2nd $				%	

		%	2	3	Comments
1	GROSS SCHEDULED RENTAL INCOME				
2	Plus: Other Income				
3	TOTAL GROSS INCOME			63 960	
4	Less: Vacancy and Credit Losses			3 840	
5	GROSS OPERATING INCOME			60 120	
6	Less: Operating Expenses				
7	Accounting and Legal				
8	Advertising, Licenses and Permits				
9	Property Insurance				
10	Property Management				
11	Payroll - Resident Management				
12	Other				
13	Taxes-Workmen's Compensation				
14	Personal Property Taxes				
15	Real Estate Taxes				
16	Repairs and Maintenance				
17	Services - Elevator				
18	Janitorial				
19	Lawn				
20	Pool				
21	Rubbish				
22	Other				
23	Supplies				
24	Utilities - Electricity				
25	Gas and Oil				
26	Sewer and Water				
27	Telephone				
28	Other				
29	Miscellaneous				
30					
31	TOTAL OPERATING EXPENSES			23 650	
32	NET OPERATING INCOME			36 470	
33	Less: Total Annual Debt Service			27 190	
34	CASH FLOW BEFORE TAXES			9 280	

One last limitation which must be addressed is that concerning investor's tax situation. To make an after-tax analysis, the tax bracket of the investor must be taken into account. Even if the investor and his tax bracket are known, his tax position can change in later years. The projector can then make the assumption of a constant tax bracket or a changing one. It is less important what the projector compared to how the reader or user interprets the projection.

It must be understood that a projection can be extremely conservative or overly optimistic.

However, if the reader of a projection understands the assumption under which it was made, he can make his own judgment based on what he feels the probabilities of the projection becoming reality are.

For example, if a study shows that an investor can expect a 15% yield if the property doubles in value and 11% yield if the property value stays the same and an 8% return if the property declines 25% of the value, the investor can make his judgment to buy or not based on some correlation of all the alternatives and not just the optimistic one.

Cash procedure analysis

In the example the following assumptions will be used.

1. Projection period—15 years

2. Net operating income will remain level.

3. Tax bracket of investor will be 40%.

4. Capital gains will be 25% on the first $50,000; 30% on the excess above $50,000.

5. Depreciation will be 125% declining balance for 25-year economic life.

6. Resale price will be the original purchase price.

7. Purchase price $365,000; cash down to a new potential mortgage of $270,000

8. Resale costs—7%

To assist the reader the step-by-step analysis procedures are outlined on a portion of the Cash Flow Analysis form. The method of completing the form is shown in Figs. 4 through 10 and a composite form in Fig. 11.

Step 1 (Fig. 4): enter basic data from Broker's Reconstructed Statement for potential client using the assumptions previously discussed.

Fig. 4

Cash Flow Analysis

Name: _Potential Client_ Date: _____ Purpose: _15 Yr. Study_

Mortgage Data

	Encumbrances	Amount	Remaining Term	Payment Period	Interest Rate	Payment Period	Remarks
1	1st Mortgage	270 000	25 Yr.	140	9	2 265 83	
2	2nd Mortgage						
3	3rd Mortgage						

		(1) Year: 1	(2) Year: 2	(3) Year: 3	(4) Year: 4	(5) Year: 5	(6) Year: 6
4	Initial Investment	95 000					
5	1st Mortgage	270 000					
6	2nd Mortgage						
7	3rd Mortgage						
8	Total Encumbrances						
9	Principal Reduction						

Ownership Analysis of Property Income: Taxable Income

10	Total Gross Income	63 960					
11	− Vacancy & Credit Loss	3 840					
12	− Operating Expenses	23 650					
13	Net Operating Income	36 470					
14	− Non-Operating Expense						
15	− Interest 9%						
16	− Depreciation 25 Yr.	125%					
17	Taxable Income						

Cash Flows

18	Net Operating Income	36 470					
19	− Princp. & Int. Pymts.	27 190					
20	− Funded Reserves						
21	− Capital Additions						
22	Cash Flow before Taxes	9 280	9 280	9 280	9 280	9 280	9 280
23	− Income Tax 40%						
24	Cash Flow after Taxes						

Analysis of Sales Proceeds Year:

	Adjusted Basis				Excess Depreciation			Tax on Gain %			
25	Original Basis				Total Depr.			Excess			
26	+ Capital Improvements				S/L Depr.			Cap. Gain			
27	+ Costs of Sale				Excess Depr.			Cap. Gain			
28	Sub-Total							Total Tax Liab.			
29	− Depreciation				Gain			Sales Proceeds			
30	− Partial Sales				Sales Price			Sales Price			
31	AB at Sale				− AB			− Sales Costs			
32					Gain			− Mortgage			
33					− Excess			Proceeds before Taxes			
34					Cap. Gain			− Total Tax Liab.			
								Proceeds after Taxes			

Step 2 (Fig. 5): Calculate the interest payable each year under the mortgage. This is done by calculating and entering the mortgage balance each year (line 5), determining the principal reduction each year (line 9) and deducting this from the annual amortization to obtain interest (line 15). It should be noted that the balance shown on line 5 in each year column refers to the mortgage balance at the beginning of the year. Therefore, the mortgage balance shown at the beginning of year sixteen is the same as at the end of year fifteen, the year the property is projected to resell. The interest shown on line 15 shows the amount of interest paid during the year. The cash flow after taxes on line 24 is the net benefit at the end of each year. Mortgage balances may be calculated from amortization schedules or with any calculator that is programmed with compound interest functions.

The monthly payments on the loan are $2,265.83 (line 1); the annual payment rounded is $27,190 (line 19).

The annual mortgage balances are as follows.

		Mortgage balance
B.O.Y.	1	$270,000
	2	266,988
	3	263,693
	4	260,089
	5	256,147
	6	251,836
	7	247,119
	8	241,961
	9	236,318
	10	230,147
	11	223,396
	12	216,012
	13	207,935
	14	199,101
	15	189,438
B.O.Y.	16	178,868

Enter these on the Cash Flow Study (line 5), then calculate the interest (line 15).

Fig. 5

Cash Flow Analysis

Name: **Potential Client** Date: _____ Purpose: **15 Yr. Study**

Mortgage Data

	Encumbrances	Amount	Remaining Term	Payment Period	Interest Rate	Payment Period	Remarks
1	1st Mortgage	270 000	25 Yr.	Mo	9%	2 265 83	
		(1)	(2)	(3)	(4)	(5)	(6)

		Year: 1	Year: 2	Year: 3	Year: 4	Year: 5	Year: 6
4	Initial Investment	95 000					
5	1st Mortgage	270 000	266 988	263 693	260 089	256 147	257 836
9	Principal Reduction	3 012	3 295	3 604	3 942	4 311	4 717

Ownership Analysis of Property Income: **Taxable Income**

		Year: 1	Year: 2	Year: 3	Year: 4	Year: 5	Year: 6
10	Total Gross Income	63 960					
11	− Vacancy & Credit Loss	3 840					
12	− Operating Expenses	23 650					
15	− Interest 9%	24 178	23 895	23 586	23 248	22 879	22 473
16	− Depreciation 25 Yr. 125%						

Cash Flows

		Year: 1	Year: 2	Year: 3	Year: 4	Year: 5	Year: 6
18	Net Operating Income	36 470					
19	− Princp. & Int. Pymts.	27 190					
22	Cash Flow before Taxes	9 280	9 280	9 280	9 280	9 280	9 280
23	− Income Tax 40%						
24	Cash Flow after Taxes						
		(1)	(2)	(3)	(4)	(5)	(6)

		Year: 7	Year: 8	Year: 9	Year: 10	Year: 11	Year: 12
4	Initial Investment						
5	1st Mortgage	247 119	241 961	236 318	230 147	223 396	216 012
9	Principal Reduction	5 158	5 643	6 171	6 751	7 384	8 077
13	Net Operating Income	36 470					
14	− Non-Operating Expense						
15	− Interest 9%	22 032	21 547	21 019	20 439	19 806	19 113
16	− Depreciation 25 Yr. 125%						
22	Cash Flow before Taxes	9 280	9 280	9 280	9 280	9 280	9 280
23	− Income Tax 40%						
24	Cash Flow after Taxes						
		(1)	(2)	(3)	(4)	(5)	(6)

		Year: 13	Year: 14	Year: 15	Year: 16	Year:	Year:
4	Initial Investment						
5	1st Mortgage	207 935	199 101	189 438	178 868		
9	Principal Reduction	8 834	9 663	10 570			
13	Net Operating Income	36 470					
14	− Non-Operating Expense						
15	− Interest 9%	18 356	17 527	16 620			
16	− Depreciation 25 Yr. 125%						
22	Cash Flow before Taxes	9 280	9 280	9 280			

Step 3 (Fig. 6): Calculate depreciation for the fifteen-year period. When the Broker's Reconstructed Statement was made the following assessed values and percentages were entered.

Land	$15,200	21.5%
Improvements	54,280	76.8%
Personal property	1,130	1.7%
Total	$70,610	100 %

The investment broker can use these allocations to determine depreciation amounts for projection studies (providing these give logical numbers). This would mean that on a $365,000 acquisition price the allocation would be as follows.

Land	$ 78,475	21.5%
Improvements	280,325	76.8%
Personal property	6,200	1.7%
Total	$365,000	100 %

If the improvement is depreciated at 125% declining balance for 25 years and the personal property 10 years straight line, the following are the amounts of depreciation for each year. (Salvage value has been disregarded for simplicity of projection.)

Year	Improvement $280,325	Personal property $6,200	Total
1	14,016	620	$14,636
2	13,315	620	13,935
3	12,650	620	13,270
4	12,017	620	12,637
5	11,416	620	12,036
6	10,846	620	11,466
7	10,303	620	10,923
8	9,788	620	10,408
9	9,299	620	9,919
10	8,834	620	9,454
11	8,392		8,392
12	7,972		7,972
13	7,574		7,574
14	7,195		7,195
15	6,835		6,835
	Total depreciation		$156,652

Enter these amounts on line 16, then deduct line 15 and 16 from Net Operating Income to obtain Taxable Income (line 17).

Step 4: Calculate Cash Flow After Taxes (See Fig. 7). Line 17 has the annual entry for Taxable Income. Taxable Income multiplied by the tax bracket of the Potential Client (40%) will result in annual income tax attributable to the real estate income. This will be entered on line 23 (Income Tax) then deducted from Cash Flow Before Taxes (line 22) to obtain Cash Flow After Taxes (line 24).

Fig. 6

Cash Flow Analysis

Name: **Potential Client** Date _____ Purpose: **15 Yr. Study**

		(1) Year: 1	(2) Year: 2	(3) Year: 3	(4) Year: 4	(5) Year: 5	(6) Year: 6
	Ownership Analysis of Property Income:		**Taxable Income**				
10	Total Gross Income						
11	− Vacancy & Credit Loss						
12	− Operating Expenses						
13	Net Operating Income						
14	− Non-Operating Expense						
15	− Interest						
16	− Depreciation 25 Yr. 125%	14 636	13 935	13 270	12 637	12 036	11 466
17	Taxable Income	⟨2 344⟩	⟨1 360⟩	⟨386⟩	585	1 555	2 531

		Year: 7	Year: 8	Year: 9	Year: 10	Year: 11	Year: 12
16	− Depreciation 25 Yr. 125%	10 923	10 408	9 919	9 454	8 392	7 972
17	Taxable Income	3 515	4 515	5 532	6 577	8 272	9 385

		Year: 13	Year: 14	Year: 15	Year:	Year:	Year:
16	− Depreciation 25 Yr. 125%	7 574	7 195	6 835			
17	Taxable Income	10 540	11 748	13 015			

Fig. 7

Cash Flow Analysis

Name _____ Date _____ Purpose _____

		(1) Year: 1	(2) Year: 2	(3) Year: 3	(4) Year: 4	(5) Year: 5	(6) Year: 6
	Ownership Analysis of Property Income:		**Taxable Income**				
10	Total Gross Income						
11	− Vacancy & Credit Loss						
12	− Operating Expenses						
13	Net Operating Income						
14	− Non-Operating Expense						
15	− Interest						
16	− Depreciation						
17	Taxable Income	⟨2 344⟩	⟨1 360⟩	⟨386⟩	585	1 555	2 531
	Cash Flows						
18	Net Operating Income						
19	− Princp. & Int. Pymts.						
20	− Funded Reserves						
21	− Capital Additions						
22	Cash Flow before Taxes	9 280	9 280	9 280	9 280	9 280	9 280
23	− Income Tax 40%	⟨938⟩	⟨544⟩	⟨154⟩	234	622	1 012
24	Cash Flow after Taxes	10 218	9 824	9 434	9 046	8 658	8 268

		Year: 7	Year: 8	Year: 9	Year: 10	Year: 11	Year: 12
17	Taxable Income	3 515	4 515	5 532	6 577	8 272	9 385
22	Cash Flow before Taxes	9 280	9 280	9 280	9 280	9 280	9 280
23	− Income Tax 40%	1 406	1 806	2 213	2 631	3 309	3 754
24	Cash Flow after Taxes	7 874	7 474	7 067	6 649	5 971	5 526

		Year: 13	Year: 14	Year: 15	Year:	Year:	Year:
17	Taxable Income	10 540	11 748	13 015			
22	Cash Flow before Taxes	9 280	9 280	9 280			
23	− Income Tax 40%	4 216	4 699	5 206			
24	Cash Flow after Taxes	5 064	4 581	4 074			

229

Step 5: Calculation of resale proceeds. (Figs. 8, 9, 10) Assume the following.

1. Resale is a purchase price of $365,000.

2. Resale costs 7%.

3. Capital Gains Taxes 25% are on the first $50,000 and 30% over $50,000.

As additional studies, resale proceeds are also calculated as though the property would sell for $315,000 and $415,000.

Fig. 8

Analysis of Sales Proceeds Year: 15

	Adjusted Basis			Excess Depreciation			Tax on Gain	%			
25	Original Basis	365	000	Total Depr.	156	652	Excess				
26	+ Capital Improvements			S/L Depr.	174	395	Cap. Gain 50,000	25		12	500
27	+ Costs of Sale 7%	25	550	Excess Depr.	—0—		Cap. Gain 81,102	30		24	331
28	Sub-Total	390	550				Total Tax Liab.			36	831
29	− Depreciation	156	652		Gain			Sales Proceeds			
30	− Partial Sales			Sales Price	365	000	Sales Price			365	000
31	AB at Sale	233	898	− AB	233	898	− Sales Costs			25	550
32				Gain	131	102	− Mortgage			178	868
33				− Excess	—0—		Proceeds befpre Taxes			160	582
34				Cap. Gain	131	102	− Total Tax Liab.			36	831
							Proceeds after Taxes			123	751

Fig. 9

Analysis of Sales Proceeds Year: 15

	Adjusted Basis			Excess Depreciation			Tax on Gain	%			
25	Original Basis	365	000	Total Depr.			Excess				
26	+ Capital Improvements			S/L Depr.			Cap. Gain 50,000	25		12	500
27	+ Costs of Sale 7%	22	050	Excess Depr.	—0—		Cap. Gain 34,602	30		10	381
28	Sub-Total	387	050				Total Tax Liab.			22	881
29	− Depreciation	156	652		Gain			Sales Proceeds			
30	− Partial Sales			Sales Price	315	000	Sales Price			315	000
31	AB at Sale	230	398	− AB	230	398	− Sales Costs			22	050
32				Gain	84	602	− Mortgage			178	868
33				− Excess	—0—		Proceeds before Taxes			114	082
34				Cap. Gain	84	602	− Total Tax Liab.			22	881
							Proceeds after Taxes			91	201

Fig. 10

Analysis of Sales Proceeds Year: 15

	Adjusted Basis			Excess Depreciation			Tax on Gain	%			
25	Original Basis	365	000	Total Depr.			Excess				
26	+ Capital Improvements			S/L Depr.			Cap. Gain 50,000	25		12	500
27	+ Costs of Sale 7%	29	050	Excess Depr.	—0—		Cap. Gain 127,602	30		58	281
28	Sub-Total	394	050				Total Tax Liab.			50	781
29	− Depreciation	156	652		Gain			Sales Proceeds			
30	− Partial Sales			Sales Price	415	000	Sales Price			415	000
31	AB at Sale	237	398	− AB	237	398	− Sales Costs			29	050
32				Gain	177	602	− Mortgage			178	868
33				− Excess	—0—		Proceeds before Taxes			207	082
34				Cap. Gain	177	602	− Total Tax Liab.			50	781
							Proceeds after Taxes			156	301

231

Fig. 11

Cash Flow Analysis

Date_____

Name __POTENTIAL CLIENT_____ Purpose __15 Yr. STUDY_____

Mortgage Data

	Encumbrances	Amount	Remaining Term	Payment Period	Interest Rate	Payment Period	Remarks
1	1st Mortgage	270 000	25 Yr.	Mo.	9 %	2 265 83	
2	2nd Mortgage						
3	3rd Mortgage						

		(1) Year: 1	(2) Year: 2	(3) Year: 3	(4) Year: 4	(5) Year: 5	(6) Year: 6
4	Initial Investment	95 000					
5	1st Mortgage	270 000	266 988	263 693	260 089	256 147	251 836
9	Principal Reduction	3 012	3 295	3 604	3 942	4 311	4 717

Ownership Analysis of Property Income: Taxable Income

10	Total Gross Income	63 960					
11	– Vacancy & Credit Loss	3 840					
12	– Operating Expenses	23 650					
13	Net Operating Income	36 470	36 470	36 470	36 470	36 470	36 470
14	– Non-Operating Expense						
15	– Interest 9%	24 178	23 895	23 586	23 248	22 879	22 473
16	– Depreciation 25 Yr. 125% DB	14 636	13 935	13 270	12 637	12 036	11 466
17	Taxable Income	‹2 344›	‹1 360›	‹386›	585	1 555	2 531

Cash Flows

18	Net Operating Income	36 470	36 470	36 470	36 470	36 470	36 470
19	– Princp. & Int. Pymts.	27 190	27 190	27 190	27 190	27 190	27 190
20	– Funded Reserves						
21	– Capital Additions						
22	Cash Flow before Taxes	9 280	9 280	9 280	9 280	9 280	9 280
23	– Income Tax 40%	‹938›	‹544›	‹154›	234	622	1 012
24	Cash Flow after Taxes	10 218	9 824	9 434	9 046	8 658	8 268

Analysis of Sales Proceeds   Year:

	Adjusted Basis			Excess Depreciation			Tax on Gain %		
25	Original Basis			Total Depr.			Excess		
26	+ Capital Improvements			S/L Depr.			Cap. Gain		
27	+ Costs of Sale			Excess Depr.			Cap. Gain		
28	Sub-Total						Total Tax Liab.		
29	– Depreciation			Gain			Sales Proceeds		
30	– Partial Sales			Sales Price			Sales Price		
31	AB at Sale			– AB			– Sales Costs		
32				Gain			– Mortgage		
33				– Excess			Proceeds before Taxes		
34				Cap. Gain			– Total Tax Liab.		
							Proceeds after Taxes		

		Year: 7		Year: 8		Year: 9		Year: 10		Year: 11		Year: 12	
4	Initial Investment												
5	1st Mortgage	247	119	241	961	236	318	230	147	223	396	216	012
9	Principal Reduction	5	158	5	643	6	171	6	751	7	384	8	077

Ownership Analysis of Property Income: Taxable Income

13	Net Operating Income	36	470	36	470	36	470	36	470	36	470	36	470
14	− Non-Operating Expense												
15	− Interest 9%	22	032	21	547	21	019	20	439	19	806	19	113
16	− Depreciation 25 yr 125%	10	923	10	408	9	919	9	454	8	392	7	972
17	Taxable Income	3	515	4	575	5	532	6	577	8	272	9	385

Cash Flows

18	Net Operating Income	36	470	36	470	36	470	36	470	36	470	36	470
19	− Princp. & Int. Pymts.	27	190	27	190	27	190	27	190	27	190	27	190
22	Cash Flow before Taxes	9	280	9	280	9	280	9	280	9	280	9	280
23	− Income Tax 40%	1	406	1	806	2	213	2	631	3	309	3	754
24	Cash Flow after Taxes	7	874	7	474	7	067	6	649	5	971	5	526

		Year: 13		Year: 14		Year: 15		Year: 16		Year:		Year:	
4	Initial Investment												
5	1st Mortgage	207	935	199	101	189	438	178	868				
9	Principal Reduction	8	834	9	663	10	570						

Ownership Analysis of Property Income: Taxable Income

13	Net Operating Income	36	470	36	470	36	470						
14	− Non-Operating Expense												
15	− Interest	18	356	17	527	16	620						
16	− Depreciation	7	574	7	195	6	835						
17	Taxable Income	10	540	11	748	13	015						

Cash Flows

18	Net Operating Income	36	470	36	470	36	470						
19	− Princp. & Int. Pymts.	27	190	27	190	27	190						
22	Cash Flow before Taxes	9	280	9	280	9	280						
23	− Income Tax 40%	4	216	4	699	5	206						
24	Cash Flow after Taxes	5	064	4	581	4	074						

Analysis of Sales Proceeds — Year: 15

	Adjusted Basis			Excess Depreciation			Tax on Gain %		
25	Original Basis	365	000	Total Depr.	156	652	Excess		
26	+ Capital Improvements			S/L Depr.	174	395	Cap. Gain 50,000 25	12	500
27	+ Costs of Sale 7%	25	550	Excess Depr.		0	Cap. Gain 81,102 30	24	331
28	Sub-Total	390	550				Total Tax Liab.	36	831
29	− Depreciation	156	652	**Gain**			**Sales Proceeds**		
30	− Partial Sales			Sales Price	365	000	Sales Price	365	000
31	AB at Sale	233	898	− AB	233	898	− Sales Costs	25	550
32				Gain	131	102	− Mortgage	178	868
33				− Excess		0	Proceeds before Taxes	160	582
34				Cap. Gain	131	102	− Total Tax Liab.	·36	831
							Proceeds after Taxes	123	751

Internal rate of return calculation

The broker has completed the one-year before-tax analysis (Broker's Reconstructed Statement) and the 15-year after-tax cash flow analysis.

The final calculation is now made to determine the investor's yield *under the projected assumptions.* Everything done thus far has been estimated, projected or assumed. The final step, which is arithmetic in nature, will give a definitive number. But the validity of the number is only as good as the earlier input estimates. The Internal Rate of Return worksheet simplifies the calculation procedure. (Fig. 12) All entries come from the cash flow analysis previously filled out. First enter the data as indicated.

By definition, the Internal Rate of Return is that rate which discounts an income stream so that the total equals the initial investment. The purpose of our calculation is to find an interest rate which will discount the total income stream so that the total present values will equal the initial investment (investment amount).

We do not know which rate will do this. As a starting point, a rate is selected, say 10%. Each annual income flow as indicated in the projection will be multiplied by the present value of 1 discounted at 10% for the year in which the income is receivable. Those amounts are entered under the amount (discount of 10%).

The calculations indicate that the present value of the income stream when discounted at 10% is $90,333. This is less than the initial investment of $95,000. Therefore, the amount discounted is too great.

Again, the cash flows are discounted but this time at 5%, which gives a total discounted value of $139,533, thereby indicating the rate is between 5 and 10%. Interpolation indicates that 9.58% will discount the cash flows to $95,000, the amount of initial investment. Therefore, the Internal Rate of Return to the investor if he acquires the property on the terms indicated and the property performs as projected is approximately 9.6% after income taxes. In order to give a final evaluation for this study, the Internal Rate of Return was calculated under the projected 15-year cash flows but under assumptions of resale price of $50,000 lower and at $50,000 higher than the purchase price. These are shown in Figs. 13 and 14. The indicated Internal Rates of Return for all the assumed resale prices are as follows.

Terminal value	IRR
$315,000	8.54%
365,000	9.58
415,000	10.61

Fig. 12

Internal Rate of Return Worksheet

Date _____

Name __POTENTIAL CLIENT__ Property __24UNIT APT. 16752 CEDAR WAY__

Net Sale Proceeds $ __123,751 (365,000)__ Investment Amount $ __95,000__

End of Year	Cash Flow	Discount at 5%		Discount at 10%		Discount at 15%		
		P.V. of 1	Amount	P.V. of 1	Amount	P.V. of 1	Amount	P.V. of 1
1	10,218	.952381	9,731	.909091	9,289	.869565		.833333
2	9,824	.907029	8,911	.826446	8,119	.756144		.694444
3	9,434	.863838	8,149	.751315	7,088	.657516		.578704
4	9,046	.822702	7,442	.683013	6,179	.571753		.482253
5	8,658	.783526	6,784	.620921	5,376	.497177		.401878
6	8,268	.746215	6,170	.564474	4,667	.432328		.334898
7	7,874	.710681	5,596	.513158	4,041	.375937		.279082
8	7,474	.676839	5,059	.466507	3,487	.326902		.232568
9	7,067	.644609	4,555	.424098	2,997	.284262		.193807
10	6,649	.613913	4,082	.385543	2,563	.247185		.161506
11	5,971	.584679	3,491	.350494	2,093	.214943		.134588
12	5,526	.556837	3,077	.318631	1,761	.186907		.112157
13	5,064	.530321	2,686	.289664	1,467	.162528		.093464
14	4,581	.505068	2,314	.263331	1,206	.141329		.077887
15	4,074	.481017	1,960	.239392	975	.122894		.064905
16		.458112		.217629		.106865		.054088
17		.436297		.197845		.092926		.045073
18		.415521		.179859		.080805		.037561
19		.395734		.163508		.070265		.031301
20		.376889		.148644		.061100		.026085
Reversion Year 15	123,751	.481019	59,526	.239392	29,625			
Reversion Year ___								
Reversion Year ___								
TOTALS			139,533		90,933			

INTERPOLATION

% Rate		$ Present Value Amount
Smaller __5__	$ __139,533__	→ $ __139,533__
Larger __10__	$ __90,433__	Investment Amount $ __95,000__

[Absolute Difference __5__ − $ __48,600__ x $ __44,533__] + Smaller Rate __5__ = __9.58__ %

Prepared by _____

235

Fig. 13

Internal Rate of Return Worksheet

Date _____

Name __POTENTIAL CLIENT__   Property _____

Net Sale Proceeds $ _91,201 (315,000)_   Investment Amount $ _95,000_

End of Year	Cash Flow	Discount at 5%		Discount at 10%		Discount at 15%		Discount at 20%	
		P.V. of 1	Amount	P.V. of 1	Amount	P.V. of 1	Amount	P.V. of 1	Amount
1	10,218	.952381		.909091		.869565		.833333	
2	9,824	.907029		.826446		.756144		.694444	
3	9,434	.863838		.751315		.657516		.578704	
4	9,046	.822702		.683013		.571753		.482253	
5	8,658	.783526		.620921		.497177		.401878	
6	8,268	.746215		.564474		.432328		.334898	
7	7,874	.710681		.513158		.375937		.279082	
8	7,474	.676839		.466507		.326902		.232568	
9	7,067	.644609		.424098		.284262		.193807	
10	6,649	.613913		.385543		.247185		.161506	
11	5,971	.584679		.350494		.214943		.134588	
12	5,526	.556837		.318631		.186907		.112157	
13	5,064	.530321		.289664		.162528		.093464	
14	4,581	.505068		.263331		.141329		.077887	
15	4,074	.481017		.239392		.122894		.064905	
16		.458112		.217629		.106865		.054088	
17		.436297		.197845		.092926		.045073	
18		.415521		.179859		.080805		.037561	
19		.395734		.163508		.070265		.031301	
20		.376889		.148644		.061100		.026085	
Reversion Year 15	91,201	.481017		.239392	21,833				
Reversion Year __									
Reversion Year __									
TOTALS		123,876			83,141				

INTERPOLATION

	% Rate	$ Present Value Amount
Smaller	5	$ 123,876 → $ 123,876
Larger	10	$ 83,141 Investment Amount $ 95,000

[Absolute Difference __5__ ÷ $ 40,735 × $ 28,876] + Smaller Rate __5__ = 8.54 %

Prepared by _____

Fig. 14

Internal Rate of Return Worksheet

Date _____

Name _____ Property _____

Net Sale Proceeds $ 156,301 (415,000)   Investment Amount $ 95,000

End of Year	Cash Flow	Discount at 5%		Discount at 10%		Discount at 15%		Discount at 20%
		P.V. of 1	Amount	P.V. of 1	Amount	P.V. of 1	Amount	P.V. of 1
1	10,218	.952381		.909091	9,289	.869565	8,885	.833333
2	9,824	.907029		.826446	8,119	.756144	7,428	.694444
3	9,434	.863838		.751315	7,084	.657516	6,203	.578704
4	9,046	.822702		.683013	6,179	.571753	5,172	.482253
5	8,658	.783526		.620921	5,376	.497177	4,305	.401878
6	8,268	.746215		.564474	4,667	.432328	3,574	.334898
7	7,874	.710681		.513158	4,041	.375937	2,960	.279082
8	7,474	.676839		.466507	3,487	.326902	2,443	.232568
9	7,067	.644609		.424098	2,997	.284262	2,009	.193807
10	6,649	.613913		.385543	2,563	.247185	1,644	.161506
11	5,971	.584679		.350494	2,093	.214943	1,283	.134588
12	5,526	.556837		.318631	1,761	.186907	1,033	.112157
13	5,064	.530321		.289664	1,467	.162528	823	.093464
14	4,581	.505068		.263331	1,206	.141329	647	.077887
15	4,074	.481017		.239392	975	.122894	501	.064905
16		.458112		.217629		.106865		.054088
17		.436297		.197845		.092926		.045073
18		.415521		.179859		.080805		.037561
19		.395734		.163508		.070265		.031301
20		.376889		.148644		.061100		.026085
Reversion Year 15	156,301			.239392	37,417		19,209	
Reversion Year ___								
Reversion Year ___								
TOTALS					98,725		68,119	

INTERPOLATION

% Rate	$ Present Value Amount

Smaller ___10___ $ 98,725 ──────► $ 98,725

Larger ___15___ $ 68,119   Investment Amount $ 95,000

[Absolute Difference ___5___] ÷ $ 30,606 x $ 3,725 + Smaller Rate 10 = 10.61 %

Prepared by _____

237

Evaluation of process

The step-by-step analysis creates no miraculous real estate investments. In fact, some brokers dislike the method because they say it doesn't show real estate yields as "high" as other types of analysis. The purpose of the procedure is not to show real estate investments as high or low; it is used merely to show what happens under projected circumstances. IRR uses a yield measurement that is similar to the measurement used and understood by the public on alternative investments.

In the example used, the foundation is the Broker's Reconstructed Statement, an estimate of the operations for the next year. If the broker finds reliability in this statement, his next step is to prepare the cash flow analysis. In making this analysis, the broker gives consideration to many things, the type of tenant or improvement, the location and the demographics or the area and increases or decreases of the quantity of income projected over the succeeding years and how these items will affect the durability of the income.

The exact extent of these items is impossible to accurately predict; yet both the broker and the client have some ability to project future trends. They are able to understand the present condition of the improvement and able to make some estimate as to whether it can be maintained at the cost indicated in the projection for the period indicated. They also have some idea as to whether the rents will increase or decrease due to the improvements, the neighborhood trends and so forth. They also are able to form an opinion as to whether the projected resale price being the same as the acquisition price is a reasonable, a conservative or an optimistic estimate. If the property is to sell at more or less than at acquisition, is that because of increased or decreased income or decreasing or increasing yield demands? These are all logical points of discussion between the broker and the seller or the broker and the buyer and all have the ability to have opinions on these subjects.

If the process of projections is followed, the discussion can get to that stage but if such a process is ignored, the negotiation process reduces itself to who is the best salesman. The seller?: "I won't take a cent less." "They don't build them like they used to." "This is the finest piece of real estate in the country." The buyer?: "I'm looking for a steal." "Don't talk to me about taxes; my brother-in-law is the best accountant there is." "I'll only offer $_____." "The price is too high." The salesman to the seller?: "You know the market is quiet." "You probably have over-priced." "You've got to be reasonable." To the buyer: "Real estate is the best investment." "This property really will increase in value and you'll come out well on your investment." "But you're getting shelter, etc. etc."

If a property is properly analyzed, logically projected and fairly compared with alternative investments many cliches suggesting real estate is the best of all investments are unfounded.

In one final reference to the example note the minor difference in yield if the property increases or decreases in value; this is from 8.5% at $315,000 to 10.6% of $415,000. And note, too, that all of these yields indicated are greater than many alternative investments that are available.

When buyers can be made to understand what their investment dollars can do for them even if the property doesn't increase in value and how they can beat alternative investments if the real estate they acquire reduces in value, they will have a greater confidence in real estate investments.

When a seller can be shown what yield a purchaser will obtain by acquiring his overpriced property, he will understand why it did not sell and will reduce his price. But first the broker must understand how to project yields at various prices, terms and conditions. The process is less for clients than for brokers. Only when the broker understands the process and the reason for it can he assist clients by talking in a language they already understand.

Other Commercial-Investment forms that assist in this process are available from RNMI. A complete study in their use and application is available in the many RNMI courses.

Chapter 13

Discounted Cash Flow – A Listing Tool

13

One of the most common (and often the most difficult) problems that brokers face in listing an income-producing property is offering the property at a price that will accomplish the transaction within a reasonable period of time.

Generally speaking, the disposition of investment properties is prompted by investment goals and is not concerned with the personal problems of sellers such as job transfer, divorce, death, change in family size and other reasons that permit a broker to list at a higher than market price, while waiting for the pressures of time and the seller's personal problems to bring the price in line.

Over the years, brokers have relied on gross multipliers and overall capitalization rates to try to convince sellers of the market place realities. All too often, however, the difference of 1% in overall capitalization rate stood between the seller and his agent in reaching an agreement on listing price.

The following example illustrates a situation where discounting is used as a persuasion means of bringing buyer and seller together.

The subject property is a 26-unit apartment that the owners wished to sell for $280,000. A typical property analysis indicated a Net Operating Income of $24,723 and thus an overall capitalization rate of 8.8% at the asking price. The broker recommended a sales price at $260,000 indicating a capitalization rate of 9.5%. The owners disagreed and the salesman was unable to list the property at $260,000.

A new listing approach was conceived based on the methodology and philosophy of discounted cash flows discussed earlier. The technique can be very successful and is capable of repetition.

In essence, the approach is based on the idea of placing the seller in the position of a prospective buyer. What would his income stream be if he acquired the property? This can be projected with data and assumptions on mortgage, amortization, depreciation, interest rates, tax brackets, term of holding and resale price. These become the basis of projections that would be presented to the present owner.

Mortgage amount

Although many people believe that the mortgage is always a percentage of sale price, this is not necessarily true. Although loans may be as high as 75% it is generally accepted that a $50,000 property sold at $100,000 will not necessarily command a $75,000 mortgage. So instead of estimating a maximum mortgage based on a sales price, estimate a "logical" mortgage for a logical period of time at a current interest rate. In the case here there was an existing mortgage which the sellers had recently put on the property by refinancing. It was for $170,000 payable at $1,410 monthly and interest rate at $8\frac{1}{2}\%$, which was considered a logical amount upon which to base the analysis.

Depreciation

Brokers tend to think of land-building allocations in terms of ratios or percentages. Such thinking conditions them to believe that as price rises so does the amount of depreciation. It is possible to change thinking habits to establish a logical amount of depreciation with a change in the price being a change in land value. Under such a premise, depreciation becomes a constant amount at various projected sale prices.

In this case improvements were estimated at $215,600 and a 25-year 125% declining balance method was selected.

Terms of projection

Experience will show that the internal rate of return in year one is usually negative and increases until some time between 12 and 16 years where it levels off, then declines. For this case, 15 years was selected as the projection period.

Tax bracket of the investor

It is unusual to find low tax bracket investors buying million dollar buildings and, conversely, not too many duplexes are acquired by high tax bracket investors.

In this case it was assumed a property in the $200,000–$300,000 bracket would be sold to someone with a 40% marginal tax rate.

Reversion (resale proceeds)

Estimating the future value of a property 15 years hence is not as difficult as estimating current value, at least from the viewpoint of present value of money. An error in judgment as to future value is minimized in terms of present value by the discounting process.

In this case the future value at time of sale was estimated at $260,000. Marketing costs were estimated at 8% and capital gains taxes were calculated at 25% for the first $50,000 and 30% for all over $50,000. No excess depreciation was considered because by the 15th year straight line depreciation exceeds 125%.

Based on the above assumptions a 15-year projection of after-tax cash flows were calculated (after-tax cash flows are net operating income less amortization and income tax). Net sale proceeds at end of year 15 were calculated as follows.

Resale Price	$260,000
Adjusted basis	144,285
Sales cost (8%)	20,800
Gain	$ 94,915

Capital gains tax—$50,000 @ 25% =	$ 12,500
$44,915 @ 30% =	13,475
Total tax	$ 25,975

Sales Price	$260,000
Less: Sales cost	20,800
Capital gains tax	25,975
Mortgage balance	96,132
Proceeds	$117,093

The resulting income stream was projected.

EOY	$
1	$7,929
2	7,701
3	7,473
4	7,248
5	7,022
6	6,795
7	6,567
8	6,336
9	6,100
10	5,860
11	5,732
12	5,472
13	5,202
14	4,923
15	4,632 + $117,093 (Reversion)

The income stream becomes the total future benefits to a prospective purchaser. It therefore follows his yield will depend upon the price he pays for the stream.

The income stream was discounted at five different rates to determine equity values *over* the proposed mortgage. The results were as follows.

Yield	Equity Value	Mortgage	Investment Value
6%	$112,760	$170,000	$282,760
8%	93,875	170,000	263,875
10%	79,200	170,000	249,200
12%	67,675	170,000	237,675
14%	58,535	170,000	228,535

A conference was held with the seller at which time it was pointed out that a buyer of his property at $280,000 could only expect a 6% yield and that no one (including him) buys real estate for that yield. He agreed that 10% was a minimum return considering competitive investments and the property was listed at $245,000, in spite of the fact he had previously refused to list at $260,000.

Within six days a client who had been searching for an investment for many months was shown the analysis from his viewpoint. He wanted to offer $230,000 but it was brought to his attention that his offer would in effect return a yield of 14% which was much higher than he could expect from competitive investments. It was also pointed out his equity funds were now earning only 5% (before taxes) and that his yield could be dramatically increased by acquiring the property. His purchase at $245,000 confirmed the broker's analysis.

Chapter 14

Speculative Land
Investments

14

Vacant land is acquired for an immediate use or to hold for use or sale at a later date. Justification of the value of the property in either case is usually done by showing what "comparable property" is selling for; per acre, per square foot, etc. If the property is acquired for immediate use, it is normal to allocate to the total rent to be charged a percentage which represents a return on the land.

But when the property is acquired for future resale, the fact that its present cost is "comparable" is really no measure of whether the property is a good investment for a particular investor. When a potential investor makes this observation, many brokers counter with the cliche "You know God stopped making land but He didn't stop making people," the inference being that land values always go up. The following illustration indicates a more logical approach to "is this a good investment?" without the presumption that *all* land is a good investment. It also demonstrates that discounted cash flow analysis is the best tool for estimating the practicability of a land investment.

Land for sale

Price	$10,000
Size	20,000 sq. ft.
Down payment required	$ 2,000
Mortgage	8,000
Annual debt service	1,192.24
Interest rate	8%

Investor information assumptions

Marginal tax bracket	50%
Capital gains rate	25%

Other assumptions

Resale at end of 5 years (prior to fifth annual payment).

Step 1. Define annual income stream before taxes.

Investors must pay out:

Initial investment	$2,000.00
Annual debt service	(1,192.24)
Annual property tax	(200.00)
Total annual cash flow	($1,392.24)

EOY	Cash Flows
1	($1392.24)
2	(1392.24)
3	(1392.24)
4	(1392.24)
5	Property sale proceeds

Step 2. Calculate mortgage balance at end of each year and determine annual interest expense.

Year	Mortgage Balance	Principal Reduced	Interest Paid during Year
1	$7447.79	$552.21	$640.03
2	6851.37	596.39	595.85
3	6207.24	644.13	548.11
4	5511.58	695.66	496.58
5			440.93

Step 3. Calculate annual income tax saving.

Year	Interest	Annual Real Estate Taxes	Total Deductions	Tax Saving
1	$640.03	$200	$840.03	$420.02
2	595.85	200	795.85	397.93
3	548.11	200	748.11	374.06
4	496.58	200	696.58	348.29
5				

Step 4. Define income stream after taxes.

Year	Cash Outlay	Tax Saving	Net Outlay
1	($1392.24)	$420.02	$(972.22)
2	(1392.24)	397.93	(944.32)
3	(1392.24)	374.06	(1018.18)
4	(1392.24)	348.29	(1043.95)
5			Resale proceeds

Step 5. Redefine income stream as follows.

The original investment was $2,000. Subsequent annual investments are needed as calculated in Step 4. These amounts are discounted back at a safe rate on the assumption that if in addition to the initial investment sufficient other funds were deposited, the annual needs for the next four years could be met from the additional down payment plus accrued interest; for this example, say 5%.

The process is to discount each of the four years back to the time of purchase at 5%. The additional amounts needed to be deposited are calculated as follows.

Amount Needed End of Year		Column 4–5% Interest Table	Discounted Amount
1	$ 972.22	$.952381	$ 925.92
2	994.31	.907029	901.87
3	1018.18	.863838	879.54
4	1043.95	.822702	858.86
	Total discounted amount		$3,566.19

Step 6. Adding that amount to the initial investment gives a redefined income stream as follows.

Year	Adjusted Initial Investment $2000 + $3566.19 = $5566.19
1	0
2	0
3	0
4	0
5	Resale proceeds

Step 7. Calculate sale proceeds.

Of course no one can accurately predict the resale price five years hence; however, this fact does not preclude making assumptions about the resale price. Therefore, for the purposes of this example, assume three possible resale prices.

Possible resale price	$15,000	$20,000	$25,000
Resale cost 12%	1,800	2,400	3,000
Gross proceeds	$13,200	$17,600	$22,000
Balance owed on property	5,511.58	5,511.58	5,511.58
Interest to sale date	440.93	440.93	440.93
Real estate taxes due	200.00	200.00	200.00
Net proceeds	$7,047.52	$11,447.52	$15,847.52
Gain on sale*	2,559.07	6,959.07	11,359.07
Capital gain tax @ 25%	639.77	1,739.77	2,839.77
Net proceeds after taxes	$ 6,407.75	$ 9,707.75	$13,007.75

* Resale price minus the total of original cost, sales costs, interest and taxes to date.

Step 8. Define income stream for the three possible sales prices and calculate rate of return.

	$15,000	$20,000	$25,000
Resale price			
Initial investment	5,566.19	5,566.19	5,566.19
1	0	0	0
2	0	0	0
3	0	0	0
4	0	0	0
5	6,407.75	9,707.75	13,007.75
Rate of return**	2.9%	11.8	18.5
Annual land appreciation rate	8.5%	14.5%	20.11%

** The rates were calculated by means of an electronic calculator but the compound interest tables can be used to closely estimate the rate. The calculation is as follows.

The initial investment ($5,566.21) was divided by the resale proceeds giving the following three factors for the indicated resale prices.

$15,000	$20,000	$25,000
5,566.19	5,566.19	5,566.19
6,407.72	9,707.22	13,007.72
.868672	.573409	.427916

These represent Column Four reversion factors at unknown interest rates. The annual tables are searched to find at what interest rates these factors appear at five years.

3 - %	11.75%	18 + %	**245**

Conclusion

The analysis is very revealing to the investor (and broker). Although they cannot accurately predict a resale price they can readily determine what resale price *must* be realized within 5 years in order to attain yields of approximately 3%, 12% and 18%.

A basis for value judgment has been created. The broker and investor can discuss the probabilities based on neighborhood, zoning, demographics, trends and all other possible factors. The projected yield can also be compared with alternative investments available.

Wishes and hopes can thus be tempered by what must happen in the market for them to be realized.

Chapter 15

Sandwich Lease

15

The "sandwich" lease is a further example of how value is estimated by the discounted cash flow process and in fact demonstrates that none of the other historical methods of valuation are feasible when applied to this type property.

Once a lease is executed by a tenant on a property an income stream is defined. The stream may be above, below or equal to the rent on comparable properties at the time of execution or later. Therefore, care must be taken to account for the differences between contract rent and market rent when analyzing the property as a potential investment.

When the contract rent is less than market rent an interest is established for the lessee called a leasehold interest. Such interest may be valued by the same discounted cash flow techniques employed elsewhere in this book, i.e. apply the appropriate discount factor to the future income stream. The discount rate used will reflect the quantity, quality and durability of the income of the leasehold.

The income stream is represented by the difference between the annual contract rent and market rent over the remaining period of the lease. If the lessee subleases the property the income stream is defined as the difference between the rent he pays and rent he receives.

The real estate investment broker has an opportunity to create leasehold interests for lessees and therefore should be aware of how this is done and how to measure the value of said interest.

Example

Twelve years have elapsed since Able leased his 50,000 square foot warehouse to Bon Bon Corporation of America for $2,500 per month net rent for a period of 30 years. Two years ago the space became inadequate for Bon Bon; the broker subleased the building to two local tenants as follows.

Cable T. V.	30,000 sq. ft.	Term: 20 years—$2400 per month net net
Dental Supply	20,000 sq. ft.	Term: 20 years—$1600 per month

Just recently Dental Supply moved and broker subleased their space for the balance of the term for $2,000 per month net to Farmer's Tractors.

1. Describe each lessor's and sublessor's projected income stream assuming Able's resale price at the end of the lease is $400,000.

2. Estimate the Present Value of each leasehold interest under the following assumptions.

Able's income stream is discounted at 10%.

Bon Bon stream should be discounted at 15% because of greater risk.

Dental Supply leasehold is discounted at 25% to reflect that Farmer's Tractors is a new local business with untested staying power and credit.

Able has 18 years left to collect on the original 30-year lease. Thus he will receive 216 monthly rentals of $2,500 (beginning of period). In addition it is assumed he will obtain $400,000 from resale proceeds at end of the leases.

Column 5 of the 10% monthly interest table represents the value of an ordinary annuity receivable at the end of each period. To adjust the answer to beginning of the period the Column 5 answer must be multiplied by the "base" (see Appendix B), the base in this situation being 1.008333. Therefore, the present value of $2,500 at the beginning of the month discounted is $2,500 × 10% Annuity Factor (216 months) × Base.

$2,500 × 100.02 × 1.08333 = $252,134

The resale proceeds of $400,000 is receivable at the end of the 216th period discounted at 10% monthly or

| $400,000 × .166536 = | $ 66,615 |
| Total present value of Able's interest | $318,749 |

Bon Bon leased to Cable T.V. and Dental Supply for a total of $4,000 per month ($48,000 annually) but after paying its obligation on its lease to Able ($2,500 per month; $30,000 annually) Bon Bon's income stream is $1,500 monthly for 216 months. Bon Bon will have no reversion; therefore its leasehold has a present value discounted at 15% monthly of the following.

$1,500 × 15% Annuity Factor (216 months) × Base
$1,500 × 74.532824 × 1.0125 = $113,197

The calculation was done by electronic calculator having compound interest functions. Typical compound interest tables at 15% or over are usually for annual values only. The following are the annual calculations for both EOY and BOY.

Present value for $18,000 annual EOY for 18 years discounted at 15%: $18,000 × 6.127966 = $110,303

Present value for $18,000 annual BOY for 18 years discounted at 15%: $18,000 × 6.127966 × 1.15 = $126,849.

Dental Supply became a sublessor when it subleased to Farmer's Tractors. The lease called for Dental to receive $2,000 per month while it in turn continued to pay Bon Bon $1,600 monthly.

Dental Supply's leasehold is $400 per month for 216 months and is discounted at 25% BOY.

By electronic calculator: PV = $400   47.441536 × 1.020833 = $19,372

By Annual Tables 25% EOY: PV = $4,800 × 3.927940 = $18,854

By Annual Tables 25% BOY: PV = $4,800 × 3.927404 × 1.25 = $23,564

Chapter 16

Construction Year Costs

16

The real estate investment broker who is knowledgeable of both the tax laws and the discounting process can effect significant permissible changes in the income stream an investment will produce. This might have some effect on yield. Recognizing that each transaction depends on the specific facts of ownership, the broker can weigh alternatives to structure a transaction to create the best possible yield for his investor.

Chapter 8 discussed some items of cost incurred in the construction of a new project that might either be expensed or capitalized. The following example demonstrates and compares two alternative income streams for the same project.

An apartment house to be built is for sale. Some facts and assumptions include the following.

Projection "A"

Project sales price	$500,000
Mortgage loan available	375,000
Equity required	125,000
Mortgage terms	20 years, 8.5% interest
	3,254.25 per month
	39,051 annual
Net operating income	50,000
Land	100,000
Improvement	400,000
Depreciation schedule	33 years, 200% declining balance
Time of purchase	upon completion
Holding period	13 years
Resale price	500,000

The after-tax cash flows are indicated as Projection "A".

All the facts and assumptions of Projection "A" are used with the following exceptions.

Projection "B"

Improvements	$400,000
Expensed (interest, fees, sales tax)	47,000
Capitalized and depreciated	353,000
Time of purchase	prior to construction
Holding period	after 13 years of operation

The after-tax cash flows are indicated as Projection "B".

Cash Flow Analysis

Date_____

Name **Projection A**   Purpose_____

Mortgage Data

	Encumbrances	Amount	Remaining Term	Payment Period	Interest Rate	Payment Period	Remarks
1	1st Mortgage	375 000	20 Yr.	Mo.	8.5	3 254	
2	2nd Mortgage						
3	3rd Mortgage						

		(1) Year: 0	(2) Year: 1	(3) Year: 2	(4) Year: 3	(5) Year: 4	(6) Year: 5
4	Initial Investment	125 000					
5	1st Mortgage	375 000	375 000	367 538	359 416	350 576	340 955

Ownership Analysis of Property Income: Taxable Income

10	Total Gross Income						
11	— Vacancy & Credit Loss						
12	— Operating Expenses						
13	Net Operating Income		50 000	50 000	50 000	50 000	50 000
14	— Non-Operating Expense						
15	— Interest		31 589	30 929	30 212	29 430	28 579
16	— Depreciation		24 244	22 774	21 394	20 097	18 879
17	Taxable Income		‹5 833›	‹3 703›	‹1 606›	973	2 542

Cash Flows

18	Net Operating Income		50 000	50 000	50 000	50 000	50 000
19	— Princp. & Int. Pymts.		39 057	39 057	39 057	39 057	39 051
20	— Funded Reserves						
21	— Capital Additions						
22	Cash Flow before Taxes		10 949	10 949	10 949	10 949	10 949
23	— Income Tax		‹2 917›	‹1 852›	‹803›	237	1 271
24	Cash Flow after Taxes		13 866	12 801	11 752	10 712	9 678

		Year: 6	Year: 7	Year: 8	Year: 9	Year: 10	Year: 11
4	Initial Investment						
5	1st Mortgage	330 483	319 086	306 682	293 181	278 486	262 493
13	Net Operating Income	50 000	50 000	50 000	50 000	50 000	50 000
14	— Non-Operating Expense						
15	— Interest	27 653	26 645	25 549	24 356	23 059	21 642
16	— Depreciation	17 735	16 660	15 650	14 701	13 810	12 973
17	Taxable Income	4 612	6 695	8 801	10 943	13 131	15 385

Cash Flows

18	Net Operating Income	50 000	50 000	50 000	50 000	50 000	50 000
19	— Princp. & Int. Pymts.	39 057	39 057	39 057	39 057	39 057	39 057
20	— Funded Reserves						
21	— Capital Additions						
22	Cash Flow before Taxes	10 949	10 949	10 949	10 949	10 949	10 949
23	— Income Tax	2 306	3 348	4 401	5 472	6 566	7 693
24	Cash Flow after Taxes	8 643	7 601	6 548	5 477	4 383	3 256

Cash Flow Analysis

Name **Projection A** Date _____ Purpose _____

Mortgage Data

	Encumbrances	Amount	Remaining Term	Payment Period	Interest Rate	Payment Period	Remarks
1	1st Mortgage						
2	2nd Mortgage						
3	3rd Mortgage						

		(1) Year: *12*	(2) Year: *13*	(3) Year: *14*	(4) Year:	(5) Year:	(6) Year:
4	Initial Investment						
5	1st Mortgage	245 086	226 141	205 521			
6	2nd Mortgage						
7	3rd Mortgage						
8	Total Encumbrances						
9	Principal Reduction						

Ownership Analysis of Property Income: Taxable Income

10	Total Gross Income						
11	− Vacancy & Credit Loss						
12	− Operating Expenses						
13	Net Operating Income	50 000	50 000				
14	− Non-Operating Expense						
15	− Interest	20 109	18 429				
16	− Depreciation	12 187	11 448				
17	Taxable Income	17 709	20 123				

Cash Flows

18	Net Operating Income	50 000	50 000				
19	− Princp. & Int. Pymts.	39 051	39 051				
20	− Funded Reserves						
21	− Capital Additions						
22	Cash Flow before Taxes	10 949	10 949				
23	− Income Tax	8 855	10 062				
24	Cash Flow after Taxes	2 094	887				

Analysis of Sales Proceeds Year: *13*

	Adjusted Basis			Excess Depreciation		Tax on Gain %		
25	Original Basis	500 000	Total Depr.	222 552	Excess 28,592 50		14 296
26	+ Capital Improvements		S/L Depr.	157 570	Cap. Gain 193,960 25		48 490
27	+ Costs of Sale		Excess Depr.	64 982	Cap. Gain		
28	Sub-Total				Total Tax Liab.		62 786
29	− Depreciation	222 552	Gain		Sales Proceeds		
30	− Partial Sales		Sales Price	500 000	Sales Price		500 000
31	AB at Sale	277 448	− AB	277 448	− Sales Costs		
32			Gain	222 552	− Mortgage		205 521
33			− Excess	28 592	Proceeds before Taxes		294 479
34			Cap. Gain	193 960	− Total Tax Liab.		62 786
					Proceeds after Taxes		231 643

Cash Flow Analysis

Name _Projection B_   Date_____ Purpose_____

Mortgage Data

	Encumbrances	Amount	Remaining Term	Payment Period	Interest Rate	Payment Period	Remarks
1	1st Mortgage	375 000	20 Yr.	Mo.	8.5	3254	
2	2nd Mortgage						
3	3rd Mortgage						

		(1) Year: 0	(2) Year: 1	(3) Year: 2	(4) Year: 3	(5) Year: 4	(6) Year: 5
4	Initial Investment	125 000					
5	1st Mortgage	375 000	375 000	367 538	359 416	350 576	340 955

Ownership Analysis of Property Income: Taxable Income

10	Total Gross Income						
11	— Vacancy & Credit Loss						
12	— Operating Expenses						
13	Net Operating Income		50 000	50 000	50 000	50 000	50 000
14	— Non-Operating Expense	47 000					
15	— Interest		31 589	30 929	30 212	29 430	28 579
16	— Depreciation		21 395	20 098	18 880	17 736	16 661
17	Taxable Income	<47 000>	<2 984>	<1 027>	908	2 834	4 760

Cash Flows

18	Net Operating Income	0	50 000	50 000	50 000	50 000	50 000
19	— Princp. & Int. Pymts.	0	39 051	39 051	39 051	39 051	39 051
20	— Funded Reserves						
21	— Capital Additions						
22	Cash Flow before Taxes	0	10 949	10 949	10 949	10 949	10 949
23	— Income Tax 50%	<23 500>	<1 492>	<514>	454	1 417	2 380
24	Cash Flow after Taxes	23 500	12 441	11 463	10 495	9 531	8 569

		Year: 6	Year: 7	Year: 8	Year: 9	Year: 10	Year: 11
4	Initial Investment						
5	1st Mortgage	330 483	319 086	306 682	293 181	278 486	262 493
13	Net Operating Income	50 000	50 000	50 000	50 000	50 000	50 000
14	— Non-Operating Expense						
15	— Interest	27 653	26 645	25 549	24 356	23 059	21 648
16	— Depreciation	15 651	14 702	13 811	12 974	12 188	11 449
17	Taxable Income	6 696	8 653	10 640	12 670	14 753	16 909

Cash Flows

18	Net Operating Income	50 000	50 000	50 000	50 000	50 000	50 000
19	— Princp. & Int. Pymts.	39 051	39 051	39 051	39 051	39 051	39 051
20	— Funded Reserves						
21	— Capital Additions						
22	Cash Flow before Taxes	10 949	10 949	10 949	10 949	10 949	10 949
23	— Income Tax	3 398	4 327	5 320	6 335	7 377	8 455
24	Cash Flow after Taxes	7 601	6 622	5 629	4 614	3 572	2 494

Cash Flow Analysis

Name **Projection B**   Date_____   Purpose_____

Mortgage Data

	Encumbrances	Amount	Remaining Term	Payment Period	Interest Rate	Payment Period	Remarks
1	1st Mortgage						
2	2nd Mortgage						
3	3rd Mortgage						

		(1) Year: 12	(2) Year: 13	(3) Year: 14	(4) Year: 15	(5) Year:	(6) Year:
4	Initial Investment						
5	1st Mortgage	245 086	226 141	205 521	183 078		
6	2nd Mortgage						
7	3rd Mortgage						
8	Total Encumbrances						
9	Principal Reduction						

Ownership Analysis of Property Income: **Taxable Income**

10	Total Gross Income						
11	− Vacancy & Credit Loss						
12	− Operating Expenses						
13	Net Operating Income	50 000	50 000	50 000	50 000		
14	− Non-Operating Expense						
15	− Interest	20 104	18 429	16 608	19 625		
16	− Depreciation	10 755	10 103	9 491	8 915		
17	Taxable Income	19 141	21 468	23 901	26 460		

Cash Flows

18	Net Operating Income	50 000	50 000	50 000	50 000		
19	− Princp. & Int. Pymts.	39 051	39 051	39 051	39 051		
20	− Funded Reserves						
21	− Capital Additions						
22	Cash Flow before Taxes	10 949	10 949	10 949	10 949		
23	− Income Tax	9 571	10 734	11 951	13 230		
24	Cash Flow after Taxes	1 378	215	⟨1 002⟩	⟨2 282⟩		

Analysis of Sales Proceeds   Year:

	Adjusted Basis		Excess Depreciation		Tax on Gain	%		
25	Original Basis	453 000	Total Depr.	196 403	Excess	50	12 615	
26	+ Capital Improvements		S/L Depr.	139 061	Cap. Gain	25	54 543	
27	+ Costs of Sale		Excess Depr.	57 342	Cap. Gain			
28	Sub-Total				Total Tax Liab.		67 158	
29	− Depreciation	196 403	**Gain**		**Sales Proceeds**			
30	− Partial Sales		Sales Price	500 000	Sales Price		500 000	
31	AB at Sale	256 597	− AB	256 597	− Sales Costs			
32			Gain	243 403	− Mortgage		205 521	
33			− Excess 41%	25 230	Proceeds before Taxes		294 479	
34			Cap. Gain	218 173	− Total Tax Liab.		67 158	
					Proceeds after Taxes		227 321	

253

A comparison of the two projections is summarized.

Cash Flow Projection
$125,000 Initial Investment

Year	Projection "A"	Projection "B"
0 (Construction)	$	$ 23,500
1 (Operating)	13,865	12,441
2	12,801	11,463
3	11,751	10,495
4	10,711	9,531
5	9,678	8,569
6	8,643	7,601
7	7,602	6,622
8	6,549	5,629
9	5,477	4,614
10	4,381	3,572
11	3,258	2,494
12	2,095	1,378
13	888	215
13 (Resale proceeds)	231,693	227,320

Projection "A"   Purchased after construction, all costs capitalized and held for 13 years of operation

Projection "B"   Purchased prior to construction, permissible costs expensed and held for 13 years of operation
(A case could be made for 12 years of operation so both projections would be for a total of 13 years.)

It should be noted that Projection "B" provides a greater earlier cash flow but a lesser sale proceeds, the latter being due to a lower basis at time of sale which resulted in a higher income tax upon disposition.

This fact of earlier cash return is appealing to many investors and brokers. A calculation was made to determine the IRR with the following results.

Year	Projection "A" $125,000.00 Cash Flows	Year	Projection "B" $125,000.00 Cash Flows
		0	$23,500
1	$13,865	1	12,441
2	12,801	2	11,463
3	11,751	3	10,495
4	10,711	4	9,531
5	9,678	5	8,569
6	8,643	6	7,601
7	7,602	7	6,622
8	6,549	8	5,629
9	5,477	9	4,614
10	4,381	10	3,572
11	3,258	11	2,494
12	2,095	12	1,378
13	232,581	13	227,535
	10.5% IRR		10.7% IRR

Note that the IRR for Projection "B" is not dramatically higher than most investors (and brokers) believe it is. (Some other sets of conditions could result in a greater difference.) The point is that alternatives must be measured by comparison rather than by assuming results.

One last observation: although the IRRs are practically identical the alternatives can be given one further review.

Assume that all the cash flows are reinvested until the time of resale at a safe rate of 5%. This would mean first year's cash flows would accrue interest for 12 years; 2nd year's cash flows, 11 years and so forth. The cash flows would grow to the following.

Year	Projection "A"	Projection "B"
0	$	$ 44,312.75
1	24,899.55	22,342.25
2	21,894.05	19,605.62
3	19.141.14	17,095.25
4	16,616.28	14,785.71
5	14,298.81	12,660.32
6	12,161.57	10,695.37
7	10,187.41	8,874.11
8	8,358.37	7,184.19
9	6,657.31	5,608.35
10	5,071.56	4,135.04
11	3,591.95	2,749.64
12	2,199.75	1,446.90
13	232,581.00	227,535.00
Totals	$377,658.75	$399,030.50

Therefore, although the Internal Rates of Return are similar, the total value produced on a Financial Management basis is greater.

Again, it is apparent that the broker's responsibility is to explore all alternatives.

Chapter 17

Multiple Exchange

17

The following detailed example involves a multi-faceted exchange, commonly referred to as a multiple exchange. The multiple exchange is nothing more than a series of exchanges calculated and executed at one time. Thus, while the following example deals with a three-way exchange and the techniques involved in bringing one about, all the requirements of executing a simple two-way exchange or a more complicated multiple exchange may be extracted from it.

The forms are used to put the mechanics of how the exchange is to be made and how the new ownership of each property will affect and serve the investor after the exchanges are completed and closed in orderly fashion.

The first property

Mike Mulder, a married man, owns a 200′ × 300′ parcel of land zoned for multiple units. He paid $15,000 for the land and has owned it for three years. During these three years the ground has grown in value to $30,000. There is a loan on it with a remaining balance of $10,000. He has taken the taxes and interest payments each year as tax deductions and, therefore, has an adjusted cost basis of $15,000 at the time of the exchange.

Mulder is a musician and earns $16,000 yearly. He has come to a knowledgeable real estate broker because he is paying too much income tax and is tired of making the $100 per month payments on the loan secured by the land. Mulder will list the land with him; it is rising in value at 10% per year.

(This is the basis of all exchanges: a client with a problem, time to do something about solving the problem and a sufficient equity or money to solve his immediate problem. As with any real estate or financial problem, the first step is to "inventory" the client and then the property.)

After preparing an Owner's Statement and a subsequent Broker's Reconstructed Statement, the broker is able to understand the client's present position and look around for other real estate that will give answers to the client's wishes, namely, to stop cash outgo and lower the client's income tax liability.

Second property

Mr. and Mrs. Stitt own an 11-unit apartment building. The Stitts have an income of $25,000 yearly and wish to retire in ten years. The 11-unit was not giving them enough tax shelter or cash flow. In order to reach their retirement goal they want to get into a larger income property that will give them tax shelter now and a larger potential return.

Annual Property Operating Data

Purpose **Broker's Reconstructed Statement**

Name **Mike Mulder**

Location **142 W. 98th St.**

Type of Property **Vacant Lot**

Date _____

Price $ **30,000**

Loans $ **10,000**

Equity $ **20,000**

Assessed/Appraised Values

Land	$ **10,000**	**10** %
Improvement	$ _____	____ %
Personal Property	$ _____	____ %
Total	$ **10,000**	**100** %

Adjusted Basis as of **10 / 11 / 7—** $ **15,000**

FINANCING

	Balance	Payment	Period	Interest	Term
Existing $	**10,000**	**1,200**	**Annual**	**7** %	
1st $				%	
2nd $				%	
3rd $				%	
Potential					
1st $				%	
2nd $				%	

		%	2	3	Comments
1	GROSS SCHEDULED RENTAL INCOME			—0—	
2	Plus: Other Income				
3	TOTAL GROSS INCOME			—0—	
4	Less: Vacancy and Credit Losses				
5	GROSS OPERATING INCOME			—0—	
6	Less: Operating Expenses				
7	Accounting and Legal				
8	Advertising, Licenses and Permits				
9	Property Insurance		40		
10	Property Management				
11	Payroll - Resident Management				
12	Other				
13	Taxes-Workmen's Compensation				
14	Personal Property Taxes				
15	Real Estate Taxes		150		
16	Repairs and Maintenance				
17	Services - Elevator				
18	Janitorial				
19	Lawn				
20	Pool				
21	Rubbish				
22	Other				
23	Supplies				
24	Utilities - Electricity				
25	Gas and Oil				
26	Sewer and Water				
27	Telephone				
28	Other				
29	Miscellaneous				
30					
31	TOTAL OPERATING EXPENSES			190	
32	NET OPERATING INCOME			‹190›	
33	Less: Total Annual Debt Service			1,200	
34	CASH FLOW BEFORE TAXES			1,390	

Mr. Stitt calls the broker and asks him to appraise his property for an immediate sale. The Stitts know nothing about exchanging and never mentioned to the broker that they were going to take the proceeds from a sale and reinvest them in another income property.

The broker does as Mr. Stitt requests and collects the necessary data to appraise the 11-unit. Between the financial data given to him by Stitt's accountant and the facts he collects in the field, the broker is able to fill in Stitt's present position on the

257

Annual Property Operating Data

Purpose **Broker's Reconstructed Statement**
Name **Harold Stitt**

Location _____
Type of Property **11-Unit Apartment Building**
Assessed/Appraised Values

Date _____

Price $ **81,000**
Loans $ **41,500**
Equity $ **39,500**

Land	$ **4,455**	**15** %
Improvement	$ **25,245**	**85** %
Personal Property	$	%
Total	$ **29,700**	**100** %

Adjusted Basis as of _____ $ **57,000**

FINANCING	Balance	Payment	Period	Interest	Term
Existing	$ **41,500**	**5,368**	**Annual**	**6.5** %	
1st	$			%	
2nd	$			%	
3rd	$			%	
Potential 1st	$ **60,000**	**6,246**	**Annual**	**8.5** %	
2nd	$			%	

		%	2	3	Comments
1	GROSS SCHEDULED RENTAL INCOME			13 680	
2	Plus: Other Income				
3	TOTAL GROSS INCOME			13 680	
4	Less: Vacancy and Credit Losses			684	
5	GROSS OPERATING INCOME			12 996	
6	Less: Operating Expenses				
7	Accounting and Legal				
8	Advertising, Licenses and Permits		50		
9	Property Insurance		200		
10	Property Management		1 094		
11	Payroll - Resident Management				
12	Other				
13	Taxes-Workmen's Compensation				
14	Personal Property Taxes				
15	Real Estate Taxes		2 100		
16	Repairs and Maintenance		684		
17	Services - Elevator				
18	Janitorial				
19	Lawn				
20	Pool				
21	Rubbish				
22	Other		75		
23	Supplies		100		
24	Utilities - Electricity		1 400		
25	Gas and Oil				
26	Sewer and Water				
27	Telephone				
28	Other				
29	Miscellaneous				
30					
31	TOTAL OPERATING EXPENSES			5 703	
32	NET OPERATING INCOME			7 293	
33	Less: Total Annual Debt Service				
34	CASH FLOW BEFORE TAXES				

The statements and figures presented herein, while not guaranteed, are secured from sources we believe authoritative. Prepared by_____

Annual Property Operating Data form. It is apparent to the broker that a new owner would not have these same sets of circumstances.

At this point, he prepares a Brokers Reconstructed Statement to analyze the property's income, expenses and cash flow potential. From these studies (not included here) the broker concluded that the property should be marketed at $81,000.

After the research, the broker called the Stitts into his office to discuss his opinion and their personal situation. He pointed out to them that an exchange could save them from paying capital gains taxes they would obviously pay on an outright sale. Also, from the broker's appraisal of the 11-unit, the Stitts agreed to market the property for a tax-deferred exchange at the market value of $81,000.

The broker now has the following elements necessary to effect a multiple exchange.

1. A client motivated to exchange his present property and the time and equity necessary to perform

2. Another client ready, willing and able to exchange his property

The exchange-minded broker now determines that the Stitts' property is just what Mulder needs. There is no doubt, however, that Mulder's property will not solve any of the Stitts' problems.

The broker approaches Mulder with the idea of exchanging his vacant land for Stitts' 11-unit apartment building and the broker's cash flow analysis convinces Mulder to make an offer to exchange.

The exchange must first be balanced out to determine who will owe what to whom. The Exchange Recapitulation form is designed to help determine the equities and how to balance them. Here are the steps to complete that form.

1. Inventory Mulder's property; determine his equity. Determine his transaction costs and commission. Calculate Mulder's net equity by subtracting commissions and transaction costs from the equity.

2. Inventory the property Mulder is to receive and maximize the financing. Mulder will have to put enough equity and/or boot and cash into the transaction to purchase the equity in the 11-unit.

3. On the next line, under the "Property" column, show the effects of his receiving the 11-unit with the new loan on the property of $60,000. Mulder will pay the commission, transaction costs and differences in equities in cash. Thus, his $17,000 net equity plus $4,000 in cash is what will be required to satisfy the equity in the 11-unit of $21,000.

4. Under the "Cash, Gives" column show that Mulder will give the $4,000 cash.

With this step of the exchange balanced, we need not go on with the Exchange Recapitulation form at this point. It has now been determined how the first leg of the transaction will look; the exchange offer to be made by Mulder is drafted and executed by Stitt giving the broker sufficient time to get acceptance.

While Mulder is ready to exchange for the Stitt property, Stitt is not about to accept the contract from Mulder. The Stitts' "no" is the broker's clue to find another leg to the exchange. Eventually, the owner of property for which the Stitts will exchange will sign the offer from Mulder as "owner under contract."

Annual Property Operating Data

Purpose **Brokers Reconstructed Statement**
Name **West King + Lyon**
Location **765 Beach St.**
Type of Property **OFFICE Building**

Assessed/Appraised Values

Land	$ 15,000	20 %
Improvement	$ 60,000	80 %
Personal Property	$	%
Total	$ 75,000	100 %

Adjusted Basis as of _____ $178,000

Date _____

Price	$ 250,000
Loans	$ 175,000
Equity	$ 75,000

FINANCING

	Balance	Payment	Period	Interest	Term
Existing	$175,000	16,281	Annual	7 %	
1st	$			%	
2nd	$			%	
3rd	$			%	
Potential					
1st	$			%	
2nd	$			%	

		%	2	3	Comments
1	GROSS SCHEDULED RENTAL INCOME			45 714	
2	Plus: Other Income			—	
3	TOTAL GROSS INCOME			45 714	
4	Less: Vacancy and Credit Losses			2 742	
5	GROSS OPERATING INCOME			42 972	
6	Less: Operating Expenses				
7	Accounting and Legal				
8	Advertising, Licenses and Permits		300		
9	Property Insurance		600		
10	Property Management		2 014		
11	Payroll - Resident Management				
12	Other		3 200		
13	Taxes-Workmen's Compensation		800		
14	Personal Property Taxes				
15	Real Estate Taxes		5 250		
16	Repairs and Maintenance		1 786		
17	Services - Elevator				
18	Janitorial				
19	Lawn				
20	Pool				
21	Rubbish		750		
22	Other		150		
23	Supplies		460		
24	Utilities - Electricity		1 800		
25	Gas and Oil		2 100		
26	Sewer and Water				
27	Telephone				
28	Other				
29	Miscellaneous		960		
30					
31	TOTAL OPERATING EXPENSES			19 670	
32	NET OPERATING INCOME			23 302	
33	Less: Total Annual Debt Service				
34	CASH FLOW BEFORE TAXES				

The statements and figures presented
herein, while not guaranteed, are secured
from sources we believe authoritative. Prepared by _____

The third property

Another broker calls a new listing he has obtained to the first broker's attention. The listing is an office building. The income and expenses of the property are shown on an Annual Property Operating Data form.

From this form, the first broker recognizes that the property would probably do for the Stitts; at least the basic economics are present.

Property	Market Value 2	Existing Loans 3	Equity 4	Cash Gives (In) 5	Cash Gets (Out) 6	Paper Gives 7	Paper Gets 8	Comm. 9	Trans. Costs 10	Net Equity 11	New Loan 12	Old Loan 13	Net Loan Proceeds 14
Vacant Land (Mulder)	30,000	10,000	20,000	4,000				2,500	500	21,000			
Gets 11-Unit	81,000	60,000	21,000							21,000			
11-Unit (Stitt)	81,000	41,500	39,500	5,670				4,860	810	39,500	60,000	41,500	18,500
Gets Off. Bldg.	250,000	175,000	75,000			35,500				39,500			
Off. Blds. (Lawyers)	250,000	175,000	75,000					15,000	2,500	57,500			
Get Vac. Land	30,000	10,000	20,000		2,000		35,500			57,500			
				7,670	2,000	35,500	35,500	22,360	3,810				18,500
				18,500	3,810	-0-		22,360	3,810				18,500
								22,360		-0-			-0-
				28,170	28,170								
				-0-									

The other broker informs the first broker that the owners of the building are three very old lawyers in the firm of West, King and Lyon. Their only motive is to dispose of the office building and get into a management-free investment. This tells the first broker that vacant land will answer the older lawyers' desires and that is what he needs, an owner for Mulder's land.

In order to start working the exchange, the first broker goes back to the Exchange Recapitulation form to balance the exchange.

Stitt will pay the commission and transaction costs from his available cash but wants to keep all the rest of his available cash for his children's college expenses. On the Exchange Recapitulation form, Stitt's position is inventoried as follows.

Market value		$81,000
Present loan		41,500
Equity		$39,500
Less: Commission	$4,860	
Transaction costs	810	5,670
		33,830
Cash paid		5,670
Net equity		$39,500

Next the net loan proceeds are calculated.

Since the office building cannot be refinanced, the Stitts will have to acquire the existing equity of $75,000 in the office building. Because the Stitts want to keep all their cash over and above transaction costs and commissions, the equity will have to be balanced in second loan paper. The paper will amount to $35,000.

To work with the office building, under the "Property" column of the Exchange Recapitulation form drop down a few spaces and inventory the office building to show and arrive at the net equity in the building. This is calculated to be $57,500. **261**

Immediately under the words "Office Building" inventory Mulder's land. In order to balance out the exchange it is obvious that the older lawyers will have to receive a net of $57,500.

In completing the multiple exchange on the Exchange Recapitulation form, the following steps should be followed to insure proper accounting and distribution of paper and cash involved in the multiple exchange.

Step 1. Total columns 5, 6, 7, 8, 9, 10 and 14.

Step 2. Transfer total of net loan proceeds, column 14, to column 5; enter this amount beneath the total of column 5; indicate in column 14 that the net loan proceeds have been distributed to the cash-in column by writing the amount of the net loan proceeds withdrawn and then zeroing it out as indicated.

Step 3. Since the totals of columns 9 and 10 have to be paid out, transfer them to column 6; indicate the transfer by duplicating each of the totals of columns 9 and 10 and zero out.

Step 4. Columns 7 and 8 should be equal; if they are, paper is in balance.

Step 5. Total columns 5 and 6 beneath the double-line and cash-in and cash-out should equal; if these two columns equal each other (cash paid in-cash paid out), the exchange is in balance.

In the final results, the older lawyers received the following for their net equity of $57,500.

$20,000 equity in Mulder's vacant land
  2,000 in cash
$35,000 second loan secured by their office building
$57,500

The Stitts received for their $39,500 net equity the $39,500 equity in the office building.

Mulder received $21,000 equity in 11-unit for which he gave his $20,000 equity
                                            plus $ 1,000 cash
                                                  $21,000

All accounts are balanced.

Exchange basis adjustment

For each of the three parties to the exchange, basis must be calculated for the new property. The rules for calculating basis are explained on page 18.

A sample Exchange Basis Adjustment form is presented for Mike Mulder.

Exchange Basis Adjustment

Name _Mike Mulder_   Date _____

Property Conveyed _Vacant Lot_ _____

	LINE NO.		(1) PROPERTY		(2) PROPERTY		(3) PROPERTY		(4) PROPERTY	
INDICATED GAIN	1	Market Value of Property Conveyed	30	000						
	2	Less: Adjusted Basis	18	000						
	3	Less: Capitalized Transaction Costs	3	000						
	4	INDICATED GAIN	9	000						
	5	Equity Conveyed	20	000						
	6	Equity Acquired	21	000						
BALANCE EQUITIES	7	Difference	1	000						
	8	Cash or Boot Received	— 0 —							
	9	Cash or Boot Paid	1	000						
DETERMINE RECOGNIZED GAIN	10	Old Loans	10	000						
	11	Less: New Loans	60	000						
	12	NET LOAN RELIEF	— 0 —							
	13	Less: Cash or Boot Paid (L9)	1	000						
	14	Recognized Net Loan Relief	— 0 —							
	15	Plus: ~~Cash or~~ Net Cash Boot Received (L8) _minus (L5)_	— 0 —							
	16	TOTAL UNLIKE PROPERTY RECEIVED	— 0 —							
	17	Recognized Gain LESSER OF L4 or L16	— 0 —							

Transfer of Basis

	LINE NO.		(1)		(2)		(3)		(4)	
TRANSFER OF BASIS	18	Adjusted Basis (L2) Plus (L3)	21	000						
	19	Plus: New Loans (L11)	60	000						
	20	Plus: Cash or Boot Paid (L9)	1	000						
	21	Plus: Recognized Gain (L17)	— 0 —							
	22	Total Additions	82	000						
	23	Less Old Loans (L10)	10	000						
	24	Less: Cash or Boot Received (L8)	— 0 —							
	25	NEW ADJUSTED BASIS	72	000						

New Allocation and Depreciation

	LINE NO.		(1)		(2)		(3)		(4)	
ALLOCATION	26	Land Allocation								
	27	Improvement Allocation								
	28	Personal Property Allocation								

			PP	IMP	PP	IMP	PP	IMP	PP	IMP
DEPRECIATION	29	Estimated Useful Life in Years								
	30	Depreciation Method								
	31	ANNUAL DEPRECIATION IMPROVEMENTS								
	32	ANNUAL DEPRECIATION PERSONAL PROPERTY								

The statements and figures presented herein, while not guaranteed, are secured from sources we believe authoritative.   Prepared by_____

Chapter 18

Sensitivity Analysis

18

One of the most useful applications of IRR analysis is in the area of forecasting in which the question What if? is asked. Seldom is there such a degree of accuracy concerning the future performance of the property being analyzed that a single investment value or rate of return estimate can be used with 100% confidence. Risk is inherent, with varying degrees, in all forms of investments.

In evaluating the future cash flows associated with a real estate investment, some care should be made to isolate those elements of the stream of future cash flows that are most subject to error in forecasting. Once isolated, the values that these elements take on may be varied to represent the most likely range of future estimates. Questions like *What if* property taxes increase steadily throughout the holding period of the investment rather than remain stable? may be examined. The reasonable or possible expenses, both high and low, as well as the most likely value that the various components of the cash flows may take on can be used in making alternative estimates of the investment value of the property or of the IRR of the investment.

In essence, these alternative measures of the investment worth of a particular property provide at least two helpful analytical tools to the investment broker. First, it allows the broker/analyst to determine just how sensitive the value or rate of return of the property is to changes in the assumed value of one or more elements in the cash flow. This can be most helpful in determining how critical a specific assumption is in the investment decision, whatever the assumed conditions. For example, the assumptions regarding the resale price of a property at the end of a long-term lease may have little effect on either the investment value or the IRR of the property because of the time value of waiting for the reversion.

A second way in which this form of analysis can be used is to determine the value of IRR under the most pessimistic and optimistic estimates of key cash flow components. While this procedure does not directly improve the objective measurement of risk associated with the investment, it does place magnitudes on the extreme outcomes that could occur so that a more rational approach may be used in investment decision-making.

As an illustration of this concept of sensitivity analysis, the following is an example of an 8-unit apartment property that is being considered by a prospective investor. The prospective investor, Mr. Smith, has $15,000 available for investment. (For this problem, a marginal tax rate of 40% will be utilized when computing the investor's income tax liability.)

The selling price of the property is $95,000. Presently, an $80,000 mortgage loan is available at an 8% annual interest rate with monthly payments over a 20-year term. A projected holding period of 10 years is assumed for this property and resale costs are estimated at 7% of the resale price. (These data will remain constant throughout the example.)

First, utilizing the given information, sensitivity analysis will be employed to illustrate the effect of different resale prices on the IRR. This is shown as Case 1. In this analysis, NOI is projected to be $8,490 per year over the entire holding period. The property will be depreciated for tax purposes using the 125% declining balance method over the 20-year depreciable life of the improvement.

Since the investor has been able to obtain an $80,000 mortgage with monthly payments of $669, his yearly payments, therefore, amount to $8,028. By the end of the 10-year projected holding period, principal payments will have amounted to $24,860, leaving a mortgage balance outstanding of $55,140.

In Case 1, the IRR for the property is calculated for three alternative resale prices: $95,000 (the same as the original selling price); $127,672 (a 3% annual growth rate); and $80,000 (a decline of $15,000 in total property value).

As indicated, the respective IRRs are as follows.

Resale Price	IRR
$ 80,000	6.7%
$ 95,000	11.4%
$127,672	17.8%

This now provides a range from the most likely "bottom" yield to the most likely (and optimistic) ceiling yield, all on a comparable after-tax basis. Although this does not measure risk, it does provide a range of yields that the investor will find useful in evaluating the investment.

Case 2 illustrates the impact of alternative estimates of NOI on the calculated IRR of this same property, with the resale price assumed to be the same as the purchase price. In this case, the calculated IRRs are as follows.

NOI	IRR
$8,090	9.8%
$8,490	11.4%
$8,890	12.8%

As indicated, a $400 drop in NOI produces a 14% drop in IRR from 11.4% to 9.8%; a $400 increase produces a similar but smaller increase in IRR. Thus, for this property, small changes in NOI produce significant changes in the rate of return. If $400 is a valid estimate of the probable range of fluctuations in NOI, the resulting IRRs provide a minimum/maximum range of most likely rates of return.

Cash Flow Analysis
Case 1

	Year: 1	Year: 2	Year: 3	Year: 4	Year: 5	Year: 6
Ownership Analysis of Property Income:		Taxable Income				
10 Total Gross Income						
11 − Vacancy & Credit Loss						
12 − Operating Expenses						
13 Net Operating Income	8490	8490	8490	8490	8490	8490
14 − Non-Operating Expense						
15 − Interest	6319	6197	6046	5880	5703	5509
16 − Depreciation	5047	4732	4433	4159	3900	3658
17 Taxable Income	(2876)	(2439)	(1989)	(1549)	(1113)	(677)
			Cash Flows			
18 Net Operating Income	8490	8490	8490	8490	8490	8490
19 − Princp. & Int. Pymts.	8028	8028	8028	8028	8028	8028
20 − Funded Reserves						
21 − Capital Additions						
22 Cash Flow before Taxes	462	462	462	462	462	462
23 − Income Tax	(1150)	(976)	(776)	(620)	(445)	(271)
24 Cash Flow after Taxes	1612	1438	1258	1082	907	733

	Year: 7	Year: 8	Year: 9	Year: 10	Year:	Year:
Ownership Analysis of Property Income:		Taxable Income				
10 Total Gross Income						
11 − Vacancy & Credit Loss						
12 − Operating Expenses						
13 Net Operating Income	8490	8490	8490	8490		
14 − Non-Operating Expense						
15 − Interest	5300	5074	4829	4563		
16 − Depreciation	3424	3214	3012	2826		
17 Taxable Income	(234)	202	649	1101		
			Cash Flows			
18 Net Operating Income	8490	8490	8490	8490		
19 − Princp. & Int. Pymts.	8028	8028	8028	8028		
20 − Funded Reserves						
21 − Capital Additions						
22 Cash Flow before Taxes	462	462	462	462		
23 − Income Tax	(94)	(81)	(260)	(440)		
24 Cash Flow after Taxes	556	381	202	22		

Analysis of Sales Proceeds — Year:

	Adjusted Basis			Excess Depreciation			Tax on Gain	%			
25	Original Basis	95	000	Total Depr.	38	405	Excess				
26	+ Capital Improvements			S/L Depr.	40	375	Cap. Gain 50%	40	17	805	
27	+ Costs of Sale 7%	5	600	Excess Depr.	—		Cap. Gain				
28	Sub-Total	100	600				Total Tax Liab.		3	561	
29	− Depreciation	38	405		Gain			Sales Proceeds			
30	− Partial Sales	—		Sales Price	80	000	Sales Price		80	000	
31	AB at Sale	62	195	− AB	62	195	− Sales Costs 7%		5	600	
32				Gain	17	805	− Mortgage		55	140	
33				− Excess	—		Proceeds before Taxes		19	260	
34				Cap. Gain	17	805	− Total Tax Liab.		3	561	
							Proceeds after Taxes		15	699	

Analysis of Sales Proceeds — Year: 10

	Adjusted Basis			Excess Depreciation			Tax on Gain	%			
25	Original Basis	95	000	Total Depr.	38	405	Excess				
26	+ Capital Improvements	—		S/L Depr.	40	375	Cap. Gain 50%	40	31	750	
27	+ Costs of Sale 7%	6	650	Excess Depr.	—		Cap. Gain				
28	Sub-Total	101	650				Total Tax Liab.		6	351	
29	− Depreciation	38	405		Gain			Sales Proceeds			
30	− Partial Sales	—		Sales Price	95	000	Sales Price		95	000	
31	AB at Sale	63	245	− AB	63	245	− Sales Costs 7%		6	650	
32				Gain	31	755	− Mortgage		55	140	
33				− Excess	—		Proceeds before Taxes		33	210	
34				Cap. Gain	31	755	− Total Tax Liab.		6	351	
							Proceeds after Taxes		26	859	

Analysis of Sales Proceeds — Year: 10

	Adjusted Basis			Excess Depreciation			Tax on Gain	%			
25	Original Basis	95	000	Total Depr.	38	405	Excess				
26	+ Capital Improvements	—		S/L Depr.	40	375	Cap. Gain 50%	40	62	140	
27	+ Costs of Sale 7%	8	937	Excess Depr.	—		Cap. Gain				
28	Sub-Total	103	937				Total Tax Liab.		12	428	
29	− Depreciation	38	405		Gain			Sales Proceeds			
30	− Partial Sales	—		Sales Price	127	672	Sales Price		127	672	
31	AB at Sale	65	532	− AB	65	532	− Sales Costs 7%		8	937	
32				Gain	62	140	− Mortgage		55	140	
33				− Excess	—		Proceeds before Taxes		63	595	
34				Cap. Gain	62	140	− Total Tax Liab.		12	428	
							Proceeds after Taxes		51	167	

Internal Rate of Return Worksheet
Case 1

Date _____

Name **Mr. Smith**   Property **8-Unit Apartment**

Net Sale Proceeds $ **See below**   Investment Amount $ **15,000**

End of Year	Cash Flow	Discount at 5%		Discount at 10%		Discount at 15%		Discount at 20%	
		P.V. of 1	Amount	P.V. of 1	Amount	P.V. of 1	Amount	P.V. of 1	Amount
1	1,612	.952381	1,535	.909091	1,465	.869565	1,402	.833333	1,343
2	1,438	.907029	1,304	.826446	1,188	.756144	1,087	.694444	999
3	1,258	.863838	1,087	.751315	995	.657516	827	.578704	728
4	1,082	.822702	890	.683013	739	.571753	619	.482253	522
5	907	.783526	711	.620921	563	.497177	451	.401878	365
6	733	.746215	547	.564474	414	.432328	317	.334898	245
7	556	.710681	395	.513158	285	.375937	209	.279082	155
8	381	.676839	258	.466507	178	.326902	125	.232568	89
9	202	.644609	130	.424098	86	.284262	57	.193807	39
10	22	.613913	14	.385543	8	.247185	5	.161506	4
11		.584679		.350494		.214943		.134588	
12		.556837		.318631		.186907		.112157	
13		.530321		.289664		.162528		.093464	
14		.505068		.263331		.141329		.077887	
15		.481017		.239392		.122894		.064905	
16		.458112		.217629		.106865		.054088	
17		.436297		.197845		.092926		.045073	
18		.415521		.179859		.080805		.037561	
19		.395734		.163508		.070265		.031301	
20		.376889		.148644		.061100		.026085	
Reversion Year 10	15,699	.613913	9,638	.385543	6,053				
Reversion Year 10	26,859			.385543	10,355	.247185	6,639		
Reversion Year 10	51,167					.247185	12,648	.161506	8,264
TOTALS	15,699		16,509		11,924				
TOTALS	26,859				16,226		11,738		
TOTALS	51,167						17,747		12,753

IRR Calculations
Case 1

INTERPOLATION

	% Rate		$ Present Value Amount	
Smaller	5%	$ 16,509	⟶ $ 16,509	
Larger	10%	$ 11,924	Investment Amount $ 15,000	

| Absolute Difference | 5% | ÷ $ 4,585 | $ 1,509 | + | Smaller Rate | 5% = 6.65 % |

INTERPOLATION

	% Rate		$ Present Value Amount	
Smaller	10%	$ 16,226	⟶ $ 16,226	
Larger	15%	$ 11,738	Investment Amount $ 15,000	

| Absolute Difference | 5% | ÷ $ 4,488 | x | $ 1,226 | + | Smaller Rate | 10% = 11.37 % |

INTERPOLATION

	% Rate		$ Present Value Amount	
Smaller	15%	$ 17,747	⟶ $ 17,747	
Larger	20%	$ 12,753	Investment Amount $ 15,000	

| Absolute Difference | 5% | ÷ $ 4,994 | x | $ 2,747 | + | Smaller Rate | 15% = 17.75 % |

Cash Flow Analysis
Case 2

		Year: 1	Year: 2	Year: 3	Year: 4	Year: 5	Year: 6
	Ownership Analysis of Property Income:			Taxable Income			
13	Net Operating Income	8 090	8 090	8090	8090	8090	8090
14	− Non-Operating Expense						
15	− Interest	6 319	6197	6046	5886	5703	5509
16	− Depreciation	5047	4732	4433	4159	3900	3658
17	Taxable Income	⟨3 276⟩	⟨2 839⟩	⟨2 389⟩	⟨1 949⟩	⟨1 513⟩	⟨1 077⟩
				Cash Flows			
18	Net Operating Income	8 090	8090	8090	8090	8090	8090
19	− Princp. & Int. Pymts.	8 028	8 028	8 028	8 028	8 028	8 028
22	Cash Flow before Taxes	62	62	62	62	62	62
23	− Income Tax	⟨1 310⟩	⟨1 136⟩	⟨956⟩	⟨780⟩	⟨605⟩	⟨431⟩
24	Cash Flow after Taxes	1 372	1 198	1 018	842	667	493

		Year: 7	Year: 8	Year: 9	Year: 10	Year:	Year:
	Ownership Analysis of Property Income:			Taxable Income			
13	Net Operating Income	8 090	8090	8090	8090		
14	− Non-Operating Expense						
15	− Interest	5 300	5 074	4 829	4 563		
16	− Depreciation	3 421	3 214	3012	2 824		
17	Taxable Income	⟨631⟩	⟨198⟩	249	701		
				Cash Flows			
18	Net Operating Income	8 090	8 090	8 090	8 090		
19	− Princp. & Int. Pymts.	8 028	8 028	8 028	8 028		
22	Cash Flow before Taxes	62	62	62	62		
23	− Income Tax	⟨254⟩	⟨79⟩	100	280		
24	Cash Flow after Taxes	316	141	⟨38⟩	⟨218⟩		

		Year: 1	Year: 2	Year: 3	Year: 4	Year: 5	Year: 6
	Ownership Analysis of Property Income:		**Taxable Income**				
13	Net Operating Income	8 890	8 890	8 890	8 890	8 890	8 890
14	— Non-Operating Expense						
15	— Interest	6 319	6 197	6 046	5 880	5 703	5 509
16	— Depreciation	5 047	4 732	4 433	4 159	3 900	3 658
17	Taxable Income	⟨2 476⟩	⟨2 039⟩	⟨1 589⟩	⟨1 149⟩	⟨713⟩	⟨277⟩
			Cash Flows				
18	Net Operating Income	8 890	8 890	8 890	8 890	8 890	8 890
19	— Princp. & Int. Pymts.	8 028	8 028	8 028	8 028	8 028	8 028
22	Cash Flow before Taxes	862	862	862	862	862	862
23	— Income Tax	⟨990⟩	⟨816⟩	⟨636⟩	⟨460⟩	⟨285⟩	⟨111⟩
24	Cash Flow after Taxes	1 852	1 678	1 498	1 322	1 147	973

		Year: 7	Year: 8	Year: 9	Year: 10	Year:	Year:
	Ownership Analysis of Property Income:		**Taxable Income**				
13	Net Operating Income	8 890	8 890	8 890	8 890		
14	— Non-Operating Expense						
15	— Interest	5 300	5 074	4 829	4 563		
16	— Depreciation	3 429	3 214	3 012	2 826		
17	Taxable Income	166	602	1 315	1 501		
			Cash Flows				
18	Net Operating Income	8 890	8 890	8 890	8 890		
19	— Princp. & Int. Pymts.	8 028	8 028	8 028	8 028		
22	Cash Flow before Taxes	862	862	862	862		
23	— Income Tax	66	241	526	600		
24	Cash Flow after Taxes	796	621	334	262		

Internal Rate of Return Worksheet
Case 2

No. 1: $ 8,090　　　　　　　　　　　　Date _____

Name Mr. Smith　　　　　　　　　　　Property 8- Unit Apartment

Net Sale Proceeds $ _____　　Investment Amount $ 15,000

End of Year	Cash Flow	Discount at 5%		Discount at 10%		Discount at 15%		Discount at 20%	
		P.V. of 1	Amount	P.V. of 1	Amount	P.V. of 1	Amount	P.V. of 1	Amount
1	1372	.952381	1307	.909091	1247	.869565		.833333	
2	1198	.907029	1087	.826446	990	.756144		.694444	
3	1018	.863838	879	.751315	765	.657516		.578704	
4	842	.822702	693	.683013	575	.571753		.482253	
5	667	.783526	523	.620921	414	.497177		.401878	
6	493	.746215	368	.564474	278	.432328		.334898	
7	316	.710681	225	.513158	162	.375937		.279082	
8	141	.676839	95	.466507	66	.326902		.232568	
9	(38)	.644609	(25)	.424098	(16)	.284262		.193807	
10	(218)	.613913	(134)	.385543	(84)	.247185		.161506	
11		.584679		.350494		.214943		.134588	
12		.556837		.318631		.186907		.112157	
13		.530321		.289664		.162528		.093464	
14		.505068		.263331		.141329		.077887	
15		.481017		.239392		.122894		.064905	
16		.458112		.217629		.106865		.054088	
17		.436297		.197845		.092926		.045073	
18		.415521		.179859		.080805		.037561	
19		.395734		.163508		.070265		.031301	
20		.376889		.148644		.061100		.026085	
Reversion Year 10	26,859	.613913	16,489						
Reversion Year 10	26,859			.385543	10,355				
Reversion Year ___									
TOTALS			21,507		14,752				

INTERPOLATION

　　　　% Rate　　　　　　　　　　$ Present Value Amount

Smaller　5%　　　　$ 21,507　　——→ $ 21,507

Larger　10%　　　　$ 14,752　　Investment Amount $ 15,000

[Absolute Difference　5%　÷ $ 6,755　×　$ 6,507]　+　Smaller Rate　5% = 9.82 %

Prepared by _____

Internal Rate of Return Worksheet
Case 2

No.1: $ 8,890   Date _____

Name Mr. Smith   Property 8-Unit Apartment

Net Sale Proceeds $ _____   Investment Amount $ 15,000

End of Year	Cash Flow	Discount at 5%		Discount at 10%		Discount at 15%		Discount at 20%	
		P.V. of 1	Amount	P.V. of 1	Amount	P.V. of 1	Amount	P.V. of 1	Amount
1	1852	.952381		.909091	1684	.869565	1610	.833333	
2	1678	.907029		.826446	1397	.756144	1269	.694444	
3	1498	.863838		.751315	1125	.657516	985	.578704	
4	1322	.822702		.683013	903	.571753	756	.482253	
5	1147	.783526		.620921	712	.497177	570	.401878	
6	973	.746215		.564474	549	.432328	421	.334898	
7	796	.710681		.513158	408	.375937	299	.279082	
8	621	.676839		.466507	290	.326902	203	.232568	
9	336	.644609		.424098	143	.284262	96	.193807	
10	262	.613913		.385543	101	.247185	65	.161506	
11		.584679		.350494		.214943		.134588	
12		.556837		.318631		.186907		.112157	
13		.530321		.289664		.162528		.093464	
14		.505068		.263331		.141329		.077887	
15		.481017		.239392		.122894		.064905	
16		.458112		.217629		.106865		.054088	
17		.436297		.197845		.092926		.045073	
18		.415521		.179859		.080805		.037561	
19		.395734		.163508		.070265		.031301	
20		.376889		.148644		.061100		.026085	
Reversion Year 10	26,859			.385543	10,355				
Reversion Year 10	26,859					.247185	6,639		
Reversion Year ___									
TOTALS					17,657		12,913		

INTERPOLATION

% Rate		$ Present Value Amount	
Smaller	10%	$ 17,657	→ $ 17,657
Larger	15%	$ 12,913	Investment Amount $ 15,000

[Absolute Difference ___5%___ ÷ $ 4,744   x $ 2,657] + Smaller Rate ___10%___ = 12.8 %

Prepared by _____

Appendix A

Compound Interest Tables

The tables are reprinted from *Ellwood Tables for Real Appraising and Financing*, 3rd edition, Part II, by the late L. W. Ellwood with the permission of the American Institute of Real Estate Appraisers.

EFFECTIVE RATE = 5/12%   **BASE = 1.00416666+**

MONTHS	1 AMOUNT OF 1 AT COMPOUND INTEREST $S^n = (1+i)^n$	2 ACCUMULATION OF 1 PER PERIOD $S_{\overline{n}|} = \dfrac{S^n - 1}{i}$	3 SINKING FUND FACTOR $1\,S_{\overline{n}|} = \dfrac{i}{S^n - 1}$	4 PRES. VALUE REVERSION OF 1 $V^n = \dfrac{1}{S^n}$	5 PRESENT VALUE ORD. ANNUITY 1 PER PERIOD $a_{\overline{n}|} = \dfrac{1 - V^n}{i}$	6 INSTALMENT TO AMORTIZE 1 $1/a_{\overline{n}|} = \dfrac{i}{1 - V^n}$	n MONTHS
1	1.004167	1.000000	1.000000	.995851	.995851	1.004167	1
2	1.008351	2.004167	.498960	.991718	1.987569	.503127	2
3	1.012552	3.012517	.331948	.987603	2.975173	.336115	3
4	1.016771	4.025070	.248443	.983506	3.958678	.252610	4
5	1.021008	5.041841	.198340	.979425	4.938103	.202507	5
6	1.025262	6.062848	.164939	.975361	5.913463	.169106	6
7	1.029534	7.088110	.141081	.971313	6.884777	.145248	7
8	1.033824	8.117644	.123188	.967283	7.852060	.127355	8
9	1.038131	9.151467	.109272	.963269	8.815329	.113439	9
10	1.042457	10.189599	.098139	.959272	9.774602	.102306	10
11	1.046800	11.232055	.089031	.955292	10.729894	.093198	11
YEARS							
1	1.051162	12.278855	.081441	.951328	11.681222	.085608	12
2	1.104941	25.185921	.039705	.905025	22.793898	.043872	24
3	1.161472	38.753336	.025804	.860976	33.365701	.029971	36
4	1.220895	53.014885	.018863	.819071	43.422956	.023030	48
5	1.283359	68.006083	.014705	.779205	52.990706	.018872	60
6	1.349018	83.764259	.011938	.741280	62.092777	.016105	72
7	1.418036	100.328653	.009967	.705201	70.751835	.014134	84
8	1.490585	117.740513	.008493	.670877	78.989441	.012660	96
9	1.566847	136.043196	.007351	.638225	86.826108	.011518	108
10	1.647010	155.282280	.006440	.607161	94.281350	.010607	120
11	1.731274	175.505671	.005698	.577609	101.373733	.009865	132
12	1.819849	196.763730	.005082	.549496	108.120917	.009249	144
13	1.912956	219.109392	.004564	.522751	114.539704	.008731	156
14	2.010826	242.598300	.004122	.497308	120.646077	.008289	168
15	2.113704	267.288945	.003741	.473103	126.455243	.007908	180
16	2.221845	293.242810	.003410	.450076	131.981666	.007577	192
17	2.335519	320.524524	.003120	.428170	137.239108	.007287	204
18	2.455008	349.202023	.002864	.407331	142.240661	.007031	216
19	2.580611	379.346717	.002636	.387505	146.998780	.006803	228
20	2.712640	411.033670	.002433	.368645	151.525313	.006600	240
21	2.851424	444.341789	.002251	.350702	155.831531	.006418	252
22	2.997308	479.354014	.002086	.333633	159.928159	.006253	264
23	3.150656	516.157530	.001937	.317394	163.825396	.006104	276
24	3.311850	554.843985	.001802	.301946	167.532948	.005969	288
25	3.481290	595.509712	.001679	.287250	171.060047	.005846	300
26	3.659400	638.255975	.001567	.273269	174.415476	.005734	312
27	3.846622	683.189218	.001464	.259968	177.607590	.005631	324
28	4.043422	730.421330	.001369	.247315	180.644338	.005536	336
29	4.250291	780.069928	.001282	.235278	183.533282	.005449	348
30	4.467744	832.258641	.001202	.223827	186.281617	.005369	360
31	4.696323	887.117429	.001127	.212933	188.896185	.005294	372
32	4.936595	944.782896	.001058	.202569	191.383497	.005225	384
33	5.189161	1005.398638	.000995	.192709	193.749748	.005162	396
34	5.454648	1069.115596	.000935	.183330	196.000829	.005102	408
35	5.733719	1136.092435	.000880	.174407	198.142346	.005047	420
36	6.027066	1206.495936	.000829	.165918	200.179632	.004996	432
37	6.335423	1280.501414	.000781	.157843	202.117759	.004948	444
38	6.659555	1358.293153	.000736	.150160	203.961554	.004903	456
39	7.000270	1440.064865	.000694	.142852	205.715609	.004861	468
40	7.358417	1526.020172	.000655	.135899	207.384290	.004822	480
41	7.734888	1616.373117	.000619	.129284	208.971754	.004786	492
42	8.130620	1711.348689	.000584	.122992	210.481953	.004751	504
43	8.546598	1811.183392	.000552	.117006	211.918649	.004719	516
44	8.983858	1916.125828	.000522	.111311	213.285417	.004689	528
45	9.443489	2026.437318	.000493	.105893	214.585663	.004660	540
46	9.926636	2142.392554	.000467	.100739	215.822623	.004634	552
47	10.434501	2264.280279	.000442	.095836	216.999379	.004609	564
48	10.968350	2392.404012	.000418	.091171	218.118860	.004585	576
49	11.529512	2527.082798	.000396	.086734.	219.183853	.004563	588
50	12.119383	2668.652007	.000375	.082512	220.197012	.004542	600

5%   QUARTERLY COMPOUND INTEREST TABLE   5%
EFFECTIVE RATE = 1¼%   BASE = 1.0125

	1 AMOUNT OF 1 AT COMPOUND INTEREST $S^n = (1+i)^n$	2 ACCUMULATION OF 1 PER PERIOD $S_{\overline{n}|} = \dfrac{S^n-1}{i}$	3 SINKING FUND FACTOR $1\,S_{\overline{n}|} = \dfrac{i}{S^n-1}$	4 PRES. VALUE REVERSION OF 1 $V^n = \dfrac{1}{S^n}$	5 PRESENT VALUE ORD. ANNUITY 1 PER PERIOD $o_{\overline{n}|} = \dfrac{1-V^n}{i}$	6 INSTALMENT TO AMORTIZE 1 $1/o_{\overline{n}|} = \dfrac{i}{1-V^n}$	n
QUARTERS							QUARTERS
1	1.012500	1.000000	1.000000	.987654	.987654	1.012500	1
2	1.025156	2.012500	.496894	.975461	1.963115	.509394	2
3	1.037971	3.037656	.329201	.963418	2.926534	.341701	3
YEARS							
1	1.050945	4.075627	.245361	.951524	3.878058	.257861	4
2	1.104486	8.358888	.119633	.905398	7.568124	.132133	8
3	1.160755	12.860361	.077758	.861509	11.079312	.090258	12
4	1.219890	17.591164	.056847	.819746	14.420292	.069347	16
5	1.282037	22.562979	.044320	.780009	17.599316	.056820	20
6	1.347351	27.788084	.035987	.742197	20.624235	.048487	24
7	1.415992	33.279384	.030049	.706219	23.502518	.042549	28
8	1.488131	39.050441	.025608	.671984	26.241274	.038108	32
9	1.563944	45.115506	.022165	.639409	28.847267	.034665	36
10	1.643619	51.489557	.019421	.608413	31.326933	.031921	40
11	1.727354	58.188337	.017186	.578920	33.686395	.029686	44
12	1.815355	65.228388	.015331	.550856	35.931481	.027831	48
13	1.907839	72.627097	.013769	.524153	38.067734	.026269	52
14	2.005034	80.402736	.012437	.498745	40.100431	.024937	56
15	2.107181	88.574508	.011290	.474568	42.034592	.023790	60
16	2.214532	97.162593	.010292	.451563	43.874992	.022792	64
17	2.327353	106.188201	.009417	.429673	45.626178	.021917	68
18	2.445920	115.673621	.008645	.408844	47.292474	.021145	72
19	2.570529	125.642280	.007959	.389025	48.877995	.020459	76
20	2.701485	136.118795	.007347	.370167	50.386657	.019847	80
21	2.839113	147.129040	.006797	.352223	51.822185	.019297	84
22	2.983753	158.700206	.006301	.335148	53.188125	.018801	88
23	3.135761	170.860868	.005853	.318902	54.487850	.018353	92
24	3.295513	183.641059	.005445	.303443	55.724570	.017945	96
25	3.463404	197.072342	.005074	.288733	56.901339	.017574	100
26	3.639849	211.187886	.004735	.274737	58.021064	.017235	104
27	3.825282	226.022551	.004424	.261419	59.086509	.016924	108
28	4.020162	241.612973	.004139	.248746	60.100305	.016639	112
29	4.224971	257.997654	.003876	.236688	61.064957	.016376	116
30	4.440213	275.217058	.003633	.225214	61.982847	.016133	120
31	4.666421	293.313711	.003409	.214297	62.856242	.015909	124
32	4.904154	312.332304	.003202	.203909	63.687298	.015702	128
33	5.153998	332.319805	.003009	.194024	64.478068	.015509	132
34	5.416572	353.325577	.002830	.184619	65.230505	.015330	136
35	5.692519	375.401494	.002664	.175669	65.946467	.015164	140
36	5.982526	398.602077	.002509	.167153	66.627722	.015009	144
37	6.287308	422.984621	.002364	.159051	67.275953	.014864	148
38	6.607617	448.609342	.002229	.151340	67.892760	.014729	152
39	6.944246	475.539523	.002103	.144004	68.479668	.014603	156
40	7.298021	503.841671	.001985	.137023	69.038124	.014485	160
41	7.669821	533.585681	.001874	.130381	69.569509	.014374	164
42	8.060563	564.845011	.001770	.124061	70.075135	.014270	168
43	8.471211	597.696857	.001673	.118047	70.556250	.014173	172
44	8.902779	632.222352	.001582	.112324	71.014042	.014082	176
45	9.356334	668.506759	.001496	.106879	71.449643	.013996	180
46	9.832996	706.639689	.001415	.101698	71.864128	.013915	184
47	10.333941	746.715313	.001339	.096768	72.258520	.013839	188
48	10.860408	788.832603	.001268	.092078	72.633794	.013768	192
49	11.413695	833.095572	.001200	.087614	72.990876	.013700	196
50	11.995169	879.613534	.001137	.083367	73.330064	.013637	200
51	12.606267	928.501369	.001077	.079326	73.653950	.013577	204
52	13.248498	979.879811	.001021	.075480	73.961580	.013521	208
53	13.923447	1033.875745	.000967	.071821	74.254296	.013467	212
54	14.632781	1090.622520	.000917	.068340	74.532824	.013417	216
55	15.378253	1150.260278	.000869	.065027	74.797849	.013369	220
56	16.161704	1212.936303	.000824	.061875	75.050027	.013324	224
57	16.985067	1278.805378	.000782	.058875	75.289980	.013282	228
58	17.850377	1348.030176	.000742	.056021	75.518302	.013242	232
59	18.759771	1420.781655	.000704	.053306	75.735556	.013204	236
60	19.715494	1497.239482	.000668	.050722	75.942278	.013168	240

EFFECTIVE RATE = 2½%   BASE = 1.025

	1 AMOUNT OF 1 AT COMPOUND INTEREST $S^n = (1+i)^n$	2 ACCUMULATION OF 1 PER PERIOD $S_{\overline{n}|} = \frac{S^n-1}{i}$	3 SINKING FUND FACTOR $1/S_{\overline{n}|} = \frac{i}{S^n-1}$	4 PRES. VALUE REVERSION OF 1 $v^n = \frac{1}{S^n}$	5 PRESENT VALUE ORD. ANNUITY 1 PER PERIOD $a_{\overline{n}|} = \frac{1-v^n}{i}$	6 INSTALMENT TO AMORTIZE 1 $1/a_{\overline{n}|} = \frac{i}{1-v^n}$	n
HALF YEARS							HALF YEARS
1	1.025000	1.000000	1.000000	.975610	.975610	1.025000	1
YEARS							
1	1.050625	2.025000	.493827	.951814	1.927424	.518827	2
2	1.103813	4.152516	.240818	.905951	3.761974	.265818	4
3	1.159693	6.387737	.156550	.862297	5.508125	.181550	6
4	1.218403	8.736116	.114467	.820747	7.170137	.139467	8
5	1.280085	11.203382	.089259	.781198	8.752064	.114259	10
6	1.344889	13.795553	.072487	.743556	10.257765	.097487	12
7	1.412974	16.518953	.060537	.707727	11.690912	.085537	14
8	1.484506	19.380225	.051599	.673625	13.055003	.076599	16
9	1.559659	22.386349	.044670	.641166	14.353364	.069670	18
10	1.638616	25.544658	.039147	.610271	15.589162	.064147	20
11	1.721571	28.862856	.034647	.580865	16.765413	.059647	22
12	1.808726	32.349038	.030913	.552875	17.884986	.055913	24
13	1.900293	36.011708	.027769	.526235	18.950611	.052769	26
14	1.996495	39.859801	.025088	.500878	19.964889	.050088	28
15	2.097568	43.902703	.022778	.476743	20.930293	.047778	30
16	2.203757	48.150278	.020768	.453771	21.849178	.045768	32
17	2.315322	52.612885	.019007	.431905	22.723786	.044007	34
18	2.432535	57.301413	.017452	.411094	23.556251	.042452	36
19	2.555682	62.227297	.016070	.391285	24.348603	.041070	38
20	2.685064	67.402554	.014836	.372431	25.102775	.039836	40
21	2.820995	72.839808	.013729	.354485	25.820607	.038729	42
22	2.963808	78.552323	.012730	.337404	26.503849	.037730	44
23	3.113851	84.554034	.011827	.321146	27.154170	.036827	46
24	3.271490	90.859582	.011006	.305671	27.773154	.036006	48
25	3.437109	97.484349	.010258	.290942	28.362312	.035258	50
26	3.611112	104.444494	.009574	.276923	28.923081	.034574	52
27	3.793925	111.756996	.008948	.263579	29.456829	.033948	54
28	3.985992	119.439694	.008372	.250879	29.964858	.033372	56
29	4.187783	127.511329	.007842	.238790	30.448407	.032842	58
30	4.399790	135.991590	.007353	.227284	30.908656	.032353	60
31	4.622529	144.901164	.006901	.216332	31.346728	.031901	62
32	4.856545	154.261786	.006482	.205908	31.763091	.031482	64
33	5.102407	164.096289	.006094	.195986	32.160563	.031094	66
34	5.360717	174.428663	.005733	.186542	32.538311	.030733	68
35	5.632103	185.284114	.005397	.177554	32.897857	.030397	70
36	5.917228	196.689122	.005084	.168998	33.240078	.030084	72
37	6.216788	208.671509	.004792	.160855	33.565809	.029792	74
38	6.531513	221.260504	.004520	.153104	33.875844	.029520	76
39	6.862170	234.486817	.004265	.145726	34.170940	.029265	78
40	7.209568	248.382713	.004026	.138705	34.451817	.029026	80
41	7.574552	262.982087	.003803	.132021	34.719160	.028803	82
42	7.958014	278.320556	.003593	.125659	34.973620	.028593	84
43	8.360888	294.435534	.003396	.119605	35.215819	.028396	86
44	8.784158	311.366333	.003212	.113841	35.446348	.028212	88
45	9.228856	329.154253	.003038	.108356	35.665768	.028038	90
46	9.696067	347.842687	.002875	.103135	35.874616	.027875	92
47	10.186931	367.477223	.002721	.098165	36.073400	.027721	94
48	10.702644	388.105758	.002577	.093435	36.262606	.027577	96
49	11.244465	409.778612	.002440	.088933	36.442694	.027440	98
50	11.813716	432.548654	.002312	.084647	36.614105	.027312	100
51	12.411786	456.471430	.002191	.080569	36.777257	.027191	102
52	13.040132	481.605296	.002076	.076686	36.932546	.027076	104
53	13.700289	508.011564	.001968	.072991	37.080354	.026968	106
54	14.393866	535.754649	.001867	.069474	37.221039	.026867	108
55	15.122556	564.902228	.001770	.066126	37.354944	.026770	110
56	15.888135	595.525404	.001679	.062940	37.482398	.026679	112
57	16.692472	627.698877	.001593	.059907	37.603710	.026593	114
58	17.537528	661.501133	.001512	.057021	37.719177	.026512	116
59	18.425366	697.014628	.001435	.054273	37.829080	.026435	118
60	19.358150	734.325993	.001362	.051658	37.933687	.026362	120

5%   **ANNUAL COMPOUND INTEREST TABLE**   **5%**

EFFECTIVE RATE = 5%   **BASE = 1.05**

YEARS	1 AMOUNT OF 1 AT COMPOUND INTEREST $S^n = (1+i)^n$	2 ACCUMULATION OF 1 PER PERIOD $S_{\overline{n}} = \frac{S^n-1}{i}$	3 SINKING FUND FACTOR $1/S_{\overline{n}} = \frac{i}{S^n-1}$	4 PRES. VALUE REVERSION OF 1 $V^n = \frac{1}{S^n}$	5 PRESENT VALUE ORD. ANNUITY 1 PER PERIOD $a_{\overline{n}} = \frac{1-V^n}{i}$	6 INSTALMENT TO AMORTIZE 1 $1/a_{\overline{n}} = \frac{i}{1-V^n}$	n YEARS
1	1.050000	1.000000	1.000000	.952381	.952381	1.050000	1
2	1.102500	2.050000	.487805	.907029	1.859410	.537805	2
3	1.157625	3.152500	.317209	.863838	2.723248	.367209	3
4	1.215506	4.310125	.232012	.822702	3.545951	.282012	4
5	1.276282	5.525631	.180975	.783526	4.329477	.230975	5
6	1.340096	6.801913	.147017	.746215	5.075692	.197017	6
7	1.407100	8.142008	.122820	.710681	5.786373	.172820	7
8	1.477455	9.549109	.104722	.676839	6.463213	.154722	8
9	1.551328	11.026564	.090690	.644609	7.107822	.140690	9
10	1.628895	12.577893	.079505	.613913	7.721735	.129505	10
11	1.710339	14.206787	.070389	.584679	8.306414	.120389	11
12	1.795856	15.917127	.062825	.556837	8.863252	.112825	12
13	1.885649	17.712983	.056456	.530321	9.393573	.106456	13
14	1.979932	19.598632	.051024	.505068	9.898641	.101024	14
15	2.078928	21.578564	.046342	.481017	10.379658	.096342	15
16	2.182875	23.657492	.042270	.458112	10.837770	.092270	16
17	2.292018	25.840366	.038699	.436297	11.274066	.088699	17
18	2.406619	28.132385	.035546	.415521	11.689587	.085546	18
19	2.526950	30.539004	.032745	.395734	12.085321	.082745	19
20	2.653298	33.065954	.030243	.376889	12.462210	.080243	20
21	2.785963	35.719252	.027996	.358942	12.821153	.077996	21
22	2.925261	38.505214	.025971	.341850	13.163003	.075971	22
23	3.071524	41.430475	.024137	.325571	13.488574	.074137	23
24	3.225100	44.501999	.022471	.310068	13.798642	.072471	24
25	3.386355	47.727099	.020952	.295303	14.093945	.070952	25
26	3.555454	51.113454	.019564	.281241	14.375185	.069564	26
27	3.733456	54.669126	.018292	.267848	14.643034	.068292	27
28	3.920129	58.402583	.017123	.255094	14.898127	.067123	28
29	4.116136	62.322712	.016046	.242946	15.141074	.066046	29
30	4.321942	66.438848	.015051	.231377	15.372451	.065051	30
31	4.538039	70.760790	.014132	.220359	15.592811	.064132	31
32	4.764941	75.298829	.013280	.209866	15.802677	.063280	32
33	5.003189	80.063771	.012490	.199873	16.002549	.062490	33
34	5.253348	85.066959	.011755	.190355	16.192904	.061755	34
35	5.516015	90.320307	.011072	.181290	16.374194	.061072	35
36	5.791816	95.836323	.010434	.172657	16.546852	.060434	36
37	6.081407	101.628139	.009840	.164436	16.711287	.059840	37
38	6.385477	107.709546	.009284	.156605	16.867893	.059284	38
39	6.704751	114.095023	.008765	.149148	17.017041	.058765	39
40	7.039989	120.799774	.008278	.142046	17.159086	.058278	40
41	7.391988	127.839763	.007822	.135282	17.294368	.057822	41
42	7.761588	135.231751	.007395	.128840	17.423208	.057395	42
43	8.149667	142.993339	.006993	.122704	17.545912	.056993	43
44	8.557150	151.143006	.006616	.116861	17.662773	.056616	44
45	8.985008	159.700156	.006262	.111297	17.774070	.056262	45
46	9.434258	168.685164	.005928	.105997	17.880067	.055928	46
47	9.905971	178.119422	.005614	.100949	17.981016	.055614	47
48	10.401270	188.025393	.005318	.096142	18.077158	.055318	48
49	10.921333	198.426663	.005040	.091564	18.168722	.055040	49
50	11.467400	209.347996	.004777	.087204	18.255925	.054777	50
51	12.040770	220.815395	.004529	.083051	18.338977	.054529	51
52	12.642808	232.856165	.004294	.079096	18.418073	.054294	52
53	13.274949	245.498974	.004073	.075330	18.493403	.054073	53
54	13.938696	258.773922	.003864	.071743	18.565146	.053864	54
55	14.635631	272.712618	.003667	.068326	18.633472	.053667	55
56	15.367412	287.348249	.003480	.065073	18.698545	.053480	56
57	16.135783	302.715662	.003303	.061974	18.760519	.053303	57
58	16.942572	318.851445	.003136	.059023	18.819542	.053136	58
59	17.789701	335.794017	.002978	.056212	18.875754	.052978	59
60	18.679186	353.583718	.002828	.053536	18.929290	.052828	60

10% MONTHLY COMPOUND INTEREST TABLE 10%

EFFECTIVE RATE = 5/6%   BASE = 1.00833333

MONTHS	1 AMOUNT OF I AT COMPOUND INTEREST $S^n = (1+i)^n$	2 ACCUMULATION OF I PER PERIOD $S_{\overline{n}|} = \frac{S^n - 1}{i}$	3 SINKING FUND FACTOR $1/S_{\overline{n}|} = \frac{i}{S^n - 1}$	4 PRES. VALUE REVERSION OF I $V^n = \frac{1}{S^n}$	5 PRESENT VALUE ORD.ANNUITY 1 PER PERIOD $a_{\overline{n}|} = \frac{1 - V^n}{i}$	6 INSTALMENT TO AMORTIZE I $1/a_{\overline{n}|} = \frac{i}{1 - V^n}$	n MONTHS
1	1.008333	1.000000	1.000000	.991735	.991735	1.008333	1
2	1.016736	2.008333	.497925	.983539	1.975274	.506258	2
3	1.025208	3.025069	.330570	.975410	2.950685	.338904	3
4	1.033752	4.050278	.246896	.967349	3.918035	.255229	4
5	1.042366	5.084030	.196694	.959355	4.877390	.205027	5
6	1.051053	6.126397	.163228	.951426	5.828817	.171561	6
7	1.059812	7.177450	.139325	.943563	6.772380	.147658	7
8	1.068643	8.237262	.121399	.935765	7.708146	.129732	8
9	1.077549	9.305906	.107458	.928031	8.636177	.115791	9
10	1.086528	10.383456	.096307	.920362	9.556540	.104640	10
11	1.095583	11.469984	.087184	.912755	10.469295	.095517	11

YEARS

1	1.104713	12.565568	.079582	.905212	11.374508	.087915	12
2	1.220390	26.446915	.037811	.819409	21.670854	.046144	24
3	1.348181	41.781821	.023933	.741739	30.991235	.032267	36
4	1.489354	58.722491	.017029	.671432	39.428160	.025362	48
5	1.645308	77.437072	.012913	.607788	47.065369	.021247	60
6	1.817594	98.111313	.010192	.550177	53.978665	.018525	72
7	2.007920	120.950418	.008267	.498027	60.236667	.016601	84
8	2.218175	146.181075	.006840	.450820	65.901488	.015174	96
9	2.450447	174.053712	.005745	.408088	71.029355	.014078	108
10	2.707041	204.844978	.004881	.369406	75.671163	.013215	120
11	2.990504	238.860492	.004186	.334391	79.872985	.012519	132
12	3.303648	276.437875	.003617	.302695	83.676528	.011950	144
13	3.649584	317.950100	.003145	.274003	87.119542	.011478	156
14	4.031743	363.809198	.002748	.248031	90.236200	.011082	168
15	4.453919	414.470344	.002412	.224521	93.057438	.010746	180
16	4.920303	470.436373	.002125	.203239	95.611258	.010459	192
17	5.435523	532.262776	.001878	.183974	97.923008	.010212	204
18	6.004693	600.563212	.001665	.166536	100.015632	.009998	216
19	6.633463	676.015596	.001479	.150750	101.909902	.009812	228
20	7.328073	759.368830	.001316	.136461	103.624619	.009650	240
21	8.095418	851.450237	.001174	.123526	105.176801	.009507	252
22	8.943114	953.173772	.001049	.111817	106.581857	.009382	264
23	9.879575	1065.549089	.000938	.101218	107.853729	.009271	276
24	10.914096	1189.691570	.000840	.091624	109.005045	.009173	288
25	12.056944	1326.833392	.000753	.082939	110.047230	.009087	300
26	13.319464	1478.335753	.000676	.075078	110.990629	.009009	312
27	14.714186	1645.702391	.000607	.067961	111.844605	.008940	324
28	16.254954	1830.594505	.000546	.061519	112.617636	.008879	336
29	17.957060	2034.847238	.000491	.055688	113.317391	.008824	348
30	19.837399	2260.487900	.000442	.050409	113.950820	.008775	360
31	21.914633	2509.756088	.000398	.045631	114.524207	.008731	372
32	24.209382	2785.125915	.000359	.041306	115.043244	.008692	384
33	26.744421	3089.330559	.000323	.037390	115.513083	.008657	396
34	29.544911	3425.389403	.000291	.033846	115.938387	.008625	408
35	32.638649	3796.638004	.000263	.030638	116.323378	.008596	420
36	36.056343	4206.761180	.000237	.027734	116.671875	.008571	432
37	39.831913	4659.829611	.000214	.025105	116.987341	.008547	444
38	44.002835	5160.340233	.000193	.022725	117.272903	.008527	456
39	48.610506	5713.260852	.000175	.020571	117.531398	.008508	468
40	53.700662	6324.079483	.000158	.018621	117.765390	.008491	480
41	59.323823	6998.858807	.000142	.016856	117.977204	.008476	492
42	65.535802	7744.296352	.000129	.015258	118.168940	.008462	504
43	72.398257	8567.790939	.000116	.013812	118.342502	.008450	516
44	79.979301	9477.516170	.000105	.012503	118.499611	.008438	528
45	88.354179	10482.501530	.000095	.011318	118.641830	.008428	540
46	97.606016	11592.721980	.000086	.010245	118.770568	.008419	552
47	107.826641	12819.197020	.000078	.009274	118.887103	.008411	564
48	119.117499	14174.100030	.000070	.008395	118.992592	.008403	576
49	131.590658	15670.879080	.000063	.007599	119.088082	.008397	588
50	145.369919	17324.390450	.000057	.006879	119.174520	.008391	600

10 % QUARTERLY COMPOUND INTEREST TABLE 10 %

EFFECTIVE RATE = 2½%   BASE = 1.025

	1	2	3	4	5	6	
	AMOUNT OF I AT COMPOUND INTEREST	ACCUMULATION OF I PER PERIOD	SINKING FUND FACTOR	PRES. VALUE REVERSION OF I	PRESENT VALUE ORD.ANNUITY 1 PER PERIOD	INSTALMENT TO AMORTIZE I	n
	$S^n = (1 + i)^n$	$S_{\overline{n}} = \frac{S^n - 1}{i}$	$1/S_{\overline{n}} = \frac{i}{S^n - 1}$	$V^n = \frac{1}{S^n}$	$a_{\overline{n}} = \frac{1 - V^n}{i}$	$1/a_{\overline{n}} = \frac{i}{1 - V^n}$	
QUARTERS							QUARTERS
1	1.025000	1.000000	1.000000	.975610	.975610	1.025000	1
2	1.050625	2.025000	.493827	.951814	1.927424	.518827	2
3	1.076891	3.075625	.325137	.928599	2.856024	.350137	3
YEARS							
1	1.103813	4.152516	.240818	.905951	3.761974	.265818	4
2	1.218403	8.736116	.114467	.820747	7.170137	.139467	8
3	1.344889	13.795553	.072487	.743556	10.257765	.097487	12
4	1.484506	19.380225	.051599	.673625	13.055003	.076599	16
5	1.638616	25.544658	.039147	.610271	15.589162	.064147	20
6	1.808726	32.349038	.030913	.552875	17.884986	.055913	24
7	1.996495	39.859801	.025088	.500878	19.964889	.050088	28
8	2.203757	48.150278	.020768	.453771	21.849178	.045768	32
9	2.432535	57.301413	.017452	.411094	23.556251	.042452	36
10	2.685064	67.402554	.014836	.372431	25.102775	.039836	40
11	2.963808	78.552323	.012730	.337404	26.503849	.037730	44
12	3.271490	90.859583	.011006	.305671	27.773154	.036006	48
13	3.611112	104.444494	.009574	.276923	28.923081	.034574	52
14	3.985992	119.439695	.008372	.250879	29.964858	.033372	56
15	4.399590	135.991590	.007353	.227284	30.908657	.032353	60
16	4.856545	154.261786	.006482	.205908	31.763692	.031482	64
17	5.360717	174.428664	.005733	.186542	32.538311	.030733	68
18	5.917228	196.689123	.005084	.168998	33.240078	.030084	72
19	6.531513	221.260505	.004520	.153104	33.875844	.029520	76
20	7.209568	248.382713	.004026	.138705	34.451817	.029026	80
21	7.958014	278.320556	.003593	.125659	34.973620	.028593	84
22	8.784158	311.366333	.003212	.113841	35.446348	.028212	88
23	9.696067	347.842688	.002875	.103135	35.874616	.027875	92
24	10.702644	388.105759	.002577	.093435	36.262606	.027577	96
25	11.813716	432.548655	.002312	.084647	36.614105	.027312	100
26	13.040132	481.605297	.002076	.076686	36.932546	.027076	104
27	14.393866	535.754651	.001867	.069474	37.221039	.026867	108
28	15.888135	595.525406	.001679	.062940	37.482398	.026679	112
29	17.537528	661.501135	.001512	.057021	37.719177	.026512	116
30	19.358150	734.325996	.001362	.051658	37.933687	.026362	120
31	21.367775	814.711016	.001227	.046799	38.128022	.026227	124
32	23.586026	903.441037	.001107	.042398	38.304081	.026107	128
33	26.034559	1001.382378	.000999	.038410	38.463581	.025999	132
34	28.737282	1109.491294	.000901	.034798	38.608080	.025901	136
35	31.720583	1228.823308	.000814	.031525	38.738989	.025814	140
36	35.013588	1360.543523	.000735	.028560	38.857586	.025735	144
37	38.648450	1505.937994	.000664	.025874	38.965030	.025664	148
38	42.660657	1666.426286	.000600	.023441	39.062368	.025600	152
39	47.089383	1843.575332	.000542	.021236	39.150552	.025542	156
40	51.977868	2039.114732	.000490	.019239	39.230442	.025490	160
41	57.373841	2254.953642	.000443	.017430	39.302818	.025443	164
42	63.329985	2493.199414	.000401	.015790	39.368388	.025401	168
43	69.904454	2756.178168	.000363	.014305	39.427790	.025363	172
44	77.161438	3046.457506	.000328	.012960	39.481606	.025328	176
45	85.171790	3366.871582	.000297	.011741	39.530361	.025297	180
46	94.013719	3720.548769	.000269	.010637	39.574530	.025269	184
47	103.773555	4110.942208	.000243	.009636	39.614545	.025243	188
48	114.546588	4541.863516	.000220	.008730	39.650797	.025220	192
49	126.438000	5017.520012	.000199	.007909	39.683639	.025199	196
50	139.563895	5542.555784	.000180	.007165	39.713393	.025180	200
51	154.052426	6122.097036	.000163	.006491	39.740348	.025163	204
52	170.045054	6761.802144	.000148	.005881	39.764768	.025148	208
53	187.697922	7467.916888	.000134	.005328	39.786892	.025134	212
54	207.183386	8247.335444	.000121	.004827	39.806934	.025121	216
55	228.691692	9107.667692	.000110	.004373	39.825092	.025110	220
56	252.432838	10057.313520	.000099	.003961	39.841542	.025099	224
57	278.638621	11105.544820	.000090	.003589	39.856445	.025090	228
58	307.564901	12262.596050	.000082	.003251	39.869946	.025082	232
59	339.494103	13539.764110	.000074	.002946	39.882178	.025074	236
60	374.737967	14949.518680	.000067	.002669	39.893259	.025067	240

10% **SEMI-ANNUAL** COMPOUND INTEREST TABLE **10**%

EFFECTIVE RATE = 5%   BASE = 1.05

	1 AMOUNT OF I AT COMPOUND INTEREST $S^n = (1 + i)^n$	2 ACCUMULATION OF I PER PERIOD $S_{\overline{n}|} = \frac{S^n - 1}{i}$	3 SINKING FUND FACTOR $1/S_{\overline{n}|} \frac{i}{S^n - 1}$	4 PRES. VALUE REVERSION OF I $V^n = \frac{1}{S^n}$	5 PRESENT VALUE ORD. ANNUITY 1 PER PERIOD $a_{\overline{n}|} = \frac{1 - V^n}{i}$	6 INSTALMENT TO AMORTIZE I $1/a_{\overline{n}|} = \frac{i}{1 - V^n}$	n
HALF YEARS							HALF YEARS
1	1.050000	1.000000	1.000000	.952381	.952381	1.050000	1
YEARS							
1	1.102500	2.050000	.487805	.907029	1.859410	.537805	2
2	1.215506	4.310125	.232012	.822702	3.545951	.282012	4
3	1.340096	6.801913	.147017	.746215	5.075692	.197017	6
4	1.477455	9.549109	.104722	.676839	6.463213	.154722	8
5	1.628895	12.577893	.079505	.613913	7.721735	.129505	10
6	1.795856	15.917127	.062825	.556837	8.863252	.112825	12
7	1.979932	19.598632	.051024	.505068	9.898641	.101024	14
8	2.182875	23.657492	.042270	.458112	10.837770	.092270	16
9	2.406619	28.132385	.035546	.415521	11.689587	.085546	18
10	2.653298	33.065954	.030243	.376889	12.462210	.080243	20
11	2.925261	38.505214	.025971	.341850	13.163003	.075971	22
12	3.225100	44.501999	.022471	.310068	13.798642	.072471	24
13	3.555673	51.113454	.019564	.281241	14.375185	.069564	26
14	3.920129	58.402583	.017123	.255094	14.898127	.067123	28
15	4.321942	66.438847	.015051	.231377	15.372451	.065051	30
16	4.764941	75.298829	.013280	.209866	15.802677	.063280	32
17	5.253348	85.066959	.011755	.190355	16.192904	.061755	34
18	5.791816	95.836323	.010434	.172657	16.546852	.060434	36
19	6.385477	107.709546	.009284	.156605	16.867893	.059284	38
20	7.039989	120.799774	.008278	.142046	17.159086	.058278	40
21	7.761588	135.231751	.007395	.128840	17.423208	.057395	42
22	8.557150	151.143005	.006616	.116861	17.662773	.056616	44
23	9.434258	168.685164	.005928	.105997	17.880066	.055928	46
24	10.401270	188.025393	.005318	.096142	18.077158	.055318	48
25	11.467400	209.347996	.004777	.087204	18.255925	.054777	50
26	12.642808	232.856165	.004294	.079096	18.418073	.054294	52
27	13.938696	258.773922	.003864	.071743	18.565146	.053864	54
28	15.367412	287.348249	.003480	.065073	18.698545	.053480	56
29	16.942572	318.851445	.003136	.059023	18.819542	.053136	58
30	18.679186	353.583718	.002828	.053536	18.929290	.052828	60
31	20.593802	391.876049	.002552	.048558	19.028834	.052552	62
32	22.704667	434.093344	.002304	.044044	19.119124	.052304	64
33	25.031896	480.637912	.002081	.039949	19.201019	.052081	66
34	27.597665	531.953298	.001880	.036235	19.275301	.051880	68
35	30.426426	588.528511	.001699	.032866	19.342677	.051699	70
36	33.545134	650.902683	.001536	.029811	19.403788	.051536	72
37	36.983510	719.670208	.001390	.027039	19.459218	.051390	74
38	40.774320	795.486404	.001257	.024525	19.509495	.051257	76
39	44.953688	879.073761	.001138	.022245	19.555098	.051138	78
40	49.561441	971.228821	.001030	.020177	19.596460	.051030	80
41	54.641489	1072.829775	.000932	.018301	19.633978	.050932	82
42	60.242241	1184.844827	.000844	.016600	19.668007	.050844	84
43	66.417071	1308.341422	.000764	.015056	19.698873	.050764	86
44	73.224821	1444.496418	.000692	.013657	19.726869	.050692	88
45	80.730365	1594.607301	.000627	.012387	19.752262	.050627	90
46	89.005227	1760.104549	.000568	.011235	19.775294	.050568	92
47	98.128263	1942.565265	.000515	.010191	19.796185	.050515	94
48	108.186410	2143.728204	.000466	.009243	19.815134	.050466	96
49	119.275517	2365.510344	.000423	.008384	19.832321	.050423	98
50	131.501258	2610.025154	.000383	.007604	19.847910	.050383	100
51	144.980137	2879.602732	.000347	.006897	19.862050	.050347	102
52	159.840601	3176.812012	.000315	.006256	19.874875	.050315	104
53	176.224262	3504.485244	.000285	.005675	19.886508	.050285	106
54	194.287249	3865.744982	.000259	.005147	19.897060	.050259	108
55	214.201692	4264.033842	.000235	.004668	19.906630	.050235	110
56	236.157366	4703.147310	.000213	.004234	19.915311	.050213	112
57	260.363496	5187.269910	.000193	.003841	19.923184	.050193	114
58	287.050754	5721.015076	.000175	.003484	19.930326	.050175	116
59	316.473456	6309.469122	.000158	.003160	19.936804	.050158	118
60	348.911985	6958.239706	.000144	.002866	19.942679	.050144	120

10% ANNUAL COMPOUND INTEREST TABLE 10%

EFFECTIVE RATE = 10%   BASE = 1.10

YEARS	1 AMOUNT OF I AT COMPOUND INTEREST $S^n = (1+i)^n$	2 ACCUMULATION OF I PER PERIOD $S_{\overline{n}|} = \frac{S^n-1}{i}$	3 SINKING FUND FACTOR $1/S_{\overline{n}|} = \frac{i}{S^n-1}$	4 PRES. VALUE REVERSION OF I $v^n = \frac{1}{S^n}$	5 PRESENT VALUE ORD. ANNUITY I PER PERIOD $a_{\overline{n}|} = \frac{1-v^n}{i}$	6 INSTALMENT TO AMORTIZE I $1/a_{\overline{n}|} = \frac{i}{1-v^n}$	n YEARS
1	1.100000	1.000000	1.000000	.909091	.909091	1.100000	1
2	1.210000	2.100000	.476190	.826446	1.735537	.576190	2
3	1.331000	3.310000	.302115	.751315	2.486852	.402115	3
4	1.464100	4.641000	.215471	.683013	3.169865	.315471	4
5	1.610510	6.105100	.163797	.620921	3.790787	.263797	5
6	1.771561	7.715610	.129607	.564474	4.355261	.229607	6
7	1.948717	9.487171	.105405	.513158	4.868419	.205405	7
8	2.143589	11.435888	.087444	.466507	5.334926	.187444	8
9	2.357948	13.579477	.073641	.424098	5.759024	.173641	9
10	2.593742	15.937425	.062745	.385543	6.144567	.162745	10
11	2.853117	18.531167	.053963	.350494	6.495061	.153963	11
12	3.138428	21.384284	.046763	.318631	6.813692	.146763	12
13	3.452271	24.522712	.040779	.289664	7.103356	.140779	13
14	3.797498	27.974983	.035746	.263331	7.366687	.135746	14
15	4.177248	31.772482	.031474	.239392	7.606080	.131474	15
16	4.594973	35.949730	.027817	.217629	7.823709	.127817	16
17	5.054470	40.544703	.024664	.197845	8.021553	.124664	17
18	5.559917	45.599173	.021930	.179859	8.201412	.121930	18
19	6.115909	51.159090	.019547	.163508	8.364920	.119547	19
20	6.727500	57.274999	.017460	.148644	8.513564	.117460	20
21	7.400250	64.002499	.015624	.135131	8.648694	.115624	21
22	8.140275	71.402749	.014005	.122846	8.771540	.114005	22
23	8.954302	79.543024	.012572	.111678	8.883218	.112572	23
24	9.849733	88.497327	.011300	.101526	8.984744	.111300	24
25	10.834706	98.347059	.010168	.092296	9.077040	.110168	25
26	11.918177	109.181765	.009159	.083905	9.160945	.109159	26
27	13.109994	121.099942	.008258	.076278	9.237223	.108258	27
28	14.420994	134.209936	.007451	.069343	9.306567	.107451	28
29	15.863093	148.630930	.006728	.063039	9.369606	.106728	29
30	17.449402	164.494023	.006079	.057309	9.426914	.106079	30
31	19.194342	181.943425	.005496	.052099	9.479013	.105496	31
32	21.113777	201.137767	.004972	.047362	9.526376	.104972	32
33	23.225154	222.251544	.004499	.043057	9.569432	.104499	33
34	25.547670	245.476699	.004074	.039143	9.608575	.104074	34
35	28.102437	271.024368	.003690	.035584	9.644159	.103690	35
36	30.912681	299.126805	.003343	.032349	9.676508	.103343	36
37	34.003949	330.039486	.003030	.029408	9.705917	.103030	37
38	37.404343	364.043434	.002747	.026735	9.732651	.102747	38
39	41.144778	401.447778	.002491	.024304	9.756956	.102491	39
40	45.259256	442.592556	.002259	.022095	9.779051	.102259	40
41	49.785181	487.851811	.002050	.020086	9.799137	.102050	41
42	54.763699	537.636992	.001860	.018260	9.817397	.101860	42
43	60.240069	592.400692	.001688	.016600	9.833998	.101688	43
44	66.264076	652.640761	.001532	.015091	9.849089	.101532	44
45	72.890484	718.904837	.001391	.013719	9.862808	.101391	45
46	80.179532	791.795321	.001263	.012472	9.875280	.101263	46
47	88.197485	871.974853	.001147	.011338	9.886618	.101147	47
48	97.017234	960.172338	.001041	.010307	9.896926	.101041	48
49	106.718957	1057.189572	.000946	.009370	9.906296	.100946	49
50	117.390853	1163.908529	.000859	.008519	9.914814	.100859	50
51	129.129938	1281.299382	.000780	.007744	9.922559	.100780	51
52	142.042932	1410.429320	.000709	.007040	9.929599	.100709	52
53	156.247225	1552.472252	.000644	.006400	9.935999	.100644	53
54	171.871948	1708.719477	.000585	.005818	9.941817	.100585	54
55	189.059142	1880.591425	.000532	.005289	9.947106	.100532	55
56	207.965057	2069.650567	.000483	.004809	9.951915	.100483	56
57	228.761562	2277.615624	.000439	.004371	9.956286	.100439	57
58	251.637719	2506.377186	.000399	.003974	9.960260	.100399	58
59	276.801490	2758.014905	.000363	.003613	9.963873	.100363	59
60	304.481640	3034.816395	.000330	.003284	9.967157	.100330	60

EFFECTIVE RATE = 15%   BASE = 1.15

YEARS	1 AMOUNT OF 1 AT COMPOUND INTEREST $S^n = (1+i)^n$	2 ACCUMULATION OF 1 PER PERIOD $S_{\overline{n}} = \frac{S^n - 1}{i}$	3 SINKING FUND FACTOR $1/S_{\overline{n}} = \frac{i}{S^n - 1}$	4 PRES. VALUE REVERSION OF 1 $v^n = \frac{1}{S^n}$	5 PRESENT VALUE ORD. ANNUITY 1 PER PERIOD $o_{\overline{n}} = \frac{1 - v^n}{i}$	6 INSTALMENT TO AMORTIZE 1 $1/o_{\overline{n}} = \frac{i}{1 - v^n}$	n YEARS
1	1.150000	1.0000	1.000000	.869565	.869565	1.150000	1
2	1.322500	2.1500	.465116	.756144	1.625709	.615116	2
3	1.520875	3.4725	.287976	.657516	2.283225	.437976	3
4	1.749006	4.9934	.200265	.571753	2.854978	.350265	4
5	2.011357	6.7424	:148315	.497177	3.352155	.298315	5
6	2.313061	8.7537	.114236	.432328	3.784483	.264236	6
7	2.660020	11.0668	.090360	.375937	4.160420	.240360	7
8	3.059023	13.7268	.072850	.326902	4.487322	.222850	8
9	3.517876	16.7858	.059574	.284262	4.771584	.209574	9
10	4.045558	20.3037	.049252	.247185	5.018769	.199252	10
11	4.652391	24.3493	.041068	.214943	5.233712	.191068	11
12	5.350250	29.0017	.034480	.186907	5.420619	.184480	12
13	6.152788	34.3519	.029110	.162528	5.583147	.179110	13
14	7.075706	40.5047	.024688	.141329	5.724476	.174688	14
15	8.137062	47.5804	.021017	.122894	5.847370	.171017	15
16	9.357621	55.7175	.017947	.106865	5.954235	.167947	16
17	10.761264	65.0751	.015366	.092926	6.047161	.165366	17
18	12.375454	75.8364	.013186	.080805	6.127966	.163186	18
19	14.231772	88.2118	.011336	.070265	6.198231	.161336	19
20	16.366537	102.4436	.009761	.061100	6.259331	.159761	20
21	18.821518	118.8101	.008416	.053131	6.312462	.158416	21
22	21.644746	137.6316	.007265	.046201	6.358663	.157265	22
23	24.891458	159.2764	.006278	.040174	6.398837	.156278	23
24	28.625176	184.1678	.005429	.034934	6.433771	.155429	24
25	32.918953	212.7930	.004699	.030378	6.464149	.154699	25
26	37.856796	245.7120	.004069	.026415	6.490564	.154069	26
27	43.535315	283.5688	.003526	.022970	6.513534	.153526	27
28	50.065612	327.1041	.003010	.019974	6.535508	153010	28
29	57.575454	377.1697	.002651	.017369	6.550877	.152651	29
30	66.211772	434.7451	.002300	.015103	6.565980	.152300	30

20%   ANNUAL COMPOUND INTEREST TABLE   20%

EFFECTIVE RATE = 20%   BASE = 1.20

	1 AMOUNT OF 1 AT COMPOUND INTEREST $S^n = (1+i)^n$	2 ACCUMULATION OF 1 PER PERIOD $S_{\overline{n}|} = \dfrac{S^n-1}{i}$	3 SINKING FUND FACTOR $1/S_{\overline{n}|} = \dfrac{i}{S^n-1}$	4 PRES. VALUE REVERSION OF 1 $v^n = \dfrac{1}{S^n}$	5 PRESENT VALUE ORD. ANNUITY 1 PER PERIOD $a_{\overline{n}|} = \dfrac{1-v^n}{i}$	6 INSTALMENT TO AMORTIZE 1 $1/a_{\overline{n}|} = \dfrac{i}{1-v^n}$	
YEARS							**YEARS**
1	1.200000	1.000000	1.000000	.833333	.833333	1.200000	1
2	1.440000	2.200000	.454545	.694444	1.527777	.654545	2
3	1.728000	3.640000	.274725	.578704	2.106481	.474725	3
4	2.073600	5.368000	.186289	.482253	2.588734	.386289	4
5	2.488320	7.441600	.134380	.401878	2.990612	.334380	5
6	2.985984	9.929920	.100706	.334898	3.325510	.300706	6
7	3.583181	12.915904	.077424	.279082	3.604592	.277424	7
8	4.299817	16.499085	.060609	.232568	3.837160	.260609	8
9	5.159780	20.798902	.048079	.193807	4.030967	.248079	9
10	6.191736	25.958682	.038523	.161506	4.192473	.238523	10
11	7.430083	32.150418	.031104	.134588	4.327061	.231104	11
12	8.916100	39.580501	.025265	.112157	4.439218	.225265	12
13	10.699320	48.496601	.020620	.093464	4.532682	.220620	13
14	12.839184	59.195921	.016893	.077887	4.610569	.216893	14
15	15.407021	72.035105	.013882	.064905	4.675474	.213882	15
16	18.488514	87.442126	.011436	.054088	4.729562	.211436	16
17	22.186217	105.930640	.009440	.045073	4.774635	.209440	17
18	26.623460	128.116857	.007805	.037561	4.812196	.207805	18
19	31.948153	154.740317	.006462	.031301	4.843497	.206462	19
20	38.337783	186.688470	.005357	.026085	4.869582	.205357	20
21	46.005340	225.026253	.004444	.021737	4.891319	.204444	21
22	55.206408	271.031593	.003690	.018114	4.909433	.203690	22
23	66.247690	326.238001	.003065	.015095	4.924528	.203065	23
24	79.497228	392.485691	.002548	.012579	4.937107	.202548	24
25	95.396675	471.982919	.002119	.010483	4.947590	.202119	25
26	114.476010	567.379594	.001762	.008735	4.956325	.201762	26
27	137.371212	681.855604	.001467	.007280	4.963605	.201467	27
28	164.845454	819.226816	.001221	.006066	4.969671	.201221	28
29	197.814545	984.072270	.001016	.005055	4.974726	.201016	29
30	237.377454	1181.886815	.000846	.004213	4.978939	.200846	30

25%   ANNUAL COMPOUND INTEREST TABLE   25%

EFFECTIVE RATE = 25%   BASE = 1.25

	1 AMOUNT OF 1 AT COMPOUND INTEREST $S^n = (1+i)^n$	2 ACCUMULATION OF 1 PER PERIOD $S_{\overline{n}|} = \dfrac{S^n-1}{i}$	3 SINKING FUND FACTOR $1/S_{\overline{n}|} = \dfrac{i}{S^n-1}$	4 PRES. VALUE REVERSION OF 1 $v^n = \dfrac{1}{S^n}$	5 PRESENT VALUE ORD. ANNUITY 1 PER PERIOD $a_{\overline{n}|} = \dfrac{1-v^n}{i}$	6 INSTALMENT TO AMORTIZE 1 $1/a_{\overline{n}|} = \dfrac{i}{1-v^n}$	
YEARS							**YEARS**
1	1.250000	1.000000	1.000000	.800000	.800000	1.250000	1
2	1.562500	2.250000	.444444	.640000	1.440000	.694444	2
3	1.953125	3.812500	.262295	.512000	1.952000	.512295	3
4	2.441406	5.765625	.173442	.409600	2.361600	.423442	4
5	3.051758	8.207031	.121847	.327680	2.689280	.371847	5
6	3.814697	11.258789	.088819	.262144	2.951424	.338819	6
7	4.768372	15.073486	.066342	.209715	3.161139	.316342	7
8	5.960465	19.841858	.050399	.167772	3.328911	.300399	8
9	7.450581	25.802323	.038756	.134218	3.463129	.288756	9
10	9.313226	33.252904	.030073	.107374	3.570503	.280073	10
11	11.641532	42.566130	.023493	.085899	3.656402	.273493	11
12	14.551915	54.207662	.018448	.068719	3.725121	.268448	12
13	18.189893	68.759577	.014544	.054976	3.780097	.264544	13
14	22.737366	86.949470	.011501	.043980	3.824077	.261501	14
15	28.421708	109.686836	.009117	.035184	3.859261	.259117	15
16	35.527134	138.108544	.007241	.028147	3.887408	.257241	16
17	44.408918	173.635678	.005759	.022518	3.909926	.255759	17
18	55.511147	218.044596	.004586	.018014	3.927940	.254586	18
19	69.388934	273.555743	.003656	.014412	3.942352	.253656	19
20	86.736167	342.944677	.002916	.011529	3.953881	.252916	20
21	108.420208	429.680844	.002327	.009223	3.963104	.252327	21
22	135.525260	538.101052	.001858	.007379	3.970483	.251858	22
23	169.406575	673.626312	.001485	.005903	3.976386	.251485	23
24	211.758219	843.032887	.001186	.004722	3.981108	.251186	24
25	264.697727	1054.791106	.000948	.003778	3.984886	.250948	25

Appendix B

Conversion and Expansion of Tables

The compound interest tables, as published in *Ellwood Tables—Part II*, may be modified or expanded quite simply for use in solving an even greater variety of compound interest and discount problems.

Converting table factors from EOP to BOP

In many instances, compound interest problems involve the receipt or investment of funds at the "beginning of the period" (BOP) rather than at the end of the period (EOP). Of course, Column 1 Factors are already based upon the assumption that the investment takes place at the beginning of the period or at the present. Thus, there is generally no need to convert such factors to BOP, although it is possible to do so.

Of much greater relevance is the conversion of those columns that are based upon either receipt or payment (investment) at EOP, Columns 2 through 6. Conversion of all columns may be accomplished using the Base of the factor as follows.

Columns					
1	2	3	4	5	6
$F_1 \div$ Base	$F_2 \times$ Base	$F_3 \div$ Base	$F_4 \times$ Base	$F_5 \times$ Base	$F_6 \div$ Base

As an example, suppose that an investor wishes to invest \$10,000 today and each year thereafter for 3 years at 10% compounded annually. How much is accumulated by the end of the third year? It is not appropriate to use the Column 2 Factor at 10% compounded annually for 3 years because this factor of 3.310000 is based upon the assumption that the first investment takes place at the end of the first period, not the beginning.

EOP	Amount Invested	Interest Earned From Prior Period	EOP Balance
1	\$10,000	–0–	\$10,000
2	\$10,000	\$1,000	\$21,000
3	\$10,000	\$2,100	\$33,100

The case described, however, indicates that the first \$10,000 investment is made at the beginning of the first period, or at the period zero (0), as follows.

287

BOP	Amount Invested	Interest Earned During Period	EOP Balance
1	$10,000	$1,000	$11,000
2	$10,000	$2,100	$23,100
3	$10,000	$3,310	$36,410

It may be seen that when the series of three investments of $10,000 each is made at the beginning of each period rather than at the end, the amount accumulated by the end of three years with 10% annual compounding is $36,410. This same result is achieved using the procedure outlined as follows.

$$\frac{\text{EOP Factor } 10\%, n = 3}{3.310000} \times \frac{\text{Base (Annual, 10\%)}}{(1.10)} = \frac{\text{BOP Factor } 10\%, n = 3}{3.641000}$$

and

$$3.641000 \times \$10,000 = \$36,410$$

The conversion of all factors at 10%, annual compounding, $n = 3$, is shown as follows.

Column	EOP Factors	Function	Base	BOP Factors
1	1.331000	÷	1.1	1.210000
2	3.310000	×	1.1	3.641000
3	.302115	÷	1.1	.274650
4	.751315	×	1.1	.826447
5	2.486852	×	1.1	2.735537
6	.402115	÷	1.1	.365559

Converting EOP to BOP factors for compounding periods of less than a year is accomplished in exactly the same manner as used for annual compounding. It is also possible to convert the present value of a variable income stream from EOP to BOP receipts by multiplying the proper base value times the present value (originally calculated using EOP factors).

Expansion of compound interest factors

It is often necessary to obtain factors that extend into periods beyond the published tables. This situation can occur if a factor is needed for a number of periods that is greater than that provided by the table. A similar situation occurs when a factor is needed for a fractional compounding period beyond one year (such as 9 years, 7 months) since only annual factors are provided beyond the first year. In either situation, the expansion procedure is exactly the same.

Columns 1 and 4

These columns may be expanded *directly* by multiplication of those factors where the sum of the number of periods is equal to the desired number of periods. For example, suppose that a Column 1 Factor at 10% annual compounding is needed for the period of 65 years. This may be calculated as follows.

Column 1 Factor (10%, n = 60)		Column 1 Factor (10%, n = 5)	Column 1 Factor (10%, n = 65)
304.481640	×	1.610510	490.37072

or

Column 1 Factor (10%, n = 35)		Column 1 Factor (10%, n = 30)		Column 1 Factor (10%, n = 65)
28.102437	×	17.449402	=	490.37072

or

any combination of two or more factors whose periods' sum is equal to $n = 65$ multiplied times each other.

$$F_1^n \times F_1^m = F_1^{n+m}$$

and

$$F_4^n \times F_4^m = F_4^{n+m}$$

If a Column 1 Factor for 3 years, 7 months, (43 months) at 5% compounded monthly is needed, it would be calculated in the following manner.

Column 1 Factor (5%, n = 36)		Column 1 Factor (5%, n = 7)		Column 1 Factor (5%, n = 43)
1.161472	×	1.029534	=	1.195775

Columns 2 and 3

The procedure for expanding Columns 2 and 3 may be generalized as follows.

$$F_2^n + (F_1^n \times F_2^m) = F_2^{n+m}$$

and

$$\frac{1}{F_2^{n+m}} = F_3^{n+m}$$

Thus, the Column 2 Factor for 3 years, 7 months, (43 months) at 5% compounded monthly is calculated as shown.

Column 2 Factor (5%, n = 36)		Column 1 Factor (5%, n = 36)		Column 2 Factor (5%, n = 7)	Column 2 Factor (5%, n = 43)
38.753336	+	(1.161472	×	7.088110) =	46.985977

To calculate the comparable Column 3 Factor, simply find the reciprocal.

$$\frac{1}{46.985977} = .021283 = F_3^{43}$$

Columns 5 and 6

Expanding Columns 5 and 6 may be generalized.

$$F_5^n + (F_4^n \times F_5^{n+m})$$

and

$$\frac{1}{F_5^{n+m}} = F_6^{n+m}$$

Thus, the Column 5 Factor for 3 years, 7 months, (43 months) at 5% compounded monthly would be calculated.

Column 5 Factor (5%, n = 36)		Column 4 Factor (5%, n = 36)		Column 5 Factor (5%, n = 7)		Column 5 Factor (5%, n = 43)
33.365701	+	(.860976	×	6.884777)	=	39.293328

To calculate the comparable Column 6 Factor, simply find the reciprocal.

$$\frac{1}{39.293328} = .0254496 = F_6^{43}$$

Interpolation

It is often necessary to "interpolate" between compound interest rates as a means of estimating an intermediate value not found in the tables or as a short-cut means of finding an approximate rate of return. The concept of interpolation is simple; it involves applying proportionate distances between known quantities so that the corresponding values found between such quantities can be estimated. For example, suppose that the following relationships are given.

	Production Time	Output of Product
	10.0 hours	90 units
	4.0 hours	30 units
Distance (value dffi.)	6.0 hours	60 units

Question: how much time would be required to produce 45 units?

The distance between the lower production level and 45 units is 15 units or a distance of 25% (15 ÷ 60) of the total distance. The same percentage of distance on the time scale would be 25% of the total distance; 1.5 (6 × .25). When this amount is added to the minimum time of 4 hours, the suggested solution is that it would take 5.5 hours to produce 45 units.

The same technique may be used to *estimate* compound interest factors but again it must be recognized that the method of estimation assumes a proportionate (linear) relationship between factors and values which does not actually exist. Thus, while the technique is reasonably useful, it loses accuracy as the distance between rates increases. For example, suppose the following rates and factors were given.

n	Rate	Factor (Column 1)
10	15	4.045558
	10	
10	5	1.628895
Diff.	$\overline{10}$	2.416663

Suppose now that the interpolation method is used to calculate the factor for 10%. The estimated factor would be as follows.

$$5 \div 10 \times 2.416663 = 1.208332$$
$$+ \underline{1.628895}$$
$$2.837227$$

However, the actual factor is 2.593742. If the same estimate of the 10 year 10% Factor is made with an interpolation between 20% and 5%, the resulting solution is 3.149842, producing an even greater error than the earlier estimate.

Perhaps the most useful and frequent application of the interpolation technique is the calculation of IRR. Assume an investment of $10,000 in return for the following after-tax cash flows.

n	After-Tax Cash Flows
1	$2,000
2	1,500
3	1,200
4	1,000
5	800
6	600
7	300 + $10,700 sales proceeds

Present Values of After-Tax Cash Flows

End of Year	After-Tax Cash Flow	Discounted at 10%		Discounted at 15%	
		P.V. of 1	Amount	P.V. of 1	Amount
1	$ 2,000	.909091	$ 1,818	.869565	$1,739
2	1,500	.826446	1,240	.756144	1,134
3	1,200	.751315	902	.657516	789
4	1,000	.683013	683	.571753	572
5	800	.620921	497	.497177	398
6	600	.564474	339	.432328	259
7	11,000	.513158	5,645	.375937	4,135
Total			$11,124		$9,026

Interpolation

% Rate		Present Value Amount	
Smaller	.10	$11,124 ——————→	$11,124
Larger	.15	$ 9,026 Initial Investment	$10,000

Absolute Difference $\left[.05 \div \$2{,}098 \right] \times \$1{,}124 +$ Smaller Rate $.10 = .126787$

or

12.68% IRR (correct answer is 12.48%)

Short-cut method for calculating the present value of a variable cash flow

The typical method of calculating the present value of a variable stream of cash flows is to find the sum of the present values of each cash flow using the appropriate Column 4 Factors. For example, the following procedure would be used to calculate the present value of the indicated cash flows with a discount rate of 8.5%.

EOP (Year)	Cash Flows	×	Discount Factor Column 4, 8.5%	=	Present Value
1	$ 2,000		.921659		$1,843.32
2	–0–		—		–0–
3	(3,000)		.782908		(2,348.72)
4	11,000		.721574		7,937.31
					$7,431.91

The "short-cut" procedure is designed for speed of calculation but also eliminates the need for any compound interest tables, thus reducing the risk of errors from coping factors. The procedure is based upon the following observation.

EOP (Years)	Cash Flows	×	Discount Factors	=	Present Value
1	$ 2,000	×	$1/(1+i)$	=	PV
2	–0–	×	$1/(1+i) \times 1/(1+i)$	=	PV
3	(3,000)	×	$1/(1+i) \times 1/(1+i) \times 1/(1+i)$	=	PV
4	11,000	×	$1/(1+i) \times 1/(1+i) \times 1/(1+i) \times 1/(1+i) =$		PV

Thus, by utilizing the following procedure, each cash flow is divided by $(1+i)$ "n" times according to when it is received. The steps are as follows.

Step 1. Enter the *last* period cash flow and divide by the appropriate base. (Enter the base in the calculator as a constant if possible.)

$11,000 \div 1.085 = \$10{,}138.25$

Step 2. Add *next* cash flow to the previously calculated product and divide the sum by the constant base.

$(\$3{,}000) + \$10{,}138.25 = \$7{,}138.25$

292 $\$7{,}138.25 \div 1.085 = \$6{,}579.03$

Step 3. Repeat Step 2 for each remaining cash flow.

0 + $6,579.03 = $6,579.03

$6,579.03 ÷ 1.085 = $6,063.62

$\qquad$ and

$2,000 + $6,063.62 = $8,063.62

$8.063.62 ÷ 1.085 = $7,431.91

The procedure illustrates the treatment of positive, zero and negative cash flows and can save a considerable amount of time in most present value calculations. For example, the cash flows in the previous problem under "Interpolation" were the following.

n	$
1	$ 2,000
2	1,500
3	1,200
4	1,000
5	800
6	600
7	11,000

The present value of this cash flow stream discounted at 10% may be calculated, with modest practice, in less than 40 seconds using the short-cut procedure. Compare this time with the conventional method using Column 4 Factors.

Appendix C

Depreciation Tables

The following tables indicate the amount of annual and accumulated depreciation for various useful lives under different depreciation methods and are useful in planning. The tables assume that the basis of the asset is $100 and there is no salvage value.

To find an annual deduction or an amount of accumulated depreciation after a specified number of years, turn to the table covering the useful life of the asset. (There are tables for 10, 15, 20, 25, 30, 33⅓, 40 and 50-year useful lives.) Find the columns for the depreciation method and look at the year of ownership required.

To find the amount applicable, multiply the figure in the table by the number of 100s in the actual basis. If the basis is $25,000, multiply the figure in the table by 250. The result of the calculation will be a close approximation but not the exact amount that would result from an actual computation. This is generally sufficient for planning purposes.

Switchover to straight line depreciation

IRS regulations require that upon switchover to straight line the remaining basis, *reduced by estimated salvage value*, be allocated equally over the remaining useful life of the property. Because the straight line rate is to be calculated in this fashion (rather than merely deducting each year the amount of straight line depreciation that would have been available annually if straight line had been adopted at the outset), there is no point at which a switchover from sum-of-the-years-digits to straight line will increase the depreciation deductions for future years. However, annual depreciation deductions for future years can be increased by switching from declining balance to straight line.

It must be remembered, however, that in calculating declining balance depreciation, basis is not first reduced by estimated salvage value. (Instead, depreciation deductions should no longer be taken when the salvage value is reached.) If, however, there is a substantial salvage value to be taken into account when switching to straight line, the advantage of switching may be diminished or eliminated entirely. Also, the point at which it may be advantageous to switch may be reached at a different year than the year when switchover would become advantageous were salvage value equal to zero. (See page 161 for a discussion of salvage values.)

In the tables that follow, an asterisk (*) appears in each of the declining balance columns indicating the year *following which* it would be advantageous to switch to straight line *if salvage value is zero*. This indication should be used merely as a guideline and be considered in conjunction with the realistic salvage value situation that applies to the particular instance.

294

Comparisons of Depreciation Methods
Cost of Asset - $100 Salvage Value - Zero
10 Year Useful Life

Year Number	Straight Line Rate: 10%		150% Declining Balance Rate: 15%		Double Declining Balance Rate: 20%		Sum-of-the-Years - Digits	
	Per Year	Total	Per Year	Total	Per Year	Total	Per Year	Total
1	10.000	10.000	15.000	15.000	20.000	20.000	18.182	18.182
2	10.000	20.000	12.750	27.750	16.000	36.000	16.364	34.546
3	10.000	30.000	10.838	38.588	12.800	48.800	14.545	49.091
4	10.000	40.000	9.212	47.800*	10.240	59.040	12.727	61.818
5	10.000	50.000	7.830	55.630	8.192	67.232	10.909	72.727
6	10.000	60.000	6.656	62.286	6.554	73.786*	9.091	81.818
7	10.000	70.000	5.657	67.943	5.243	79.029	7.273	89.091
8	10.000	80.000	4.809	72.752	4.194	83.223	5.455	94.546
9	10.000	90.000	4.087	76.839	3.355	86.578	3.636	98.182
10	10.000	100.000	3.474	80.313	2.684	89.262	1.818	100.000

15 Year Useful Life

Year Number	Straight Line Rate: 6-2/3%		150% Declining Balance Rate 10%		Double Declining Balance Rate: 13-1/3%		Sum-of-the-Years - Digits	
	Per Year	Total	Per Year	Total	Per Year	Total	Per Year	Total
1	6.667	6.667	10.000	10.000	13.333	13.333	12.500	12.500
2	6.666	13.333	9.000	19.000	11.556	24.889	11.667	24.167
3	6.667	20.000	8.100	27.100	10.015	34.904	10.833	35.000
4	6.666	26.666	7.290	34.390	8.679	43.583	10.000	45.000
5	6.666	33.333	6.561	40.951	7.522	51.105	9.167	54.167
6	6.666	39.999	5.905	46.856*	6.519	57.624	8.333	62.500
7	6.667	46.666	5.314	52.170	5.650	63.274	7.500	70.000
8	6.666	53.332	4.783	56.953	4.897	68.171*	6.667	76.667
9	6.667	59.999	4.305	61.258	4.244	72.415	5.833	82.500
10	6.666	66.665	3.874	65.132	3.678	76.093	5.000	87.500
11	6.667	73.332	3.487	68.619	3.188	79.281	4.167	91.667
12	6.666	79.998	3.138	71.757	2.763	82.044	3.333	95.000
13	6.667	86.665	2.824	74.581	2.394	84.438	2.500	97.500
14	6.666	93.331	2.542	77.123	2.075	86.513	1.667	99.167
15	6.667	99.998	2.288	79.411	1.798	88.311	.833	100.000

*Year *after* which switch to straight line should be considered.

Comparisons of Depreciation Methods
Cost of Asset - $100 Salvage Value - Zero
20 Years Useful Life

Year Number	Straight Line Rate: 5%		125% Declining Bal. Rate: 6.25%		150% Declining Bal. Rate: 7.5%		Double Declining Bal. Rate: 10%		Sum-of-the-Years - Digits	
	Per Year	Total	Per Year	Total	Per Year	Total	Per Year	Total	Per Year	Total
1	5.000	5.000	6.250	6.250	7.500	7.500	10.000	10.000	9.524	9.524
2	5.000	10.000	5.859	12.109	6.938	14.438	9.000	19.000	9.048	18.572
3	5.000	15.000	5.493	17.602	6.417	20.855	8.100	27.100	8.571	27.143
4	5.000	20.000	5.149	22.751	5.936	26.791	7.290	34.390	8.095	35.238
5	5.000	25.000	4.828	27.579*	5.491	32.282	6.561	40.951	7.619	42.857
6	5.000	30.000	4.526	32.105	5.079	37.361	5.905	46.856	7.143	50.000
7	5.000	35.000	4.243	36.348	4.698	42.059*	5.314	52.170	6.667	56.667
8	5.000	40.000	3.978	40.326	4.346	46.405	4.783	56.953	6.190	62.857
9	5.000	45.000	3.729	44.055	4.020	50.425	4.305	61.258	5.714	68.571
10	5.000	50.000	3.496	47.551	3.718	54.143	3.874	65.132	5.238	73.809
11	5.000	55.000	3.278	50.829	3.439	57.582	3.487	68.619*	4.762	78.571
12	5.000	60.000	3.073	53.902	3.181	60.763	3.138	71.757	4.287	82.858
13	5.000	65.000	2.881	56.783	2.943	63.706	2.824	74.581	3.809	86.667
14	5.000	70.000	2.701	59.484	2.722	66.428	2.542	77.123	3.333	90.000
15	5.000	75.000	2.532	62.016	2.518	68.946	2.288	79.411	2.857	92.857
16	5.000	80.000	2.374	64.390	2.329	71.275	2.059	81.470	2.381	95.238
17	5.000	85.000	2.225	66.615	2.154	73.429	1.853	83.323	1.905	97.143
18	5.000	90.000	2.086	68.701	1.993	75.422	1.668	84.991	1.429	98.572
19	5.000	95.000	1.956	70.657	1.843	77.265	1.501	86.492	.952	99.924
20	5.000	100.000	1.833	72.490	1.705	78.970	1.351	87.843	.476	100.000

*Year *after* which switch to straight line should be considered.

Comparisons of Depreciations Methods
Cost of Asset - $100 Salvage Value - Zero
25 Years Useful Life

Year Number	Straight Line Rate: 4% Per Year	Total	125% Declining Bal. Rate: 5% Per Year	Total	150% Declining Bal. Rate: 6% Per Year	Total	Double Declining Bal. Rate: 8% Per Year	Total	Sum-of-the-Years - Digits Per Year	Total
1	4.000	4.000	5.000	5.000	6.000	6.000	8.000	8.000	7.692	7.692
2	4.000	8.000	4.750	9.750	5.640	11.640	7.360	15.360	7.385	15.077
3	4.000	12.000	4.512	14.262	5.302	16.942	6.773	22.133	7.077	22.154
4	4.000	16.000	4.286	18.548	4.983	21.925	6.229	28.362	6.769	28.923
5	4.000	20.000	4.072	22.620	4.685	26.610	5.731	34.093	6.462	35.385
6	4.000	24.000	3.869	26.489 *	4.403	31.013	5.273	39.366	6.154	41.539
7	4.000	28.000	3.675	30.164	4.139	35.152	4.851	44.217	5.846	47.385
8	4.000	32.000	3.491	33.655	3.891	39.043	4.463	48.680	5.538	52.923
9	4.000	36.000	3.317	36.972	3.657	42.700 *	4.106	52.786	5.231	58.154
10	4.000	40.000	3.151	40.123	3.438	46.138	3.777	56.563	4.923	63.077
11	4.000	44.000	2.993	43.116	3.232	49.370	3.475	60.038	4.615	67.692
12	4.000	48.000	2.844	45.960	3.038	52.408	3.197	63.235	4.308	72.000
13	4.000	52.000	2.702	48.662	2.856	55.264	2.941	66.176 *	4.000	76.000
14	4.000	56.000	2.566	51.228	2.684	57.948	2.706	68.882	3.692	79.692
15	4.000	60.000	2.438	53.666	2.523	60.471	2.489	71.371	3.385	83.077
16	4.000	64.000	2.316	55.982	2.372	62.843	2.290	73.661	3.077	86.154
17	4.000	68.000	2.200	58.182	2.229	65.072	2.107	75.768	2.769	88.923
18	4.000	72.000	2.090	60.272	2.096	67.168	1.939	77.707	2.462	91.385
19	4.000	76.000	1.986	62.258	1.970	69.138	1.783	79.490	2.154	93.539
20	4.000	80.000	1.887	64.145	1.852	70.990	1.641	81.131	1.846	95.385
21	4.000	84.000	1.792	65.937	1.741	72.731	1.510	82.641	1.538	96.923
22	4.000	88.000	1.703	67.640	1.636	74.367	1.389	84.030	1.231	98.154
23	4.000	92.000	1.618	69.258	1.538	75.905	1.278	85.308	.923	99.077
24	4.000	96.000	1.537	70.795	1.446	77.351	1.175	86.483	.615	99.692
25	4.000	100.000	1.460	72.255	1.359	78.710	1.081	87.564	.308	100.000

*Year *after* which switch to straight line should be considered.

Comparison of Depreciation Methods
Cost of Asset - $100 Salvage Value - Zero
30 Years Useful Life

Year Number	Straight Line Rate: 3-1/3%		125% Declining Bal. Rate: 4.16%		150% Declining Bal. Rate: 5%		Double Declining Bal. Rate: 6-2/3%		Sum-of-the-Years-Digits	
	Per Year	Total	Per Year	Total	Per Year	Total	Per Year	Total	Per Year	Total
1	3.333	3.333	4.160	4.160	5.000	5.000	6.667	6.667	6.452	6.452
2	3.333	6.666	3.986	8.146	4.750	9.750	6.222	12.889	6.237	12.689
3	3.334	10.000	3.821	11.967	4.513	14.263	5.807*	18.696	6.022	18.711
4	3.333	13.333	3.662	15.629	4.287	18.550	5.420	24.116	5.806	24.517
5	3.333	16.666	3.509	19.138	4.073	22.623	5.059	29.175	5.591	30.108
6	3.334	20.000	3.363	22.501	3.869	26.492	4.722	33.897	5.376	35.484
7	3.333	23.333	3.223	25.724*	3.675	30.167	4.407	38.304	5.161	40.645
8	3.333	26.666	3.089	28.813	3.492	33.659	4.113	42.417	4.946	45.591
9	3.334	30.000	2.961	31.774	3.317	36.976	3.839	46.256	4.731	50.322
10	3.333	33.333	2.838	34.612	3.151	40.127	3.583	49.849	4.516	54.838
11	3.333	36.666	2.720	37.332	2.994	43.121	3.344	53.183	4.301	59.139
12	3.334	40.000	2.606	39.938	2.844	45.965 *	3.121	56.304	4.086	63.225
13	3.333	43.333	2.498	42.436	2.702	48.667	2.913	59.217	3.871	67.096
14	3.333	46.666	2.394	44.830	2.567	51.234	2.719	61.936	3.656	70.752
15	3.334	50.000	2.295	47.125	2.438	53.672	2.538	64.474	3.441	74.193
16	3.333	53.333	2.199	49.324	2.316	55.988	2.368	66.842*	3.226	77.419
17	3.333	56.666	2.108	51.432	2.201	58.189	2.211	69.053	3.011	80.430
18	3.334	60.000	2.020	53.452	2.091	60.280	2.063	71.116	2.796	83.226
19	3.333	63.333	1.936	55.388	1.986	62.266	1.926	73.042	2.581	85.807
20	3.333	66.666	1.855	57.243	1.887	64.153	1.797	74.839	2.366	88.173
21	3.334	70.000	1.778	59.021	1.792	65.945	1.677	76.516	2.151	90.324
22	3.333	73.333	1.704	60.725	1.703	67.648	1.566	78.082	1.935	92.259
23	3.333	76.666	1.633	62.358	1.618	69.266	1.461	79.543	1.720	93.979
24	3.334	80.000	1.565	63.923	1.537	70.803	1.364	80.907	1.505	95.484
25	3.333	83.333	1.500	65.423	1.460	72.263	1.273	82.180	1.290	96.774
26	3.333	86.666	1.438	66.861	1.387	73.650	1.188	83.368	1.075	97.849
27	3.334	90.000	1.378	68.239	1.318	74.968	1.109	84.477	.860	98.709
28	3.333	93.333	1.321	69.560	1.252	76.220	1.035	85.512	.645	99.354
29	3.333	96.666	1.266	70.826	1.189	77.409	.966	86.478	.430	99.784
30	3.334	100.000	1.213	72.039	1.130	78.539	.901	87.309	.216	100.000

*Year *after* which switch to straight line should be considered.

Comparison of Depreciation Methods
Cost of Asset - $100 Salvage Value - Zero
33-1/3 Years Useful Life

Year Number	Straight Line Rate: 3% Per Year	Total	125% Declining Bal. Rate: 3.75% Per Year	Total	150% Declining Bal. Rate 4.50% Per Year	Total	200% Declining Bal. Rate: 6% Per Year	Total	Sum-of-the Years - Digits Per Year	Total
1	3.000	3.000	3.750	3.750	4.500	4.500	6.000	6.000	5.830	5.830
2	3.000	6.000	3.609	7.359	4.298	8.798	5.640	11.640	5.650	11.480
3	3.000	9.000	3.474	10.833	4.104	12.902	5.302	16.942	5.479	16.959
4	3.000	12.000	3.343	14.176	3.919	16.821	4.983	21.925	5.306	22.265
5	3.000	15.000	3.218	17.394	3.743	20.564	4.685	26.610	5.131	27.396
6	3.000	18.000	3.097	20.491	3.575	24.139	4.403	31.013	4.952	32.348
7	3.000	21.000	2.981	23.472 *	3.414	27.583	4.139	35.152	4.783	37.131
8	3.000	24.000	2.869	26.341	3.259	30.842	3.891	39.043	4.602	41.733
9	3.000	27.000	2.762	29.103	3.112	33.954	3.657	42.700	4.428	46.161
10	3.000	30.000	2.658	31.761	2.972	36.926	3.438	46.138	4.253	50.414
11	3.000	33.000	2.558	34.319	2.838	39.764	3.232	49.370	4.081	54.495
12	3.000	36.000	2.463	36.782	2.711	42.475 *	3.038	52.408	3.904	58.399
13	3.000	39.000	2.370	39.152	2.589	45.064	2.856	55.264	3.727	62.126
14	3.000	42.000	2.281	41.433	2.472	47.536	2.684	57.948	3.586	65.712
15	3.000	45.000	2.196	43.629	2.361	49.897	2.523	60.471	3.378	69.090
16	3.000	48.000	2.113	45.742	2.255	52.152	2.372	62.843	3.202	72.292
17	3.000	51.000	2.034	47.776	2.153	54.305	2.229	65.072 *	3.026	75.318
18	3.000	54.000	1.958	49.734	2.056	56.361	2.096	67.168	2.851	78.169
19	3.000	57.000	1.884	51.618	1.964	58.325	1.970	69.138	2.676	80.845
20	3.000	60.000	1.814	53.432	1.875	60.200	1.852	70.990	2.502	83.347
21	3.000	63.000	1.746	55.178	1.791	61.991	1.741	72.731	2.326	85.673
22	3.000	66.000	1.680	56.858	1.710	63.701	1.636	74.367	2.152	87.825
23	3.000	69.000	1.617	58.475	1.633	65.334	1.538	75.905	1.977	89.802
24	3.000	72.000	1.557	60.032	1.560	66.894	1.446	77.351	1.802	91.604
25	3.000	75.000	1.498	61.530	1.490	68.384	1.359	78.710	1.627	93.231
26	3.000	78.000	1.442	62.972	1.423	69.807	1.277	79.987	1.452	94.683
27	3.000	81.000	1.388	64.360	1.359	71.166	1.201	81.188	1.277	95.960
28	3.000	84.000	1.336	65.696	1.298	72.464	1.129	82.317	1.102	97.062
29	3.000	87.000	1.286	66.982	1.239	73.703	1.061	83.378	.927	97.989
30	3.000	90.000	1.238	68.220	1.183	74.886	.997	84.375	.752	98.741
31	3.000	93.000	1.191	69.411	1.130	76.016	.938	85.313	.577	99.318
32	3.000	96.000	1.147	70.558	1.079	77.095	.881	86.194	.402	99.720
33	3.000	99.000	1.104	71.662	1.031	78.126	.828	87.022	.228	99.948
33-1/3	1.000	100.000	.351	72.013	.328	78.454	.260	87.282	.052	100.000

*Year *after* which switch to straight line should be considered.

Comparison of Depreciation Methods
Cost of Asset - $100 Salvage Value - Zero
40 Years Useful Life

Year Number	Straight Line Rate. 2.5% Per Year	Total	125% Declining Bal. Rate: 3.125% Per Year	Total	150% Declining Bal. Rate: 3.75% Per Year	Total	200% Declining Bal. Rate: 5% Per Year	Total	Sum-of-the-Years - Digits Per Year	Totals
1	2.500	2.500	3.125	3.125	3.750	3.750	5.000	5.000	4.878	4.878
2	2.500	5.000	3.027	6.152	3.609	7.359	4.750	9.750	4.756	9.634
3	2.500	7.500	2.932	9.084	3.474	10.833	4.513	14.263	4.634	14.268
4	2.500	10.000	2.840	11.924	3.344	14.177	4.287	18.550	4.512	18.780
5	2.500	12.500	2.752	14.676	3.218	17.395	4.073	22.623	4.390	23.170
6	2.500	15.000	2.666	17.342	3.098	20.493	3.869	26.492	4.268	27.438
7	2.500	17.500	2.582	19.924	2.982	22.475	3.674	30.166	4.146	31.584
8	2.500	20.000	2.502	22.426	2.870	26.345	3.492	33.658	4.024	35.608
9	2.500	22.500	2.424	24.850*	2.762	29.107	3.317	36.975	3.902	39.510
10	2.500	25.000	2.348	27.198	2.658	31.765	3.151	40.126	3.780	43.290
11	2.500	27.500	2.274	29.472	2.559	34.324	2.994	43.120	3.659	46.949
12	2.500	30.000	2.203	31.675	2.463	36.787	2.844	45.964	3.537	50.486
13	2.500	32.500	2.134	33.809	2.370	39.157	2.702	48.666	3.415	53.901
14	2.500	35.000	2.068	35.877	2.282	41.439*	2.567	51.233	3.293	57.194
15	2.500	37.500	2.003	37.880	2.196	43.635	2.438	53.671	3.171	60.365
16	2.500	40.000	1.941	39.821	2.114	45.749	2.316	55.987	3.049	63.414
17	2.500	42.500	1.880	41.701	2.034	47.783	2.201	58.188	2.927	66.341
18	2.500	45.000	1.821	43.522	1.958	49.741	2.091	60.279	2.805	69.146
19	2.500	47.500	1.764	45.286	1.885	51.626	1.986	62.265	2.683	71.829
20	2.500	50.000	1.709	46.995	1.814	53.440	1.887	64.152	2.561	74.390
21	2.500	52.500	1.656	48.651	1.746	55.440	1.792	65.944*	2.439	76.829
22	2.500	55.000	1.604	50.255	1.681	56.867	1.703	67.647	2.317	79.146
23	2.500	57.500	1.554	51.809	1.617	58.484	1.618	69.265	2.195	81.341
24	2.500	60.000	1.505	53.314	1.551	60.041	1.537	70.802	2.073	83.414
25	2.500	62.500	1.458	54.772	1.498	61.539	1.460	72.262	1.951	85.365
26	2.500	65.000	1.413	56.185	1.442	62.981	1.387	73.649	1.829	87.194
27	2.500	67.500	1.369	57.554	1.388	64.369	1.318	74.967	1.707	88.901
28	2.500	70.000	1.326	58.880	1.336	65.705	1.252	76.219	1.585	90.486
29	2.500	72.500	1.284	60.164	1.285	66.990	1.189	77.408	1.463	91.949
30	2.500	75.000	1.244	61.408	1.238	68.228	1.130	78.538	1.341	93.290
31	2.500	77.500	1.205	62.613	1.191	69.419	1.073	79.611	1.220	94.510
32	2.500	80.000	1.168	63.781	1.147	70.566	1.019	80.630	1.098	95.608
33	2.500	82.500	1.131	64.912	1.104	71.670	.969	81.599	.976	96.584
34	2.500	85.000	1.096	66.008	1.062	72.732	.920	82.519	.854	97.438
35	2.500	87.500	1.062	67.070	1.023	73.755	.874	83.393	.732	98.170
36	2.500	90.000	1.028	68.098	.984	74.739	.830	84.223	.610	98.780
37	2.500	92.500	.996	69.094	.947	75.686	.789	85.012	.488	99.268
38	2.500	95.000	.965	70.059	.912	76.598	.749	85.761	.366	99.634
39	2.500	97.500	.935	70.994	.878	77.476	.712	86.473	.244	99.878
40	2.500	100.000	.906	71.900	.845	78.321	.676	87.149	.122	100.000

*Year after which switch to straight line should be considered.

Comparison of Depreciation Methods
Cost of Asset - $100 Salvage Value - Zero
50 Years Useful Life

Year Number	Straight Line Rate: 2%		125% Declining Bal. Rate: 2.5%		150% Declining Bal. Rate: 3%		200% Declining Bal. Rate: 4%		Double Declining Bal. Switch to Straight Line		Sum-of-the-Years-Digits	
	Per Year	Total	Per Year	Total	Per Year	Total	Per Year	Total	Per Year	Total	Per Year	Total
1	2.000	2.000	2.500	2.500	3.000	3.000	4.000	4.000	4.000	4.000	3.921	3.921
2	2.000	4.000	2.437	4.937	2.910	5.910	3.840	7.840	3.840	7.840	3.843	7.764
3	2.000	6.000	2.376	7.313	2.823	8.733	3.686	11.526	3.686	11.526	3.765	11.529
4	2.000	8.000	2.317	9.630	2.738	11.471	3.539	15.065	3.539	15.065	3.686	15.215
5	2.000	10.000	2.259	11.889	2.656	14.127	3.397	18.462	3.397	18.462	3.608	18.823
6	2.000	12.000	2.202	14.091	2.576	16.703	3.262	21.724	3.262	21.724	3.529	22.352
7	2.000	14.000	2.147	16.238	2.499	19.202	3.131	24.855	3.131	24.855	3.451	25.803
8	2.000	16.000	2.094	18.332	2.424	21.626	3.006	27.861	3.006	27.861	3.373	29.176
9	2.000	18.000	2.041	20.373	2.351	23.977	2.886	30.747	2.886	30.747	3.294	32.470
10	2.000	20.000	1.990	22.363	2.281	26.258	2.770	33.517	2.770	33.517	3.216	35.686
11	2.000	22.000	1.940	24.303*	2.212	28.470	2.659	36.176	2.659	36.176	3.137	38.823
12	2.000	24.000	1.892	26.195	2.146	30.616	2.553	38.729	2.553	38.729	3.059	41.882
13	2.000	26.000	1.845	28.040	2.082	32.698	2.451	41.180	2.451	41.180	2.980	44.862
14	2.000	28.000	1.799	29.839	2.019	34.717	2.353	43.533	2.353	43.533	2.902	47.764
15	2.000	30.000	1.754	31.593	1.958	36.675	2.259	45.792	2.259	45.792	2.824	50.588
16	2.000	32.000	1.710	33.303	1.900	38.575	2.168	47.960	2.168	47.960	2.745	53.333
17	2.000	34.000	1.667	34.970	1.843	40.418*	2.082	50.042	2.082	50.042	2.667	56.000
18	2.000	36.000	1.625	36.595	1.788	42.206	1.998	52.040	1.998	52.040	2.588	58.588
19	2.000	38.000	1.585	38.180	1.734	43.940	1.918	53.958	1.918	53.958	2.510	61.098
20	2.000	40.000	1.545	39.725	1.682	45.622	1.841	55.799	1.841	55.799	2.431	63.529
21	2.000	42.000	1.506	41.231	1.631	47.253	1.768	57.567	1.768	57.567	2.353	65.882
22	2.000	44.000	1.469	42.700	1.583	48.835	1.697	59.264	1.697	59.264	2.275	68.157
23	2.000	46.000	1.432	44.132	1.535	50.370	1.629	60.893	1.629	60.893	2.196	70.353
24	2.000	48.000	1.396	45.528	1.489	51.859	1.564	62.457	1.564	62.457	2.118	72.471
25	2.000	50.000	1.361	46.889	1.444	53.303	1.502	63.959	1.502	63.959	2.039	74.510
26	2.000	52.000	1.327	48.216	1.401	54.704	1.442	65.401	1.442	65.401*	1.961	76.471
27	2.000	54.000	1.294	49.516	1.359	56.063	1.384	66.785	1.442	66.843	1.882	78.353
28	2.000	56.000	1.262	50.772	1.318	57.381	1.329	68.114	1.442	68.285	1.804	80.151
29	2.000	58.000	1.230	52.002	1.279	58.660	1.275	69.389	1.441	69.726	1.725	81.882
30	2.000	60.000	1.199	53.201	1.240	59.900	1.224	70.613	1.442	71.168	1.647	83.529
31	2.000	62.000	1.169	54.370	1.203	61.103	1.175	71.788	1.441	72.609	1.569	85.098
32	2.000	64.000	1.140	55.510	1.167	62.270	1.128	72.916	1.442	74.051	1.490	86.588
33	2.000	66.000	1.112	56.622	1.132	63.402	1.083	73.999	1.441	75.492	1.412	88.000
34	2.000	68.000	1.084	57.706	1.098	64.500	1.040	75.039	1.442	76.934	1.333	89.333
35	2.000	70.000	1.057	58.763	1.065	65.565	.998	76.037	1.441	78.375	1.255	90.588
36	2.000	72.000	1.030	59.793	1.033	66.598	.959	76.996	1.442	79.817	1.176	91.764
37	2.000	74.000	1.005	60.798	1.002	67.600	.920	77.916	1.442	81.259	1.098	92.863
38	2.000	76.000	.980	61.778	.972	68.572	.883	78.799	1.442	82.701	1.020	93.882
39	2.000	78.000	.955	62.733	.943	69.515	.848	79.647	1.441	84.142	.941	94.823
40	2.000	80.000	.931	63.664	.915	70.432	.814	80.461	1.442	85.584	.863	95.686
41	2.000	82.000	.908	64.572	.887	71.317	.782	81.243	1.442	87.025	.784	96.470
42	2.000	84.000	.885	65.447	.860	72.177	.750	81.993	1.442	88.467	.706	97.176
43	2.000	86.000	.863	66.320	.835	73.012	.720	82.713	1.441	89.908	.627	97.823
44	2.000	88.000	.842	67.162	.810	73.822	.691	83.404	1.442	91.350	.549	98.352
45	2.000	90.000	.820	67.982	.785	74.607	.664	84.068	1.442	92.791	.471	98.823
46	2.000	92.000	.800	68.782	.761	75.368	.637	84.705	1.442	94.233	.392	99.215
47	2.000	94.000	.780	69.562	.739	76.107	.612	85.317	1.441	95.674	.314	99.529
48	2.000	96.000	.760	70.322	.717	76.824	.587	85.904	1.442	97.116	.235	99.764
49	2.000	98.000	.741	71.063	.695	77.519	.564	86.468	1.442	98.558	.157	99.921
50	2.000	100.000	.723	71.786	.674	78.193	.541	87.009	1.442	100.000	.079	100.000

*Year after which switch to straight line should be considered.

Appendix D

Limited Partnership

The use of the partnership form of ownership and the significance of the limited partnership were discussed beginning on page 111.

Because the limited partnership is of special significance to real estate ventures, especially where a substantial investor participation is involved such as the real estate syndicate, the tax aspects of this form of ownership will be examined in some detail.

Major reasons for using the limited partnership

Before going into a detailed explanation of the limited partnership, it is appropriate to review the principal reasons for using this form of ownership in syndications.

1. The liability of the limited partners, i.e. the investors, is limited to the amount of the investment they agree to make. This is similar to the treatment of stockholders in a corporation.

2. There is no double taxation on operating income of gains from sales; the partnership is a mere conduit and is not a tax-paying entity. Profits and capital gains pass directly through to the partners without first being taxed.

3. Losses, as well as profits, pass directly through to the partners. These losses include tax losses generated by non-cash outlays such as depreciation. Thus, while the partnership may have an actual cash surplus over cash outlay for the year (and the cash may be distributed to the partners), a tax loss is available to the partners to offset their other personal income.

In this respect, the availability of increased basis to each partner for his share of the partnership's liabilities becomes important because a partner may not deduct his share of partnership losses that exceed his basis. While a limited partner may not increase his basis for a share of liabilities that are specifically those of the partnership, he *may* increase his basis by a share of the liabilities that are of a non-recourse nature (i.e. those liabilities secured by liens on the partnership property where the *only* recourse of the creditor in case of default is to foreclose on the property and where the creditor has no recourse to the other partnership assets or to the assets of any of the partners). The availability of non-recourse loans to increase limited partners' bases is the heart of many real estate limited partnership syndications and of the so-called "tax shelters" provided by these forms of investment.

Comparison with corporation

A corporation offers the shareholders limited liability but it presents the problem of double taxation. The corporation is a tax-paying entity so that income and gains realized by the corporation are subject to corporate income tax and there may be another tax on distribution to the shareholders. Further, because the corporation is a separate entity, losses and deductions of the corporation do not pass through to the shareholders.

The Subchapter S corporation

Some of the tax objections to a corporation can be avoided if the corporation elects Subchapter S status. In that case, the shareholders retain the benefits of limited liability, avoid the corporate income tax and obtain the benefit of a pass-through of losses and deductions. However, in a Subchapter S corporation the liabilities of the corporation or the liens on the corporation's property do not enter into the calculation of the basis of the shareholder's stock as in the case of a limited partnership. Yet, as in the case of a partnership, a Subchapter S shareholder may not deduct losses in excess of his basis.

There may be other objections to the use of Subchapter S. A Subchapter S corporation is limited to ten investors whereas there is no such limitation in the case of a limited partnership. There is also a number of troublesome rules applicable to the use of Subchapter S for a real estate investment. More than 20% of the gross receipts of a Subchapter S corporation may not come from passive investment income and passive investment income includes rents. Thus most real estate syndications would not quality for Subchapter S status.

Assuring partnership status

If the limited partnership is chosen as the vehicle for a real estate investment, it is essential that the partnership be classified by the tax law as a partnership rather than what the law calls an association which is taxed as a corporation. (As will be explained, even though a business form is a partnership under state law, it may still be treated as a corporation under the tax law if it has enough "corporate attributes.")

Avoiding corporate status

Fortunately, IRS has formulated rules which make it relatively easy to obtain the tax status of a limited partnership and to avoid being labelled as a corporation for tax purposes. These rules were formulated at a time when the Treasury was trying very hard to prevent doctors and other professionals from forming unincorporated organizations that could qualify as corporations for tax purposes. State laws, at that time, prevented most professionals from forming corporations. So in order to obtain pension plans and other "fringe benefits," doctors formed organizations which they claimed qualified as corporations for tax purposes. The government countered by adopting Regulations under which it became very difficult for an unincorporated organization to be a corporation and very easy for it to be a partnership. Although the original controversy has now been stilled by state statutes permitting professionals to incorporate, the Regulations adopted at the time of the controversy still remain in force.

The Treasury Regulations (Reg. Section 301.7701-2(a)(b)) provide four criteria for determining whether an association is a corporation or a partnership. These four criteria are (1) continuity of life, (2) centralized management, (3) transferability of interest and (4) limited liability. The Regulations further say that the unincorporated organization will not be considered a corporation unless it has more corporate characteristics than partnership characteristics. Thus, if an organization resembles a corporation as to two of the tests and resembles a partnership as to the other two, the Regulations say that the organization is to be classified as a partnership.

Consider the four criteria in greater detail. "Continuity of life" is a corporate characteristic. It means, say the Regulations, that the death, resignation, etc. of a member does not cause the dissolution of the organization. In a partnership agreement, provision can be made for the continuation of the venture despite the death, resignation, etc. of a general partner. But the Regulation says that the partnership agreement for continuity does not control. If under state law, death or resignation, etc. causes a technical dissolution of the partnership, that is it. The partnership does not meet the "continuity of life" test. Under just about every state law, death, resignation, etc. of a general partner *does* create a technical dissolution.

On centralized management, the Regulations take the position that it exists only if management is substantially divorced from ownership. So in a limited partnership there is centralized management only if the general partner has a 20% or less investment interest. The 20%, of course, is only a rule of thumb. In any event, most of the limited partnerships meet the centralized management standard. Usually the limited partners supply the bulk of the investment and the general partners operate the partnership without any voice in management by the limited partners.

The Regulations seem to indicate that if there is any substantial restriction on transfer of interest (i.e. if the approval of the general partner is needed before a limited partner may transfer his interest or the general partner has a right of first refusal) the transferability-of-interest test may not be met. The Regulations are not specific here; they simply indicate that a substantial restriction on transferability of the interest may prevent the organization from being considered a corporation.

The last test is limited liability, a corporate characteristic. An organization has the characteristic of limited liability if there is *no* member who is personally liable for the debts of the organization. In a limited partnership, limited liability would exist if the general partner is not a person with substantial assets other than his interest in the partnership or if he is a mere dummy, an agent for the limited partners.

IRS attitude on partnership status

Although, under the Regulations discussed previously, it would seem relatively simple to assure partnership status of a limited partnership real estate syndicate, imaginative maneuvering on the part of syndicate promoters in setting up many of these arrangements has caused IRS to take a careful look at this area. It has imposed restrictions, indirectly, through its power to issue advance ruling.

It is common for the syndicators to seek an advance ruling from IRS regarding the partnership status of the proposed syndicate. Sophisticated investors and their advisers will often insist on such a ruling to assure the deductibility of losses that are expected to pass to the limited partners in the early years. While IRS will issue advance rulings on proposed transactions, it can also refuse to rule. This is a powerful tool in the hands of IRS. In a specific case, the Government may feel it does not have sufficient basis to rule adversely. However, if the facts do not meet IRS guidelines for a favorable ruling, it can refuse any ruling at all. Thus, while ostensibly the guidelines for issuing favorable rulings deal only with whether IRS will or will not issue a ruling, its power to withhold a ruling can have the practical effect of an adverse ruling.

Furthermore, although the guidelines for issuing a ruling technically do not affect the substance of a transaction, tax practitioners often feel that they will still influence revenue agents examining returns. For example, a taxpayer need not get an advance ruling to proceed with a transaction. He may feel he is on safe ground or he may be advised by counsel that his syndicate will meet the requirements of partnership status. Subsequently, when the tax return is examined, although the IRS guidelines for rulings were not issued as substantive rules, many tax advisers fear that the revenue agent examining the return will apply those guidelines in determining the status of the already existing syndicate.

Two sets of guidelines for favorable rulings regarding limited partnership status that IRS has issued take on substantial significance. One of these sets of guidelines (*Rev. Proc. 74-17*) deals in general with when IRS will rule with regard to limited partnership status. The other (*Rev. Proc. 72-13*) sets forth requirements for the recognition of a corporation as a general partner of a limited partnership.

General requirements of a limited partnership

Rev. Proc. 74-17, issued May 3, 1974, provides that IRS will refuse to rule that a limited partnership will be taxed as a partnership and not as a corporation unless the following requirements are met.

1. The interests of all the general partners, taken together, in each material item of partnership income, gain, loss, deduction or credit is equal to at least one percent of each such item at all times during the existence of the partnership. In determining the general partners' interests in such items, limited partnership interests owned by the general partners shall not be taken into account.

2. The aggregate deductions to be claimed by the partners as their distributive shares of partnership losses for the first two years of operation of the limited partnership will not exceed the amount of equity capital invested in the limited partnership.

3. A creditor who makes a non-recourse loan to the limited partnership must not have or acquire, at any time as a result of making the loan, any direct or indirect interest in the profits, capital or property of the limited partnership other than as a secured creditor.

The first of these requirements is apparently aimed at the arrangements under which all of the partnership losses are attempted to be allocated to the limited partners or other special allocations of the various items made in order to make the investment in the syndicate more attractive. This requirement that the general partners must have at least a one percent interest in each item can be significant where the total amounts are substantial.

The second requirement seems to be an attempt to curb the practice of promising investors loss deductions far in excess of their cash investments (via large depreciation and other deductions) made possible by substantial increases of limited partners' bases via non-recourse loans.

The third requirement, which is consistent with other IRS rulings, is aimed at preventing the boosting of partners' bases via non-recourse loans when these loans come from investors in the project. IRS apparently does not want to recognize the validity of a non-recourse loan unless it is from a true outsider.

As mentioned previously, and as must be emphasized, these requirements are ostensibly *not* substantive requirements. They are merely the guidelines IRS has set up for issuing favorable advance rulings. Taxpayers are free to set up limited partnerships that do not meet these requirements and may very well prevail on the ground that they meet the tests of the Regulations (i.e. that the organization does not have more corporate attributes than partnership attributes). Nevertheless, the absence of an advance ruling may affect the marketability of the limited partnership interests. Consequently, syndicators presumably will attempt to meet the IRS requirements although they and their tax advisers may believe that the IRS requirements are unwarranted by law.

Corporation as a general partner

Rev. Proc. 72-13 deals with the current tendency to use a corporation as the general partner in a limited partnership. As was pointed out, an organization is treated as having limited liability (a corporate characteristic) if no member of the organization is personally liable for the debts of the organization.

Since most states now permit corporations to be partners in partnerships, the idea arose to have a corporation be the general partner. In a limited partnership of this type, the only partner with personal liability is the corporate general partner. The limited partners do not have personal liability and the shareholders of the general-partner corporation (as in the case of the shareholders of *any* corporation) do not have personal liability.

If the corporation is the only entity personally liable for the debts of the limited partnership, will the organization be classified as a partnership or taxed as a coporation? IRS, in *Rev. Proc. 72-13*, provides the guidelines as to when IRS will issue a ruling that a limited partnership with a corporation as general partner is taxable as a partnership and not as a corporation.

1. The limited partners may not own more than 20% of the stock of the general-partner corporation or its affiliates. Attribution rules apply in determining stock ownership (i.e. one is deemed to own stock owned by his spouse, children, etc.).

2. The corporate general partner must have a net worth *at all times* of at least 15% of the total contributions to the limited partnership or $250,000, whichever is less, if the total contributions to the partnership are less than $2,500,000. If total contributions to the partnership are $2,500,000 or more, the corporation's net worth must at all times be at least 10% of the total contributions.

3. The net worth computation is based on current market values but *excludes* the corporation's interest in the partnership as well as receivables from and payables to the partnership.

4. If the corporation has interests in more than one limited partnership, the minimum net worth must equal the aggregate of the amounts required for each individual partnership.

5. The purchase of an interest in a limited partnership may not carry with it the right or obligation to purchase a security of the general-partner corporation or its affiliates.

Again, these are IRS guidelines for issuing favorable advance rulings rather than substantive rules which result in the reluctance of investors (or their advisers) to enter syndications without the assurance of an advance ruling that the partnership status will be recognized.

In addition, the guidelines issued by the IRS require that the specific minimum capital requirements of the corporate partner be met "at all times." This requirement undoubtedly gives tax advisers a difficult time. What kind of assurances and guarantees should they insist that their investor clients get to assure that the corporate general partner retain the capital levels "at all times" in the future?

Even if the syndicate promoters give contractural assurances to the investors, the failure to maintain the minimum capital levels in the corporate general partner might destroy the tax shelter to the investor (if the IRS guideline is subsequently upheld as a proper substantive criterion as well as a guideline for advance ruling). The investor (limited partner) may have a lawsuit against the syndicator but that may be small solace (or of limited economic value, depending on the liquidity of the syndicator) to the investor.

Basis of limited partner's interest

As previously explained (see page 302), the limited partnership has great appeal as a vehicle for tax-sheltered investments because of the potential for increasing the limited partner's basis far beyond his investment. A partner, including a limited partner, can deduct partnership losses only to the extent of his basis. However, the tax rules say that a limited partner's basis includes his share of those liabilities of the partnership for which *no* partner is personally liable, so called "subject to" or non-recourse liabilities.

The rule is stated in Reg. Section 1.752-1(e) and it is worth quoting that portion of the Regulation in full.

"(e) *Partner's share of partnership liabilities.* A partner's share of partnership liabilities shall be determined in accordance with his ratio for sharing losses under the partnership agreement. In the case of a limited partnership, a limited partner's share of partnership liabilities shall not exceed the difference between his actual contribution credited to him by the partnership and the total contribution which he is obligated to make under the limited partnership agreement. However, where none of the partners have any personal liability with respect to a partnership liability (as in the case of a mortgage on real estate acquired by the partnership without the assumption by the partnership or any of the partners of any liability on the mortgage), then all partners, including limited partners, shall be considered as sharing such liability under Section 752(c) in the same proportion as they share the profits. The provisions of this paragraph may be illustrated by the following example.

"G is a general partner in partnership GL. Each makes equal contributions of $20,000 cash to the partnership upon its formation. Under the terms of the partnership agreement, they are to share profits equally but L's liabilities are limited to the extent of his contribution. Subsequently, the partnership pays $10,000 for real property which is subject to a mortgage of $5,000. Neither the partnership nor any of the partners assumes any liability on the mortgage. The basis of such property to the partnership is $15,000. The basis of G and L for their partnership interests is increased by $2,500 each, since each partner's share of the partnership liability (the $5,000 mortgage) has increased by that amount. However, if the partnership had assumed the mortgage so that G had become personally liable thereunder, G's basis for his interest would have been increased by $5,000 and L's basis would remain unchanged."

Partnership liabilities are normally allocated for basis purposes in accordance with the ratio for sharing losses. If the partnership agreement provides one ratio for losses and another for profits, the loss ratio may be used. When the limited partnership has non-recourse liabilities, the Regulations require that the profit ratio be used.

If any of the partners are personally liable for a partnership liability, that liability cannot increase the limited partner's basis beyond his subscription liability. If no one is personally liable, then the limited partner can increase his basis by his share of that liability.

To understand why the partnership Regulations permit the limited partner to increase his basis by an allocated share of the non-recourse liabilities of the partnership, comparison can be made to the purchase of real estate by an individual. If he purchases real estate subject to a mortgage, the basis of the real estate includes the mortgage. He is considered to have incurred the mortgage liability even though he is not personally liable. Similarly, if a partnership purchases property subject to a mortgage, the partners are deemed to have incurred the mortgage liability and the liability is reflected in the basis of the partnership interests.

If the partnership were legally liable on the mortgage (i.e. if it were not a non-recourse liability), the general partner would be personally liable and no part of the mortgage liability would be allocated to the limited partner. When the mortgage is non-recourse, why should the liability be allocated solely to the general partner if he is no more liable than the limited partner? That is why the non-recourse liabilities are allocated among all the partners, limited as well as general.

Non-recourse liabilities must have some property, some assets, that the creditor can look to for payment, i.e. property on which the liability is a lien. Otherwise, the transaction may be subject to attack as fictitious or sham and designed solely for its tax consequences. There is no problem when the non-recourse debt is a mortgage on real estate. Since the debt is secured by valuable real estate, the debt is bona-fide even though there is no personal liability.

Consequences of including liabilities in the basis of a partner's interest

We have seen that a partner's allocable share of the liabilities of the partnership enter into the computation of the basis of his partnership interest. To the extent that a partner shares partnership liabilities, it is the same as if he made a money contribution to the partnership and that is exactly what Section 752 of the Code says. Correspondingly, any decrease in a partner's share of partnership liabilities is considered the same as a distribution of money to the partner by the partnership.

Partnership agreements in many tax-sheltered transactions provide that limited partners shall have allocated to them a high proportion of the profits during the early years of the venture. During its early years, the venture is going to operate at a substantial loss because of the use of accelerated depreciation and other initial deductible expenses. By allocating a high proportion of the profits to the limited partners, they are able to use almost all of the losses. As was pointed out previously, a limited partner adds to his basis a proportion of the partnership's non-recourse liabilities *in accordance with the profit ratio.* So if, say, 90% of the profits are allocated to the limited partners, then the limited partners can include in their basis 90% of the non-recourse liabilities of the partnership. However, while the general partner may not object to giving the limited partners the profits for the years when there will be losses, he likely wants a larger share of the profits in the years when there will be profits. So these arrangements often provide that down the line the profit ratio will change. The limited partner's share of the profits will change, say from 90% to 50%. *This change may be a trap for the limited partners.*

Suppose a limited partner has invested $10,000 and partnership non-recourse liabilities amount to $100,000. Because of the 90% profit ratio, $90,000 of the liabilities are allocated to the limited partner and the basis of his interest is $100,000. Losses pass through to him and, over the years, he takes deductions of $50,000. Let us assume that at that time partnership non-recourse liabilities stand at $70,000. The basis of the limited partner's interest, the 90% profit ratio still being in effect, is $23,000 (investment, $10,000, plus share of liabilities, $63,000, minus losses deducted, $50,000). Now there is a profit switch to 50%. The limited partner is considered to have received a distribution from the partnership of $28,000 since his allocable share of partnership liabilities has been reduced from $63,000 to $35,000. To the extent that this constructive distribution exceeds his basis before the distribution, he realizes a gain which is considered a gain from the sale of his partnership interest. Thus, all of a sudden, because of a profit switch and without receiving any real money, the limited partner will incur a tax.

Disposition of property or partnership interest

It is quite clear that if the property of the partnership were sold for a price that exceeded the amount of the mortgage or other non-recourse liability to which it was subject, the partnership would realize a gain allocable among the partners, general and limited, according to the partnership agreement.

Suppose, however, that the property has declined in value, that debt service payments cannot be met and the mortgage is foreclosed. Assume that the market value of the property is less than the mortgage liability outstanding at that time. This could easily happen in the case of low-income housing projects which are the subject of many tax-sheltered partnership investments. Nevertheless, on a disposition of the property or a foreclosure, the partnership would be regarded as receiving income to the extent of the liability of which it was relieved. For example, suppose there is a non-recourse mortgage of $500,000 on the partnership real estate and the limited partner had an original basis of $90,000. Over the years, he deducted losses of $70,000 and reduced his basis to $20,000. On foreclosure of the mortgage, the partner is relieved of his $50,000 share of the liability. That is treated as a sale for $50,000 and since the limited partner's basis has been reduced to $20,000, he has a taxable gain of $30,000.

Additional illustrations of the principle under which the partner's relief of non-recourse liabilities creates a taxable gain to him can be found in IRS ruling *Rev. Rul. 74-40* issued in 1974. Three examples are given.

The first situation involves a limited partner who invested $10,000 cash and whose share of the partnership's non-recourse liabilities was $15,000. He later sells his interest for $10,000 cash. At the time of the sale, his basis for his interest is $20,000. (Presumably, he reduced his original $25,000 basis by deducting a $5,000 loss.) Although he receives the same amount of cash as he invested ($10,000), he is treated as having realized a taxable gain of $5,000. The sales price of his partnership interest is calculated to be $25,000 ($10,000 cash plus $15,000 of partnership liabilities of which he is now relieved). Subtracting his $20,000 basis, he has a $5,000 gain.

The second situation is the same as the first except that, instead of selling his partnership interest, he receives $10,000 from the partnership in liquidation of his interest. The tax result is the same as in the first situation.

In the third example, the taxpayer has claimed sufficient losses to bring his basis down to zero. At that point, he simply withdraws from the partnership and *receives nothing* for his interest. He is treated as having realized a taxable gain of $15,000. The $15,000 of liabilities of which he is relieved is considered as an amount received by him. He has no basis to subtract from that so the whole $15,000 is taxable gain.

Note that the gains in each of the three instances can be capital gains if the partnership had no unrealized receivables, no substantially appreciated inventory and there was no depreciation recapture at the time of disposition.

Allocation of income and deductions

It is quite common for a real estate syndication that is intended to offer the limited partners a tax shelter to provide for a plan for sharing of profits and losses which has the effect of providing losses to the limited partner in the beginning years of the venture with, as previously explained, the probability of income realization in the future, preferably capital gain.

The tax law (Section 702) is flexible in that it permits a partnership agreement to make special allocations of particular items of income, deduction or credit among the partners. If, however, the Government determines that the principal purpose of a special allocation is the avoidance or evasion of income tax, the item must be allocated in accordance with the general profit and loss ratio. The Treasury Regulations list various factors going into this determination among which are "whether the partnership or a partner individually has a business purpose for the allocation; whether the allocation has 'substantial economic effect,' that is, whether the allocation may actually affect the dollar amount of the partners' shares of the total partnership income or loss, independently of tax consequences . . . ."

The courts have been called upon to interpret these Regulations. For example, the *Orrisch* case, 55 T.C. 395, dealt with a real estate general partnership in which both partners originally had equal interest with profits and losses being shared equally. At some point, Orrisch's other income was substantial while his partner already had losses. At this point, they conceived the idea of amending their partnership agreement to provide that depreciation deductions would be specifically allocated to Orrisch but that, in the event that the property was sold at a gain, the specially allocated depreciation deduction would be "charged back" to Orrisch and he would pay the tax on the gain attributable thereto. The Tax Court held that, in the circumstances, the only purpose and effect of the special allocation was to enable Orrisch to obtain present deductions at the cost of future capital gain and so was lacking business purpose.

That result is exactly what happens in some tax-sheltered real estate offerings. The limited partner realizes present tax losses at the expense of greater capital gain in the future. A very large part of the present loss is attributable to depreciation. Can the government use the *Orrisch* holding to attack the arrangement? The statutory pattern permits the special allocation to be set aside in favor of the general ratio of sharing profits and losses and Orrisch fell within this pattern. Suppose *Orrisch's* amendment had simply altered the general ratio to provide the same effect. Would the government then have been precluded from attacking the division?

The Government argued exactly that position in *Kresser*, 54 T.C. 1621, where all of the partnership income for one year was allocated to a partner who had a net operating loss expiring in that year. The Tax Court held for the Government on the ground that the modification of the general profit-sharing ratio to 100–0 was a sham. However, the Tax Court recognized that the problem in general was a difficult one and that the language of the law supported the taxpayer's right to alter the overall profit-sharing scheme (without allocation of specific items) if there was no sham involved.

Besides the statutory pattern, there may be business purposes that support the profit and loss ratios in a tax shelter partnership. For example, the general partner's purpose is to avoid advancing his own funds to the partnership and the limited partner would not make the investment without such an arrangement.

Retroactive allocations

Suppose a limited partner were to enter after a partnership has started and after some of the initial deductible expenses, such as interest and taxes during construction, have been paid. Can the new partner get the benefit of these deductions, assuming, of course, that he comes in before the end of the partnership year? Reg. Section 1.706-1(c)(4) states that where a partner's interest is reduced, the partnership taxable year continues but his varying partnership interests are taken into account in computing his taxable income. But Reg. Section 1.761-1(c) permits a partnership agreement to be modified before the due date of its return. Resolution of the question is uncertain. The strongest position might be if the new partner does not purchase the interest of a previous partner and if, on formation, the limited partnership reserved interests for new partners with the initial partners entitled to use only losses attributable to their initial interests.

Appendix E

Corporate Liquidations/ Reorganizations

In the discussion of the forms of ownership of real estate, it was pointed out that real estate is often acquired in corporate form in order to avoid personal liability but that in some situations corporate ownership may create tax disadvantages that could outweigh whatever advantages may flow from limited liability. (See the material beginning on page 116.) In other situations, corporate ownership may present an opportunity for tax-free diversification of the investment.

One of the major problems of corporate ownership arises when disposition of the property owned by the corporation is desired. The problem is especially acute when the corporation is owned by just one or a few shareholders, i.e. the so-called closely-held corporation. Since the corporation is a separate entity, any gain realized on the disposition will be taxable to the corporate entity. However, if corporate reinvestment is not intended at that point and if each of the shareholders would like to reinvest his share in different investments and not in conjunction with the other shareholders, the problem arises of how to get the after-tax proceeds into the hands of the shareholders. As was pointed out on page 105, distributions to the shareholders by the corporation of after-tax corporate profits are again taxed to the shareholders as dividends.

This problem of double taxation may be solved in some cases by astute use of the rule applying to corporate liquidations.

In some cases, an investor may be seeking to diversify his investments. However, he may be deterred by the tax cost involved in disposing of his current holdings to acquire the funds with which to reinvest. In some cases, if he holds the property in unincorporated form this problem may be solved via so-called "like-kind" exchanges (described in detail beginning on page 195). In other situations, the fact that the property is held in corporate form may present an opportunity to diversify without incurring a tax. This result may be achieved via a corporate reorganization.

Corporate liquidations

The general tax rule pertaining to complete liquidations of corporations must first be understood in order to apply the special rules that are available to avoid double taxation.

If a corporation is completely liquidated, the shareholders receive all of the corporate assets in exchange for their shares in the corporation. The transaction is treated as a sale or exchange. Assuming the shareholder has held his stock for more than six months, he will realize a long-term capital gain or loss on the transaction (it is treated as if he sold his stock to the corporation for the assets he received). The gain or loss will be equal to the difference between the market value of everything he receives from the corporation and the basis for the stock he surrenders. Even though the corporation has accumulated earnings which, if distributed to the stockholder as a dividend would be taxed to him as ordinary income, if these earnings are paid to the shareholder as part of the total liquidation of the corporation, they are part of the total proceeds used to measure his long-term capital gain on liquidation.

The corporation is normally not taxable on the transaction. However, if the corporation distributes depreciable property as part of the liquidation, whatever depreciation recapture would have arisen had it sold the property to a third party at its market value at that time arises upon the liquidation distribution. (The rules pertaining to depreciation recapture are explained beginning on page 175.) Although the corporation is completely liquidated, it may still be liable for some taxes attributable to the distribution of property on which depreciation recapture is realized. (If the corporation has not retained assets with which to pay the taxes, IRS may pursue each of the shareholders who received a distribution in liquidation for his pro rata share of the taxes payable by the corporation.)

The twelve-month (Section 337) liquidation

The problem with the corporate liquidation rules as a vehicle for the sale of property held in a corporation can be seen from the following oversimplified example.

Assume a corporation with two equal stockholders holds a piece of property worth $1,000,000. Its basis for the property is $200,000. If it sells the property it will realize a gain of $800,000. (For illustrative purposes, assume that there is no depreciation recapture and that the entire gain qualifies as a Section 1231 gain.) The corporation has a long-term capital gain of $800,000 and pays a 30% tax or $240,000. The corporation now has $760,000 in cash and the two equal shareholders would like to get that money. The corporation can now go through a complete liquidation, distributing $380,000 to each shareholder. If each shareholder has a basis for his stock of $80,000, each will have a long-term capital gain of $300,000. Taking into account each shareholder's other income, assume each pays an effective overall rate on his capital gain of 30% or $90,000. (The rules for taxing long-term capital gains are complex involving a combination of the alternative tax on $50,000 of the gain, reporting half of the balance of the gain and possibly paying a 10% excise tax on part of the gain as tax preference income. Hence, a reasonable assumption of a 30% rate is made. The rules for calculating the tax on long-term capital gains are set forth beginning on page 91.) Thus, the $800,000 gain on the sale of the property by the corporation is subject to a total tax of $420,000 ($240,000 on the corporate level and $90,000 on the shareholder level).

With this problem of double taxation before them, taxpayers attempted to circumvent the double tax by going through the liquidation prior to the sale. Had the corporation in the example distributed the property to the shareholders in total liquidation, they would have had a capital gain on the distribution of $840,000 (the $1,000,000 market value of the property received minus the combined basis of the stock in the hands of both shareholders of $160,000). Again, assuming a 30% tax on the capital gains, the tax would come to $252,000. If the shareholders then sold the property for $1,000,000 they would have no gain or loss on the transaction since their bases for the property would be $1,000,000, the value they picked up in computing their taxable capital gain on the liquidation.

If the corporation liquidated the property and the stockholders then sold it, they would have cash remaining after taxes of $748,000 ($1,000,000 sales proceeds minus the $252,000 capital gains tax paid on the liquidation) or $374,000 each. **313**

On the other hand, where the corporation sold the property first each received a distribution of $380,000, paid a capital gains tax of $90,000 and had $290,000 left after taxes.

Obviously, the preferred tax route was to liquidate first and then sell. However, a famous U. S. Supreme Court decision, the *Court Holding Company* case, presented a major problem. In that case, the Court agreed with IRS that although the liquidation took place before the sale, the negotiations prior to the transaction made it clear that the sale was really being made on behalf of the corporation. So the court said the case should be decided on what it considered to be the *substance* of the transaction, not its formal form, and it treated the transaction as if the sale was made by the corporation and then the liquidation took place; hence the double tax. In a later case, the *Cumberland Public Service Company* case, the Supreme Court held that the facts concerning sales negotiations there indicated that the liquidation took place first and the sale was truly made by the shareholders after liquidation; a double tax was avoided.

The result of these cases was to create great uncertainty; fine distinctions between fact patterns made all the difference and no one could be sure exactly how the facts in his case would ultimately be interpreted. Finally, Congress came to the rescue and enacted Section 337 of the Internal Revenue Code.

Section 337 is intended to take the uncertainty out of the result and remove the problems that would arise if it were ultimately determined that the fact pattern resembled *Court Holding Company* rather than *Cumberland Public Service.*

If the rules of Section 337 are met, the corporation makes the sale. However, the gain to the corporation is not taxed to the corporation. On the liquidation that follows, the shareholders apply the regular rules applying to corporate liquidations and a report a capital gain for the difference between the proceeds they receive and the basis for their stock.

If Section 337 were applied to the example here, the corporation would sell the property for $1,000,000. It would not recognize any gain on the transaction and thus pay no tax. It could then distribute the $1,000,000 to the two shareholders who would have a combined capital gain of $840,000, a combined capital gain tax of $252,000 and proceeds remaining of $748,000 or $374,000 each; these are the same results that would arise if they liquidated first and then sold (and were not subsequently upset by the *Court Holding Company* rule).

Section 337 rules   For Section 337 to apply, certain rules must be followed. First, a plan of complete liquidation must be adopted. This can be a simple matter of having a corporate resolution passed by the Board of Directors. While the Treasury Regulations will recognize some informal arrangements as having the effect of the adoption of a plan of liquidation (especially where the existence of such a plan will produce adverse tax effects), if a Section 337 liquidation is desired, it is the safe and prudent practice to have the formal adoption of a plan in writing.

The next requirement is to liquidate the entire corporation (i.e. all of its assets distributed to the shareholders) within one year of the adoption of the plan of liquidation. The corporation may retain such assets as are required to meet its liabilities which are not distributed.

Within the one-year period, gains and losses on the sale of property by the corporation are not recognized for tax purposes, i.e. they are tax-free. Property here means all property other than inventory. (Thus, if the corporation were a dealer in real estate, see page 172, sale of individual pieces of real estate would be taxable to the corporation as sale of inventory.) If, however, the entire inventory is sold to one customer in one transaction, gain or loss on that sale, too, is not recognized for tax purposes.

Note that the non-recognition applies to both gains and losses. If some of the property sold by the corporation during the one year after the adoption of the plan of liquidation were sold at a loss, that loss would not be deductible by the corporation to offset other income. To avoid this result it is advisable to sell the loss property prior to the adoption of the plan of liquidation. After the sale at a loss, the plan can be adopted and subsequent sales by the corporation at gains within the one-year period would not be taxable at the corporate level. (It is important here to avoid any informal understanding that resembles a plan of liquidation before the loss property is sold. It is in these situations that IRS may seek to establish that *in fact* a plan of liquidation was adopted prior to the sale of the loss property and thus deny the corporation a deduction for those losses.)

Problems in Section 337 liquidations   While Section 337 may be a useful vehicle for selling corporate property and getting the proceeds into the hands of the stockholders at the cost of one tax, it is not a suitable device to use if installment sale reporting is desired.

The corporation can make a sale within the one-year period that qualifies for installment sale reporting (see page 181 for the installment sale rules). Under the rules of Section 337, the corporation will not have any recognized gain. However, when the corporation is completely liquidated (as it must be within one year), the installment obligations will be distributed to the shareholders. (Because the liquidation qualifies under Section 337, the corporation will not be taxed on the difference between its basis for the installment obligations and their market value. In an ordinary complete liquidation, the corporation *is* taxed if it distributes installment obligations.) The shareholders, however, in computing their capital gains on the liquidation will have to include the full market value of the installment obligations they receive at the time they receive those obligations. Hence, they will be taxable on the gain inherent in the market value of those installment obligations at the time of liquidation even though they may not collect on some of the installment obligations for a number of years. While there is only one tax on the gain of the sale of the property by the corporation (at the stockholder level at the time of liquidation), the deferral of the gain over the period of collection that is available in the installment method of reporting is destroyed when the installment obligations are distributed in the liquidation of the corporation.

The one-month Section 333 liquidation

This special form of liquidation is designed to permit the property to be distributed to the shareholders in a transaction in which the shareholders do not recognize any gain. However, they retain as the basis for the property they have received the basis of the stock they have surrendered. On subsequent sale, the gain is taxable to the shareholders (since they have then sold their own property). In this situation the shareholder can make his own installment sale and report the gain under the installment method of reporting if the installment sale rules are met.

The foregoing is a simplified explanation of the one-month liquidation rules. As may be expected, there are a number of complexities in this section. Certain rules must be followed and notwithstanding the foregoing broad description of the purpose of Section 333, there are situations where part or all of the gain to the shareholders on liquidation may be taxed, even as ordinary income.

Before getting into the specific rules of Section 333, it should be noted that this section is most beneficial when the corporation holds the property that has appreciated considerably in value and has little or no earnings and profits (accumulated or current) and little or no cash or securities acquired after 1954.

To qualify a liquidation under Section 333, a plan of liquidation has to be adopted. Thereafter, at least 80% of the shareholders must consent to the liquidation. If enough shareholders consent, those who do not consent treat their distributions in liquidation under the general rules pertaining to liquidations (they realize capital gain or loss for the difference between the market value of what they receive in the liquidation and the bases for their shares in the corporation).

Once the plan is adopted and the necessary consents obtained, the complete liquidation of the corporation must take place within one calendar month. Note that the entire distribution must take place within that one month (a calendar month and *not* a 30-day period spanning two calendar months).

If the Section 333 rules are met, the shareholder computes his gain in the usual manner, i.e. the difference between the market value of what he receives and the basis for the stock he surrenders. However, all or part of that gain may not be recognized.

1. If, at the time of the liquidation, the corporation had earnings and profits accumulated from prior years or current year's earnings or both, he is deemed to have received his pro rata share of those earnings and profits. The portion of his gain equal to his pro rata share of earnings and profits is taxable to him as a dividend (ordinary income).

2. If the distribution to the shareholder includes cash, stock or securities acquired by the corporation after 1954, that portion of his gain remaining (after applying the rules on earnings and profits) that is equal to the value of such cash and stock or securities is taxable to him as a capital gain.

3. Any remaining gain, after applying the rules in 1 and 2, is not recognized. The bases for these items are allocable portions of the remaining basis of his stock.

Obviously, if there are little or no earnings and profits and no cash or securities, then most or all of the gain on liquidation is not recognized. Thereafter, the shareholder can sell the property to a third party, recognize the gain and pay the tax. Also, the transaction can be structured as an installment sale.

Note that if this form of liquidation is used to bring about an installment sale, care must be taken that there are no negotiations to sell prior to the liquidation or if there are such negotiations, it must be clear that the corporation refuses to sell and the sale can only take place if, as and when the shareholders acquire the property first and the sale will be made by them for their own account. Otherwise, it is possible for the *Court Holding Company* rules to apply here and the transaction will be treated as if the sale was made by the corporation.

Earnings and profits   When a one-month liquidation is employed and if the corporation distributes depreciable property, depreciation recapture on the corporate level can occur. The corporation is deemed to have the same amount of depreciation recapture as it would have had had it sold the property at the time of liquidation at a price equal to the market value at the time of liquidation. If depreciation recapture occurs, the corporation has income and a tax to pay. In addition, the income remaining after the tax adds to the corporation's earnings and profits and thereby creates (or adds to) a dividend to the shareholders at the time of liquidation.

Basis It was explained earlier that in a Section 333 liquidation the shareholders allocate their bases for their stock to the properties received in the liquidation (where gain is not recognized). It should be noted that where the property is subject to a mortgage or other lien, the liability that comes with the property is added to the basis of the property received thus increasing the shareholder's basis.

Corporate reorganizations

In the context of the real estate investor, the corporate reorganization can provide a means of diversification of investment without reducing the amount available for reinvestment.

For example, if an investor should sell his current investment, he is left with *after-tax* proceeds for reinvestment. On the other hand if he is able to combine his corporation with another and thereby become an investor in the combined enterprise (thereby diversifying or expanding his investment) without paying a tax, he has the full value of the original investment working for him. This latter result can be accomplished via a corporate reorganization.

From a potential seller's viewpoint, the corporate reorganization is most attractive when the seller's corporation (usually closely-held) is acquired by a much larger corporation whose stock is publicly traded. After the acquisition, the former shareholder of the closely-held company is now a stockholder in a corporation whose stock is traded publicly. He is now in a position to dispose of part of his investment as the situation dictates, picking up capital gains along the way. He is also in a position to make gifts and otherwise plan his estate using determined values (stock quotations).

Statutory pattern of reorganization

The tax law in this area is very complex. What follows, therefore, is an outline of the structures of the various forms of corporate reorganization and the basic rules without an examination of all of the fine points and complexities.

There are six forms of reorganizations. Only three will be considered here, the "A," "B" and "C" types. The other three do not apply to the acquisition type of transactions.

Basically, in a corporate reorganization, the shareholders and bondholders of the corporation that is being acquired end up as shareholders or bondholders of the corporation doing the acquiring. Part or all of the gain on the transaction may be non-recognized (i.e. not currently taxed) depending on how the transaction is structured.

Typically, if a shareholder gets stock only in return for his stock, the gain on the transaction is not taxed. If he gets securities (i.e. bonds, notes, etc.), they are considered "boot" to the extent that the face amount of the securities received exceeds the face amount of the securities surrendered (obviously, if no securities are surrendered, the face amount of any securities received constitutes "boot"). Cash and property other than stock or securities also constitute "boot." Basically,   **317** "boot" is taxable to the extent it does not exceed the total gain. ("Boot" is further explained under each type of reorganization.)

"A" type of reorganization

The "A" type is defined as a "statutory merger or consolidation." Evidently all that is required to consummate an "A" type reorganization is to effect, under the corporation laws of any state, a merger of two or more corporations whereby one retains its corporate existence and absorbs the others.

Unlike the "B" and "C" types, in an "A" reorganization no restrictions are imposed by the tax law as to the amount of money or other property that may be used nor the type of stock or securities that may be issued. True, any money or other property will constitute "boot" and result in some tax incidence but the issuance of "boot" in and of itself will not disqualify the transaction as an "A" reorganization.

Thus, considerable flexibility is available in an "A" reorganization. Should some shareholders want cash and others stock it can be worked out within the framework of an "A" type. However, there is some peril inherent in this very flexibility. Excessive use by the acquiring or resulting corporation of bonds, cash and other property may violate the requirement of "continuity of interest." This concept requires that there be a continuity of interest through stock ownership in the acquiring corporation on the part of the former stockholders of the acquired corporation. How much "boot," therefore, may be given and yet preserve the reorganization?

IRS takes the position that the "continuity of interest" is satisfied if at least 50% in value of the former stock interest is continued in the acquiring corporation. IRS would thus permit not more than 50% of the value of the stock to be exchanged for "boot."

Note, also, that after receiving the required stock interest in the acquiring corporation, it is necessary to retain it for a relatively reasonable period of time. Otherwise IRS will probably argue that there was a pre-existing plan to sell off the stock thereby destroying the "continuity of interest" at the time of the reorganization.

Treatment of "boot" in "A" reorganizations If "boot" is given in an otherwise qualifying reorganization, gain is recognized to the recipient of the "boot" but in an amount not in excess of the "boot." A loss sustained on the reorganization is not deductible whether or not "boot" is received. If gain is recognized, it is treated as a dividend to the extent of the recipient's share of the corporation's accumulated earnings and profits.

"B" type of reorganization

In this type of reorganization, the acquiring corporation acquires the stock of the acquired corporation directly from that corporation's stockholders. The acquiring corporation must have at least 80% control of the acquired corporation after the exchange. In effect, the acquiring corporation ends up with a subsidiary corporation which it controls.

What do the shareholders of the acquired corporation get? They must get voting stock *only* in the acquiring corporation or its parent *and nothing else*.

Should the acquiring corporation issue any cash or "boot" to finance the redemption or purchase of the stock of any dissenting shareholders, that will destroy the

"B" type reorganization status and a fully taxable transaction will result.

Minimal cash may be given in lieu of fractional shares. If any other amount of "boot" is given, the *entire* transaction is fully taxable and the gain is to be reported as capital gain to the extent the value of the stock and other property received by the shareholder exceeds his basis in the stock exchanged. IRS has ruled that the issuance of contingent rights to receive additional shares will not violate the "solely for voting stock" requirement provided the right is not represented by a negotiable certificate. The acquiring corporation may acquire debentures of the acquired corporation for cash or by issuance of its own bonds without invalidating the reorganization.

"C" type of reorganization

A "C" type of reorganization resembles an "A" type in that it generally achieves a merger of the assets of the acquired corporation with that of the acquiring corporation although it need not go that far.

In a "C" type there must be an acquisition of substantially all of the properties of the acquired corporation in exchange solely for voting stock of either the acquiring corporation or its parent corporation. The assets received may also be transferred directly to a subsidiary of the acquiring corporation.

Initially, the exchange is between the two corporations; one corporation transfers its assets in exchange for the other corporation's stock. After the exchange, the corporation whose assets were acquired usually distributes the stock received to its shareholders in liquidation of the corporation. This second exchange is taxfree to the shareholders (subject to the "boot" provisions). After the liquidation of the corporation whose assets were acquired, there is, in effect, the same result as in a merger. In fact, the "C" reorganization followed by the liquidation is often referred to as a "practical merger."

Unlike an "A" reorganization, the "C" type lacks flexibility in that *solely voting stock* must be used. Peculiarly, here the statute expands the phrase "solely for voting stock" to permit a limited amount of "boot" to be given by the acquiring corporation.

As mentioned, in an "A" reorganization the "continuity of interest" requirement acts as the only limitation on the issuance of "boot." In a "C" type, the acquired corporation or its shareholders may receive cash or other property in addition to voting stock but only up to a value equal to 20% of the total value of the corporation's property. On the face of it, this would seem to allow for a sizable amount of "boot." However, there is this additional provision: in applying this 20% "boot" test, liabilities taken over are treated as if they constituted cash paid to the transferor corporation. Yet, where no "boot" whatsoever is given in addition to the voting stock, the liabilities taken over will *not* be treated as cash. In other words, if the acquiring corporation gives no "boot," only voting stock, then it can take over the liabilities regardless of the amount involved. But should any amount of "boot" be given, say $100 in cash, then *all* liabilities taken over suddenly become the equivalent of cash for the purposes of the 20% test.

As can be assumed, most corporations will have liabilities equal to at least 20% of the value of the assets. Hence, a "C" reorganization in practical effect precludes the issuance of any "boot."

Another problem may arise in a "C" reorganization with reference to the require- **319** ment for a transfer of "substantially all" of the acquired company's properties. Obviously, where all assets are taken over without exception, no question arises. But should the acquiring corporation reject some of the assets, the "substantially all" requirement may prevent consummation of a "C" reorganization. Although courts have found that 86% of the acquired corporation's net worth is "substantially all," while 68% is not, IRS maintains no percentage is controlling and that the facts in each case will be studied.

Appendix F

Gift and Estate Planning

Throughout this book we have been concerned with the income stream and cash flow from a property (including the income and cash flow arising from the disposition of the property). In doing so, we have necessarily taken into account the impact of the Federal income tax on these cash flows.

The types of dispositions of property with which we have been concerned thus far are sales and exchanges. However, there are other types of dispositions that should be considered: lifetime gifts and dispositions arising because of death. Each of these types of dispositions may have federal (and, in most cases, state) tax consequences. The taxes involved are the gift and estate taxes.

The real estate broker should have some familiarity with these taxes because just about every investor with substantial amount of property will be concerned about passing his estate on to his family or other objects of his bounty. In the vast majority of cases he will want to pass on the maximum amount possible. Consequently, he will be concerned with planning devices that will reduce the estate and gift taxes as much as possible. (It should be emphasized that the property owner's personal desires should take precedence over tax savings. There are numerous situations where personal and family considerations, emotional or otherwise, may call for plans that save less taxes than other available alternatives.) Knowing the gift and estate tax rules will help the real estate broker understand the needs of the investor and thereby enable the broker to present purchase or sales situations intelligently and usefully.

Federal estate tax

A Federal estate tax is imposed on all taxable estates in excess of $60,000. In arriving at the taxable estate, the starting point is the gross estate, i.e. the market value of all the property the decedent owned at his death. From the gross estate is first subtracted debts of the decedent and the costs of administering the estate. At this point, the amount remaining is the Adjusted Gross Estate. Amounts left outright to the decedent's spouse or in a trust form that, for tax purposes, is deemed to be outright (i.e. income from the trust to go to the surviving spouse for life, with the surviving spouse having the power to designate who is to get the trust property after the spouse's death) are eligible for the "marital deduction." The marital deduction, which may not exceed one-half the Adjusted Gross Estate, is deducted from the Adjusted Gross Estate. The remaining amount is further reduced by any charitable bequests that were made by the decedent. Finally, a flat $60,000 (the statutory allowance) is deducted. The remaining amount is the taxable estate subject to the estate tax (a graduated tax, with increasing rates as the size of the estate increases). After the estate tax is calculated, the tax is reduced by the amount of State death taxes imposed. There is, however, a maximum credit for State taxes allowed for each tax bracket regardless of the actual amount of the state death taxes. Of course, the credit can never exceed the actual amount of state death taxes imposed on the estate.

The foregoing explanation of the estate tax structure may be summarized as follows.

Gross Estate (market value of all property owned by decedent at time of death) $_____

Less: Funeral expenses $_____ .
      Debts of decedent _____
      Administration expenses of estate _____ _____

Adjusted Gross Estate _____

Less: Marital deduction (amount left outright to spouse, or equivalent, but not more than $\frac{1}{2}$ adjusted gross estate) _____

Resulting amount _____

Less: Charitable bequests _____
      Statutory allowance 60,000 _____

Taxable estate _____

Estate tax: Appropriate rates × taxable estate _____

Less: Credit for state death taxes (lower of amount actually due to state or federal statutory credit geared to size of taxable estate) _____

Estate Tax Due $_____

Alternate valuation date

It was previously stated that the gross estate consists of the market value of all the property owned by the decedent at the time of his death. However, the estate has a choice as of which of two dates it shall use to determine the value of the property: date of death or six months after date of death (referred to as the alternate valuation date).

The alternate valuation date may be selected only if the estate is required to file an estate tax return, i.e. the gross estate exceeds $60,000. If the alternate valuation date is selected, *all* property in the estate must be valued as of the alternate valuation date. It is not permissible to value some of the property as of the date of death and other property as of the alternate valuation date. Furthermore, if the alternate valuation date is chosen and if some of the estate's property is sold or distributed between the date of death and the alternate valuation date, the value of such property for estate tax purposes is its sales price or the value on the date of distribution.

Why choose the alternate valuation date? Obviously, the value of the property in the estate (or some significant portion of it) may have gone up or down six months after the date of death. If the value has gone down, the alternate valuation date may be used to reduce the value of the estate and thereby reduce the amount of the estate tax due.

However, the alternate valuation date may also be deemed an advisable choice when the value of the property has increased between the date of death and six months thereafter. As was pointed out on page 121, when property is inherited, it takes as its basis the market value at the date of death or the alternate valuation date (whichever date is used for estate tax purposes). The higher the basis assigned

322

to the property, the lower the potential capital gain on disposition by the heir who inherited the property. Hence, if the income tax bracket of the person inheriting the property is such that the tax on a capital gain by him would exceed the estate's tax on the difference between the date-of-death value and the higher alternate-valuation-date value, the use of the alternate valuation date will be favored by that beneficiary.

Choosing the alternate valuation date to benefit one or a few of the beneficiaries can be done with impunity if there are no other beneficiaries who would be hurt by the choice of the alternate valuation date. (For example, some beneficiaries may be entitled to cash bequests and have no interest in the property whose value has increased in the six months following the decedent's death. The choice of the alternate valuation date means a higher estate tax overall and, if their bequests are to share in the estate's tax burden, a smaller net bequest than they would have received had date-of-death valuation been used). If some beneficiaries would be burdened by a larger estate tax under the alternate-valuation-date valuation than by date-of-death valuation, many State courts have determined that the beneficiaries who benefit from the alternate-valuation-date valuation have to make good to the other beneficiaries the additional estate tax those other beneficiaries had to bear.

Amount of property passing to beneficiaries

Obviously, the amount of property that passes to the decedent's beneficiaries is the net amount after the estate taxes are paid. Consequently, the usual strategy for people with large estates is to embark on programs that will reduce the tax impact on the property being transferred.

Maximum marital deduction   Because half the Adjusted Gross Estate escapes tax if it qualifies for the marital deduction, it is common (especially if one spouse has a much larger estate than the other) for a married person to use the maximum marital deduction and, in effect, split the estate approximately in half. The object of such planning is to cause approximately half the estate to be taxable on the death of the first spouse (usually, the husband, who is the spouse more likely to have the larger estate and who, statistically, is apt to be the first to die) and the balance of the estate to be taxable in the estate of the second spouse. Since the estate tax, like the income tax, is a graduated tax, splitting the estate in this manner removes property in the first estate from higher brackets and transfers it to the lower brackets of the estate of the second spouse. In addition each estate is entitled to its own $60,000 exemption further reducing the combined tax in both estates (as compared to the estate tax that would be payable if the entire property remained in the first estate).

If the husband (for example) wishes to have his wife enjoy the benefits of the entire estate during her lifetime, he can still get the benefit of the full marital deduction and, in effect, split the estate by following this two-part procedure.

1. He leaves half the estate (maximum marital deduction) to his wife outright or in a trust that pays the income to the wife for her lifetime and gives her the power to name who shall receive the trust property on her death. This portion of the estate qualifies for the marital deduction and escapes tax in the husbands' estate. It is then included in the wife's estate on her death if she still possesses it.

2. He leaves the balance of the estate in trust with the income of the trust to go to to the wife during her lifetime. On her death, the trust property passes to the bene-   **323**

ficiaries named by the husband. This portion of the estate is taxable in the husband's estate but under the estate tax rules, it is *not* included in the wife's estate.

Lifetime gifts

Another method of reducing the estate tax on death is to remove property from the estate during lifetime. This is done by making gifts, usually to those beneficiaries who would inherit the property after the death of the donor had he not made the gifts (generally children, grandchildren and other relatives).

Since removing the property from the estate via lifetime gifts reduces the ultimate estate tax, to protect the Treasury against this loss of revenue, there is a gift tax imposed on lifetime gifts. However, because of the rate structure and other provisions applying to gift taxes, there is an overall tax saving available when lifetime gifts are made.

How the gift tax works

There is a graduated federal gift tax imposed on gifts. However, the gift tax rates are 75% of the rates on equivalent amounts under the estate tax rate table.

In addition, the gift tax structure provides for its own exemptions and exclusions. Only the value of the gifts in excess of the exclusions and exemptions are subject to gift taxes. Note that the amount of a gift other than cash is the market value on the date of the gift of the property. These gifts will be referred to as taxable gifts. Consequently, it is often possible to remove from the estate a considerable amount of property and give it away free of gift taxes thus escaping all taxes on that portion given away.

How to calculate taxable gifts

Annual exclusion Each person is entitled to an *annual* gift tax exclusion of $3,000 *per donee* per year. Thus, if an individual makes ten $3,000 gifts to 10 different donees (e.g. children, grandchildren) in one year (a total of $30,000), no part of those gifts would be subject to the gift tax. And he could repeat the process every year.

Split gifts If a married person makes a gift (and his spouse consents by signing the consent clause on the gift tax return), the annual exclusion on that gift is increased to $6,000. This is so even if only one spouse owns the property being given away and the other merely "consents." Thus, in the preceding example if the donor's wife consented, he could give away a total of $60,000 per year without any gift tax liability.

Gift tax marital deduction If one spouse makes a gift to the other spouse, one-half of the gift is deducted as a gift tax marital deduction and is not subject to the gift tax. Thus, if a husband makes a gift to his wife of $6,000, half or $3,000 would be deducted as a marital deduction. The other $3,000 would be eligible for the annual exclusion. Hence, the entire $6,000 could be given without any gift tax cost.

Lifetime exemptions Each person is entitled to a lifetime exemption from gift taxes of $30,000. This exemption is only applied to the portion of the gift that exceeds the annual exclusion. Once the full $30,000 is exhausted, there is no further exemption. However, the exemption may be spread out over as many years as the taxpayer desires during his lifetime. Any unused lifetime exemption remaining at his death is no longer available to anyone.

Combining the annual exclusions, split gifts and each spouse's lifetime exemption and applying them in one year to ten donees (as in our example) a total of $120,000 can be given in one year without gift tax ($60,000 in annual exclusions on split gifts plus $60,000 in lifetime exemptions by combining husband's and wife's lifetime exemptions).

As a practical matter there are no gift taxes to be paid until the donor exhausts his lifetime exemption.

Taxable gifts   The taxable gifts are those in excess of the annual exclusions and lifetime exemption.

Mr. Brown, a widower, makes a gift of $50,000 to his son. He reduces the $50,000 by the $3,000 annual exclusion. Assume he still has $20,000 of his lifetime exemption unused and he further reduces the gift by that $20,000. Hence, the taxable gift is $27,000. He pays the gift tax on $27,000.

The following year he makes a $25,000 gift to his son. Again, he deducts the $3,000 exclusion. Since he has no lifetime exemption left, the taxable gift is $22,000. Because the gift tax is a graduated tax, the tax rates increase as the taxable gifts pile up. Therefore, Brown must first add the $22,000 current taxable gift to his $27,000 prior total of taxable gifts and determine the gift tax on gifts totalling $49,000. From this amount he subtracts all previous gift taxes paid (the tax on the $27,000 taxable gift of the prior year). The difference is the tax he owes on the current gift of $22,000.

If he made another taxable gift the following year of $20,000 (after exclusion of $3,000), he would first find the tax on the total of $69,000 ($49,000 prior taxable gifts plus $20,000 current taxable gift). From this he would subtract the total gift taxes paid in the prior two years. The difference would then be the current gift tax he owed on the $20,000.

Appendix G

Charitable Contributions

Both the Federal income tax and estate tax provisions allow substantial deductions for charitable contributions. As is explained on page 86, charitable contributions reduce adjusted gross income in arriving at taxable income. Also charitable bequests (see page 321) reduce the estate subject to estate taxes.

While there is no limit on charitable bequests as reductions of the estate, the income tax law does provide a series of limitations regarding the charitable contribution deduction for income tax purposes.

Income tax limitations on charitable deductions

The deductible amount of charitable contributions made to public charities (those which receive their financial support from the public, e.g. the Red Cross, Boy Scouts of America, local churches and synagogues) is limited to 50% of adjusted gross income. (Adjusted gross income is defined on page 82.) Contributions to private foundations (entities qualifying as charitable organizations but which do not look to the public for support; generally, foundations set up by individuals for specific charitable purposes whose financial support comes from the founder and a few others) are deductible to the extent of 20% of adjusted gross income. If more than the limit is contributed to a public charity in one year, the excess may be carried forward and be treated as charitable deductions (within the allowable limits) for the following five years.

Contributions of property other than cash

Charitable contributions need not be made in cash in order to be deductible. Thus contributions of real estate, for example, may be made. In some cases, making such a contribution may be considered an attractive alternative to selling since the donor can thereby satisfy his charitable inclinations and at the same time enjoy tax benefits thus reducing the economic impact of parting with the property. Since, in some cases, not only does he get a deduction for the value of the property he gives away but also avoids the capital gains tax on the appreciation (a tax he would have had to pay had he sold the property), the tax savings can be substantial.

As might have been expected, there are a number of technical rules that have the effect of limiting the tax benefits available from contributions of appreciated property. These limitations may be summarized as follows.

1. *Gift to a public charity of appreciated property which, had it been sold, would have produced a long-term capital gain.* The taxpayer gets a deduction for the fair market value of the property and pays no tax on the appreciation. However, in this case the ceiling on deductible contributions is 30% of adjusted gross income instead of 50%. Any unused deduction may be carried forward for five years. (The taxpayer may use the 50% limitation if he is willing to treat the amount of the gift

as the market value of the property minus one-half the appreciation.) The rules of this category of gift apply not only to real estate but to stocks and securities as well. They do not apply to tangible personal property. (See item 4.)

Note that if any part of the gain (had the property been sold) would have been treated as ordinary income due to depreciation recapture, the market value of the property must be reduced by the depreciation recapture in determining the amount of the contribution.

2. *Same as item 1 except the gift is to a private foundation.* The amount of the charitable contribution is equal to the fair market value of the property minus one-half the appreciation. Again, the taxpayer is not taxed on the appreciation. If part of the gain, had the property been sold, would have been ordinary income because of depreciation recapture, the amount of the contribution must be reduced by the depreciation recapture.

3. *Gift of appreciated property, which if sold, would have resulted in ordinary income or short-term capital gain.* The amount of the contribution is equal to the donor's basis. While the appreciation is not taxed neither is it included in the amount of the contribution.

4. *Gift of tangible personal property, which if sold, would have produced a long-term capital gain.* The amount of the contribution is the market value of the property minus one-half the capital gain that would have been realized had it been sold. However, if the property contributed is related to the function of the charity receiving it (e.g. a painting to an art museum) the full market value of the property is the amount of the contribution. In neither situation is the appreciation taxable to the donor.

Gift of real estate subject to liens

If property contributed to a charity is subject to liens, e.g. a mortgage, liens for taxes, etc, the value of the gift is the difference between its market value and the amount of the liens. (Then, the preceding rules are applied to determine the amount of the deduction available.)

Bargain sale to charity

Suppose, instead of making an outright gift of the property, the donor sells appreciated property to the charity for his basis. In this way, he recovers his cost and, in effect, is making a gift of the appreciation. At least that was the way the tax law was applied prior to 1970.

Under current law, such a sale is treated as two transactions: a sale and a gift, with the donor's basis allocated between the two transactions. Thus, he gets a charitable contribution deduction but he also ends up with a taxable capital gain.

Stimson owns property for more than six months with a basis of $40,000 and a market value of $100,000. He sells it to a charity for $40,000. As a result he has the following.

1. A sale at $40,000 of a portion of the property having a basis of $16,000. (Since the $40,000 sales price is 40% of the total value of the property, 40% of the $40,000 basis or $16,000 is allocable to the portions of the property sold.) Hence, he has a taxable long-term capital gain of $24,000.

2. A charitable contribution of $60,000 for the balance of the property subject to the limitations described in (1) relating to the contribution of appreciated property. **327**

Mortgage in excess of basis   If the property contributed to a charity is subject to a mortgage in excess of basis, it is likely to be treated as a bargain sale of the property. The amount of the mortgage will probably be treated as proceeds received on the transfer and will result in a capital gain for the difference between the mortgage and the portion of the basis allocable to the same percentage of the property as the mortgage is a percentage of the total value of the property transferred.

Green has property with a basis of $20,000 and a value of $100,000. He obtains an $80,000 mortgage on the property and transfers the property to a charity subject to the mortgage.

The transaction will probably be considered a sale for $80,000. Hence, he would have a capital gain of $64,000 ($80,000 minus $16,000; 80% of the $20,000 basis). He would also have a charitable contribution deduction (subject to the limitations previously described) of $20,000.

Bibliography

Advanced Real Estate Taxation and Marketing Tools for Investment Real Estate. 1975 REALTORS® National Marketing Institute Educational Course.

Bierman, Harold Jr. and Smidt, Seymour. *The Capital Budgeting Decision: Economic Analysis and Financing of Investment Projects.* New York: The Macmillan Company, 1966.

Bittker, Boris I. and Eustice, James S. *Federal Income Taxation of Corporations and Shareholders.* Boston: Warren, Gorham & Lamont, Inc., 1971.

Bleck, Erich K. "Real Estate Investments and Rates of Return." *The Appraisal Journal.* October, 1973.

Case Studies in Commercial and Investment Real Estate Brokerage. 1975 REALTORS® National Marketing Institute Educational Course.

Casey, William J. *Real Estate Investment Planning.* New York: Institute for Business Planning, Inc., monthly updated loose-leaf service.

Cooper, James R. *Real Estate Investment Analysis.* Lexington, Mass.: Lexington Books, 1974.

Cooper, James R. and Pyhrr, Stephen A. "Forecasting the Rates of Return on an Apartment Investment: A Case Study." *The Appraisal Journal.* July, 1973.

Dasso, Jerome J., Kinnard, William N. Jr. and Messner, Stephen D. "Lender Participation Financing: Applications of Sensitivity and Investment Analysis." *The Real Estate Appraiser.* July–August, 1971.

_____ "Lender Participation Financing: Case Applications in Appraising Participation Financed Properties." *The Real Estate Appraiser.* May–June, 1971.

_____ "Lender Participation Financing: Its Nature and Significance to Appraisers." *The Real Estate Appraiser.* March–April, 1971.

_____ *Valuation and Analysis of Interests in Participation Financed Properties.* Chicago: Society of Real Estate Appraisers, 1972.

Dilmore, Gene. *The New Approach to Real Estate Appraising.* Englewood Cliffs, N. J.: Prentice-Hall, Inc., 1971.

Effective Communications for Commercial-Investment Real Estate Brokerage. 1975 REALTORS® National Marketing Institute Educational Course.

329

Ellwood, L. W. *Ellwood Tables*. Chicago: American Institute of Real Estate Appraisers, 1970.

Erler, Raymond L. "Rate of Return and Financial Leverage: A Paradigm for Sensitivity Analysis." *The Appraisal Journal*. July, 1972.

Federal Tax Course. Chicago: Commerce Clearing House, Inc., issued annually.

Fundamentals of Creating a Real Estate Investment. 1975 REALTORS® National Marketing Institute Educational Course.

Fundamentals of Real Estate Investment and Taxation. 1975 REALTORS® National Marketing Institute.

Hershman, Mendes. "The New Look in Real Estate Financing Techniques." *The Appraisal Journal*, April, 1972.

Introduction to Commercial & Investment Real Estate. 1975 REALTORS® National Marketing Institute.

Jackson, R. Peter. "All Leverage Isn't Positive." *real estate today*®. February, 1975.

Journal of Real Estate Taxation, The. Boston: Warren, Gorham & Lamont, Inc., quarterly journal.

Kaufman, Arnold. "The Sell/Hold Decision Process in Real Estate Liquidation." *The Real Estate Appraiser*. November–December, 1972.

Kinnard, William N. Jr. *Income Property Valuation*. Lexington, Mass.: Heath Lexington Books, 1971.

Klock, Joseph P. *To Sell or Not to Sell*. Chicago: REALTORS® National Marketing Institute, 1975.

_____ *To Buy or Not to Buy*. Chicago: REALTORS® National Marketing Institute, 1975.

Kornfield, Leo and Malaga, Stanley. *Estate Planner's Complete Guide and Workbook*. Greenvale, N. Y.: Panel Publishers, 1975.

Latane, H. "Criteria for Choice among Risky Ventures." *Journal of Political Economy*. April, 1959.

Lyon, Victor L. "DCF or IRR—A Better Yardstick." *real estate today*. November, 1972.

Martin, Wendell H. "Tax Shelter and the Real Estate Analyst." *The Appraisal Journal*. January, 1975.

Messner, Stephen D. and Findlay, M. Chapman III. "Real Estate Investment Analysis: IRR Versus FMRR." *The Real Estate Appraiser*. July–August, 1975.

Pyle, Jack C. "The Effects of Leverage." *real estate today*. April, 1973.

Rams, Edwin M. "Investment Mechanics vs. Investment Analysis." *The Appraisal Journal*. January, 1974.

real estate today®. Chicago: REALTORS® National Marketing Institute, magazine published ten times per year.

Ring, Alfred A. *The Valuation of Real Estate*. Englewood Cliffs, N. J.: Prentice-Hall, Inc., 1970.

Roulac, Stephen E. "Truth in Real Estate Reporting." *Real Estate Review*. Spring, 1974.

_____ "Life Cycle of a Real Estate Investment." *Real Estate Review*. Fall, 1974.

Schreiber, Irving (ed). *How to Plan for Tax Savings in Real Estate Transactions*. Greenvale, N. Y.: Panel Publishers, periodically supplemented loose-leaf service.

_____ *How to Take Money Out of a Closely-Held Corporation*. Greenvale, N. Y.: Panel Publishers, periodically supplemented loose-leaf service.

Schreiber, Irving and Sullivan, Joseph (eds). *How to Use Tax Shelters Today*. Greenvale, N. Y.: Panel Publishers, periodically supplemented loose-leaf service.

Seldin, Maury and Swesnik, Richard H. *Real Estate Investment Strategy*. New York: John Wiley and Sons, Inc., 1970.

Smith, Keith V. and Eiteman, David K. *Essentials of Investing*. Homewood, Ill.: Richard D. Irwin, Inc., 1974.

Thorne, Oakleigh J. "Real Estate Financial Analysis—The State of the Art." *The Appraisal Journal*. January, 1974.

Troxel, Jay C. "Rates: Capitalization and Interest." *The Appraisal Journal*. January, 1975.

Wendt, Paul F. and Cerf, Alan R. *Real Estate Investment Analysis and Taxation*. New York: McGraw-Hill, Inc., 1969.

Index

339

343

345

351

Marketing
Investment
Real Estate

2nd Supplement

Tax Update
through Revenue Act of 1978

NATIONAL ASSOCIATION OF REALTORS®
developed in cooperation with its affiliate, the
REALTORS NATIONAL MARKETING INSTITUTE®
of the NATIONAL ASSOCIATION OF REALTORS®
Chicago, Illinois

International Standard Book Number: 0-913652-07-5
Library of Congress Catalog Card Number: 75-25213
REALTORS NATIONAL MARKETING INSTITUTE®
Catalog Number: BK 119

Printed in the United States of America
First printing, 1976, 10,240
Second printing, 1978, 1,102

Second supplement
First printing, 1979, 15,000

Introduction

The Tax Reform Act of 1976 made sweeping changes in the federal income, gift and estate tax provisions. The Tax Reduction and Simplification Act of 1977 made significant rate changes and changed the structure of the income tax rate tables. The Revenue Act of 1978 (and other miscellaneous legislation passed at the same time) enacted many additional sweeping changes, including modifications to the Tax Reform Act of 1976. It also further reduced income tax rates.

Real estate investment escaped some of the restrictions put on so-called tax shelters, namely the "at-risk" limitations. On the other hand, real estate investments will probably be adversely affected by the requirements for capitalizing (and amortizing) construction period interest and taxes. Major revisions affecting capital gains taxation will also affect real estate investment planning.

The following summary sets forth, for each item identified (by page number and "catch line"), the gist of the new tax law change that directly affects the material identified. The nature of this publication necessarily limits the discussion to a short summary whose primary purpose is to alert the reader of the book to the changes made that affect the book and its examples.

Page 82—Nature of taxable income

Alimony is deductible among the adjustments in arriving at adjusted gross income (it used to be deducted as an itemized deduction). This change became effective for taxable years beginning after 1976. The standard deduction has been replaced by a zero bracket amount adjustment (see the reference to page 86—standard deduction). The capital gains calculations have been changed (see the reference to page 93—long-term capital gain treatment for individuals). For changes in the rules for exemptions, see the reference to page 87.

Page 84—Cash method

Prepaid interest paid by cash basis taxpayers is no longer deductible for taxable years beginning after 1975. This is more fully discussed in the reference to page 137.

Page 86—Standard deduction

Permanent rates were put into the law for 1976. The standard deduction became 16% of adjusted gross income, with a maximum of $2,800 on joint returns ($1,400 for each spouse if they file separate returns) and

TABLE A (For taxable years 1977 and 1978)

Schedule I — Single Taxpayers Not Qualifying as Heads of Households

If taxable income is: Not over $2,200 . . . . . The tax is: —0—

Over—	But not over—	The tax is:	of the amount over—
$2,200	$2,700	14%	$2,200
$2,700	$3,200	$70+15%	$2,700
$3,200	$3,700	$145+16%	$3,200
$3,700	$4,200	$225+17%	$3,700
$4,200	$6,200	$310+19%	$4,200
$6,200	$8,200	$690+21%	$6,200
$8,200	$10,200	$1,110+24%	$8,200
$10,200	$12,200	$1,590+25%	$10,200
$12,200	$14,200	$2,090+27%	$12,200
$14,200	$16,200	$2,630+29%	$14,200
$16,200	$18,200	$3,210+31%	$16,200
$18,200	$20,200	$3,830+34%	$18,200
$20,200	$22,200	$4,510+36%	$20,200
$22,200	$24,200	$5,230+38%	$22,200
$24,200	$28,200	$5,990+40%	$24,200
$28,200	$34,200	$7,590+45%	$28,200
$34,200	$40,200	$10,290+50%	$34,200
$40,200	$46,200	$13,290+55%	$40,200
$46,200	$52,200	$16,590+60%	$46,200
$52,200	$62,200	$20,190+62%	$52,200
$62,200	$72,200	$26,390+64%	$62,200
$72,200	$82,200	$32,790+66%	$72,200
$82,200	$92,200	$39,390+68%	$82,200
$92,200	$102,200	$46,190+69%	$92,200
$102,200	. . . . . .	$53,090+70%	$102,200

Schedule II — Married Taxpayers Filing Joint Returns and Certain Widows and Widowers

If taxable income is: Not over $3,200 . . . . . The tax is: —0—

Over—	But not over—	The tax is:	of the amount over—
$3,200	$4,200	14%	$3,200
$4,200	$5,200	$140+15%	$4,200
$5,200	$6,200	$290+16%	$5,200
$6,200	$7,200	$450+17%	$6,200
$7,200	$11,200	$620+19%	$7,200
$11,200	$15,200	$1,380+22%	$11,200
$15,200	$19,200	$2,260+25%	$15,200
$19,200	$23,200	$3,260+28%	$19,200
$23,200	$27,200	$4,380+32%	$23,200
$27,200	$31,200	$5,660+36%	$27,200
$31,200	$35,200	$7,100+39%	$31,200
$35,200	$39,200	$8,660+42%	$35,200
$39,200	$43,200	$10,340+45%	$39,200
$43,200	$47,200	$12,140+48%	$43,200
$47,200	$55,200	$14,060+50%	$47,200
$55,200	$67,200	$18,060+53%	$55,200
$67,200	$79,200	$24,420+55%	$67,200
$79,200	$91,200	$31,020+58%	$79,200
$91,200	$103,200	$37,980+60%	$91,200
$103,200	$123,200	$45,180+62%	$103,200
$123,200	$143,200	$57,580+64%	$123,200
$143,200	$163,200	$70,380+66%	$143,200
$163,200	$183,200	$83,580+68%	$163,200
$183,200	$203,200	$97,180+69%	$183,200
$203,200	. . . . . .	$110,980+70%	$203,200

Schedule III — Married Taxpayers Filing Separate Returns

If taxable income is: Not over $1,600 . . . . . The tax is: —0—

Over—	But not over—	The tax is:	of the amount over—
$1,600	$2,100	14%	$1,600
$2,100	$2,600	$70+15%	$2,100
$2,600	$3,100	$145+16%	$2,600
$3,100	$3,600	$225+17%	$3,100
$3,600	$5,600	$310+19%	$3,600
$5,600	$7,600	$690+22%	$5,600
$7,600	$9,600	$1,130+25%	$7,600
$9,600	$11,600	$1,630+28%	$9,600
$11,600	$13,600	$2,190+32%	$11,600
$13,600	$15,600	$2,830+36%	$13,600
$15,600	$17,600	$3,550+39%	$15,600
$17,600	$19,600	$4,330+42%	$17,600
$19,600	$21,600	$5,170+45%	$19,600
$21,600	$23,600	$6,070+48%	$21,600
$23,600	$27,600	$7,030+50%	$23,600
$27,600	$33,600	$9,030+53%	$27,600
$33,600	$39,600	$12,210+55%	$33,600
$39,600	$45,600	$15,510+58%	$39,600
$45,600	$51,600	$18,990+60%	$45,600
$51,600	$61,600	$22,590+62%	$51,600
$61,600	$71,600	$28,790+64%	$61,600
$71,600	$81,600	$35,190+66%	$71,600
$81,600	$91,600	$41,790+68%	$81,600
$91,600	$101,600	$48,590+69%	$91,600
$101,600	———	$55,490+70%	$101,600

Schedule IV — Unmarried Taxpayers Qualifying as Heads of Households

If taxable income is: Not over $2,200 . . . . . The tax is: —0—

Over—	But not over—	The tax is:	of the amount over—
$2,200	$3,200	14%	$2,200
$3,200	$4,200	$140+16%	$3,200
$4,200	$6,200	$300+18%	$4,200
$6,200	$8,200	$660+19%	$6,200
$8,200	$10,200	$1,040+22%	$8,200
$10,200	$12,200	$1,480+23%	$10,200
$12,200	$14,200	$1,940+25%	$12,200
$14,200	$16,200	$2,440+27%	$14,200
$16,200	$18,200	$2,980+28%	$16,200
$18,200	$20,200	$3,540+31%	$18,200
$20,200	$22,200	$4,160+32%	$20,200
$22,200	$24,200	$4,800+35%	$22,200
$24,200	$26,200	$5,500+36%	$24,200
$26,200	$28,200	$6,220+38%	$26,200
$28,200	$30,200	$6,980+41%	$28,200
$30,200	$34,200	$7,800+42%	$30,200
$34,200	$38,200	$9,480+45%	$34,200
$38,200	$40,200	$11,280+48%	$38,200
$40,200	$42,200	$12,240+51%	$40,200
$42,200	$46,200	$13,260+52%	$42,200
$46,200	$52,200	$15,340+55%	$46,200
$52,200	$54,200	$18,640+56%	$52,200
$54,200	$66,200	$19,760+58%	$54,200
$66,200	$72,200	$26,720+59%	$66,200
$72,200	$78,200	$30,260+61%	$72,200
$78,200	$82,200	$33,920+62%	$78,200
$82,200	$90,200	$36,400+63%	$82,200
$90,200	$102,200	$41,440+64%	$90,200
$102,200	$122,200	$49,120+66%	$102,200
$122,200	$142,200	$62,320+67%	$122,200
$142,200	$162,200	$75,720+68%	$142,200
$162,200	$182,200	$89,320+69%	$162,200
$182,200	. . . . . .	$103,120+70%	$182,200

TABLE B (For taxable years 1979 and thereafter)

Schedule I
Single Taxpayers Not Qualifying as Heads of Households

If taxable income is:
Not over $2,300 . . . . . . —0—

Over—	But not over—	The tax is:	of the amount over—
$2,300	$3,400	14%	$2,300
$3,400	$4,400	$154+16%	$3,400
$4,400	$6,500	$314+18%	$4,400
$6,500	$8,500	$692+19%	$6,500
$8,500	$10,800	$1,072+21%	$8,500
$10,800	$12,900	$1,555+24%	$10,800
$12,900	$15,000	$2,059+26%	$12,900
$15,000	$18,200	$2,605+30%	$15,000
$18,200	$23,500	$3,565+34%	$18,200
$23,500	$28,800	$5,367+39%	$23,500
$28,800	$34,100	$7,434+44%	$28,800
$34,100	$41,500	$9,766+49%	$34,100
$41,500	$55,300	$13,392+55%	$41,500
$55,300	$81,800	$20,982+63%	$55,300
$81,800	$108,300	$37,677+68%	$81,800
$108,300	. . . . . .	$55,697+70%	$108,300

Schedule II
Married Taxpayers Filing Joint Returns and Certain Widows and Widowers

If taxable income is:
Not over $3,400 . . . . . . —0—

Over—	But not over—	The tax is:	of the amount over—
$3,400	$5,500	14%	$3,400
$5,500	$7,600	$294+16%	$5,500
$7,600	$11,900	$630+18%	$7,600
$11,900	$16,000	$1,404+21%	$11,900
$16,000	$20,200	$2,265+24%	$16,000
$20,200	$24,600	$3,273+28%	$20,200
$24,600	$29,900	$4,505+32%	$24,600
$29,900	$35,200	$6,201+37%	$29,900
$35,200	$45,800	$8,162+43%	$35,200
$45,800	$60,000	$12,720+49%	$45,800
$60,000	$85,600	$19,678+54%	$60,000
$85,600	$109,400	$33,502+59%	$85,600
$109,400	$162,400	$47,544+64%	$109,400
$162,400	$215,400	$81,464+68%	$162,400
$215,400	. . . . . .	$117,504+70%	$215,400

Schedule III
Married Taxpayers Filing Separate Returns

If taxable income is:
Not over $1,700 . . . . . . —0—

Over—	But not over—	The tax is:	of the amount over—
$1,700	$2,750	14%	$1,700
$2,750	$3,800	$147+16%	$2,750
$3,800	$5,950	$315+18%	$3,800
$5,950	$8,000	$702+21%	$5,950
$8,000	$10,100	$1,132.50+24%	$8,000
$10,100	$12,300	$1,636.50+28%	$10,100
$12,300	$14,950	$2,252.50+32%	$12,300
$14,950	$17,600	$3,100.50+37%	$14,950
$17,600	$22,900	$4,081+43%	$17,600
$22,900	$30,000	$6,360+49%	$22,900
$30,000	$42,800	$9,839+54%	$30,000
$42,800	$54,700	$16,751+59%	$42,800
$54,700	$81,200	$23,772+64%	$54,700
$81,200	$107,700	$40,732+68%	$81,200
$107,700	. . . . . .	$58,752+70%	$107,700

Schedule IV
Unmarried Taxpayers Qualifying as Heads of Households

If taxable income is:
Not over $2,300 . . . . . . —0—

Over—	But not over—	The tax is:	of the amount over—
$2,300	$4,400	14%	$2,300
$4,400	$6,500	$294+16%	$4,400
$6,500	$8,700	$630+18%	$6,500
$8,700	$11,800	$1,026+22%	$8,700
$11,800	$15,000	$1,708+24%	$11,800
$15,000	$18,200	$2,476+26%	$15,000
$18,200	$23,500	$3,308+31%	$18,200
$23,500	$28,800	$4,951+36%	$23,500
$28,800	$34,100	$6,859+42%	$28,800
$34,100	$44,700	$9,085+46%	$34,100
$44,700	$60,600	$13,961+54%	$44,700
$60,600	$81,800	$22,547+59%	$60,600
$81,800	$108,300	$35,055+63%	$81,800
$108,300	$161,300	$51,750+68%	$108,300
$161,300	. . . . . .	$87,790+70%	$161,300

$2,400 for single persons. The low income allowance became $2,100 on joint returns ($1,050 for each spouse if they file separate returns) and $1,700 for single persons.

Beginning in 1977, the terms "standard deduction" and "low income allowance" were eliminated from the tax law. A new concept, zero bracket amount, was instituted. A flat amount (instead of a percentage standard deduction) became subject to a "zero" tax. This concept was built into the tax tables for those who would have claimed the standard deduction. Instead of claiming the standard deduction, reference to the tax table with the adjusted gross income yields a tax that taxed the first bracket (equal to the zero bracket amount) at zero. For 1977 and 1978, the zero bracket amounts were: $3,200 on joint returns ($1,600 for each spouse filing separately) and $2,200 for single taxpayers and heads of households. Beginning in 1979, the flat amounts are: $3,400 on a joint return ($1,700 for each spouse filing separately) and $2,300 for single taxpayers and heads of households. (See the reference to page 87—computing the tax.)

Page 87—Exemptions for individuals

In 1976, the $30-per-exemption credit was changed to a $35-per-exemption credit or a credit of 2% of the first $9,000 of taxable income, whichever was larger. This new credit applied for the years 1976, 1977 and 1978. The $750 deduction per exemption and dependency deduction remained unchanged during those three years. Beginning in 1979, the $750 deduction has been increased to $1,000 and the credit has been eliminated.

Page 87—Computing the tax

The tax rates were affected by the 1976, 1977, and 1978 tax laws. As indicated above, in the reference to page 86, the standard deduction was increased each time. In addition, in the 1978 Act the rates were reduced by widening the tax brackets.

Beginning in 1977 (as indicated above in the reference to page 86), the zero bracket amount was introduced into the tax rate structure. The first bracket in the tax tables is subject to a "zero" tax. When the standard deduction is claimed, the zero bracket concept is built into the tables. If itemized deductions are taken, the tax tables nevertheless include the "zero" bracket. To compensate for this, in computing his taxable income, a taxpayer must first reduce his itemized deductions by an amount equal to the zero bracket amount, thus increasing his taxable income by that amount. The tax table then compensates for this increase by subjecting that increase to a "zero" tax in the first bracket of the tax table.

Schedules I-IV referred to on page 88 have been revised to reflect the introduction of the zero bracket amount by the 1977 and 1978 legislation. Table A (in this supplement) should be used for 1977 and 1978 tax returns; Table B, for 1979 and thereafter.

Page 88—Computing the tax (example)

The following example illustrates the application of the new rules for computing the tax:

Assume that for 1979, Jones, an unmarried individual, has salary income of $25,000 and security income of $7,000. He has personal, itemized deductions of $4,000. To arrive at his taxable income, he first reduces his $4,000 of itemized deductions by the $2,300 zero bracket amount for 1979. He reduces his $32,000 (combined salary and security) income by the remaining $1,700 of itemized deductions, to $30,300. He further reduces this figure by his $1,000 exemption. Then, to find his tax, he goes to Schedule I of Table B (of this supplement).

In the bracket "over $28,800 but not over $34,100," he will find the tax to be $7,434 plus 44% of the excess over $28,800. The tax on that excess (44% of $500) is $220. Thus, his total tax is $7,654. (In Schedule I, the first $2,300 of Jones' income was subject to a "zero" tax, thus compensating for the reduction of his itemized deductions by $2,300.)

Pages 90 and 91—Holding periods for long-term capital gains and losses

The more-than-six-months holding period requirement for Section 1231 assets and for capital assets has been changed to a more-than-nine-month holding period for 1977 and a more-than-one-year holding period for 1978 and thereafter. While the techniques for determining net long-term and short-term capital gains and losses remain unchanged, bear in mind that all the examples on page 91–93 use the more-than-six-months holding period as the criterion for long-term gains and losses and the nine-month and one-year criteria should be substituted for 1977 and 1978 and thereafter.

Page 93—Long-term capital gain treatment for individuals

One of the most dramatic changes enacted by the 1978 legislation was the reduction of the tax on long-term capital gains for individuals.

The *alternative tax* is completely eliminated from the tax law beginning in 1979. (There is, however, a new alternative minimum tax that may apply as a penalty in some cases for unusually large reductions in the capital gains tax. See the discussion in reference to page 101.) But beginning with transactions taking place after October 31, 1978, under the *regular method* of calculating taxes on long-term capital gains, only 40% (rather than 50%) of the net gain is added to ordinary income.

Because the new rule that includes only 40% of the gain in income affects transactions taking place after October 31, 1978, there is a special computation for 1978 only. You determine the net long-term capital gain for the entire year (including November and December). You also calculate the net long-term capital gain for November and December only. You include in ordinary income 40% of the *lower* of these two gains. The difference between these two gains is included at 50%.

Page 97—Capital losses for individuals

The $1,000 limitation of ordinary income that can be offset by capital losses has been increased. For 1977, the limit becomes $2,000. For 1978, the limit is increased to $3,000. The rule that requires $2 of long-term gain to offset $1 of ordinary income continues to be in effect.

The 1978 change under which only 40% of net long-term capital gains are included in ordinary income make it more advantageous to use long-term losses to offset ordinary income (within the limits allowed) than to use such losses to offset long-term capital gains.

For example, assume a taxpayer has a $2,000 long-term capital loss in 1979 and is in a position to acquire a $2,000 long-term gain in 1979 or to postpone it until 1980. If he takes the gain in 1979, it will be offset by the $2,000 loss he has already realized that year. However, were there no loss to offset that gain, only 40% of the gain would be included in ordinary income. So, the $2,000 long-term loss, in effect, offset $800 of ordinary income (40% of $2,000). Had the $2,000 long-term gain been postponed until 1980, the $2,000 loss in 1979 would have offset $1,000 of ordinary income.

Page 100—Maximum tax on earned income (impact of tax preferences)

Both the 1976 and 1978 Acts affected the maximum tax on earned income. The 50% maximum tax remains intact. However, for taxable years beginning after 1976, the amount of earned income eligible for maximum tax treatment had to be reduced by the *full* amount of tax preferences. (This rule was further modified for taxable years beginning after 1978; see below.) Under the law in effect before 1977, the earned income eligible for maximum tax had to be reduced by the amount of tax preferences in excess of $30,000. Consequently, under the 1976 law, if, for example, a taxpayer had $100,000 of earned income and long-term capital gains of $50,000, only $75,000 of the earned income would be eligible for treatment under the maximum tax rule (one-half of the $50,000 capital gain is a tax preference and reduces the income eligible for maximum tax). In addition, some new items were added to the tax preference list which could further reduce the advantages of the maximum tax. (See the discussion, in reference to page 101, on the changes affecting tax preferences.) On the other side of the coin, the 1976 law provided that some pension, annuity and deferred income payments be among the items eligible for the maximum tax.

The 1978 legislation made a major pro-taxpayer change in the maximum tax computation. Beginning with net long-term capital gains arising after October 31, 1978, *no part* of long-term capital gains are treated as tax preferences. Therefore, the income eligible for maximum tax treatment is (after October 31, 1978) no longer reduced by any part of long-term capital gains.

Page 101—Minimum tax on tax preferences

Both the 1976 and the 1978 Acts affected the rules on tax preferences. For taxable years beginning after 1975, the rules for taxing tax preferences were made tougher. But there was some relief for taxable years beginning after 1978. Beginning after 1975, the 10% rate was increased to 15%. Also, the old exemption of $30,000 plus the regular tax liability was drastically reduced to the larger of $10,000 or half the regular tax liability. Further, three items were added to the list of tax preferences: (1) The excess of accelerated depreciation over straightline depreciation on *all* leased personal (i.e., non-real estate) property. (The old law applied only to property leased under a net lease.) (2) The excess of intangible drilling costs over the deductible amount under either cost depletion or a 10-year amortization. (3) That portion of itemized deductions that exceeds 60% of adjusted gross income. However, for this purpose, medical expenses and casualty losses are not included in itemized deductions.

For taxable years beginning after 1978, two items were removed from the list of tax preferences: (1) the portion of the long-term capital gain not included in ordinary income; (2) the total of the itemized deductions in excess of 60% of adjusted gross income.

New Alternative Minimum Tax

With the elimination of the untaxed portion of the capital gains and the excess itemized deductions from the list of tax preferences, Congress (in the 1978 legislation) added a new minimum alternative tax aimed at those taxpayers who might benefit too greatly from these liberalizing changes. As indicated, the new minimum tax is an *alternative* tax. It applies only when it is greater than the total of the regular income tax plus the tax on tax preferences. In that case the alternative minimum tax is paid *instead of* the other two taxes. The alternative minimum tax is imposed for taxable years beginning after 1978.

The alternative minimum tax is imposed on alternative minimum taxable income (AMTI). AMTI is the total of the taxable income *plus* the 60% of the net long-term capital gain not included in ordinary income *plus* the amount by which itemized deductions exceed 60% of adjusted gross income. (In determining the amount of the total itemized deductions for this purpose, state and local taxes, medical expenses, and casualty losses are omitted.) The following tax rates apply to AMTI:

> First $20,000 . . . . 0%
> Next $40,000 . . . . 10%
> Next $40,000 . . . . 20%
> AMTI in excess of $100,000 . . . . 25%

Page 103—Partnership tax returns

Although partnerships pay no income taxes, they are required to file information returns. There was no penalty in the tax law for failure to file such information returns. For partnership taxable years beginning after 1978, a penalty is imposed for failure to file a timely partnership return (unless reasonable cause for such failure is shown). The penalty is $50 per month or fraction thereof (not to exceed five months) that the return is late. The penalty is then multiplied by the number of partners in the partnership during the taxable year for which the return was due.

The 1978 Act also has a provision extending the statute of limitations for assessing tax deficiencies on partners (and extending the period during which refunds can be claimed). This extension of the statute of limitations applies only to "federally registered partnerships"—i.e., those partnerships in which interests were offered for sale in an offering requiring S.E.C. registration or which are or have been subject to annual reporting requirements of the S.E.C. Prior to this statute of limitations extension, assessment and refund time limitations were generally three years from the time a partner's tax return was due (or when he filed it, if filed after the due date). The due date of the partnership return was irrelevant for this purpose. Under the new rule, the statute of limitations as to each partner is four years after the partnership return is filed. To repeat: this rule applies only to federally registered partnerships. This new rule applies as to partnership items (on the partner's return) arising in partnership taxable years beginning after 1978.

Page 104—Bonus depreciation for partnerships

A partnership is limited to bonus depreciation of 20% on $10,000 of eligible property per year, a maximum deduction of $2,000 per year for the entire partnership. Under the old rule, each partner could deduct his own bonus depreciation of 20% on his share of the partnership eligible property or a maximum of $4,000 per partner who filed a joint return. This rule became effective for partnership taxable years beginning after 1975.

Page 104—Non-recourse liabilities of partnerships

Beginning after 1976, *except for real estate partnerships,* all partners' deductible losses (whether they are general or limited partners) were limited to the amount they had "at risk" in the partnership. In other words, non-recourse liabilities of the partnerships did not add to the bases of any of the partners. "At risk" liability is the amount contributed to the partnership by a partner plus amounts borrowed for which he is personally liable. *Note again: this rule did not apply to partnerships whose principal activity is investing in real estate activities;* for them, the old non-recourse rules still applied.

Four specific types of investments were also made subject to the at-risk rules, whether they were made by partnerships or any other type of investors (individuals, tenants in common, trusts, etc.). These were farming; exploring for gas or oil as a trade or business or for production of income; holding, producing or distributing motion pictures or video tape; and leasing of personal property.

For taxable years beginning after 1978, the at-risk rules are made applicable to *all types* of investments (not merely the four listed above) *except for real estate investments,* whether made by individuals, partnerships, or closely-held corporations. Hence, the previous rule dealing specifically with partnerships was repealed.

Page 104—Corporate tax rates

The tax rates listed as applying after 1974 and before 1976 were extended through the end of 1978. After 1978, corporate tax rates are further reduced, as follows:

First $25,000 of taxable income 17%
Next $25,000 . . . . 20%
Next $25,000 . . . . 30%
Next $25,000 . . . . 40%
Taxable income in excess of $100,000 . . . . . 46%

Keep these rates in mind when reading the examples that appear in later pages of the book.

Page 107—Taxation of corporate capital gains

After 1978, the corporate alternative tax rate is 28%.

Page 110—Individual ownership

The discussion dealing with adding mortgages to basis must be read in conjunction with the discussion above concerning non-recourse liability. The discussion on page 110 is valid under the new laws in terms of real estate. In other cases, check the non-recourse liability rules.

Page 111—Joint ownership

The rules discussed in the last paragraph under "Joint ownership" have been modified by the new law. See the discussion relating to page 121.

Page 112—Partnerships

See the discussion relating to page 104 regarding the new rules on non-recourse liabilities of partners.

Page 116—Subchapter S corporations

The Tax Reform Act of 1976 provided that for taxable years beginning after 1976, a Subchapter S corporation that had retained that status for five consecutive years was permitted to have 15 shareholders. Even though a Subchapter S corporation had not yet had that status for five consecutive years, it was permitted to have 15 shareholders if the extra shareholders acquired that status by inheriting the Subchapter S stock. Furthermore, voting trusts and trusts in which the creator of the trust was treated as the owner of the trust property because he had retained too much control over it, were allowed to be shareholders. Also, if a trust received Subchapter S stock under a will it was permitted to remain a shareholder for 60 days.

The Revenue Act of 1978 made further modifications to the Subchapter S requirements (effective after 1978, except as otherwise noted):

(1) The Subchapter S corporation is permitted to have 15 shareholders no matter how long it has been in existence.

(2) Husband and wife are treated as one shareholder regardless of the form of ownership each has for the stock.

(3) Subchapter S elections can be made during the entire year preceding the year in which the election is to become effective. The election may also be made within the first 75 days of the year in which it is to become effective.

(4) The rule under the 1976 law (see above) allowing trusts in which the creator is treated as owner to be a Subchapter S shareholder applies only if the creator of the trust is a U.S. citizen or resident. The creator of the trust is the one who is considered to be the shareholder in this case.

Also, if the creator of the trust dies, the trust may continue to be a Subchapter S shareholders for 60 days. The 60-day period is extended to two years if the entire trust property is included in the trust creator's estate. The rules in this paragraph are effective for taxable years beginning after 1976.

Page 119—Basis for purchased property

The discussion of the new rules affecting non-recourse liability (relating to page 104) indicated that in specific instances deductible losses cannot exceed "at-risk" investment. While, for the purposes of limiting the amount of deductible loss, basis cannot include non-recourse indebtedness, apparently that rule applies only for limiting the deductible loss. Basis for other purposes (i.e., for figuring depreciation or gain or loss on sale) still would include the non-recourse loans.

Page 120—Basis of inherited property

The Tax Reform Act of 1976 made a drastic change in the rules for calculating basis of inherited property. This rule was to go into effect for property passing from a decedent who died after 1976. The Revenue Act of 1978 postponed the effective date of these new rules to property passing from a decedent who dies after 1979. There is still considerable controversy over this new rule and there is speculation that the rule will be modified, repealed, or have its effective date postponed further. That, of course, remains to be seen.

The main import of this new rule (that has been postponed until after 1979) is to carry over the decedent's basis (with certain modifications) to the heirs instead of "stepping up" the basis to the property's value at the time of the decedent's death. Those heirs who inherited property after 1976 and before the 1978 Act went into effect may have incurred capital gains taxes on the sale of inherited property because they used carryover bases. To the extent that such gains reflected the difference between the carryover basis and the date-of-death value, a tax refund may be available.

Under the carryover basis rule (as it stands after the enactment of the Revenue Act of 1978), for property inherited from a decedent dying after 1979, the heir takes as his basis a carryover basis—that is, the decedent's basis (rather than the date-of-death value). In other words, any appreciation in the property at date of death will be subject to tax when it is disposed by the heir or legatee. There are several adjustments to this rule, however:

(1) If the property was held by the decedent on December 31, 1976, for purposes of determining gain on subsequent disposition by the heir or

legatee, the carryover basis of the property becomes its market value on December 31, 1976 (if that is greater than the adjusted basis of the decedent on date of death). But in no event can the carryover basis be greater than date-of-death value. Note that the 1976 date remains in the law for this purpose even after the effective date of the carryover basis was deferred to property of decedents dying after 1979.)

Marketable securities' value on December 31, 1976 is determined from quoted listings. Other property's December 31, 1976 value is determined by a formula:

(a) The difference between decedent's adjusted basis on date of death and market value at date of death is determined.

(b) A fraction is used, the numerator of which is the total days the decedent held the property through December 31, 1976, and the denominator of which is the total number of days the decedent held the property until death.

(c) The amount determined in (a) is multiplied by the fraction determined in (b).

(d) The carryover basis is the amount determined in (c) plus the decedent's adjusted basis plus any depreciation the decedent deducted from the time he acquired the property through December 31, 1976.

(2) Federal and State estate tax attributable to the appreciation in the decedent's property is added to the carryover basis.

(3) If the total carryover basis of all properties in the decedent's estate is less than $60,000, a $60,000 basis is assigned to the aggregate estate and allocated among the items in proportion to their net increases in value over the decedent's basis.

Page 121—Basis of jointly-held property

Under the 1976 law, for joint interests created after 1976, if, when the joint interest is created, it is treated as a gift from one spouse to the other, only one-half of the property's value will be included in the estate of the first spouse to die. Under the 1978 law, joint tenancies of spouses created before 1977 can also be eligible for this 50–50 rule if a gift tax return is filed in any quarter of 1977, 1978, or 1979 reporting the gift of half the property to the other spouse. The taxable gift will be the entire value of the gift, or the appreciation of the value of the gift since the original gift was reported (if, in fact, it was reported as a gift when the joint tenancy was created).

Note that the basis of the portion of the property that was included in the estate of the first spouse to die and which automatically passes to the surviving spouse will be the carryover basis, rather than a stepped-up basis, when the carryover basis rules go into effect.

Page 123—Community property

The carryover basis rules discussed above in relation to the material on page 120 applies both to the portion of the community property included in the decedent's estate and the portion of the community property that belonged to the surviving spouse as his or her share of the community property before the other spouse died. Under the old law there was a step-up in basis of both portions of the community property.

Page 123—Life estates

If the life estate is acquired by inheritance after the new carryover basis rules go into effect, the initial basis used by the life tenant would be determined under the carryover basis rules discussed above in connection with inherited property (page 120). In all other respects the rule as stated in the book remains unchanged.

Page 130—Involuntary conversion of real estate

In the case where the special rule for real property used in a trade or business or held for production of income applies, the two-year period for replacement has been lengthened to three years. In all other involuntary conversion situations, the two-year rule continues in effect. The new rule applies to disposition of converted property after 1974.

Page 132—Construction period interest and real estate taxes

Although the rules that permit capitalization of carrying charges, interest and taxes continue in the tax law, a new section *requires* the capitalization of interest and real estate taxes incurred during the construction period. This rule applies to individuals and Subchapter S corporations. When in full effect, it will require the capitalization of construction period interest and real estate taxes and a write-off (amortization) of the capitalized amount over a 10-year period. There are three different starting dates of the new provision, depending on the nature of the property: For non-residential property, the new provisions apply to construction beginning in taxable years that begin after 1975; for residential property other than low-income housing, it is 1978; for low-income housing, it is 1982. During the first six years in which the new rule is effective as to each type of property, the write-offs are allowed at a faster rate than 10% per year, according to the following table:

If the amount is paid or accrued in a taxable year beginning in—

Non-residential real property	Residential real property	Low-income housing	The percentage of such amount allowable for such amortization year shall be the following percentage of such amount
1976	—	—	*
—	1978	1982	25
1977	1979	1983	20
1978	1980	1984	16-2/3
1979	1981	1985	14-2/7
1980	1982	1986	12-1/3
1981	1983	1987	11-1/9
after 1981	after 1983	after 1987	10

* 50% for 1976; 16-2/3% for each of the succeeding three years.

Page 137—Prepaid interest

The Tax Reform Act of 1976 put an end to the deduction of prepaid interest. All interest paid after 1975 is deductible only to the extent that the payment deducted covers a period of time falling within the year in which the deduction is taken. This rule applies to all taxpayers— individuals, corporations, estates, trusts. There is one small exception: mortgage "points" paid in advance are deductible but only if the mortgage is on the taxpayer's principal residence.

Page 139—Excess investment interest

For taxable years beginning after 1975, the computation of excess investment interest is changed substantially. In Step 1, the old $25,000 figure is changed to $10,000. Step 3 and Step 4 are eliminated altogether. Hence to the extent the investment interest exceeds the total of $10,000 plus net investment income it is disallowed. The conversion of long-term capital gains to ordinary income to preserve the interest deduction no longer applies. Nor is the excess amount first cut in half, as under the old law. However, the full amount of the disallowed interest carries over to future years without the complex calculations previously required.

Page 143—Determining and allocating adjusted basis of property

Although the new law limits the losses or deductions available to investors in certain properties to the amount they have "at-risk" (see the discussion in reference to page 104) the fact that property is acquired with the aid of non-recourse loans does not affect the basis for the property for depreciation purposes; the old rules continue to apply.

Page 159—Five-year depreciation for rehabilitation of low-income rental housing

The January 1, 1976 deadline (in item 1) was first extended to January 1, 1978, and then it was extended to January 1, 1982. The $15,000 limit (in item 2) has been raised to $20,000.

Page 165—First year "bonus" depreciation

As noted in the discussion pertaining to page 104, the new law limits the entire partnership to a total "bonus" depreciation deduction per year of $2,000 (20% of a maximum first-year eligible property of $10,000).

Page 166—Investment credit

The 10% investment credit has been made permanent. Similarly, the increased limit of $100,000 on used property has also been made permanent.

The limit on the amount of the credit allowable in one year when the tax exceeds $25,000 has been increased to $25,000 plus 60% of the excess, for 1979; plus 70% of the excess, for 1980; plus 80% of the excess, for 1981; and plus 90% of the excess, for 1982 and thereafter.

The investment credit, generally applicable to personal property, has been extended to qualified rehabilitation expenditures incurred after October 31, 1978. The credit has also been extended to certain pollution control facilities acquired or constructed after 1978. Furthermore, it was made clear that single purpose livestock or horticultural structures would qualify for the investment credit effective for taxable years ending after August 15, 1971.

Pages 176-180—Depreciation recapture on disposition of real property

The rules that previously applied to depreciation deducted after 1969 now apply to depreciation deducted for the period after 1969 and before 1976. For the period after 1975, the *entire excess depreciation* on *all* real estate is subject to recapture—except for a special rule for subsidized low-income housing. Excess depreciation on subsidized low-income housing is reduced by 1 percent for each month of holding period in excess of 100 months.

The new rules (except for low-income housing) are primarily aimed at residential rental property. The rule for commercial property after 1975 is the same as the one that applied after 1969. But after 1969, the excess depreciation on residential rental property was reduced by 1 percent for each month of holding period in excess of 100. After 1975, *all* excess depreication on residential rental property is recapturable.

Pages 249-255—Construction year costs

The assumption that construction-year interest and real estate taxes may be written off as expenses for income tax purposes (in Projection "B") must be modified in accordance with the new tax rules requiring capitalization of such costs and a write-off over a 10-year period—taking into account, of course, the starting date of this new rule for different types of property and the shorter-than-10-year amortization periods allowed during the "phase-in" years of the new law. See the discussion of this provision in reference to page 132.

Page 302—Major reasons for using limited partnership

As explained in the material dealing with page 104, for taxable years beginning after 1976, partnership non-recourse liabilities *do not* increase the basis of partnership interests of limited or general partners except if the principal partnership activity is investment in real estate. Thus the old rule remains intact for real estate partnerships.

Page 303—Subchapter S corporations

See the discussion relating to page 116 regarding the modification of the 10-shareholder rule.

Page 307—Basis of limited partner's interest

See the discussion on non-recourse loans in relation to the material on pages 104 and 302.

Page 310—Allocation of income and deductions

The 1976 law adopts the position of the Regulations which require that allocations must have "substantial economic effect." This provision applies both to the overall allocation of income or loss among the partners and to allocations of specific items of income or deduction. This rule applies to taxable years beginning after 1975. (Of course, IRS will likely argue that the rules apply for prior years under the provisions of the IRS Regulations.)

Page 311—Retroactive allocations

Retroactive allocations of partnership income or loss are prohibited by the 1976 law. The effective date of this provision is for taxable years beginning after 1975. Under this law, partnership income or loss must be allocated to the partners in terms of their varying interests throughout the partnership year. Thus a partner admitted to the partnership the last few days of the year can have income or loss allocable to him only in proportion to his interest in the partnership for the portion of the year in which he held that interest. Furthermore, if a partner's interest varies during the year (because, for example, he sold part of his interest or the partnership admitted new partners or some partners retired), the allocation of income or loss to him must take into account his varying interests during the year. The 1976 law also provides that these statutory provisions regarding allocation cannot be overridden by the provision of the partnership agreement.

Page 314—Section 337 rules

Normally, a plan of liquidation to qualify under Section 337 must be adopted before any sale or exchange of the property is made by the corporation. However, if there is an involuntary conversion (e.g., fire, condemnation), the corporation may adopt its plan of liquidation within 60 days after the involuntary conversion takes place and still apply the Section 337 rules to the gain on the involuntary conversion. This 60-day rule applies to involuntary conversions occurring after November 10, 1978.

Pages 321-325—Gift and Estate Planning

For gifts made and property passing from a decedent after 1976, the 1976 Act combines the gift and estate taxes into one unified tax. Under the old law, there were separate gift-tax tables. Lifetime gifts, in excess of annual exclusions of $3,000 per donee and a lifetime exemption of $30,000, were taxed at a progressive rate. The estate was subject to a separate tax, after applying a $60,000 exemption. Both the gift tax structure and the estate tax structure allowed for marital deductions. One-half of gifts to spouses were not included in taxable gifts; up to one-half of the adjusted gross estate was eligible for a marital deduction to reduce the estate.

Under the new law, there are no separate gift and estate taxes; there is a unified transfer tax. There is one tax rate table. In effect, the estate becomes the last "gift" of the taxpayer who had made gifts during his lifetime.

Application of new tax credit: Gifts made during lifetime continue to be subject to the annual exclusion of $3,000 (and $6,000 on gifts to which a spouse consents). In addition, gifts to spouses are subject to a gift tax marital deduction. (See the discussion below.) The gifts in excess of the exclusions and marital deduction are then subject to tax. The tax is calculated using a tax table that has increasing rates as the cumulative total of gifts increases (as is the case under the old law). When the tax on taxable gifts is determined the tax credit is then applied to reduce or eliminate the tax. Once the entire credit is used up, further gifts are subject to tax. (Of course, if the entire credit is used up during life, there will be no credit remaining to offset against the tax on the estate remaining at death.)

The credit is $30,000 in 1977. It increases annually until it reaches $47,000 in 1981. As a transitional rule for gift tax purposes, only $6,000 of the unified credit can be applied to gifts made after 1976 and before July 1, 1977.

The $47,000 credit is the equivalent of an exemption of $175,000 under the old law. Obviously, the new credit will relieve many estates from the estate tax burden that would have been taxable under the old law. This new tax structure will require much rethinking in estate planning of many smaller and moderate estates.

Calculating tax on death: On death, the taxable estate is calculated much the same way as it is under the old law. However, the marital deduction may be more substantial than under the old law (see below) and all gifts made within three years of death are to be included in the estate *together with the gift tax paid on those gifts.* Once the taxable estate is determined, it is added to the total taxable gifts made during lifetime to determine the tax on the entire amount. The unified credit and any gift taxes paid during lifetime reduce the tax due.

New marital deduction: (1) The new law allows a marital deduction for the full amount of gifts to spouses up to $100,000, no marital deduction on the next $100,000 of gifts to spouses and 50% of the amount given to spouses in excess of $200,000.

(2) The maximum marital deduction for estate tax purposes is the greater of one-half the adjusted gross estate or $250,000. This maximum is reduced by any gift tax marital deduction allowed under the new law which exceeded 50% of the lifetime gifts to spouses under the new law. Thus, if the decedent took a total of $100,000 gift tax marital deduction on $100,000 of gifts, the maximum estate tax marital deduction is reduced by $50,000.

(3) An adjustment is made in the $250,000 estate tax marital deduction ceiling in community property states to maintain a parity between community property and common law states as prevailed under the old law.